P9-APL-488

Educational Psychology
04/05

Nineteenth Edition

EDITORS

Kathleen M. Cauley
Virginia Commonwealth University

Kathleen M. Cauley received her Ph.D. in educational studies/human development from the University of Delaware in 1985. Her research interests center on applying cognitive developmental research to school learning. Currently, she is studying children's mathematical understanding.

Fredric Linder
Virginia Commonwealth University

Fredric Linder received a B.A. in American civilization from the University of Miami, Florida, an M.A. in psychology from the New School for Social Research, and a Ph.D. in educational psychology from the State University of New York at Buffalo. His research focuses on the values and cognitive learning styles of students.

James H. McMillan
Virginia Commonwealth University

James H. McMillan received his bachelor's degree from Albion College in 1970, an M.A. from Michigan State University in 1972, and a Ph.D. from Northwestern University in 1976. He has reviewed and written extensively in educational psychology.

McGraw-Hill/Dushkin
2460 Kerper Blvd., Dubuque, IA 52001

Visit us on the Internet
http://www.dushkin.com

Credits

1. **Perspectives on Teaching**
   Unit photo—© 2003 by Cleo Freelance Photography.
2. **Development**
   Unit photo—© 2003 by PhotoDisc, Inc.
3. **Exceptional and Culturally Diverse Children**
   Unit photo—Courtesy of Pam Carley/McGraw-Hill/Dushkin.
4. **Learning and Instruction**
   Unit photo—Courtesy of New Zealand Ministry of Education.
5. **Motivation and Classroom Management**
   Unit photo—© 2003 by Cleo Freelance Photography.
6. **Assessment**
   Unit photo—Courtesy of Pam Carley/McGraw-Hill/Dushkin.

Copyright

Cataloging in Publication Data
Main entry under title: Annual Editions: Educational Psychology. 2004/2005.
1. Educational Psychology—Periodicals. I. Cauley, Kathleen M., *comp.,* Linder, Fredric, McMillan, James H., II. Title: Educational Psychology.
ISBN 0–07–286379–X   658'.05   ISSN 0731–1141

Nineteenth Edition

Cover image © 2004 by Keith Brofsky/Getty Images
Printed in the United States of America   1234567890QPDQPD0987654   Printed on Recycled Paper

Editors/Advisory Board

Members of the Advisory Board are instrumental in the final selection of articles for each edition of ANNUAL EDITIONS. Their review of articles for content, level, currentness, and appropriateness provides critical direction to the editor and staff. We think that you will find their careful consideration well reflected in this volume.

Staff

To the Reader

In publishing ANNUAL EDITIONS we recognize the enormous role played by the magazines, newspapers, and journals of the public press in providing current, first-rate educational information in a broad spectrum of interest areas. Many of these articles are appropriate for students, researchers, and professionals seeking accurate, current material to help bridge the gap between principles and theories and the real world. These articles, however, become more useful for study when those of lasting value are carefully collected, organized, indexed, and reproduced in a low-cost format, which provides easy and permanent access when the material is needed. That is the role played by ANNUAL EDITIONS.

Educational psychology is an interdisciplinary subject that includes human development, learning, intelligence, motivation, assessment, instructional strategies, and classroom management. The articles in this volume give special attention to the application of this knowledge to teaching.

Annual Editions: Educational Psychology 04/05 is divided into six units, and an overview precedes each unit, explaining how the unit articles are related to the broader issues within educational psychology.

The first unit presents issues that are central to the teaching role. The articles' authors provide perspectives on being an effective teacher and the issues facing teachers in the twenty-first century.

The second unit is concerned with child and adolescent development. It covers the biological, cognitive, social, and emotional processes of development. The essays in this unit examine the issues of parenting, moral development, the social forces affecting children and adolescents, as well as the personal and social skills needed to cope with school learning and developmental tasks.

The third unit focuses on the learning disabled, the gifted, and multicultural education. Diverse students require an individualized approach to education. The articles in this unit review the characteristics of these children and suggest programs and strategies to meet their needs.

In the fourth unit, articles about theories of learning and instructional strategies are presented. The different views of learning, such as information processing, behaviorism, and constructivist learning, represent the accumulation of years of research on the way humans change in their thinking or behavior due to experience. The principles generated by each approach have important implications for teaching. These implications are addressed in a section on instructional strategies, covering such topics as instructional methods and technology, concept mapping, and learning styles.

The topic of motivation is perhaps one of the most important aspects of school learning. Effective teachers need to motivate their students both to learn and to behave responsibly. How to manage children and what forms of discipline to use are issues that concern parents as well as teachers and administrators. The articles in the fifth unit present a variety of perspectives on motivating students and discuss approaches to managing student behavior.

The articles in the sixth unit review assessment approaches that can be used to diagnose learning and improve instruction. The focus is on how alternative assessments, such as performance assessments and portfolios, can be integrated with instruction to enhance student learning. Approaches to grading are also reviewed.

A feature that has been added to this edition are selected World Wide Web sites, which can be used to further explore the articles' topics.

This nineteenth edition of Annual Editions: Educational Psychology has been revised in order to present articles that are current and useful. Your responses to the selection and organization of materials are appreciated. Please complete and return the postage-paid article rating form on the last page of the book.

Kathleen M. Cauley

Fredric Linder

James H. McMillan
Editors

Contents

UNIT 1
Perspectives on Teaching

Four selections discuss the importance of research to the teaching process and that when based on solid research, effective teaching can take many forms.

The concepts in bold italics are developed in the article. For further expansion, please refer to the Topic Guide and the Index.

UNIT 2
Development

Four articles examine how social interaction in the classroom influences child and adolescent development.

UNIT 3
Exceptional and Culturally Diverse Children

Seven articles look at the problems and positive effects of educational programs for learning disabled, gifted and culturally diverse children.

The concepts in bold italics are developed in the article. For further expansion, please refer to the Topic Guide and the Index.

UNIT 4
Learning and Instruction

Thirteen selections explore the important types of student/teacher interaction.

The concepts in bold italics are developed in the article. For further expansion, please refer to the Topic Guide and the Index.

The concepts in bold italics are developed in the article. For further expansion, please refer to the Topic Guide and the Index.

UNIT 5
Motivation and Classroom Management

Seven selections discuss student control and motivation in the classroom.

The concepts in bold italics are developed in the article. For further expansion, please refer to the Topic Guide and the Index.

UNIT 6
Assessment

Six articles discuss the implications of educational measurements for the classroom decision-making process and for the teaching profession.

The concepts in bold italics are developed in the article. For further expansion, please refer to the Topic Guide and the Index.

Topic Guide

This topic guide suggests how the selections in this book relate to the subjects covered in your course. You may want to use the topics listed on these pages to search the Web more easily.

On the following pages a number of Web sites have been gathered specifically for this book. They are arranged to reflect the units of this *Annual Edition.* You can link to these sites by going to the DUSHKIN ONLINE support site at *http://www.dushkin.com/online/.*

ALL THE ARTICLES THAT RELATE TO EACH TOPIC ARE LISTED BELOW THE BOLD-FACED TERM.

Technology

Thinking skills

Validity

World Wide Web Sites

The following World Wide Web sites have been carefully researched and selected to support the articles found in this reader. The easiest way to access these selected sites is to go to our DUSHKIN ONLINE support site at *http://www.dushkin.com/online/*.

AE: Educational Psychology 04/05

The following sites were available at the time of publication. Visit our Web site—we update DUSHKIN ONLINE regularly to reflect any changes.

General Sources

American Psychological Association
http://www.apa.org/psychnet/

By exploring the APA's "PsychNET," you will be able to find links to an abundance of articles and other resources that are useful in the field of educational psychology.

Educational Resources Information Center
http://www.eric.ed.gov

This invaluable site provides links to all ERIC sites: clearinghouses, support components, and publishers of ERIC materials. Search the ERIC database for what is new.

National Education Association
http://www.nea.org

Something—and often quite a lot—about virtually every education-related topic can be accessed at or through this site of the 2.3-million-strong National Education Association.

National Parent Information Network/ERIC
http://npin.org

This is a clearinghouse of information on elementary and early childhood education as well as urban education. Browse through its links for information for parents.

U.S. Department of Education
http://www.ed.gov/pubs/TeachersGuide/

Government goals, projects, and grants are listed here, plus many links to teacher services and resources.

UNIT 1: Perspectives on Teaching

The Center for Innovation in Education
http://www.center.edu

The Center for Innovation in Education, self-described as a "not-for-profit, non-partisan research organization," focuses on K–12 education reform strategies. Click on its links about school privatization.

Classroom Connect
http://www.classroom.net

This is a major Web site for K–12 teachers and students, with links to schools, teachers, and resources online. It includes discussion of the use of technology in the classroom.

Education World
http://www.education-world.com

Education World provides a database of literally thousands of sites that can be searched by grade level, plus education news, lesson plans, and professional-development resources.

Goals 2000: A Progress Report
http://www.ed.gov/pubs/goals/progrpt/index.html

Open this site to survey a progress report by the U.S. Department of Education on the Goals 2000 reform initiative. It provides a sense of the goals that educators are reaching for as they look toward the future.

Teacher Talk Forum
http://education.indiana.edu/cas/tt/tthmpg.html

Visit this site for access to a variety of articles discussing life in the classroom. Clicking on the various links will lead you to electronic lesson plans, covering a variety of topic areas, from Indiana University's Center for Adolescent Studies.

UNIT 2: Development

Association for Moral Education
http://www.amenetwork.org/

AME is dedicated to fostering communication, cooperation, training, curriculum development, and research that link moral theory with educational practices. From here it is possible to connect to several sites on moral development.

Child Welfare League of America
http://www.cwla.org

The CWLA is the United States' oldest and largest organization devoted entirely to the well-being of vulnerable children and their families. This site provides links to information about issues related to morality and values in education.

Pediatric Behavioral Health Resources
http://www.earlychildhoodbehavioralhealth.com/index.htm

This Web site is dedicated to serving the needs of those working with young children and their families who are experiencing mental health or behavioral issues. Find information on Abuse & Neglect, Mental Health Disabilities, Classroom & Behavior Management, and Discipline Reactive Attachment Disorder.

Guidelines for Developmentally Appropriate Early Childhood Practice
http://www.naeyc.org/resources/position_statements/daptoc.htm

Here is a 23-page excerpt from a report, edited by Sue Bredekamp, that covers every aspect of appropriate programs that serve children from birth through 8 years of age. It is published on the Web by the National Association for the Education of Young Children (NAEYC).

The National Association for Child Development
http://www.nacd.org

This international organization is dedicated to helping children and adults reach their full potential. Its home page presents links to various programs, research, and resources into such topics as ADD/ADHD.

National Association of School Psychologists (NASP)
http://www.nasponline.org/index2.html

The NASP offers advice to teachers about how to help children cope with the many issues they face in today's world. The site includes tips for school personnel as well as parents.

Scholastic News Zone
http://www.scholasticnews.com

At this site, Scholastic Classroom magazines provide up-to-date information to children, teachers, and parents online to help explain timely issues.

www.dushkin.com/online/

UNIT 3: Exceptional and Culturally Diverse Children

The Council for Exceptional Children
http://www.cec.sped.org/index.html

This page will give you access to information on identifying and teaching gifted children, attention-deficit disorders, and other topics in gifted education.

Global SchoolNet Foundation
http://www.gsn.org

Access this site for multicultural education information. The site includes news for teachers, students, and parents, as well as chat rooms, links to educational resources, programs, and contests and competitions.

International Project: Multicultural Pavilion
http://curry.edschool.virginia.edu/curry/centers/multicultural/ papers.html

Here is a forum for sharing stories and resources and for learning from the stories and resources of others, in the form of articles on the Internet that cover every possible racial, gender, and multicultural issue that could arise in the field of multicultural education.

Let 1000 Flowers Bloom/Kristen Nicholson-Nelson
http://teacher.scholastic.com/professional/assessment/100flowers.htm

Open this page for Kristen Nicholson-Nelson's discussion of ways in which teachers can help to nurture children's multiple intelligences. She provides a useful bibliography and resources.

Multicultural Publishing and Education Catalog
http://www.mpec.org

This is the home page of the MPEC, a networking and support organization for independent publishers, authors, educators, and librarians fostering authentic multicultural books and materials. It has excellent links to a vast array of resources related to multicultural education.

National Attention Deficit Disorder Association
http://www.add.org

This site, some of which is under construction, will lead you to information about ADD/ADHD. It has links to self-help and support groups, outlines behaviors and diagnostics, answers FAQs, and suggests books and other resources.

National MultiCultural Institute (NMCI)
http://www.nmci.org

NMCI is one of the major organizations in the field of diversity training. At this Web site, NMCI offers conference data, resource materials, diversity training and consulting service information, and links to other related sites.

UNIT 4: Learning and Instruction

Education Week on the Web
http://www.edweek.org

At this page you can open archives, read special reports, keep up on current events, and access a variety of articles in educational psychology. A great deal of material is helpful in learning and instruction.

Online Internet Institute
http://www.oii.org

A collaborative project among Internet-using educators, proponents of systemic reform, content-area experts, and teachers who desire professional growth, this site provides a learning environment for integrating the Internet into educators' individual teaching styles.

Teachers Helping Teachers
http://www.pacificnet.net/~mandel/

This site provides basic teaching tips, new teaching-methodology ideas, and forums for teachers to share their experiences. It features educational resources on the Web, with new ones added each week.

The Teachers' Network
http://www.teachers.net/

Bulletin boards, classroom projects, online forums, and Web mentors are featured on this site, as well as the book *Teachers' Guide to Cyberspace* and an online, 4-week course on how to use the Internet.

UNIT 5: Motivation and Classroom Management

Canada's Schoolnet Staff Room
http://www.schoolnet.ca/home/e/

Here is a resource and link site for anyone involved in education, including special-needs educators, teachers, parents, volunteers, and administrators.

UNIT 6: Assessment

Awesome Library for Teachers
http://www.neat-schoolhouse.org/teacher.html

Open this page for links and access to teacher information on everything from assessments to child development topics.

Phi Delta Kappa International
http://www.pdkintl.org

This important organization publishes articles about all facets of education. You can check out the online archive of the journal, *Phi Delta Kappan,* which has resources such as articles having to do with assessment.

Washington (State) Center for the Improvement of Student Learning
http://www.k12.wa.us/

This Washington State site is designed to provide access to information about the state's new academic standards, assessments, and accountability system. Many resources and Web links are included.

We highly recommend that you review our Web site for expanded information and our other product lines. We are continually updating and adding links to our Web site in order to offer you the most usable and useful information that will support and expand the value of your Annual Editions. You can reach us at: *http://www.dushkin.com/annualeditions/.*

UNIT 1
Perspectives on Teaching

Unit Selections

1. **Good Teachers, Plural**, Donald R. Cruickshank and Donald Haefele
2. **What I Hope for in My Children's Teachers: A Parent's Perspective**, David Boers
3. **What Urban Students Say About Good Teaching**, Dick Corbett and Bruce Wilson
4. **Helping Children Cope With Loss, Death, and Grief: Response to a National Tragedy**, National Association of School Psychologists

Key Points to Consider

• What questions would you like to see educational psychologists study?

• Describe several characteristics of effective teachers. How is effective teaching viewed by different constituents?

• As we move into the twenty-first century, what new expectations should be placed on teachers and schools? What expectations will fade?

 **Links: www.dushkin.com/online/**
These sites are annotated in the World Wide Web pages.

The Center for Innovation in Education
http://www.center.edu

Classroom Connect
http://www.classroom.net

Education World
http://www.education-world.com

Goals 2000: A Progress Report
http://www.ed.gov/pubs/goals/progrpt/index.html

Teacher Talk Forum
http://education.indiana.edu/cas/tt/tthmpg.html

The teaching-learning process in school is enormously complex. Many factors influence pupil learning—such as family background, developmental level, prior knowledge, motivation, and, of course, effective teachers. Educational psychology investigates these factors to better understand and explain student learning. We begin our exploration of the teaching-learning process by considering the characteristics of effective teaching.

In the first three articles, perspectives on effective teaching are presented—the variety of professional perspectives as well as a parent perspective and the urban students' perspective.

The fourth article discusses the range of reactions that children and adolescents have experienced in response to the terrorism attacks of September 11, 2001, and suggests ways that educators can help them to cope and continue their schooling.

Educational psychology is a resource for teachers that emphasizes disciplined inquiry, a systematic and objective analysis of information, and a scientific attitude toward decision making.

The field provides information for decisions that are based on quantitative and qualitative studies of learning and teaching rather than on intuition, tradition, authority, or subjective feelings. It is our hope that this aspect of educational psychology is communicated throughout these readings, and that, as a student, you will adopt the analytic, probing attitude that is part of the discipline.

While educational psychologists have helped to establish a knowledge base about teaching and learning, the unpredictable, spontaneous, evolving nature of teaching suggests that the best they will ever do is to provide concepts and skills that teachers can adapt for use in their classrooms. The issues raised in these articles about effective teaching, and the issues facing teachers in the twenty-first century, help us understand the teaching role and its demands. As you read articles in other chapters, consider the demands they place on the teaching role as well.

Good Teachers, Plural

What makes a teacher good? Looking at the ways we have answered that question in the past century may place the current evaluation craze in perspective.

Donald R. Cruickshank and Donald Haefele

There are as many kinds of good teachers in our schools as there are varieties of good apples in supermarkets. Unfortunately, we tend to recognize and honor only one kind of teacher at a time. We currently glorify teachers whose students pass standardized tests (Bradley, 2000). In the 1990s, we admired those who had proven they could bring about greater student achievement. In the 1980s, good teachers were those who followed Madeline Hunter's prescriptions for teaching success (Garman & Hazi, 1998). And the list goes on.

For the first half of the 20th century, school principals, supervisors, and education professors determined the attributes of good teachers.

Let us identify some of these visions of good teachers. Only then can we begin to explore how we can value them all and how school districts can support the development of many kinds of teachers and create ways to evaluate them.

Visions of Good Teachers

Ideal teachers. For the first half of the 20th century, school principals, supervisors, and educational professors determined the attributes of good teachers. Schools, school districts, and colleges cranked out checklists and rating scales that scored such traits as professional attitude, understanding of students, creativity, control of class, planning, individualization, and pupil participation. During this period, scholar Dwight Beecher (1953) developed the popular Teaching Evaluation Record, and Arvil Barr and his associates (1961) drew up a comprehensive list of ideal attributes that included buoyancy, emotional stability, ethical behavior, expressiveness, forcefulness, and personal magnetism.

Thus, an ideal teacher met subjective standards of excellence determined by selected, significant others. Because the standards were subjective, many disagreements developed over what the standards meant and which teachers met them (Mitzel, 1960; Morsh & Wilder, 1954).

Analytic teachers. By the early 1960s, administrators encountered problems associated with measuring the attributes of ideal teachers (Cruickshank, 1990). In a search for some other way to judge teacher quality, experts soon began describing good teachers as analytic.

Analytic teachers methodically inspected what they did in the classroom. They recorded and examined their classroom practice using a variety of observation techniques (Simon & Boyer, 1968). Many teachers and observers used the Flanders System of Interactional Analysis (Flanders, 1960) to make a detailed record of the teacher-student interactions occurring during a lesson: how much and about what the teacher talked, how much and about what students talked, and the extent and nature of student silence or confusion. Teachers modified their practice on the basis of these analyses. Becoming an analytic teacher required being investigative and self-correctional. Over time, the work involved in being analytical seemed to overwhelm even proponents of this vision of good teachers.

Effective teachers. In 1966, the influential Coleman Report asserted that students' socioeconomic backgrounds influenced their learning more than their teachers did (U.S. Department of Health, Education, and Welfare). Immediately, dozens of educational researchers set out to show that teachers made a crucial difference in student achievement. First, researchers identified teachers whose students scored higher on tests than did comparable students taught by others. Next, they examined these overachieving teachers, referred to as *outliers* or *effective teachers*, to determine exactly what they were like and what they did so that other teachers might benefit from such knowledge.

The findings of many studies (Rosenshine, 1971; Rosenshine & Furst, 1971) consistently found that effective teachers carefully monitor learning activities and are clear, accepting and supportive, equitable with students, and persistent in challenging and engaging them. Nonetheless, researchers disagreed about the methods used in the studies and about whether student gain is the most important outcome of teaching (Cruickshank, 1990).

Paralleling the development of the concept of the effective teacher has been a significant increase in the amount of student-achievement testing. As a result, we have become more focused on the product—better student scores on standardized tests—and on rewarding teachers who succeed in teaching to the test. In many states, teachers and principals are deemed effective and are rewarded monetarily when students demonstrate satisfactory gains on standardized tests. Opposition to this narrow definition of teacher effectiveness is mounting (Hoff, 1999; Kohn, 1999).

Dutiful teachers. Those less than satisfied with the attributes originally assigned to effective teachers argued that teachers who do not display the typical attributes of effective teachers, such as enthusiasm, may yet bring about student learning. They asserted that studying the attributes of effective teachers can be useful, especially for guiding preservice and inservice development, but these attributes should not be used as standards for judging teacher quality. Rather, we should evaluate teachers according to how well they understand and perform their duties: knowledge of the subject matter, school, and community; demonstrated classroom skills, including testing and grading; personal characteristics that encourage learning; and service to the profession (Scriven, 1990).

Competent teachers. The U.S. accountability movement in the 1970s spurred an effort in education to identify competencies that teachers should possess. Specifically, the public wanted to know what teachers needed to know and be able to do.

To identify teacher competencies, scholars studied the early research on teacher effectiveness, analyzed what teachers do, and obtained the opinions of expert teacher practitioners and other educators. The most thorough compilation (Dodl et al., 1972) organized competencies in the areas of planning instruction, implementing instruction, assessing and evaluating students, communicating, and performing administrative duties.

The public also wanted to make certain that teachers used their knowledge and performed well in the classroom. Consequently, the teacher-testing movement was born, soon to be given a boost by the 1983 publication of *A Nation At Risk* (National Commission on Excellence in Education). Thereafter, teachers or teachers-to-be had to pass tests developed by state education departments or by such national organizations as the Educational Testing Service and the National Board for Professional Teaching Standards.

The Educational Testing Service developed the Praxis teacher competency series of tests for use in teacher preparation programs and entry into the teaching profession. Praxis assesses three areas: reading, writing, and math skills near the beginning of a preservice teaching program; professional academic and pedagogical knowledge near the end of a teaching program; and on-the-job classroom performance. Thirty-eight states currently require some Praxis testing.

The National Board for Professional Teaching Standards provides national certification for experienced teachers who meet competencies set forth by discerning teachers (King, 1994). Teachers seeking National Board certification submit portfolios that include lesson plans, videotapes of lessons taught, and samples of student work. They also come to regional sites for further inspection and testing. States now offer incentives for teachers to obtain Board certification. For example, in Massachusetts, the Veteran Teachers Board offers up to $50,000 over 10 years to any public school teacher who receives National Board certification (Bradley, 1998).

Even the National Council for Accreditation of Teacher Education is moving toward assessing the competence—the knowledge and skills—of preservice teachers and away from merely reviewing their programs of study (Bradley, 1999).

Expert teachers. In the 1980s and into the 1990s, many scholars decided that what makes a teacher good is expertise. Expert teachers are different from nonexperts in three ways: they have extensive and accessible knowledge that is organized for use in teaching; they are efficient and can do more in less time; and they are able to arrive at novel and appropriate solutions to problems (Sternberg & Horvath, 1995). Thus, expertise is more than experience. Teachers could be experienced and have less expertise than some novices.

Reflective teachers. The definition of the reflective teacher was developed at Ohio State University in the late 1970s. Reflective teachers are students of teaching, with a strong, sustained interest in learning about the art and science of teaching and about themselves as teachers (Cruickshank, 1987, 1991). Reflective teachers are introspective, examining their own practice of teaching and seeking a greater understanding of teaching by reading scholarly and professional journals and books, including teachers' autobiographies. Because they want to be thoughtful practitioners, they constantly monitor their teaching—for example, by using videotape or audiotape.

Satisfying teachers. Satisfying teachers please students, parents or caregivers, teaching colleagues, administrators, and supervisors by responding to their needs. In Rochester, New York, for example, parents rate their children's teachers on the basis of 20 questions that inquire about such qualities as the teacher's accessibility, clarity, responsiveness, and optimism (Janey, 1997).

School or parent organizations recognize satisfying teachers by presenting them with awards for good teaching. More often, however, admiration shows up in daily responses to the teacher: students advise one another to take this teacher's courses, fellow teachers look to this teacher for guidance and inspiration, most parents want their children in this teacher's class, and administrators trust this teacher to respond positively to difficult students.

Of course, knowing and meeting the expectations of others is a daunting task, and considerable disagreement can develop about what expectations are appropriate. We can all think of instructors who did or did not satisfy us or others but who were nonetheless effective teachers.

Diversity-responsive teachers. Diversity-responsive teachers take special interest in and are particularly sensitive to students who are different culturally, socially, economically, intellectually, physically, or emotionally. For example, Jacqueline Irvine and James Fraser (1998) believe that African American students are best served by "warm demanders" (p. 56). Warm demanders use a culturally specific pedagogical style that is substantively different from the approaches described in effective teaching research. Such teachers perceive themselves as parental surrogates and advocates, employ a teaching style filled with rhythmic language and rapid intonation, link students' everyday cultural experiences to new concepts, develop personal relationships with the learners, and teach with authority.

Diversity-responsive teachers are also dedicated to bettering the lives of students both inside and outside the classroom. Often working with children who have special needs, this kind of teacher demonstrates great tenderness, patience, and tact. A well-known exemplar is Annie Sullivan, Helen Keller's teacher (Peterson, 1946).

Respected teachers. Respected teachers, real and fictional, sometimes are idolized in books and films. Some of the real ones include LouAnne Johnson in *Dangerous Minds*, Jaime Escalante in *Stand and Deliver*, and Marva Collins in *The Marva Collins Story*. Fictional, virtuous teachers have been crafted in *Mr. Holland's Opus; The Prime of Miss Jean Brodie; Up the Down Staircase; To Sir, with Love;* and *Goodbye, Mr. Chips.*

Historian Richard Traina (1999) explored the autobiographies of some 125 prominent Americans to determine what qualities in teachers they valued. He notes that three attributes stand out: subject-matter competence, caring about students and their success, and distinctive character. Respected teachers possess and demonstrate virtuous qualities, including honesty, decency, fairness, devotion, empathy, and selflessness. Most such teachers also have determination, overcoming great odds to ensure student success.

Moving Forward

None of these categories is mutually exclusive. And no variation, by itself, has proven or is proving to be just right: None satisfies all education stakeholders. In a utopian world, teachers would demonstrate all aspects of teacher "goodness" and possess the attributes of all 10 visions. In the real world, we must learn how to recognize and appreciate the many models that teachers can follow to be good teachers.

Further, we need to answer some questions. Have we identified all of the possible exemplars of good teaching?

Variations of a Good Teacher

IDEAL teachers meet standards set by school principals, supervisors, and education professors.

ANALYTIC teachers use observation techniques to record how well they are meeting their instructional intentions.

EFFECTIVE teachers bring about higher student achievement.

DUTIFUL teachers perform assigned teaching duties well.

COMPETENT teachers pass tests that indicate they possess requisite teacher attributes.

EXPERT teachers have extensive and accessible knowledge and can do more in less time.

REFLECTIVE teachers examine the art and science of teaching to become more thoughtful practitioners.

SATISFYING teachers please students, parents or caregivers, colleagues, supervisors, and administrators.

DIVERSITY-RESPONSIVE teachers are sensitive to all students.

RESPECTED teachers possess and demonstrate qualities regarded as virtues.

To what extent do the exemplars overlap? Are some models more valuable than others? Who decides which exemplar is more valuable? Should all teachers be good teachers according to at least one of the 10 or so models? What should be the standard for good teachers within each vision of a good teacher? How can we prepare teachers and help them become good by some criteria? How can teachers document what kind of good teachers they are? How can we reward good teachers?

Tests for teachers were a direct result of the push to describe the competent teacher and to determine to what extent teachers measure up.

In addition, we need to conduct research. To what extent do various education stakeholders agree on what makes teachers good? How do perceptions of good teachers differ by age, gender, socioeconomic background, educational level, geographic area, and political persuasion? Which exemplars of good teachers are related to which educational outcomes? To what extent can good teachers be readily distinguished from bad teachers?

Evaluating Different Kinds of Teachers

School districts that appreciate multiple kinds of good teachers need to create teacher evaluation systems corresponding to the full range of teaching exemplars. To meet legal requirements, an evaluation system must be both formal (guided by public, written policies and procedures) and standardized (applied evenly and fairly). For example, all teachers must meet the criteria of one of the exemplars. Evaluations of *effective teachers* should require that teachers demonstrate such attributes as clarity and enthusiasm—qualities associated with student achievement. *Dutiful teachers* should be judged on such criteria as knowledge of subject matter and classroom skills.

Clearly, to judge each vision of a good teacher, we must use valid criteria that are related to the particular exemplar that the teacher strives to emulate. A good teacher evaluation system should also have predictive validity and make the desired impact on students; an evaluation of a *satisfying teacher*, for example, should include surveys of students and parents. Of course, any teacher evaluation system should require that evaluators—administrators, supervisors, teaching peers, or others—receive training so that each evaluation is objective and would result in approximately the same outcome if done by another evaluator.

Accepting Many Exemplars

Substantiating that there are all kinds of good teachers serves several useful ends. First, it dispels the traditional notion that there is only one kind of good teacher. Second, it permits teachers to describe which kind of good teacher they are and, when necessary, submit evidence to that effect. Third, it provides positive direction for teachers and persons responsible for teachers' continuing development. Finally, such knowledge enables the teaching profession to identity and remove teachers who are unable to meet any definition of what makes teachers good.

Meanwhile, Wyoming Governor Jim Geringer, chairman of the Education Commission of the States, whose membership consists of governors and top state education officials, reports that he hopes to work with the states to define what it means to be a good teacher (Sandham, 1999). Is the time right for educators, educational researchers, and elected officials to join hands in broadening the scope of this ambitious and important task?

References

Barr, A., Worcester, D., Abell, A., Beecher, C., Jenson, L., Peronto, A., Ringness, T., & Schmidt, J. (1961). Wisconsin studies of the measurement and predictability of teacher effectiveness. *Journal of Experimental Education, 30*, 1–156.

Beecher, D. (1953). *The teaching evaluation record*. Buffalo, NY: Educators Publishing Company.

Bradley, A. (1998, February 25). A better way to pay. *Education Week, 17*(24), 29–31.

Bradley, A. (1999, January 13). NCATE unveils a plan for aspiring elementary teachers. *Education Week, 18*(18), 5.

Bradley, A. (2000, March 22). L.A. proposes linking teacher pay to tests. *Education Week, 19*(28), 3.

Cruickshank, D. (1987). *Reflective teaching: The preparation of students of teaching*. Reston, VA: Association of Teacher Educators.

Cruickshank, D. (1990). *Research that informs teachers and teacher educators*. Bloomington, IN: Phi Delta Kappa Educational Foundation.

Cruickshank, D. (1991). *Reflective teaching*. Bloomington, IN: Phi Delta Kappa Educational Foundation.

Dodl, N., Elfner, E., Becker, J., Halstead, J., Jung, H., Nelson, P., Puriton, S., & Wegele, P. (1972). *Florida catalog of teacher competencies*. Tallahassee: Florida State University.

Flanders, N. (1960). *Teacher influence, pupil attitudes, and achievement: Final report*. Minneapolis: University of Minnesota.

Garman, N., & Hazi, H. (1998, May). Teachers ask: Is there life after Madeline Hunter? *Phi Delta Kappan, 69*(9), 669–672.

Hoff, D. (1999, September 22). Standards at crossroads after debate. *Education Week, 19*(3), 1, 9.

Irvine, J., & Fraser, J. (1998, May 13). Warm demanders. *Education Week, 17*(35), 56, 42.

Janey, C. (1997, October 1). Seeking customer satisfaction. *Education Week, 17*(5), 39.

King, M. (1994). Locking themselves in: National standards for the teaching profession. *Teaching and Teacher Education, 10*(1), 95–108.

Kohn, A. (1999, September 15). Confusing harder with better. *Education Week, 19*(2), 68, 52.

Mitzel, H. (1960). Teacher effectiveness. In C. Harris (Ed.), *Encyclopedia of educational research* (3rd ed.) (p. 1481). New York: MacMillan.

Morsh, J., & Wilder, E. (1954). *Identifying the effective instructor: A review of quantitative studies*. Lackland Air Force Base, TX: Air Force Personnel and Training Center.

National Commission on Excellence in Education. (1983). *A nation at risk*. Washington, DC: U.S. Department of Education.

Peterson, H. (1946). *Great teachers*. New York: Random House.

Rosenshine, B. (1971). *Teaching behaviors and student achievement*. London: National Foundation for Educational Research.

Rosenshine, B., & Furst, N. (1971). Research on teacher performance criteria. In B. O. Smith (Ed.), *Research in Teacher Education* (pp. 37–72). Englewood Cliffs, NJ: Prentice-Hall.

Sandham, J. (1999, August 4). ECS members take closer look at the teaching profession. *Education Week, 18* (43), 23.

Scriven, M. (1990, September). Can research-based teacher evaluation be saved? *Journal of Personnel Evaluation in Education, 4*(1), 19–32.

Simon, A., & Boyer, E. (1968). *Mirrors for behavior: An anthology of classroom observation instruments*. Philadelphia: Research for Better Schools.

Sternberg, R., & Horvath, J. (1995, August/September). A prototype view of expert teaching. *Educational Researcher, 24*(6), 9–17.

Traina, R. (1999, January 20). What makes a teacher good? *Education Week, 18*(19), 34.

U.S. Department of Health, Education, and Welfare. (1966). *Equality of educational opportunity: Summary report* (The Coleman report). Washington, DC: U.S. Government Printing Office.

Donald R. Cruickshank (cruickshank1@osu.edu) is Professor Emeritus and **Donald Haefele** (haefele@osu.edu) is Associate Professor of Education at Ohio State University, 2817 Wickliffe Rd., Columbus, OH 43221.

What I Hope for in My Children's Teachers

A Parent's Perspective

DAVID BOERS

Teaching today may be more difficult than it has ever been. Children still go through the critical stages that children have always gone through to attempt to establish who they are and to grow into what they can become (Santrock 1987). The difference these days is that children go through these stages at faster paces and with different types of adult guidance (Elkind 1994). Whether it is because of the media, the lack of parent involvement, the dearth of traditional families, or simply an adult-centered society, teachers often end up with classes filled with too many students with too many problems. Students seem to have difficulty in personal and logical progression through normal child developmental stages, such as the realization of self-worth, productivity, and the establishment of identity. Teachers end up trying to deal with this difficult situation. In this article I will share what, in spite of all of the above, many parents still hope for in their children's teachers.

Let us begin with the premise that parents and guardians do care deeply about their children's success in school. The myth of a lack of caring parents in America today often overshadows, perhaps obliterates, the fact that in all communities many, if not most, parents want to work with teachers for the benefit of their children (Willis 1993). And these parents genuinely want to go beyond fundraising and cheerleading to serious relationships with teachers about their children. They do not all have the "My kid's gotta go to Harvard" mentality; they just care about their children having a good experience in school.

As a parent of school-aged children, I have attempted to be supportive of my children's school experience. In doing this, I have attempted to be supportive of teachers, administrators, school programs, district initiatives, and education in general. To this end, I have regularly communicated with teachers, administrators, program coordinators, school board members, and other parents regarding educational progress in our community and for my children. After ten years, dozens of teachers and administrators, and a number of curricular and cocurricular programs, I have experienced both the extreme joy of a genuine sense of partnership and an empty sense of detachment. I have come to care deeply about strengthening the connection between teacher and parents in a way that achieves the mutual goal of providing children with the greatest chance for school and life success. For I have learned that the key to my children's success in school is the competence and professionalism of classroom teachers and the communication that develops between my children's teachers and me. In an effort to define this issue more clearly, I offer the descriptions below to form a portrait of what I hope for in my children's teachers.

Enthusiastic, Energetic, Happy, Positive

Nothing works better to get students excited about school than a teacher who loves teaching and learning. I want my children's teachers to be enthusiastic about school, about learning, and about what goes on in class so they can carry on the joy of learning we have already started and continue at home. And I want the enthusiasm to be overt and obvious, genuine, not feigned.

It takes energy to be enthusiastic. It takes energy to teach. Teaching is an active profession, and I hope my children's teachers are healthy enough both physically and mentally to have the energy for planned and spontaneous enthusiastic activity, because this energy is conveyed to the students.

In school, if the teachers are happy, my children will be happy (Boers 1995). Conversely, if the teachers are not happy, negative things can happen. The mission of all teachers should center on fostering happy, well-adjusted children who will grow up to be happy, well-adjusted adults. If my children's teachers are not happy at school,

I worry about their working with my children. If my children's teachers are happy at school, I see unlimited potential for all kinds of spontaneous learning.

Enthusiasm, energy, and happiness contribute to creating a positive environment, one in which children's basic needs—physiological needs, safety and security, love and belonging, self-esteem, and self-actualization (Santrock 1987)—are met, as are additional needs for power, freedom, and fun (Glasser 1990). A positive environment leads to greater curiosity, greater production, and higher levels of thinking. When students are empowered as valued decision makers in the classroom, the classroom is much more conducive to achievement and retention because it is a positive place to be (Glasser 1993). For those reasons, I hope my children's teachers are positive leaders.

Competent, Research-Based, Well-Read, Confident

I hope my children's teachers have a high degree of competency in the knowledge of human growth, development, and learning. I hope that they can appropriately apply methods and strategies for dealing with children in all ways, not just academically. For example, teachers know full well that children grow, develop, and learn in different ways and through individual processes. Teachers must then have the competence to perceive student levels and provide direction and instruction beginning at those levels. If my children are developmentally more immature than the others in the class, then the teacher's behavioral directions and instructional techniques need to be different for them. In this case, perhaps my children would need more specific directions and more direct instruction.

I hope my children's teachers teach from a reputable base of qualified research—that at any time, they can cite notable researchers and theorists to justify what they are saying or doing. For example, if methods such as assertive discipline (Canter 1986) or control theory (Glasser 1986) were used, I would be interested in knowing that teachers understand the research that supports those methods and are able to explain the psychology of the process that leads to the expected results. Academically, if teachers use theories of multiple intelligences (Gardner 1983), they ought to know and understand and be able to explain the human growth, development, and learning principles that are inherent in the strategies. In other words, I would prefer that teachers know what they are doing and understand why they are doing it.

Teaching is a profession, and I hope that my children's teachers read professional journals and books so that they can understand, use, and talk about current knowledge and practice. Understanding current knowledge about the brain (Jensen 1998) or quality school teaching (Glasser 1993) is vital to the effective delivery of instruction. Children, schools, and teaching are very widely studied and written about, with the hope that what occurs at school makes sense for student progress. There are no professions left that can "do it the way we've always done it." Therefore, it is important that teachers regularly read, understand, and apply ideas that work, as reported in contemporary professional writings.

I hope that my children's teachers are confident enough to listen and respond professionally to my questions and challenges, not in grudge-match fashion, but as a matter of two-way intellectualizing for the benefit of students. If my children's teachers can confidently (not brashly) carry on a two-way conversation, they will model the same in the classroom. Confidence leads to open-mindedness and a willingness to learn and share knowledge and will serve as a good model for my children's learning.

Personable, Communicative, Respectful, Welcoming

I hope my children's teachers get to know who we are as a family. They should understand our family's lifestyle and goals. For example, I'd like teachers to know that we take learning and school seriously, expect to do difficult work, and want to be challenged constantly. I will willingly share our family's joys, happiness, and sorrows with my children's teachers if given the chance. From this, I hope that my children's teachers know how my children think and act and live their lives, so they can avoid jumping to conclusions and help find possibilities and connections for my children. Teachers teach my children best when they personally know my children.

I hope my children's teachers communicate with me eagerly, early, and regularly via notes, telephone calls, e-mail. I want to know how my children are doing and how things are going. I'd like to hear teachers' opinions, comments, and advice regarding my children's growth and progress. When teachers know and care about my children and me personally, they should be eager to share whatever they know about us. Teachers have the advantage of being in school, a place where my children spend a tremendous amount of time, so they know what is going on in that part of my children's life. Teachers' communicating what they observe is an important learning tool for parents.

I hope my children's teachers are respectful of me as a parent partner. If my ideas and values are different from the teachers', they can still be heard, pondered, considered, and perhaps implemented.

In the best-case scenario my children's teachers would know me well enough to seek me out and use me as a resource. I will hang bulletin boards and supervise game day activities but would also ask that teachers use me as a guest teacher in areas of curriculum in which I have appropriate knowledge. When I take the initiative to make myself available, I would hope the teachers would follow up on the offer and even consider creating situations where I might be involved.

Student-Centered, Differentiating, Homework-Efficient, Work-Responsive

I hope my children's classrooms are student-centered, as opposed to teacher-centered or even subject-centered. My children are more important to me than social studies, foreign language, or any academic area. But I also know that when a teacher focuses on the student as a learner (rather than on the teacher as teacher), more achievement and more retention in academic endeavors occur. This is a result of increased ownership of academic material on the part of students. Student-centered classrooms have the additional advantage of increasing the opportunities for developing caring, compassionate students who see every person as a valuable individual (Kohn 1996, 101–19). I want my children and all the children they are with to be caring, compassionate people.

When my children's teachers use a multiple-modality approach that allows for different approaches to instruction (Holloway 2000), it gives my children options of different ways to achieve the class goals. If my children can convey key concepts graphically rather than in writing, they should have that opportunity. One-dimensional teaching will not accommodate my children's learning styles. This includes differentiation through assessments that are meaningful and authentic.

I hope teachers will call on my children and expect them to perform every day as a natural part of being in school. If homework is assigned, I hope that it is worth doing, clearly explained, and connected to the curriculum. Otherwise, homework can become drudgery that makes school unpleasant and unappealing (Gratz 2000). My children's teachers can encourage, via meaningful homework, my children's love for school.

Effective time management is critical for teachers. It permits them to return work in a timely fashion with specific, meaningful teacher comments. I know that my children have the teacher in mind when they do the work. They want and need to know soon whether they have met the requirements, exceeded the requirements, or have work left to do. If in fact teachers are abiding by an integrated, connected curriculum, my children need to know in a timely fashion how they are doing to better connect it to where they have been and where they are going.

Well-Planned, Conferencing-Complete, Honest, Holistic

My children's teachers need to know where they are going and how that fits into everything else taught and learned in previous years, as well as all that will follow in ensuing years. If that is too much to ask, then teachers should at least have a clear set of goals and strategies for the entire school year and for each day of that year. This does not prevent spontaneity related to course goals. Further, I hope that my children's teachers have a vision for an integrated set of school learning experiences, if not across the curriculum and cocurriculum every day in school, then at least with each teacher's own course offerings. I hope my children's teachers will not force them to learn in small, isolated, nonintegrated units, one after another, all year long. All students deserve teachers with a vision that school is good, school is meaningful, school is desired, and that every day is connected to the last one.

I hope my children's teachers have a specific, detailed plan for our conferences that goes beyond merely presenting grades. Handing out a computerized list of scores may be a start, but the teacher is so much more involved with my children's lives than to be one-dimensional in conferencing. I want to know about skill levels, academic performance, social skills, and personal happiness. I hope my children's teachers will tell me how they assess my children in those four areas.

I hope my children's teachers are honest about who they are, how they teach, and how they are working with my children. Honest teachers eliminate the see-through camouflage of teachers or systemic games that sometimes block the path to what is best for students. Honest teachers allow for an authentic discussion and a focused collaboration in educational partnerships.

I believe that my children's teachers need to have an understanding of the school experience, both as an experience unto itself and as a part of a bigger whole. Teachers should support special school events such as homecoming, harvest moon celebration, multicultural awareness week, and so on, by being involved themselves and by reducing or eliminating homework so that students are encouraged to become involved. Further, most districts have at least an unwritten agreement to reduce work on a specific evening so that children may attend religious education. It is important that teachers honor such agreements.

These are the hopes that I have for my children's teachers. I know that I am not alone in these hopes. Concerned parents love school. We want to be partners in education, and we very much respect the difficulties of being a teacher. In my experience, model teachers demonstrate the characteristics I have described in their professional approach to their important responsibility. I hope that all teachers reflect on their classrooms, contemplate refining their skills, and ponder their attitudes in making the educational experiences of all of their students the very best possible. Parents want the best for their children and will be there to support thoughtful, caring, and knowledgeable teachers as they work with the sometimes difficult classroom conditions that exist in our schools.

Key words: teachers, parent expectations, characteristics, student-teacher relationships

REFERENCES

Boers, D. 1995. *Happy classrooms: The CARTIE model for behavioral/academic success K–12*. Ripon, WI: WISC

Canter, L. and M. Canter. 1986. *Assertive discipline elementary resource materials workbook, grades K–6*. Santa Monica, CA: Canter and Associates.

Elkind, D. 1994. *Ties that stress: The new family imbalance*. Cambridge: Harvard University Press.

Gardner, H. 1983. *Frames of mind: The theory of multiple intelligences*. New York: Basic Books.

Glasser, W. 1986. *Control theory in the classroom*. New York: Harper and Row.

_____. 1990. *The quality school: Managing students without coercion*. New York: Harper and Row.

_____. 1993. *The quality school teacher*. New York: HarperPerennial.

Gratz, D. B. 2000. High standards for whom? *Phi Delta Kappan* 81 (9): 681–87.

Holloway, J. H. 2000. Preparing teachers for differentiated instruction. *Educational Leadership* 58 (1): 82–84.

Jensen, E. 1998. *Teacher with the brain in mind*. Alexandria, VA: Association for Supervision and Curriculum Development.

Kohn, A. 1996. *Beyond discipline: From compliance to community*. Alexandria, VA: Association for Supervision and Curriculum Development.

Santrock, J. 1987. *Adolescence: An introduction*. Dubuque, IA: Wm. C. Brown.

Willis, S. 1993. Teaching young children: Educators seek developmental appropriateness. *Association for Supervision and Curriculum Update*.

David Boers is a professor of graduate education at Marian College, Fond du Lac, Wisconsin.

From *The Clearing House*, September/October 2001, pp. 51-54. Reprinted with permission of the Helen Dwight Reid Educational Foundation. Published by Heldref Publications, 1319 Eighteenth St., NW, Washington, DC 20036-1802. © 2001.

What Urban Students Say About
Good Teaching

Interviews with these inner-city adolescents show that they want to learn and have a vision of the kind of teacher who can help them excel.

Dick Corbett and Bruce Wilson

What can schools do to encourage students to care more about learning? Make sure that teachers act in ways that demonstrate how much *they* care! At least, that would be the answer of nearly 400 students we interviewed from inner-city, low-income middle and high schools. In fact, the students never wavered in identifying their teachers as the main factor determining how much they learned, and they spoke with one voice when describing good teachers. Good teachers

- Made sure that students did their work.
- Controlled the classroom.
- Were willing to help students whenever and however the students wanted help.
- Explained assignments and content clearly.
- Varied the classroom routine.
- Took the time to get to know the students and their circumstances.

Significantly, students did not confuse teachers' personal qualities with their professional ones. Interviewees described "mean" good teachers and "mean" bad teachers; "funny" good teachers and "funny" bad teachers; and "boring" good teachers and "boring" bad teachers. If a teacher had the six qualities that students identified as those of a good teacher, then demeanor, sense of humor, and charisma—as well as any other personal characteristic—were unimportant.

Interviewing Students About Reform Efforts

In an effort to include students' voices in education reform efforts being implemented in Philadelphia, we interviewed inner-city middle schoolers annually for three years while their schools were undergoing a districtwide reform known as Children Achieving. The adolescents,

selected to reflect a range of attendance and achievement patterns, attended six of the lowest-income schools in the city. Each year, we asked them to talk about their daily instructional routines, the classes in which they learned the most and least (and behaved the best and worst), how they preferred to learn and which classes accommodated this preference, what they thought good teaching was, and where in their schedules they encountered it. We hoped to discover through these conversations whether school reforms had actually changed the educational experiences of students.

We also followed many of the same students into high school. In a serendipitous occurrence, several of the middle schools fed into high schools that had adopted the Johns Hopkins Talent Development Model. Because of this fortunate timing, we were able to get students' descriptions of their high school experiences before and during this reform.[1]

Throughout the years that the students talked with us, they held fast to their view that good teaching was central to the quality of their schooling experiences.

Throughout the years that the students talked with us, they held fast to their view that good teaching was central to the quality of their schooling experiences. Moreover, when they talked about the value of education reforms (specifically, the Talent Development Model's block schedule), they judged such reforms on the basis of their effects on teacher behavior that aided student learning.

What Is a Good Teacher?

Students repeatedly invoked the six qualities of good teaching in answering almost any question we asked. Students talked approvingly about "strict" teachers—those who pushed students to complete their assignments and maintained an orderly classroom. Students added that good teachers were willing to help, explained assignments and content clearly, varied classroom activities, and tried to understand students.

Good Teachers Push Students

These urban students admitted that their default response to most assignments was to ignore them, which understandably gave the impression that they cared little about learning. Nevertheless, students liked teachers who successfully combated this habit. As two students explained (in their words and syntax),

> I like the ones that don't allow excuses. It's my turn to get an education. I need to have someone to tell me when I'm tired and don't feel like doing the work that I should do it anyway.

> If they don't keep after you, you'll slide and never do the work. You just won't learn nothing if they don't stay on you.

Teachers "nagged" students in many ways—by consistently checking homework, offering quiet individual reminders, giving rewards, and calling parents. As one student boasted, "He keeps pressing me until I get it right."

Good Teachers Maintain Order

According to students, their teachers varied tremendously in how well they were able to control students, and the ones who could not maintain control bothered them a lot. As one student succinctly explained,

> The kids don't do the work. The teacher is hollering and screaming, "Do your work and sit down!" This makes the ones that want to learn go slower. It makes your grade sink down. It just messes it up for you. The teacher is trying to handle everybody and can't.

Another student pointed out the difference between strict and not-so-strict teachers:

> Teachers that just let you do what you want, they don't get a point across. Strict teachers get the point across.

And, as was typical of almost everything students had to say about good teaching, everything came back to whether they learned:

> I want a teacher strict enough for me to learn.

Good Teachers Are Willing to Help

Just as research has demonstrated that students have different learning styles, the students we interviewed had different helping styles. Some wanted help after school, some during class, some individually, some through working with peers, some through whole-class question-and-answer sessions, and some without ever having to acknowledge to anyone that they needed it. Being omnisciently adept at knowing how and when to offer help was an indelible part of being a good teacher.

> A good teacher takes time out to see if all the kids have what they're talking about and cares about how they're doing and will see if they need help.

Teachers who offered generous help often hooked students who previously had been reluctant classroom participants into working.

> One boy in the class, he do all his work now. If it wasn't for my teacher, he wouldn't do nothing. At the beginning of the year, he don't do nothing; now he does…. [It's] 'cause the teacher took time out to help him and talk to him.

Teacher help also broke the cycle of failure that we heard about from so many students. One of them explained this phenomenon and the role of teacher assistance in ameliorating it:

> Say, for instance, I didn't come to school. The next day I came in, they went over something new. There wouldn't be like time to show me what they did [the previous day]. And the teacher wouldn't make sure I understood. So, I start moving with them, but I be behind. They should have given extra help…. They could pull me to the side and ask me if I want to do it. Then it would be my choice.

Good Teachers Explain Until Everyone Understands

Many students complained about teachers who moved too fast through material or explained it only once and in one way. They much preferred to have teachers who stayed on an assignment until everyone understood, who offered multiple and repeated explanations, and who, as one student said, "feed it into our head real good; they do it step-by-step and they break it down."

Students seemed most disturbed by teachers who allowed discipline problems to affect the quality of their explanations. For example, many students referred to teachers who would say a variant of "I've already told you this; you should have listened the first time" in response to repeated requests for clarification. Although the teachers may have been justified in feeling frustrated at the lack of attention that prompted the requests, to students this phrase meant "I refuse to teach you."

By contrast, students' faces brightened considerably when they were able to say something like the following:

> The teachers are real at ease. They take the time, you know, go step-by-step. We learn it more. It seems like they got the time to explain it all. We don't have to leave anyone behind.

Good Teachers Vary Classroom Activities

Different activities appealed to different students. Students' preferences included working in groups, listening to the teacher talk, reading from a book, doing worksheets, participating in whole-class discussions, and doing hands-on activities. However, students agreed that learning was the primary reason for liking a certain approach, as the following three statements illustrate:

> I prefer working in groups. You have more fun and you learn at the same time. You learn quickly. So, you have fun and you do the work.

> My favorite subject is math because she made our work into a game and I caught on real fast doing it that way.

> I prefer to work by myself because most people don't read on the same level. I don't like to listen to others read. I might be ahead or behind where they are, whatever the case may be.

Students appreciated teachers who made the effort to see beyond students' behavior and understand who they really were.

Good Teachers Try to Understand Students

Students applauded teachers who did more than just teach content to them. They especially appreciated teachers who made the effort to see beyond students' behavior and understand who they really were. One student explained:

> I heard teachers talking about people, saying "Those kids can't do nothing." Kids want teachers who believe in them.

Students particularly valued teachers who recognized the possibility that students' misbehavior was not automatically targeted at the teachers.

> Sometimes a teacher don't understand what people go through. They need to have compassion. A teacher who can relate to students will know when something's going on with them. If like the student don't do work or don't under-

stand, the teacher will spend a lot of time with them.

Good Teaching = More Learning

Students clearly expressed the belief that good teaching was important because it made them learn better. Understand that when they said "better," students sometimes meant that they learned "something." Unfortunately, it was not unusual for these students to spend a semester or an entire year in a core subject in which they learned nothing, most often because they experienced a revolving door of substitutes or a new teacher who was not equipped to meet the challenges of an urban environment. Indeed, one student's advice to an early-career teacher was, "She should quit this job—it's too hard for her."

Students defined learning "better" as "getting the work right," "understanding something that a teacher already tried to teach," and "getting stuff we haven't had before." Despite the lack of definitional sophistication, students voiced no doubt about doing better in some teachers' classrooms than in others.

And because they cared about learning, it mattered greatly to students how often they encountered good teachers. Nearly every student in all six Philadelphia middle schools could identify a teacher whom they considered to be good; and nearly every one could describe a classroom situation where little learning, if any, took place.

Students' Views on School Reforms

Because good teachers were central in determining students' school experiences, these same students judged the changes that adults implemented in their schools on the basis of whether the reforms increased the number of good teachers. Students were keenly adept at evaluating the effects of significant instructional changes that had been made in their schools in terms of whether these changes promoted better teaching and, by extension, learning.

In that respect, therefore, the students tended to adopt the kind of single-minded, uncomplicated focus on improved school and classroom practices that the experts frequently urge education stakeholders to use when making strategic decisions. An illustration of how students perceived the value of one such change occurred after our original middle school students had moved on to two high schools that adopted a block schedule.

The Block Schedule

The students we had talked to in the middle school project were in the 10th grade when their schools became Talent Development High Schools and switched all of the grades from the traditional seven-period day to a block schedule in which students took four classes each semester, with 80–90 minutes devoted to each class. They saw a difference between their 9th grade and 10th grade experiences. Time seemed to be the theme that ran through many of their comparisons:

> Teachers last year wouldn't take as much time to help you.

> Now the teachers take time with you, and let you know what's got to be done.

Students predictably complained about the length of the classes with this new arrangement. Class got boring, they said—they had to sit too long, and sometimes the teachers talked forever. However, when we asked whether they preferred seven periods to four, 107 out of 148 9th and 10th graders said that they wanted the latter. Of the 41 who did not, six were neutral, and not a single student said that he or she learned better in the shorter classes. Even as they rolled their eyes about the tedium of having to be with one teacher for so long, the students explained their almost reluctant endorsements of the block schedule:

> There is more time for the teachers to help you. They can explain the work. We get to also work in groups and if I don't understand, someone else can help me.

> You learn more with just four classes because the teacher has a longer time to explain it right.

> We get to do more things. We get to work by ourselves, we get to work together, and we get to go over the work more.

> I become more focused. With more classes, oh God, it drove me crazy.

> You can build a relationship with the teacher. We can have more one-on-one interaction.

Readily available help… good explanations… variety… focused attention… closer student-teacher relationships—the block schedule, students felt, had almost single-handedly created a school full of good teachers! In spite of students' complaints about the "boredom" of longer class periods, the implementation of block scheduling had changed teachers' behaviors to correspond more closely with students' notions of good teaching—and that result alone was enough reason for students to support the reform.

Students Do Care

The block schedule has been the subject of intensive debates. Adults argue passionately, relying on research that cannot conclusively bolster either side. Our students exhibited much more single-mindedness in deciding that they supported this change. Unlike adults, they did not raise financial, political, occupational, legal, bureaucratic, or philosophical reasons why something that promoted student learning was nevertheless inadvisable. All that the Philadelphia high school students knew was that with the advent of longer classes, their teachers had changed. Instead of telling the students something once and leaving it up to them to choose to work or not, the teachers prodded, aided, and clarified more. And, over time, students noticed the true benefit of this development—they learned better.

When adults ask what they can do to make students care more about learning, their question implies that students do not care enough now. Adults, quite understandably, allow scowls, yawns, misbehavior, disrespect, and refusal to work to persuade them that apathy is rampant.

But our interviews with students in high-poverty schools suggest that these adolescents do care. The students we talked with cared so deeply about having good teachers that they wholeheartedly embraced a reform about which many adults are deeply divided. Students simply wanted good teachers because such teachers made them learn—often in spite of themselves.

Do students care about learning? Perhaps the question we should be asking is What can schools do to support and reinforce adult actions that demonstrate to students that the adults care as much about learning as the students do? The students' definitions of good teaching provide an excellent starting point for identifying just what those actions might look like.

Note

1. Our discussions with middle schoolers are reported in detail in *Listening to Urban Students: School Reform and the Teachers They Want* (Wilson & Corbett, 2001, State University of New York Press). Additional material from the project that followed students to high school is available in *Students' Perspectives on the Ninth Grade Academy of the Talent Development High Schools in Philadelphia: 1999–2000* (Corbett & Wilson, 2000, Philadelphia Education Fund).

Dick Corbett (610-408-9206) and **Bruce Wilson** (856-662-6424) are independent education researchers. Their most recent book (with coauthor Belinda Williams) is *Effort and Excellence in Urban Classrooms: Expecting and Getting Success with All Students* (Teachers College Press, 2002).

Helping Children Cope With Loss, Death, and Grief: Response to a National Tragedy

The security and safety that was a hallmark of our American society was shattered by the events of September 11th. Never before in our nation's history have so many lives been lost in a single day. Communities are impacted by multiple losses that stretch their capacities to cope. It is difficult to predict how students, adults and schools will be able to deal with the harsh realities of life in the coming weeks, months and years. Children who have experienced the loss of one or both parents, siblings, other relatives, friends, or neighbors are now suffering from profound grief.How can caring adults help these children deal with loss of this magnitude? How can we begin to understand and respond to the depths of their suffering? One thing we do know is that this will be an extremely difficult and painful task. Children and adolescents will need all the support they can get and they will require a long time to recover. Life may not be the same for anyone in this country, but those youngsters who have sustained personal losses may require significant assistance from trained, caring adults.

Expressions of Grief

Talking to children about death must be geared to their developmental level and their capacity to understand the related facts of the situation. Children will be aware of the reactions of significant adults as they interpret and react to information about death and tragedy. The range of reactions that children display in response to the death of significant others may include:

- *Emotional shock* and at times an apparent lack of feelings, which serve to help the child detach from the pain of the moment;
- *Regressive (immature) behaviors*, such as needing to be rocked or held, difficulty separating from parents or significant others, needing to sleep in parent's bed or an apparent difficulty completing tasks well within the child's ability level;

- *Explosive emotions and acting out behavior* that reflect the child's internal feelings of anger, terror, frustration and helplessness. Acting out may reflect insecurity and a way to seek control over a situation for which they have little or no control;
- **Asking the same questions over and over**, not because they do not understand the facts, but rather because the information is so hard to believe or accept. Repeated questions can help listeners determine if the child is responding to misinformation or the real trauma of the event.

Helping Children Cope

The following tips will help teachers and parents support children who have experienced the loss of parents or loved ones. Some of these recommendations come from Dr. Alan Wolfelt, Director of the Center for Loss and Life Transition in Fort Collins, Colorado.

- *Allow children to be the teachers about their grief experiences*: Give children the opportunity to tell their story and be a good listener.
- *Don't assume that every child in a certain age group understands death in the same way or with the same feelings*: All children are different and their view of the world is unique and shaped by different experiences. (Developmental information is provided below.)
- *Grieving is a process, not an event*: Parents and schools need to allow adequate time for each child to grieve in the manner that works for that child. Pressing children to resume "normal" activities without the chance to deal with their emotional pain may prompt additional problems or negative reactions.
- *Don't lie or tell half-truths to children about the tragic event*: Children are often bright and sensitive. They will see through false infor-

mation and wonder why you do not trust them with the truth. Lies do not help the child through the healing process or help develop effective coping strategies for life's future tragedies or losses.

- *Help all children, regardless of age, to understand loss and death*: Give the child information at the level that he/she can understand. Allow the child to guide adults as to the need for more information or clarification of the information presented. Loss and death are both part of the cycle of life that children need to understand.
- *Encourage children to ask questions about loss and death*: Adults need to be less anxious about not knowing all the answers. Treat questions with respect and a willingness to help the child find his or her own answers.
- *Don't assume that children always grieve in an orderly or predictable way*: We all grieve in different ways and there is no one "correct" way for people to move through the grieving process.
- *Let children know that you really want to understand what they are feeling or what they need*: Sometimes children are upset but they cannot tell you what will be helpful. Giving them the time and encouragement to share their feelings with you may enable them to sort out their feelings.
- *Children will need long-lasting support*: The more losses the child or adolescent suffered, the more difficult it will be to recover. This is especially true if they lost a parent who was their major source of support. Try to develop multiple supports for children who suffered significant losses.
- *Keep in mind that grief work is hard*: It is hard work for adults and hard for children as well.
- *Understand that grief work is complicated*: When death results from a terrorist act, this brings forth many issues that are difficult, if not impossible, to comprehend. Grieving will also be complicated by a need for vengeance or justice and by the lack of resolution of the current situation: Perpetrators may still be at large and our nation is at war. The sudden nature of death and the fact that many individuals were considered missing rather than dead further complicates the grieving process.
- *Be aware of your own need to grieve*: Focusing on the children in your care is important, but not at the expense of your emotional needs. Adults who have lost a loved one will be far more able to help children work through their grief if they get help themselves. For some

families, it may be important to seek family grief counseling, as well as individual sources of support.

Developmental Phases in Understanding Death

It is important to recognize that all children are unique in their understanding of death and dying. This understanding depends on their developmental level, cognitive skills, personality characteristics, religious or spiritual beliefs, teachings by parents and significant others, input from the media, and previous experiences with death. Nonetheless, there are some general considerations that will be helpful in understanding how children and adolescents experience and deal with death.

- *Infants and Toddlers*: The youngest children may perceive that adults are sad, but have no real understanding of the meaning or significance of death.
- *Preschoolers*: Young children may deny death as a formal event and may see death as reversible. They may interpret death as a separation, not a permanent condition. Preschool and even early elementary children may link certain events and magical thinking with the causes of death. As a result of the World Trade Center disaster, some children may imagine that going into tall buildings may cause someone's death.
- *Early Elementary School*: Children at this age (approximately 5–9) start to comprehend the finality of death. They begin to understand that certain circumstances may result in death. They can see that, if large planes crash into buildings, people in the planes and buildings will be killed. However, they may over-generalize, particularly at ages 5–6—if jet planes don't fly, then people don't die. At this age, death is perceived as something that happens to others, not to oneself or one's family.
- *Middle School*: Children at this level have the cognitive understanding to comprehend death as a final event that results in the cessation of all bodily functions. They may not fully grasp the abstract concepts discussed by adults or on the TV news but are likely to be guided in their thinking by a concrete understanding of justice. They may experience a variety of feelings and emotions, and their expressions may include acting out or self-injurious behaviors as a means of coping with their anger, vengeance and despair.
- *High School*: Most teens will fully grasp the meaning of death in circumstances such as the

World Trade Center or Pentagon disasters. They may seek out friends and family for comfort or they may withdraw to deal with their grief. Teens (as well as some younger children) with a history of depression, suicidal behavior and chemical dependency are at particular risk for prolonged and serious grief reactions and may need more careful attention from home and school during these difficult times.

Tips for Children and Teens with Grieving Friends and Classmates

Many children and teens have been indirectly impacted by the terrorists' attacks. They have learned of the deaths of people close to their friends and classmates—parents, siblings, other relatives and neighbors. Particularly in areas near the World Trade Center or Pentagon, it is not unusual to find several children in a given classroom who lost a family member—or even multiple family members. Additionally, all over the country, children have been impacted by the death of a family member at either the attack site or on board one of the four hijacked planes. Seeing their friends try to cope with such loss may scare or upset children who have had little or no experience with death and grieving. Some suggestions teachers and parents can provide to children and youth to deal with this "secondary" loss:

- Particularly with younger children, it will be important to help clarify their understanding of death. See tips above under "helping children cope."
- Seeing their classmates' reactions to loss may bring about some fears of losing their own parents or siblings. Children need reassurance from caretakers and teachers that their own families are safe. For children who have experienced their own loss (previous death of a parent, grandparent, sibling), observing the grief of a friend can bring back painful memories. These children are at greater risk for developing more serious stress reactions and should be given extra support as needed.
- Children (and many adults) need help in communicating condolence or comfort messages. Provide children with age-appropriate guidance for supporting their peers. Help them decide what to say (e.g., "Steve, I am so sorry about your father. I know you will miss him very much. Let me know if I can help you with your paper route…") and what to expect (see "expressions of grief" above).

- Help children anticipate some changes in friends' behavior. It is important that children understand that their grieving friends may act differently, may withdraw from their friends for a while, might seem angry or very sad, etc., but that this does not mean a lasting change in their relationship.
- Explain to children that their "regular" friendship may be an important source of support for friends and classmates. Even normal social activities such as inviting a friend over to play, going to the park, playing sports, watching a movie, or a trip to the mall may offer a much needed distraction and sense of connection and normalcy.
- Children need to have some options for providing support—it will help them deal with their fears and concerns if they have some concrete actions that they can take to help. Suggest making cards, drawings, helping with chores or homework, etc. Older teens might offer to help the family with some shopping, cleaning, errands, etc., or with babysitting for younger children.
- Encourage children who are worried about a friend to talk to a caring adult. This can help alleviate their own concern or potential sense of responsibility for making their friend feel better. Children may also share important information about a friend who is at risk of more serious grief reactions.
- Parents and teachers need to be alert to children in their care who may be reacting to a friend's loss of a loved one. These children will need some extra support to help them deal with the sense of frustration and helplessness that many people are feeling at this time.

Resources for Grieving and Traumatized Children

At times of severe stress, such as the trauma of the terrorist attacks on our country, both children and adults need extra support. Children closest to this tragedy may very well experience the most dramatic feelings of fear, anxiety and loss. They may have personally lost a loved one or know of friends and schoolmates who have been devastated by these treacherous acts. Adults need to carefully observe these children for signs of traumatic stress, depression or even suicidal thinking, and seek professional help when necessary.

Resources to help you identify symptoms of severe stress and grief reactions are available at the National Association of School Psychologist's website—*www.nasponline.org*. See also:

For Caregivers

Deaton, R.L. & Berkan, W.A. (1995). *Planning and managing death issues in the schools: A handbook*. Westport, CT: Greenwood Publishing Group.

Mister Rogers Website: *www.misterrogers.org* (see booklet on Grieving for children 4–10 years)

Webb, N.B. (1993). *Helping bereaved children: A handbook for practitioners*. New York: Guilford Press.

Wolfelt, A. (1983). *Helping children cope with grief*. Bristol, PA: Accelerated Development.

Wolfelt, A. (1997). *Healing the bereaved child: Grief gardening, growth through grief and other touchstones for caregivers*. Ft. Collins, CO: Companion.

Worden, J.W. (1996). *Children and grief: When a parent dies*. New York: Guilford Press

For Children:

Gootman, M.E. (1994). *When a friend dies: A book for teens about grieving and healing*. Minneapolis: Free Spirit Publishing.

Greenlee, S. (1992). *When someone dies*. Atlanta: Peachtree Publishing. (Ages 9–12).

Wolfelt, A.(2001). *Healing your grieving heart for kids*. Ft. Collins, CO: Companion.

UNIT 2
Development

Unit Selections

5. **Shaping the Learning Environment: Connecting Developmentally Appropriate Practices to Brain Research**, Stephen Rushton and Elizabeth Larkin
6. **To Be Successful-Let Them Play!**, Sally C. Hurwitz
7. **The School and the Child and the Child in the School**, Debra Eckerman Pitton
8. **Differing Perspectives, Common Ground: The Middle School and Gifted Education Relationship**, Hilda C. Rosselli and Judith L. Irvin

Key Points to Consider

- How do biology and environment interact to produce an intelligent human being?

- Why is an accurate perception of self important to children's self-esteem?

- How can schools and teachers provide an environment that is conducive to adolescent development?

 **Links: www.dushkin.com/online/**
These sites are annotated in the World Wide Web pages.

Association for Moral Education
http://www.amenetwork.org/

Child Welfare League of America
http://www.cwla.org

Pediatric Behavioral Health Resources
http://www.earlychildhoodbehavioralhealth.com/index.htm

Guidelines for Developmentally Appropriate Early Childhood Practice
http://www.naeyc.org/resources/position_statements/daptoc.htm

The National Association for Child Development
http://www.nacd.org

National Association of School Psychologists (NASP)
http://www.nasponline.org/index2.html

Scholastic News Zone
http://www.scholasticnews.com

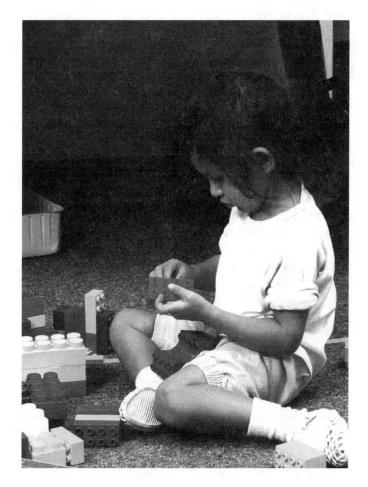

The study of human development provides us with knowledge of how children and adolescents mature and learn within the family, community, and school environments. Educational psychology focuses on description and explanation of the developmental processes that make it possible for children to become intelligent and socially competent adults. Psychologists and educators are currently studying the idea that biology as well as the environment influence cognitive, personal, social, and emotional development and involve predictable patterns of behavior.

The perceptions and thoughts that young children have about the world are often quite different when compared to adolescents and adults. That is, children may think about moral and social issues in a unique way. Children need to acquire cognitive, moral, and social skills in order to interact effectively with parents, teachers, and peers. Human development encompasses all of the above skills and reflects the child's intelligent adaptation to the environment.

Today the cognitive, moral, social, and emotional development of children takes place in a rapidly changing society. A

child must develop positive conceptions of self within the family as well as at school in order to cope with the changes and become a competent and socially responsible adult. In "Shaping the Learning Environment: Connecting Developmentally Appropriate Practices to Brain Research," the authors discuss the interaction of biology and environment. The article "To Be Successful—Let Them Play!" discusses the development of cognitive and social skills in children.

Adolescence brings with it the ability to think abstractly and hypothetically and to see the world from many perspectives. Adolescents strive to achieve a sense of identity by questioning their beliefs and tentatively committing to self-chosen goals. Their ideas about the kinds of adults they want to become and the ideals they want to believe in sometimes lead to conflicts with parents and teachers. Adolescents are also sensitive about espoused adult values versus adult behavior. The articles in this unit discuss the unique needs of young adolescents and also suggest ways in which schools and teachers can help meet these needs.

Shaping the Learning Environment: Connecting Developmentally Appropriate Practices to Brain Research

Connections are shown between recent findings in brain research and principles of Developmentally Appropriate Practices to explore the implications for early childhood learning environments and teaching practices. New research on how the growing mind learns appears to bear out the value of NAEYC's constructivist approach to early childhood education where environments are designed to gain the learner's attention, foster meaningful connections with prior understanding, and maximize both short- and long-term memory through patterns and active problem solving. Each unique learner needs to feel challenged, but not fearful, so that stimulating experiences result in an exchange of ideas and promote deeper understanding.

KEY WORDS: early childhood education; brain research; developmentally appropriate practices (DAP); learning environments.

Stephen Rushton and Elizabeth Larkin

INTRODUCTION

The past several years have seen an explosion of published articles, books, and documentaries as well as a proliferation of conferences and workshop seminars focused on connecting recent neuroscientific research findings relating the child's developing brain to educational strategies. President of the James S. McDonnell Foundation, Bruer (1998), questions the validity of this marriage, stating clearly that "brain science has little to offer education practice or policy" (p. 14). He is supported by others who warn the educational community that knowledge gleaned from today's brain science may well be out-dated in several years due to its rudimentary nature. Indeed, many educators are quick to exert pressure on the educational pendulum in order to substantiate their philosophical position. However, although brain science is relatively new, Wolfe (1998), an educational consultant and expert on brain research, postulates that the bridge between neuroscience research and education is not the job of neuroscientists, but instead, that of educators.

Studies about how the human brain learns need to be interpreted in light of the classroom environment, because children spend a great deal of their time in these settings at a critical period in their development, and expectations for our professional success carry high stakes. The good news is that new research appears to be affirming what many early childhood educators have always known about effective learning environments. The bad news is that we have yet to fully explore the implications of this rapidly expanding area of knowledge in terms of generating widely recognized practices in the field of early childhood education. This paper is a beginning attempt to draw some parallels between brain research and the early childhood classroom, and so it should be acknowledged at the outset that the connections we propose here are tentative.

The National Association for the Education of Young Children's position statement on developmentally appropriate practices (DAP) for children birth through age 8 (Bredekamp & Copple, 1997) originally stated two main objectives, namely, (a) to provide "guidance to program personnel seeking accreditation by NAEYC's National Academy of Early Childhood Programs"; and (b) to counter persistent beliefs in the prevailing traditional approach to early childhood education. The educational emphasis was on a didactic, teacher-centered approach to learning that encompassed primarily whole group instructional techniques (Bredekamp & Copple, 1997, p. v). Subsequently, DAP was revised to describe a philosophical orientation that now implies a constructivist approach to teaching young children. It is built on the premise that children are social learners who actively construct meaning and knowledge as they interact with their environment.

Research on what constitutes appropriate early learning experiences has focused during the past decade on both the social-emotional (Burts, Hart, Charlesworth, & Kirk, 1990; Hyson, Hirsh-Pasek, & Rescorla, 1990) and the cognitive (Dunn, Beach, & Kontos, 1994; Sherman & Mueller, 1996) development of young children. Studies indicate that children actively engaged in learner-centered environments score higher on measures of creativity (Hyson *et al.*, 1990), have better receptive verbal skills (Dunn *et al.*, 1994), and are more confident in their cognitive abilities (Mantzicopoulos; Neuharth-Pritchett, & Morelock, 1994; Stopek, 1993). Additionally, Frede and Barnett (1992) reported that children who attended developmentally appropriate programs in preschool performed better in first grade on standardized assessments of achievement. A study by Burts *et al.* (1993) indicated that children from low socioeconomic home environments who were enrolled in DAP kindergarten classrooms showed higher reading scores in first grade than their counterparts who attended more traditional classrooms.

Unfortunately, even with these studies, there exists a wide discrepancy between what research recommends and how children are currently being taught. Dunn and Kontos (1997) postulated that DAP programs are not the norm in early childhood programs as teachers have difficulty knowing how to implement such practices. They also reported that many parents are unaware of the significant benefits of a DAP program and therefore choose a more traditional learning environment for their children.

During the past decade a parallel body of literature has emerged, one that has potentially important implications for teachers and young children alike. Research in the fields of neuroscience (Diamond & Hopson, 1998; Fitzpatrick, 1995; Sylwester, 1997), cognitive psychology (Gardner, 1993; Goldman, 1995; LaDoux, 1996), and education (Caine & Caine, 1991, 1997; Jensen, 1998; Kovalik, 1994; Wolfe, 1998) has provided some new information for teachers to better understand the learning process with implications for how to create more effective classroom environments. Combining knowledge across these disciplines could benefit teachers seeking ideas about best practices in designing environments that are consistent with what we now know about how the human brain learns. Specifically, brain research will help provide educators with strategies that can stimulate specific areas of the brain (thalamus, amygdala, hippocampus, and the frontal cortex) in order to gain the learner's attention, foster meaningful connections with prior understanding, and maximize both short- and long-term memory.

Brain research also supports the importance of developing and implementing a curriculum that is appropriate for the learner's particular developmental age. Early childhood teachers have been acutely aware for some time now that certain periods in a young child's life are more receptive for some kinds of learning. It is exciting to observe how the literature also indicates that particular "windows of opportunities" for learning do exist when the brain's plasticity, or adaptability, allows for greater amounts of information to be processed and absorbed (Wolfe, 1998).

Many teachers who embrace the early childhood philosophy are already practicing brain research-based strategies. Rushton (in press) describes a typical early childhood setting, for example, encouraging verbal interaction, integrating curriculum content areas, and providing meaningful problem-solving opportunities. Brain research, in and of itself, does not introduce new strategies for teachers; however, it does provide very concrete and important reasons why specific approaches to teaching and certain classroom strategies are more effective than others. As we will show, brain research seems to affirm many DAP principles and the underlying early childhood educational philosophy. With each DAP principle and brain research corollary, examples are provided on how to create, organize, and/or implement a learner-centered classroom that is compatible with both bodies of research. Not all principles are addressed since clear connections are not always evident. Table I outlines the parallels between the DAP standard and what we termed Brain Research principle. Additionally, the chart provides a few classroom strategies [to] connect the two similar bodies of research.

DAP Principle 1

Domains of children's development—physical, social, emotional, and cognitive—are closely related. Development in one domain influences and is influenced by development in other domains.

Educators have known for some time that development in one area is either influenced by, or is influencing another area of development. For instance, Graves (1983), Adams (1990), Weaver (1990), and others have articulated how reading and writing are connected; as a child begins to explore letters, sounds, and writing the desire and capacity to interpret, recognize, and understand these symbols increases simultaneously. And of course, this is conditional on the child's ability to see and hear—two very separate, yet interconnecting physiological functions. With even younger children, becoming mobile increases their ability to explore and understand their immediate environment. This increased activity also helps to stimulate cognitive development as they begin to interact and make sense of their surroundings (Kostelnik, Soderman, & Whiren, 1993; Sroufe, Cooper, & DeHart, 1992).

Each region of the brain consists of a highly sophisticated neurological network of cells, dendrites, and nerves that interconnect one portion of the brain with another. New stimuli entering the body via the five senses are directed immediately to the thalamus. The thalamus acts as a sorting station and reroutes the sensory input to various parts of the brain that deal specifically with each sense. These portions of the brain, called lobes, consist of millions of cells related to the specific sense that is being stimulated. For instance, the occipital lobe relates to the receiving and processing of visual information, and is located near the rear of the brain. The temporal lobe relates to language development, writing, hearing, sensory associations, and, to some extent, memory. It is located in the mid-left portion of the brain. The parietal lobe relates to higher sensory, language, and short-term memory. Finally, the frontal lobe helps us in our ability to judge, be creative, make decisions, and plan. Learning does not take place as separate and isolated events in the brain—all these parts work together.

When a child is engaged in a learning experience a number of areas of the brain are simultaneously activated. Each lobe interacts cohesively, not as separate or isolated organs, but as interdependent collective units (Sylwester, 1997), and all of them are needed in order to read and write. For instance, reading a book requires that the child picks up a book (activating the motor cortex: movement); she looks at the words (activating the occipital lobe: vision); she attempts to decipher words (activating the temporal lobe: language); and finally, she begins to think about what the words mean (activating the frontal lobe: reasoning) (Sorgen, 1999).

We know that learning and memory are strongly connected to emotions, and thus, the learning environment needs to be both stimulating and safe. Classroom experiences can be designed to allow children to investigate, reflect, and express ideas in a variety of ways that are increasingly complex and interconnected. Gardner (1993) proposed that each individual draws on multiple intelligences and generally relies on some more than others. Thus, learners need ample opportunities to use and expand their preferred intelligences, as well as adapt to and develop the other intelligences, which are all interdependent within the one brain. Then, they need opportunities to express what they know and understand in a variety of formats.

Early childhood teachers need to recognize developmental characteristics among children in a group, as well as each learner's unique capabilities. Multiage grouping is one strategy that helps to facilitate learning for a range of abilities (Kasten & Clarke, 1993). Because all the children in the class are not the same age, children can recognize more readily how individual approaches to learning tasks are both distinctive and viable. Here, what a child knows and how he knows it is not so much a factor of age as of prior experience and learning meanings. In this, or any environment, teachers of all ages will want to foster a learning context that builds trust, promotes self-direction, and encourages students to freely exchange their feelings and ideas so that the social/emotional realm is connected positively to cognitive and physical experiences.

Table I. Different Strategies and Principles

DAP position[a]	BR principle[b]	Classroom environment[c]
1. Domains of children's development—physical, social, emotional, and cognitive—are closely related. Development in one domain influences and is influenced by development in other domains.	Each region of the brain consists of a highly sophisticated neurological network of cells, dendrites, and nerves that interconnect one portion of the brain to another. The brain's emotional center is tied to the ability to learn. Emotions, learning, and memory are closely linked as different parts of the brain are activated in the learning process.	Good curriculum naturally engages many of the five senses and activates more than one of Gardner's eight intelligences at the same time. Learning is a social activity, so children need opportunities to engage in dialogue. Multiage grouping is a strategy that can support and challenge a range of learning styles and capabilities. Good learning environments build trust, empower learners, and encourage students to explore their feelings and ideas.
2. Development occurs in a relatively orderly sequence, with later abilities, skills, and knowledge building on those already acquired.	The brain changes physiologically as a result of experience. New dendrites are formed every day, "hooking" new information to prior experiences. An enriched environment increases cell weight and branching of dendrites.	Hands-on activities stimulate the various regions of the brain, and active participation helps young children to form stronger associations with existing understanding. Different stages of play (solitary, parallel, associative, collaborative), for example, can be identified and appropriate activities designed to build increasingly complex ideas through play.
3. Development proceeds at varying rates from child to child as well as unevenly within different areas of a child's functioning.	Each brain is unique. Lock-step, assembly-line learning violates a critical discovery about the human brain: each brain is not only unique, but also is growing on its own timetable.	Environments should allow choices to accommodate a range of developmental styles and capabilities. Large blocks of time, and systems for planning and tracking work, can be organized for children to share responsibility for their activity choices. Teachers need to adjust expectations and performance standards to age-specific characteristics and unique capabilities of learners.
4. Early experiences have both cumulative and delayed effects on individual children's development. Optimal periods exist for certain types of development and learning.	Brain research indicates that certain "windows of opportunity" for learning do exist. The brain's "plasticity" allows for greater amounts of information to be processed and absorbed at certain critical periods (Wolfe, 1998). The critical period for learning a spoken language is lost by about age 10 (Sorgen, 1999).	Children need opportunities to use sensory inputs, language, and motor skills. Young children also require frequent opportunities to interact verbally with peers. Repeated opportunities to interact with materials, peers, and ideas are critical for long-term memory. Second language programs will be most successful before 5th grade and should start as early as possible.
5. Development proceeds in predictable directions toward greater complexity, organization, and internalization.	The brain is designed to perceive and generate patterns. The brain is designed to process many inputs at once and prefers multi-processing. Hence, a slower linear pace reduces understanding (Caine & Caine, 1997).	Finding patterns can be built into math, language arts, science, and other subject area curriculum. Learning environments need to be organized for both low and high order thinking skills. The use of metaphor, and repeated opportunities to compare and contrast through multiple modalities, allow children to differentiate increasingly complex schemas.
7. Children are active learners, drawing on direct physical and social experience as well as culturally transmitted knowledge to construct their own understanding of the world around them.	When a child is engaged in a learning experience, a number of areas of the brain are simultaneously activated. Children raised in nonacademically oriented environments have little experience in using decontextualized language. They are more inclined to reason with visual, hands-on strategies (Healy, 1990).	Learning should be presented in a real life context so that new information builds upon prior understanding, and then generalizes to broader concepts. Field trips, guest speakers, interactive technology, and multicultural units of study will help children better understand themselves and succeed in today's world. In environments where children can interact with diverse populations (various cultures and generations—including grandparents), and use language as well as visual-spatial strategies, their learning will be enhanced.

Table I. Different Strategies and Principles (cont.)

DAP position[a]	BR principle[b]	Classroom environment[c]
8. Development and learning result from interaction of biological maturation and the environment, which includes both the physical and social worlds that children live in.	Each of the senses can be independently or collectively affected by environmental factors that in turn will affect the brain's ability to learn. Enriched environments increase dendritic branching and synaptic responses (Diamond, 1998). The simple act of reading a book may be one of the most challenging tasks the brain must perform. Speech comes naturally, but reading does not (Sorgen, 1999).	Environments should be carefully monitored for appropriate lighting, aromas, ionization (fresh air), and noise. Water and appropriate foods should be made available to children, remembering that each person's internal clock differs. Environments should offer a wealth of materials and activity choices to explore. Children need to understand the relevance of learning to read. Learning to read should be connected to the child's speaking and writing. Reading aloud and reading for meaning are two different processes, and children need opportunities to do both.
11. Children demonstrate different modes of knowing and learning and different ways of representing what they know.	"The mental mechanisms that process music (and rhyme and rhythm) are deeply entwined with the brain's other basic functions, including emotion, perception, memory, and even language" (Sorgen, 1999, p. 56). The most powerful influences on a learner's behavior are concrete, vivid images. The brain has a primitive response to pictures, symbols, and strong, simple images (Jensen, 1995).	A classroom should provide opportunities for individual children to learn via modalities other than just verbal/linguistic or logico-mathematical tasks. Rhyme and rhythm are memory aids. Children should be able to express knowledge in a variety of forms. Dramatization, music, and the visual arts should be made readily available as modes of both learning and expression. Symbolic representation can easily be built into the arts.
12. Children develop and learn best in the context of a community where they are safe and valued, their physical needs are met, and they feel psychologically secure.	Brain research has clearly demonstrated that high levels of stress, or a perceived threat, will inhibit learning (Caine & Caine, 1997). "The brain is primarily designed to survive. No intelligence or ability will unfold until or unless given the appropriate model environment" (Jensen, 1996).	The classroom environment should connect learning experiences to positive emotions. Students need to make decisions and choices about learning that is meaningful to them. The classroom culture should support risk-taking, and view failures as a natural part of the learning process.

[a]NAEYC's positions on Developmentally Appropriate Practices (DAP)

[b]What brain research (BR) suggests about how the brain learns

[c]Strategies that incorporate both BR and DAP

DAP Principle 2

Development occurs in a relatively orderly sequence, with later abilities, skills, and knowledge building on those already acquired.

DAP Principle 3

Development proceeds at varying rates from child to child as well as unevenly within different areas of a child's functioning.

We learn to sit before we crawl, and crawl before we walk. In this way, human development is ordered and sequential. Developmental psychologists have described how stages of physical, cognitive, and social development are stable and predictable over time especially in children during the first 9 years of life. Notable pioneers such as Piaget (1952) and Erikson (1963), for example, proposed different stages of play and socialization that, providing normal development, are observable, predictable, and measurable. In these hierarchies, no stage can be skipped over as the developmental process unfolds.

Wolfe and Brandt (1998) stated that the brain changes physiologically as a result of experience. As the child experiences an event for the first time, either new dendrites are formed, or the experience is associated with a similar past event hooking new information to old understanding. Much of our behavior and development is "hardwired" through a long history of human evolution (i.e., breathing, circulation, and reflexes). However, individual brains are also "softwired" in order to adapt and create new neurological networks in response to the unique environmental stimuli encountered in our individual lives. It is in the interplay between environment and genetics, hardwired automatic behaviors and softwired developing neuronetworks, that we need to be sensitive to differences among children.

Each child's uniqueness is expressed in a number of ways: personality, temperament, learning style, maturation, speed of mastering a skill, level of enjoyment of a particular subject, attention, and memory. These attributes help to identify how a particular child will learn and what style of teaching is best suited for him or her. Further, each brain's growth is largely dictated by genetic timing, and therefore is as individualized as DNA (Sylwester, 1995). In truth, there are no homogeneous groups of children; as no two children are the same, no two brains are the same. Wolfe (1998) put it succinctly when she stated: "The environment affects how genes work, and genes determine how the environment is interpreted" (p. 10).

IMPLICATIONS FOR PRACTICE

Early childhood teachers have learned that children progress through various stages of development, knowing that each child's rate of development (and each brain) is unique and different. Providing hands-on activities that both cater to the differences among children and stimulate various regions of the brain reinforces stronger associations of meaning and makes learning inherently more interesting. Teachers who are trained to observe each child's development can establish a responsive environment for different documented stages of play (solitary, parallel, associative), and carefully design appropriate activities for the child's level. Teachers of older students can pay attention to higher order thinking skills in a similar manner, challenging students with engaging problem-solving opportunities. Teaching complex skills too soon may impede learning, and conversely, not teaching children when they are ready may result in boredom and a lack of interest.

Activities that have different levels of complexity allow every child access both to the content ideas and to conversation with peers. Creating centers around the classroom with a range of problems to solve and materials to use can accommodate the differences among learners. A general overall theme may permeate the activities in each center so that the children see connections across subject areas. A center (Rushton, in press) approach can easily be adapted from preschool to third grade, using planning sheets and individualized contracts to help children discover for themselves what their particular strengths and challenges are.

Because each learner is so different, children should be able to choose activities that fit their level of development, experience, and interest. Thus, teachers will want to use a variety of teaching methods and materials to ensure that every child becomes interested in exploring ideas, so that their auditory, visual, tactile, or emotional preferences are accounted for. More important, teachers need to remember that each child's educational experiences inside the classroom play a part in shaping a lifetime of learning habits. Different children feel challenged by different problems, and threatened by different social circumstances, and these matter in what and how they learn.

DAP Principle 4

Early experiences have both cumulative and delayed effects on individual children's development. Optimal periods exist for certain types of development and learning.

Principle 4 suggests that each learning experience lays groundwork for future learning, either positively or negatively. The child's ability to learn and interpret new information is directly related to the frequency of prior experience with related ideas. Brain research also indicates that certain windows of opportunities for learning do exist (Sorgen, 1999). In some instances, it is vital to development that a particular sense be stimulated. For instance, it has been demonstrated that some animals have had their vision obscured at key times in their development and were unable to ever see again. The blueprint, so to speak, relating to vision simply cannot be reestablished if not stimulated to grow in the first several years (Wolfe, 1998). The same can be said for developing oral language. In extreme cases in which a child has been abused, neglected, and cut off from society, speech pathologists have been unable to help those individuals speak normally.

Language and motor development both require children to actively engage with others. Conversation and physical activity are extremely important for the development of the brain. To facilitate optimal development, young children require opportunities to interact with each other regularly, encounter new vocabulary, construct arguments, express emotions, and stretch their muscles. Thus, learning environments should encourage verbal interactions, moving around the room as children work on projects or pursue a line of inquiry, and plentiful occasions to use manipulative materials including gross motor equipment.

Second language acquisition is most successful prior to fifth or sixth grade when the necessary structures in the brain for language learning are still in place. Young children seem to be particularly adept at mimicry, especially when language is rhythmic and rhyming. Also, the brain looks for patterns and connections, and repetition is critical for long-term memory. Introducing young children to more than one language is extremely beneficial, even if they do not yet understand how language is structured grammatically or written down. This early learning creates a foundation for later, more formal, study of another language.

DAP Principle 5

Development proceeds in predictable directions toward greater complexity, organization, and internalization.

The brain is designed to perceive and generate patterns and is constantly seeking to place new information into existing neurological networks. If no prior network exists, then new dendrites will be formed. Each layer of learning builds upon former networks. It has been suggested that the myelin sheath that surrounds the axons (the long tentacles of a dendrite) thicken with repeated exposure to a thought, idea, or experience. The greater the complexity of an experience, the thicker the myelin becomes. The belief is that thicker myelin results in faster recall of an event and greater memory (Diamond & Hopson, 1998). If this is true, then repetition of activities helps to thicken the myelin and thus, reinforce students' understanding.

Since no two children learn at the same rate, it is crucial that children be given repeated opportunities and ample time to explore, play, and socialize while they work in various curriculum areas (paint, blocks, dramatic play, listening center, water table, science). A typical K–3 classroom covers content in reading, writing, and mathematics, and time permitting, social studies, science, and the arts. Curriculum is often presented as separate subjects in distinct units with little overlap. Information would be better presented in a context of real life experiences where new information can build upon prior knowledge, so that learners understand how it is meaningful to them. Field trips are an excellent strategy to connect new learning to real world applications. When studying pollution, for example, students might visit the landfill, clean water treatment center, recycling plant, or local municipal garbage collection center rather than just viewing pictures and reading texts about the subject. The learner should be able to connect new information to well-established conceptual frameworks in an experiential manner, not as isolated bits of information that have no meaningful connection.

DAP Principle 7

Children are active learners, drawing on direct physical and social experience as well as culturally transmitted knowledge to construct their own understanding of the world around them.

DAP Principle 8

Development and learning result from interaction of biological maturation and the environment, which includes both the physical and social worlds that children live in.

The environment in which a child learns, both the explicit physical surroundings (people, manipulative materials, books) and the implicit cultural norms (alphabet, numerical symbols, values), shapes that child's understanding of the meaning of his or her experiences. Bredekamp and Copple (1997) stated that "young children actively learn from observing and participating with other children and adults" and that they need to "form their own hypotheses and keep trying them out through social interaction, physical manipulation, and their own thought processes" (p. 13).

The human brain is constantly seeking information from a variety of stimuli. These data are interpreted through all the senses and are then organized by the brain. Since each of the senses can be independently or collectively affected by environmental factors, they will affect the brain's overall ability to learn. Therefore, it stands to reason that the learning environment should make children physically comfortable—they need good lighting, fresh air, and a reasonable level of noise. In addition, children cannot learn when they are hungry or tired because their minds will be focused on the body's signals to eat or sleep. They need to move around to oxygenate their blood and exercise their muscles.

The social environment in a classroom relies heavily on language, and the simple act of reading is one of the most challenging tasks the brain performs. But the brain perceives patterns, and so we can help children develop language skills by looking for letter patterns in words, word patterns in sentences such as rhyming or alliteration, patterns in story sequence, and the like. Most importantly, we need to help children see the relevance of learning language and becoming competent readers, so that their motivation to learn and attention to the challenge are both high. The learning environment can reflect children's interests by including them in conversations about which books will be read.

Children who have been raised in nonacademically oriented environments have less experience using decontextualized language than their peers. In other words, they are less apt to rely on words to describe events to others outside the context where they occurred, and oral language skill development will affect later reading ability (Snow, Tabors, & Nicholson, 1995). These children may communicate more readily through using visual images, physical activity, and symbolic representation.

The curriculum can include practice in storytelling as a way to develop oral language skills and to make connections with children's real world experiences at the same time. The more children are exposed to and talk about experiences that are new to them, the more connections they can make to what they already know. Children also need opportunities to express ideas and understanding in physically active ways, such as through visual and dramatic arts. Repeated practice helps children to recall information and master physical tasks. As new information builds on prior understanding, children are able to generalize their own experiences to broader concepts.

DAP Principle II

Children demonstrate different modes of knowing and learning and different ways of representing what they know.

Gardner's (1993) work in multiple intelligences and assessment has pointed to the need for classrooms to provide more occasions for children to use music, bodily-kinesthetic, visual-spatial, and interpersonal domains to learn and express understanding. Brain research has indicated that the "mental mechanisms that process music (and rhyme and rhythm) are deeply entwined with the brain's other basic functions, including emotion, perception,

memory, and even language" (Sorgen, 1999, p. 56). If music and movement can be used to build children's social/emotional experiences in the classroom, and to reinforce memory, language development, or even mathematical skills, we are likely to reach more kinds of learners than we would if we relied solely on narrowly defined subject areas.

Jensen (1998) has said that the most powerful influences on a learner's behavior are concrete, vivid images. The brain, he added, has a primitive response to pictures, symbols, and strong, simple images. It follows, then, that our systems of symbolic representation (the alphabet and numbers) are learned better if they can be connected to concrete, vivid images such as pictures and expressive motions. Children's memories are helped by physically representing what they know in addition to using language, so the arts should hold an important place in the curriculum. Children can draw, paint, construct, and dramatize what they know and understand.

DAP Principle 12

Children develop and learn best in the context of a community where they are safe and valued, their physical needs are met, and they feel psychologically secure.

Research on the brain and learning has clearly demonstrated that high levels of stress, or a perceived threat by the child, inhibits learning (Caine & Caine, 1997). It is the brain's principal job to ensure survival. The brain's emotional center is tied to its ability to learn. The amygdala checks all incoming sensory information first to see if it fits a known impression of danger. If a threat is perceived, the ability to learn is greatly impeded as the entire body automatically gears up to defend itself.

Teachers have a central responsibility to create a learning environment that feels relaxed enough to allow children's attention to focus on the curriculum, and challenging enough to excite interest. Evaluation is one component of the educational milieu, and thus, all assessment situations need to avoid generating a perceived threat. Clearly, using a variety of methods for collecting data enhances the likelihood of matching an individual learner's ways of knowing, and provides a more complete picture of what is known and understood.

Emotions, learning, and memory are closely linked as different parts of the brain are activated in the learning process. It is crucial, especially during the first several years of the child's life, to provide a rich and safe environment that lays groundwork for this neurological network to develop. Early childhood programs ought to invite children to make choices about what and how they learn so that they are more willing to take risks and view their experiences as both relevant and positive. Children need to explore, play, and discover, in a safe and healthy environment, using all of their senses in making connections from one part of the curriculum to another.

CONCLUSION

Technological advancements during the past decade have seen the development of some sophisticated equipment that has helped to better understand the functions of the human brain. This technology and subsequent understanding of the brain, albeit overwhelming for most educators, supports many of the philosophical tenets of constructivism, rooted in the philosophy of Dewey (1964). He believed that children learn best when interacting in a rich environment. He also believed that children constructed meaning from real life applications, and further, he knew that when various senses were used simultaneously, the probability of learning would be greater. Our modern educational terminology—such as integrated curriculum, whole language, hands-on learning, authentic assessment, and developmentally appropriate practices—not only echoes brain research, but also, we believe, contains many of the underpinning beliefs, thoughts, and tenets of Dewey.

Brain research helps to explain further why constructivist educators such as Dewey (1964), Piaget and Inhelder (1969), and Vygotsky (1967) still prevail. It is hoped that with new understanding about how the brain works, combined with the tenets of Developmentally Appropriate Practice, our ability to educate future generations will be greatly enhanced. The neuroscientist's job is to better understand the workings of the mind and brain; it is our job, as educators, to carefully sift through their findings and connect them to what we know empirically about how children learn best.

REFERENCES

Adams, M. J. (1990). *Beginning to read: Thinking and learning about print.* Urbana-Champaign, IL: The Reading Research and Education Center.

Bredekamp, S., & Copple, C. (1997). *Developmentally appropriate practice in early childhood programs* (Rev. ed.). Washington, DC: National Association for the Education of Young Children.

Burts, D., Hart, C., Charlesworth, R., & Kirk, L. (1990). A comparison of frequencies of stress behaviors observed in kindergarten children in classrooms with developmentally appropriate versus developmentally inappropriate instructional practices. *Early Childhood Research Quarterly, 5,* 407–423.

Burts, D., Hart, C., Charlesworth, R., DeWolf, D., Ray, J., Manuel K., & Fleege, P. (1993). Developmental appropriateness of kindergarten programs and academic outcomes in first grade. *Journal of Research in Childhood Education, 8*(1), 23–31.

Caine, R. N., & Caine, G. (1997). *Education on the edge of possibility.* Alexandria, VA: ASCD.

Dewey, J. (1964). The relation of theory to practice in education. In R. Archamault (Ed.), *John Dewey on education: Selected writings* (pp. 313–338). New York: Random House.

Diamond, M., & Hopson, J. (1998). *Magic trees of the mind: How to nurture your child's intelligence, creativity, and healthy emotions from birth through adolescence.* New York: Penguin Putnam.

Dunn, L., Beach, S., & Kontos, S. (1994). Quality of the literacy environment in day care and children's development. *Journal of Research in Childhood Education, 9*(1), 24–34.

Elkind, D. (1981). *The hurried child.* Reading, MA: Addison-Wesley.

Erikson, E. H. (1963). *Childhood and society.* New York: Norton.

Fitzpatrick, S. (1995). Smart brains: Neuroscientists explain the mystery of what makes us human. *American School Board Journal.*

Frede, E., & Barnett, W. S. (1992). Developmentally appropriate public school preschool: A study of implementation of the High/Scope curriculum and its effects on disadvantaged children's skills at first grade. *Early Childhood Research Quarterly, 7,* 483–499.

Gardner, H. (1993). *Multiple intelligences: The theory in practice.* New York: Basic Books.

Graves, D. (1983). *Writing: Teachers and children at work.* Portsmouth, NH: Heinemann.

Hirsh-Pasek, K., Hyson, M., & Rescorla, L. (1990). Academic environments in preschool: Do they pressure or challenge young children? *Early Education and Development, 1,* 401–423.

Hyson, M., Hirsh-Pasek, K., & Rescorla, L. (1990). The classroom practices inventory: An observation instrument based on NAEYC's guidelines for developmentally appropriate practices for 4- and 5-year-old children. *Early Childhood Research Quarterly, 5,* 475–494.

Jensen, E. (1998). *Teaching with the brain in mind.* Alexandria, VA: Association for Supervision and Curriculum Development.

Kasten, W., & Clark, B. (1993). *The multi-age classroom: A family of learners.* New York: Richard C. Owen Publishers.

Kostelnik, M., Soderman, A., & Whiren, A. (1993). *Healthy young children: A manual for programs.* New York: Macmillan.

LaDoux, J. (1996). *The emotional brain: The mysterious underpinnings of emotional life.* New York: Simon & Schuster.

Piaget, J. (1952). *The origins of intelligence in children.* Toronto: George J. McLeod.

Piaget, J., & Inhelder, B. (1969). *The psychology of the child.,* New York: Basic Books.

Rushton, S. (in press). A developmentally appropriate and brain-based compatible learning environment. *Young Children.*

Sherman, C., & Mueller, D. (1996, June). *Developmentally appropriate practice and student achievement in inner-city elementary schools.* Paper presented at Head Start's Third National Research Conference, Washington, DC. (ED 401 354)

Sorgen, M. (1999, June). *Applying brain research to classroom practice.* Materials presented at the University of South Florida Brain/Mind Connections Conference, Sarasota, FL.

Spodek, B. (Ed.). (1993). *The handbook of research on the education of young children.* New York: Teachers College Press.

Snow, C. E., Tabors, P. O., & Nicholson, P. A. (1995, Fall/Winter). SHELL: Oral language and early literacy skills in kindergarten and first grade children. *Journal of Research in Childhood Education, 10,* 37–48.

Sroufe, L. A., Cooper, R. G., & DeHart, G. G. (1992). *Child development: Its nature and course* (2nd ed.). New York: Knopf.

Sylwester, R. (1997). The neurobiology of self-esteem and aggression. *Educational Leadership, 54*(5), 75–79.

Vygotsky, L. (1967). Play and its role in the mental development of the child. *Soviet Psychology, 12,* 62–76.

Weaver, C. (1990). *Understanding whole language: From principles to practice.* Portsmouth, NH: Heinemann.

Wolfe, J., & Brandt, R. (1998). What we know from brain research. *Educational Leadership, 56*(3), 8–14.

Stephen Rushton and Elizabeth Larkin are from the University of South Florida at Sarasota

Correspondence should be directed to Stephen Rushton, University of South Florida at Sarasota, 5700 N. Tamiami Trail, PMC 217, Sarasota, Florida 34243; e-mail: srushton@sar.usf.edu

From *Early Childhood Education Journal,* Vol. 29, No. 1, 2001, pp. 25-33. © 2001 by Early Childhood Education Journal.

For Parents Particularly—Mary Jane Blasi

To Be Successful—
Let Them Play!

Sally C. Hurwitz

Upon observing her son's class, a parent of a kindergarten child asked the principal, "These kids are just playing—when are they going to start learning something?"

All parents reach a point when they anxiously wait for their children to begin "real school." Up until that time, many parents view their children's activities as nothing more than mindless play. It is no surprise to parents that healthy young children devote much of their time and energy to play. After all, to adults play is just for fun; it's relaxing and recreational, not work. They perceive child's play as just that, play. And more important, many feel there is no learning value in their children's play.

Nothing could be further from the truth. Play for young children is creative, spontaneous, unpredictable, and absolutely fun. While play may seem like a frivolous activity, it is an important medium for young children's learning. It is a significant contributor to the child's cognitive, physical, emotional, and social development.

Play is the natural and best way for children to learn as they investigate for themselves and observe others at play and work. They are natural anthropologists who have a need and desire to investigate their world through real experiences and natural environments.

Take a moment to remember your own childhood. How did you spend your time? In play, of course! Outside or inside, quietly or loudly, with a big mess or no mess at all, play is the way children make sense out of the complicated and complex world in which we live. Play is the medium children use to take risks, to challenge themselves both physically and mentally, to create something new, to deal with fears, and to enjoy the moment as they construct new meanings.

For children, play is at the very heart of their learning and development. Five qualities distinguish play for young children from other activities:

- It is a process. The outcome is not as important as the process itself.
- Play is child-initiated. The activity is done for no other reason than the child wants to do it.
- In play, everything and anything can happen: a sheet over a table becomes a castle and the little girl inside is the princess. There is no question that the functions of objects are transformed during play—a process called nonliteral play.
- Play becomes the arena for testing rules, both logical and illogical. Rules freely appear and disappear in children's play; they may be simple or complex, and they are created from children's previous knowledge. An example of rules in play is the "rule" of roles. For example, when young children play in the housekeeping area, you will often hear one of the children assigning roles to each of the other children ("You be the baby").
- Play is very much an activity of the mind. Children may become deeply engrossed in their play and find it difficult to stop when asked. Engagement in play involves the mind in an active process as a child investigates, explores, and inquires during play.

Within a classroom setting, play and the curriculum should be deeply integrated; experienced teachers should be in a position to observe as children's cognitive, social, and physical learning takes place. A quality curriculum should rely heavily on play. Research supports the importance of play for young children, but it must be tempered with what we know about the individual child and what is age-appropriate for the child.

Children need multiple opportunities for meaningful play in a variety of settings and environments. Through many experiences, children begin to construct their knowledge and understanding of multiple skills, including creativity, cognitive competencies, social skills, and physical skills. These play experiences force children to constantly reexamine what they know to be true, and they challenge them to construct a new understanding based on new information. This "constructing" is repeated many times in a young child's life and helps him/her to construct a personal understanding of the world. It sounds simple enough, but the trick for parents, caregivers, and teachers is to provide multiple meaningful and appropriate experiences for the child within a safe environment.

When parents, caregivers, and teachers provide opportunities for children to play, they also are providing them with learning opportunities. During play, children may expand their expressive language proficiency; develop number sense as they build with blocks and other constructive materials; develop creativity through art activities and problem solving; and develop important social skills, such as taking turns and cooperating. They develop the eye-hand coordination necessary to hold a pencil and learn to read and write; develop a strong body through fine and gross motor activities; and develop early essential math skills, such as number concepts and classification skills. The dramatic arts area and the manipulatives area provide skills essential for an understanding of how things work, the library corner provides children a place for developing story sense and comprehension, and the ma-nipulative area offers opportunities to learn about the properties of a variety of objects. This list is not comprehensive, but it demonstrates that play is an essential for young children as they construct their own knowledge about the world in which they live.

Parents, caregivers, and teachers see children play in many ways. Learning to identify different types of play may give you further understanding of their importance. The many different play categories include:

- Practice Play—play that children do repeatedly, solely for pleasure, such as playing in sand and pouring it through their fingers.
- Constructive Play—play where children construct or create something, such as block building.
- Rough and Tumble Play—play that involves laughing and pretending; as the name implies, it can get a little rough (it is not aggressive play and, when done in a safe area, is an acceptable form of play).
- Dramatic Play—play that gives children the opportunity to take on the role of another person or of an object.
- Games With Rules—play governed by a set of rules, such as a game of "Duck, Duck, Goose."

Understanding these categories helps teachers plan appropriate play activities to meet the developmental needs of the whole child.

Many forms of learning are influenced in part by the belief that play is a beneficial component of young children's learning. A large body of research supports the value of play for a child's development. The research demonstrates that play promotes: cognitive development, problem solving, language development, creativity, discovery, reasoning and thought, group cooperation, social skills, and fine and gross motor skills. So the next time you see your children engaged in play, remember that they are practicing and developing the skills necessary to be successful students and members of the community. Let them have fun and play!

Sally C. Hurwitz is Coordinator of Field Experience, College of Education, Arizona State University West, Phoenix.

Reinventing the Middle School

The School and the Child and the Child in the School

Middle school students are still open to new ideas, still undecided about who they are and what they will ultimately be, thereby creating a wonderful opportunity for teachers to be a part of their journey into adulthood.

By Debra Eckerman Pitton

S itting in a meeting with a group of teachers who were discussing plans for the conversion of their district's junior high into a new middle school, I overheard one 8th grade teacher say, "I don't know about expecting all of this interdisciplinary teaching stuff and flexible scheduling to really make a difference. It was so much easier back a few years ago… the kids listened to you and did what you asked. Now it seems that the kids don't care, they don't do the work, or they just aren't as capable. There is so much need for discipline and…"

One of the administrators cut her off. "The kids who come in our doors are the kids we need to teach. The parents aren't keeping all the good ones at home. We have to find ways to meet students' needs, whatever they are, not pine for the 'good old days.' Yes, students are different today; our society has changed. With technology and the impact of the media, very little is the way it was 10 or 15 years ago, so why would you expect the students to remain the same?"

Unconvinced, the teacher just shook her head. I listened to the rest of the discussion, but thought for a long time about those comments. I am aware of the challenges involved in the process of moving a junior high towards a middle school philosophy, yet I wondered why this was so. I wondered if the difficulty of embracing a middle school approach was related to this perception that kids today are somehow not as capable and bright as their predecessors.

Who Are the Students in Our Schools?

Behind all of the concepts espoused by middle level philosophy lies the premise that we need a different structure for children of this age because they are developmentally different from elementary and high school students. If teachers do not recognize the impact of these developmental differences, then they will not be able to respond accordingly. Eccles, Lord, Roeser, Barber, & Josefowicz (1996) state that middle school students require different types of educational environments in order to meet each individual's developmental needs at that particular time, as well as to help them continue to develop. Students at this transitional period, between grade school and high school, need schools and classrooms that help them move through this period of adjustment.

If we know that students of this age need teaching and classroom interactions that provide them with meaning and address their developmental issues, why do many middle school classrooms still reflect a teacher focused, content directed, autocratic approach? Perhaps it is because we, as educators, have not been willing to give any real credence to the insights provided by developmental theory. As adults, we know that we work harder on things we enjoy, we learn more when we choose to do something and are involved in the decision making, and we strive to do our work well when it means something to us. Yet when we face a classroom full of young adolescents, it is easy to pull rank and dictate what *we* think is important, what *we* think is relevant and meaningful. Why is it so easy to tell young people what to do rather than to ask them?

As adults, most of us would never think of forcing another individual to follow our directives. We ask for input, we work in committees, we gather multiple perspectives and we build consensus. Even without reviewing the research on group dynamics (Johnson & Johnson, 1991), adults are aware that a higher quality work product is produced when individuals have a say in what is completed and how it is accomplished. At least here in the United States, it is a commonly held belief that if someone has a voice in a decision they are more likely to support it. Our democratic society demands active participation in making decisions that affect us as individuals. As research into group interaction and the effects of group participation identifies, being a part of group decision-making, rather than being dictated to, results in a more productive worker (or learner) and a higher quality product (Johnson, 1990; Johnson & Johnson, 1991). Well intentioned adults strive to positively interact and give everyone a voice in our communities, in the work place, and in government. So why does this not occur in many classrooms, when our purpose is to develop future citizens?

Perhaps teachers find a classroom of hormonally charged young people innately threatening, so keeping control becomes paramount. We know that all of the changes young people are going through at this time creates anxiety and often confusion and hostility. It is scary to think about unleashing all of that emotional energy in a classroom. It feels more comfortable to keep things under control, to manage all aspects of the classroom. Middle school philosophy suggests that teachers give up much of that control and begin to work with their students as they would other adults. This is asking for change that is too much for many teachers to handle. They are moving out of their comfort zones if they let go of their control of the curriculum and ask students what they would like to learn. Teachers let go of their control if they ask other teachers with differing perspectives to share in the development of curriculum. They let go of their control when they have to teach in areas that stretch them beyond current levels of knowledge and preparation. Finally, they let go of their control if they give the students opportunities to express themselves freely.

Structural changes such as teaming flexible schedules, exploratory options, interdisciplinary curriculum, and advisory groups have been identified as critical elements in creating a supportive learning environment for middle schoolers. However, several studies indicate that teachers may need to adjust the way they interact with their students for these changes to be effective. Eccles and Midgley, (1989); and Eccles, Midgley, Buchanan, Wigfield, Reuman and Mac Iver, (1993), identified that despite awareness of the physical, social, emotional and cognitive changes occurring in young people, classrooms for students between the ages 10–14 often reflect strong teacher centered control and emphasis on discipline along with limited input from students in the way the class is run. Decisions about curriculum and learning opportunities are most often left solely to the teachers. Eccles and Wigfield (1997) refer to Mac Iver and Reuman's (1988) work which concluded that this mismatch between the emerging adolescent's need for self-management and the opportunities provided for them in the classroom results in the students' lack of motivation and interest in school. These studies point out that for many young adolescents there seems to be no purpose to being in school, nor any feeling that they are being allowed to develop and have a voice. Therefore, they choose to act out.

Middle school students are at a crossroads in their educational development; failing to sense a purpose to schooling will create feelings of apathy

Middle school students are at the crossroads in their educational development, and for many, the sense that there is no purpose to their schooling creates a feeling of apathy and disinterest. This can result in failure or dropping out of school altogether. Teachers must recognize that adolescent changes cannot be downplayed. The incorporation of student choice and proactive accommodation for the young adolescents' myriad physical, emotional and social stresses must be included in every classroom. While many educators can recite a litany of young adolescent needs, their own reactions to the adolescents' push for independence and self-determination is often to try to squash the emerging sense of self with control and directives. It is easier to try and control the tensions and emotional ups and downs among students than to try and help them learn to deal with such issues. It often feels more comfortable for teachers to keep a tight hold on the reins in their class-rooms, yet it is only through the sharing of decision making that students will feel invited into the learning process. Extending an invitation to students to join in the educational process says that the teacher values them as individuals.

Changing Perceptions

Just as we know middle school students are going through an adjustment period and that they need support to accomplish a successful transition to adulthood, so too do teachers moving into a middle school concept need support as they move into a new dimension of teaching. Teacher preparation programs must provide more emphasis on the links between adolescent development and best practice in the classroom. However, McEwin and Dickinson (1995) reported that many issues, such as lack of program availability, interest, teacher resistance, and a dearth of advocates for the middle level concept has prevented widespread implementation of specialized middle school teacher preparation. Thus there are too few teachers who have studied to any extent the needs of young adolescents or the appropriate educational responses to those needs.

Atwell, noted middle school writing teacher, described an epiphany she experienced after working with a student who did not follow her prescribed writing program. Atwell wrestled with ideas from experts who suggested that she needed to let go of her extensive writing curriculum. At first she resisted, but after observing her students at work, she stated, "I saw that my creation (the curriculum) manipulated kids.... Students either found ways to make sense of, or peace with, the language arts curriculum, or they failed the course." (Atwell, 1998, p. 4.). Here was a teacher who had created a very thoughtful, detailed curriculum, and who struggled to identify what would make her teaching better. "I rationalized... what I needed were even more creative, more open topics (for writing).... I needed better students—kids who consistently made my assignments their own,... who came to me prepared by their teachers to write well. I needed better colleagues." (Atwell, 1998, p. 11).

I find it interesting that Atwell also complained about the students and felt that if only somehow the kids were different and their prior classrooms were more effective—she would be successful, just like the teacher in the planning meeting mentioned at the beginning of this article. The fact was that Atwell needed to change, just as many teachers have to change before they can truly help middle school students learn. Atwell went on to say "I didn't know how to share responsibility with my students and I wasn't too sure I wanted to. I liked the vantage of my big desk. I liked being creative, setting topic and pace... taking charge. Wasn't that my job? If responsibility for their writing shifted to my students, what would I do?" (Atwell, 1998, p. 13).

Atwell articulated the unspoken fear that many educators hold—what will my role be if I no longer dictate every move in the classroom?

Atwell articulated the unspoken fear that many educators hold—what will my role be if I no longer dictate every move in the classroom? We know what the research says about development and the needs of students. As teachers, we have to change our selves to be able to create classrooms and schools where students can learn. We need to let go of the image of what teachers *used* to do and what we *thought* kids were like. Our society has changed, and those kids who, as Atwell said, "didn't make peace with the curriculum," who used to leave school or fail, can no longer be ignored or pushed out. Society is demanding that all students be given the opportunity to learn. Standards are being set, and the expectation is that teachers can and must help students learn.

It is not easy to let go of the tightly held beliefs about teaching that shape educators' perceptions about their role and responsibilities in a classroom. However, we cannot close our eyes to what we now know about how students learn. We need to overcome our fears about giving students a voice in their own learning if we want to enable all students to reach their potential.

Becoming Responsive to Young Adolescents' Needs

Specifically, what can teachers do to move out from behind the desk and work with the students to develop appropriate educational experiences? The answer has always been out there—in the concepts proposed by the middle school model. Two primary areas to start with are the advisory program and the curriculum.

In their 25-year perspective on middle schools, McEwin, Dickinson, and Jenkins (1996) described research on the implementation of the middle school concept which indicated that teacher-based guidance programs had declined slightly from 1988 to 1993. For advisory programs that were in place, there seemed to be an increase of time allotted to them, although there was some question as to what was occurring during those advisory times. Again, lip service to the concepts of supporting young adolescent needs and creating strong connections between caring adults and adolescents seems to be the common experience. Advisory is a foreign experience for many teachers, and McEwin, Dickinson, and Jenkins' work confirmed that teachers are often opposed to this role. Lack of preparation heightens teachers' feelings of inadequacy when leading advisory activities, discussions, and lessons.

Any job that makes one stretch into areas that are uncomfortable has the potential to make them a better person.

Teaching, which addresses new ideas, knowledge, and competencies that students need to develop into adulthood, is not static. Any job that makes one stretch into areas that are uncomfortable has the potential to make them a better person as they rise to meet the new challenges. Teachers will benefit from meeting this challenge.

So what should advisory look like? It is not a good option to simply use advisory time for a study hall or revert to an administrative home room model. Students at this age need opportunities to talk about issues they are concerned about, they need to feel a sense of belonging, and they need to connect with an adult who cares. If teachers view their students as emerging adults and acknowledge the needs and concerns of young adolescents, then it makes sense that the teacher's role must also include facilitating opportunities for student discussion and skill building in the social and emotional areas. All of these things happen in a well developed and carefully facilitated advisory program.

Once middle school teachers have embraced the effective use of advisory programs to support their students, the other area where educators need to let go of their preconceived images of middle school students is in the area of curriculum. There are two important shifts that need to occur: Content has to connect to the lives of the students in order to be meaningful, and students need to have some voice in the decisions about what they will learn.

While integrated curriculum may hook students and excite them about learning, it is a scary step for many teachers.

Inviting students to share in curriculum decision making is another difficult step for teachers. Atwell (1998), describing what she had learned about curriculum for young adolescents, stated "Learning is more likely to happen when students like what they are doing. Learning is also more likely when students can be involved and active and when they can learn from and with other students" (p. 69).

Making Connections

Giving the students a voice in deciding what they learn is only part of the curriculum shift that must happen in middle school classrooms. Interdisciplinary or integrated curriculum is another way to make the learning meaningful, but it is another middle school concept that teachers often resist. Brazee (1995) stated, "While there are numerous arguments for an integrated curriculum, perhaps the most compelling one is that an integrated curriculum best addresses the unique needs of young adolescents, yet it is the least developed in practice" (p. 16). Another curriculum expert, Beane (1995), added "Curriculum integration begins with real-life problems as themes, proceeds according to the organic integration of knowledge and serves the purpose of enhancing self and world meaning" (p. 28). George, Stevenson, Thomason, and Beane (1992) suggested that middle school curriculum needs to begin by seeking out answers to young adolescent's concerns about their world, and that teachers must discuss this with their students as a part of curriculum planning. This is very different from the traditional curriculum developed and implemented by most teachers. However, while it may "hook" students and excite them about learning, it is a scary step for many teachers.

Many of us are fearful of going somewhere where we have not been before. Descriptions of appropriate middle school curriculum suggest major shifts from the way teachers have developed their lessons in the past. "The definition of who is learning in the school should be expanded to include teachers and other adults.... Adults cannot simply provide answers to powerful questions, but must seek them along with young people" (George, Stevenson, Thomason, & Beane, 1992, p. 97). This echoes what Atwell proposed: that we must be involved with our students in their learning. But if a teacher does not have everything all lined up and ready to go in the classroom because she wants to ask students for their input, then there are many opportunities for the teacher to "lose control." This is the heart of many teachers' fears: that the students will overwhelm them with their voices and energy and the teacher will lose control in the classroom.

Teaming provides an answer—holding hands and going together makes the process more comfortable. Teachers who are developing new curricula and seeking connections to provide adolescents with relevant learning experiences cannot make this change overnight. Working together they can structure class discussions on curriculum development to allow for student voice and yet maintain a focus. School systems should provide scheduling that supports teaming and does not undermine efforts to link content and help students make sense of the curriculum.

Teachers who struggle to let go of the control they traditionally have held over the curriculum and to shift their view of young adolescent learners need support. This support must come from school districts in the form of money and time. McEwin, Dickinson, and Jenkins state that the "lack of money to support two prep times for development of team teacher project(s) and no common planning time for teachers" (1996, p. 107) are major obstacles to the implementation of middle school concepts. Teachers need to discuss and reflect with their colleagues about their fears and frustrations as they work to move their classroom interactions in a new direction. Two prep periods give teachers time to plan for their own classes but also provide valuable interaction time for colleagues during team planning time. Common planning time underpins the concept of teaming and provides the opportunity for personal interactions that must be provided to teachers before they can model it for their students. Interdisciplinary curriculum cannot be generated and coordinated if the teachers involved never have a chance to talk. Districts that provide the financial means to support two prep times for faculty teams are doing their part to help teachers implement middle level concepts.

Support for Change

With all that we know about young adolescents, why is it that despite 25 years of discussion and study on the positive effects of middle schools, some districts still refuse to provide the resources that will enable students' needs to be met? A longitudinal study of middle schools involved in comprehensive school transformation identified that there was higher achievement by students in schools with high levels of implementation of the middle school concept (Felner, Jackson, Kasak, Mulhall, Brand, & Flowers, 1997). More than 15,000 students were involved in this study which showed increased levels of achievement in reading, mathematics, and language arts, The implication from this study is clear: Young people in schools that implemented middle school concepts at a high level "achieve a higher level academically than those in non-implemented schools and substantially better than those in partially implemented schools" (Felner, et. al., 1997, p. 544).

The more comprehensive the implementation of middle school concepts, the better the results for students.

Research such as this should not be ignored. We need to disseminate what we know about middle school teaching and learning so parents, teachers, and administrators are as aware of the best practices for middle schools as they are with medical research. As Felner's study indicated, the more comprehensive the implementation of middle school concepts, such as those in *Turning Points* (Carnegie Council on Adolescent Development, 1989), the better the results for students. Indeed, "the presence or absence of a particular element of the program may affect the levels of implementation of other components." (Felner, et. al., 1997, p. 543.) Middle schools and middle school teachers should not pick and choose which of the middle level components they want to use. All of the elements need to be present, especially those difficult for teachers to embrace—advisory and student centered curriculum. Time and money for teacher development and interaction are crucial to the effective implementation of all of the middle level concepts. Parents need to be informed that schools cannot simply consider what is efficient, but must find the resources to implement what is good for young people. Referendums that provide money to fund the operation of middle schools must be supported. In addition, those responsible for educational funding in our state governments need to be informed about the components of effective middle schools and their positive impact on young adolescents' educational experiences.

Making a Difference

For students to be supported in their middle school years, for them to be a part of the school, teachers need to be supported by district funding so they have the time, money, and other resources to develop their understandings of teaming, curriculum, and student centered learning. However, in describing barriers that can impede the movement towards implementation of middle school concepts, Lipsitz, Mizell, Jackson, and Austin (1997) stated that "A lack of individual will to persevere despite formidable obstacles has been the most persistent, albeit understandable, barrier to school reform." (1997, p. 539).

Ultimately, teachers must let go of their old perceptions of young adolescents, learn to enjoy and appreciate their students as young adults, and allow themselves to learn how to work in teams to implement concepts such as advisory and student centered curriculum.

Middle school students are still open to new ideas, still searching for answers and undecided about who they are and what they will ultimately be. This creates a wonderful opportunity for teachers to be a part of their journey into adulthood. But as with all adults, we cannot force the learning process, we must invite the students to join us on the journey. The children who are in our middle schools today are the best we have. There are none of those "perfect children" hidden away somewhere waiting for teachers to fill their heads with knowledge. Students today are a part of a world that is active, mobile, and ever-changing. We need to change our perception of students and help them deal with the issues they will have to face as adults.

This will only happen when we bring the child into our school, into our classroom, and make the school a place that reveals their world. Middle schools will never reach their potential until the human element, the teachers, stretch themselves and learn to focus on the students. Franklin D. Roosevelt once said "we have nothing to fear but fear itself"—a great quote for a middle school teacher. We cannot fear going forward, changing our world view, and inviting young adolescent learners into the classroom as partners. Through teacher commitment in the areas of advisory and student centered curriculum, coupled with district support, middle level classrooms can provide a meaningful learning experience for every child in the school.

References

Atwell, N. (1998). *In the middle: New understandings about writing, reading and learning.* Portsmouth, NH: Boynton/Cook.

Beane, J. A. (1995). Myths, politics and meaning in curriculum integration. In Y. Siu-Runyan & V. Faircloth (Eds.), *Beyond separate subjects: Integrative learning at the middle level* (pp. 25–38). Norwood, MA: Christopher-Gordon.

Brazee,E. (1995). An integrated curriculum supports young adolescent development. In Y. Siu-Runyan & V. Faircloth (Eds.), *Beyond separate subjects: Integrative learning at the middle level* (pp. 5–24). Norwood, MA: Christopher-Gordon.

Carnegie Council on Adolescent Development. (1989). *Turning Points: Preparing American youth for the 21st century.* New York: Carnegie Corporation.

Eccles, J. S., Midgely, C., Buchanan, C. M., Wigfield, A., Reuman, D., & Mac Iver, D. (1993). Development during adolescence: The impact of stage/environment fit. *American Psychologist, 48*(2), 90–101.

Eccles, J. S., Lord, S. E., Roeser, R. W., Barber, B. L., & Jozefowicz, D. M. H. (1996). The association of school transitions in early adolescence with developmental trajectories through high school. In J. Schulenberg, J. Maggs & K. Hurrelmann, (Eds.), *Health risks and developmental transitions during adolescence* (pp. 283–320). New York: Cambridge University Press.

Eccles, J. S., & Midgley, C. (1989). Stage environment fit: Developmentally appropriate classrooms for young adolescents. In C. Ames & R. Ames (Eds.), *Research on motivation in education* (pp. 139–186). New York: Academic Press.

Eccles, J. S. & Wigfield, A. (1997). Young adolescent development. In J. L. Irvin, (Ed.), *What current research says to the middle level practitioner* (pp. 15–29). Columbus, Ohio: National Middle School Association.

Felner, R. D., Jackson, A. W., Kasak, D., Mulhall, P., Brand, S., & Flowers, N. (1997). The impact of school reform for the middle years. *Phi Delta Kappan, 78*(7), 528–532, 541–550.

George, P. S., Stevenson, C., Thomason, J., & Beane, J. (1992). *The middle school and beyond.* Alexandria, VA: Association for Supervision and Curriculum Development.

Johnson, D. W. (1990). *Reaching out: Interpersonal effectiveness and self-actualization* (4th ed.). Englewood Cliffs: NJ: Prentice-Hall.

Johnson, D. W., & Johnson, F. P. (1991). *Joining together* (4th ed.). Englewood Cliffs: NJ: Prentice-Hall.

Lipsitz, J., Mizell, M. H., Jackson, A. W., & Austin, L. M. (1997). Speaking with one voice: A manifesto for middle-grades reform. *Phi Delta Kappan, 78*(7), 533–540.

McEwin, C. K. & Dickinson, T. S. (1995). *The professional preparation of middle level teachers: Profiles of successful programs.* Columbus, Ohio: National Middle School Association.

McEwin, C. K., Dickinson, T. S. & Jenkins, D. M. (1996). *American middle schools: Practices and progress—A 25 year perspective.* Columbus, OH: National Middle School Association.

Mac Iver, D., & Reuman, D. (1988, April). *Decision making in the classroom and early adolescents' valuing of mathematics.* Paper presented at the annual meeting of the American Educational Research Association, New Orleans.

Debra Eckerman Pitton is an associate professor of education at Gustavus Adolphus College, St. Peter, Minnesota, E-mail: dpitton@gustavus.edu

From *Middle School Journal,* September 2001, pp. 14-20. © 2001 by the National Middle School Association.

Differing Perspectives, Common Ground: The Middle School and Gifted Education Relationship

What Research Says

Middle school educators and advocates for the gifted share much common ground for addressing the needs of a wide variety of learners: flexible pacing, independent study, and teaching thinking skills.

By Hilda C. Rosselli & Judith L. Irvin

A curious relationship has evolved over the years between the fields of gifted education and middle grades education. On an initial glance, beliefs important to each field indicate an amazing overlap in philosophy and practices. However, when middle grades philosophy positioned heterogeneous grouping as one of the preeminent guideposts for policies and practices endorsed by the field, the common ground between the two fields lessened. Leaders in gifted education, unable to embrace a total abandonment of grouping, responded vehemently and expressed reservations regarding the ability of the middle school movement to meet the needs of high ability students (Gallagher, Coleman, & Nelson, 1995; Plucker & McIntire, 1996; Sicola, 1990; Tomlinson, 1992; 1994). The resulting differences reframed the relationship between experts from gifted education and middle grades education and fueled lively debates on the moral and efficacious nature of ability grouping. Others sought to re-examine the goodness of fit between the two movements by moving beyond the rhetoric of differences towards a healthier focus on programs and practices (Coleman, Gallagher, & Howard, 1993; Coleman & Gallagher, 1995; Mills & Durden, 1992; Rosselli, 1995). At the same time, with the advent of the National Research Center on the Gifted and Talented and federally funded Javits grants, a more defined research focus in gifted education provided a rich source for examining implications for middle level education. This article provides an overview of the literature that has historically framed the

debates between gifted education and middle grades education followed by discussion of research that seeks common ground between the two fields and implications relative to middle school education policies and practices that hold promise for considering the unique needs of high ability students.

Nature and definition of giftedness and intelligence

Although the field of gifted education has traditionally been grounded in the use of IQ scores for identification and definition purposes, the last twenty years has seen a growing interest in other views of intelligence and giftedness. On the heels of Howard Gardner's work (1983) has followed a redefining of gifted education by well-renowned experts (Gagne, 1995; Feldhusen, 1992; Renzulli, 1994; Treffinger, 1992) who are not convinced that traditional IQ measures are sufficient for identifying the unique and individual talents of capable youth. With the publication of National Excellence: A Case for Developing America's Talent (U.S. Department of Education, 1993), the term "talent" appeared liberally throughout the report and served as a cornerstone for encouraging more overlap between education reform and the development of individual gifts and talents. Furthermore, the 1990s saw growth in a researchable knowledge base regarding the diversity rather than the homogeneity within the gifted population (Betts & Neihart, 1988; Ford, 1993; Maker, 1996; Nielsen, Higgins, Hammond, & Williams, 1993). This work specifically focuses attention on the historically under-represented presence of students from culturally diverse backgrounds, from low socioeconomic environments, with limited English proficiency, and with two exceptionalities.

Characteristics and needs of gifted students

A number of developmental characteristics that apply to middle level adolescents apply to gifted adolescents as well, particularly: rapid physical growth, varying levels of cognitive operations, sporadic brain growth, affective ambivalence, and capacity of introspection. Like all adolescents, teens who are gifted must also cope with the achievement of independence, discovery of identity as a person, exploration and acceptance of sexuality, development of meaningful interpersonal relationships, and establishment of personal values and philosophy (Clark, 1988). Clearly, being gifted places some additional twists on the already difficult tasks of adolescent maturation. Wallace (1985) described the gifted adolescent as a doubly marginal individual. The obvious move is away from the family, which is part of the adolescent experience, as well as a move away from the system that perhaps supported and nurtured a specific gift or talent. This new autonomy may cause an additional burden or responsibility for the gifted adolescent, just at a time when he/she has few appropriate peer role models to emulate. Manaster and Powell (1983) reported that gifted adolescents may feel "out of stage" due to their perfectionism and focus on success, causing them to be out of touch with their immediate environment. In addition, alienation from their age-peer group may be influenced by gifted students' awareness of their unusual abilities or interests, causing them to feel "out of phase." Lastly, these students may feel "out of sync" as though they do not, should not, or cannot fit in. Buescher (1985) also found that ownership, or the simultaneous owning and questioning of the abilities of these youngsters, may compete with the beliefs that a debt is owed towards parents, teachers, and society.

To be gifted and to be under-challenged in school creates another undesirable combination. High ability students have reported school work being too easy (Tomlinson, 1995), spending little or no time studying, and group work leading to gifted students doing all the work (Clinkenbeard, 1991). In one study of high ability middle level students, Plucker and McIntire (1996) found that students exhibited a variety of nonconstructive behaviors such as interacting with peers, selected attention, and reduced effort when the level of stimulation or challenge was inappropriate. In addition, teachers in the study did not always recognize when high ability students were trying to stimulate themselves intel-

lectually and sometimes even allowed the students to pursue nonconstructive behaviors rather than adapt or modify instruction.

Instructional implications

Middle school instruction is intended to respond to the recognized developmental needs of young adolescent students. Earlier research on brain periodicity fueled support for a movement away from abstract types of thinking. The resulting de-emphasis on academics also acknowledged that young adolescent students do not always prize school achievement and that over-challenging students at the middle school level could contribute to poor self-concept (National Association of Secondary School Principals, 1989). Tomlinson (1992) has questioned the implications of accepting findings that only 20% of 14 year-olds use even early formal operations. In her view, this finding still creates a need to explore viable options for these 20 percenters, many of whom might be identified as gifted students. In their study of talented teenagers, Csikszentmihalyi, Rathunde, & Whalen (1993) found that students seem to benefit more from a differentiated (more complex and even competitive) learning environment than an integrated (supportive and comfortable) environment. Beane and Lipka's (1986) finding that only 25% of an individual's academic school achievement is linked to IQ while 50% is related to self-concept has posed another dilemma. For gifted students, academic success plays an important role in maintaining self-esteem. This aspect of self-concept is supported by students' intellectual peers who act as "mental catalysts and who provide realistic perspective of their abilities" (Sicola, 1990). Furthermore, Bloom (1985) found in his study that "... exceptional levels of talent development require certain types of environmental support, special experiences, excellent teaching, and appropriate motivational encouragement at each stage of development" (p. 543).

To allow any student to underachieve continually can result in a negative impact on self-concept which, in turn, can impact future performance. Ironically, it was the middle school movement that reminded educators that lockstep-graded practices "force[s] many students to compromise the integrity of their individual readiness" (NASSP, 1989, p. 7). In 1988, Chapman and McAlpine conducted a study to examine the academic self-concepts of mainstreamed intellectually gifted and average students over a two-year period. They measured perceptions of ability in the areas of math, reading, spelling, general ability, penmanship, neatness, and confidence/satisfaction at the beginning and the end of the sixth grade year and then again at the end of the seventh year. These researchers found that, with the exception of penmanship, the students identified as gifted had overall higher perceptions of general ability as well as specific academic areas. However, the gifted students showed lower perceptions of school satisfaction than the average students. Chapman and McAlpine felt that lack of challenge in a mainstreamed environment may cause boredom which could explain the lower scores.

In a qualitative study conducted in a sixth grade gifted class, Clinkenbeard (1991) found that students who were identified gifted felt that their general classroom teachers and peers held sometimes unrealistic expectations of them. Teachers expected them to achieve and behave at a gifted level consistently, some days failing to acknowledge that the students' achievements were linked to effort as well as ability. Students who participated in the study also felt that they were graded harder than were other students and their age peers were sometimes jealous and insulting. Gifted adolescents appear to develop a variety of coping strategies to deal with these types of pressures, including the use of one's abilities to help others in classes, making friends with other bright students, selecting programs and classes designed for gifted/talented students, and achieving in areas outside of academics/school. In their study of gifted adolescents' adjustment, Buescher and Higharn (1989) found gender differences indicating girls to be more at risk for avoiding or walking away from their talents during early adolescence whereas boys more often select friends that provide support for their talent areas.

Equity and excellence

The greatest philosophical difference that separates advocates of gifted education and those of the middle school concept does not lend itself to traditional research methodology. As Plowman (1988) stated, "Education of the gifted and talented is consistent with the philosophical principles and basic tenets of our educational and political systems which include: concern for individuals, individualized instruction, equal opportunity, and equal access" (p. 60). Yet, services that address the needs of high ability learners are sometimes suspect and equated with social discrimination (Johnston & Markle, 1986; McKay, 1995). Helpful to this discussion is a closer look at what Salkind (1988) addressed as two other types of equity. Horizontal equity involves the equal treatment of individuals who have similar needs while vertical equity exists when children who have different needs are treated differently; otherwise referred to as the "unequal treatment of unequals." Both types of equity must guide policy and practices involving services for high ability adolescents.

Ability grouping

As mentioned previously, the main point of disagreement between the two fields often centers around the issue of ability grouping. Kulik and Kulik's

(1987) second meta-analysis coded 82 studies of between-class and 19 within-class programs and described the outcomes on a common scale. For inclusion in their analysis, the studies had to be quantitative, include both a control group and an experimental group with a similar aptitude, and involve a classroom rather than a lab setting. In 49 studies of comprehensive between-class grouping, the effect sizes were .12 for high, .04 for middle, and .00 for low groups with the difference between the high and low groups statistically significant at $p < .05$. In 25 studies dealing with special classrooms only for talented students, variation of effect size from -.27 to 1.25 led the Kuliks to believe that factors other than grouping played a role in the outcome. Two features showing significant relationships in an analysis of total class grouping within the classroom were instructor effects and flexibility/permanence of assignment. The Kuliks concluded that the strongest and clearest effects of grouping were in programs designed especially for talented students. They also concluded that programs designed for all students in a grade, rather than only for talented students, had significantly lower effects. The Kuliks noted that their results are, in some regards, similar to those of Slavin, particularly their findings that comprehensive grouping between classes has little or no effect, either positive or negative.

As the debates have ensued, Slavin (1990) has led a discussion on the practice of "regrouping" for select subject areas as an alternative to ability grouping. To be instructionally effective, Slavin believes that regrouping plans must meet two conditions: 1) instructional level and pace must be completely adapted to student performance level, and 2) regrouping should only be done for one or two subjects so that students remain in a heterogeneous setting most of the day. The National Association for Gifted Children believes that this type of flexible use of grouping will help match students' advanced abilities and knowledge while still maintaining the important social goals of the middle school movement (National Association for Gifted Children, 1994). However, many still question the practice of keeping high ability students in a heterogeneous setting for the majority of the day if their cognitive needs require more challenge.

Revisiting program organization

Over the years a wide variety of programs have been developed to meet the needs of gifted adolescents. Gifted education has rallied around options that move beyond the traditional pull-out and self-contained programs, such as early admission or acceleration options, special schools, mentorships, continuous progress, dual enrollment, and within-class individualization. As an alternative to formal grouping, Renzulli (1994) researched the use of Talent Pools which are composed of the top 15–20 percent of the general population using either general ability or one or more specific areas of ability. Students in these talent pools are then offered opportunities to learn subjects at a faster pace using "curriculum compacting"; thus, freeing up time for enrichment within the general education class. In addition, thousands of students now participate each year in Talent Searches during which seventh and eighth grade students take the SAT. The results of these talent searches can help districts identify able students who may be in need of more academic challenge. Allowing students to take Algebra as early as seventh grade permits them to be able to take more advanced math electives during high school such as: Differential Equations, Real Analysis, Linear Algebra, or Theory of Numbers.

Regardless of the delivery model employed, certain assumptions undergirding the philosophy of gifted services must be supported at the middle school level.

All children progress through challenging material at their own pace. Gifted students often reach mastery in significantly less time than other learners.

- Achieving success for all students is not equated with achieving the same results for all students.
- Most students gain self-esteem and self-confidence from mastering work that initially seems slightly beyond their grasp.
- In addition to sometimes serving as peer role models, high ability students also need to spend time learning new material and stretching to their full potential.
- Flexible grouping of gifted learners should be offered based on students' abilities and talents in these areas.
- Professionals working with gifted students require ongoing specialized training to support their ability to work with this population of students.
- Program strategies used with gifted students should address academic as well as social and personal needs.

In 1995, Coleman and Gallagher conducted a study to identify schools where the middle school movement was blended with quality program services for students who are gifted. Successful sites used instructional grouping to offer challenges to students as well as some form of enrichment. A variety of differentiation approaches were utilized, including mentoring, flexible pacing, independent studies, interdisciplinary units, and thinking skills. In addition, each site also had at least one person on staff who was knowledgeable about the needs of gifted students.

The call for more collaboration between the gifted and the middle school movements will be enhanced if schools first explore the common ground existing between the two fields (Coleman & Gallagher, 1992), namely, that both are committed to meeting the unique developmental needs of students during early adolescence. As programs for the middle school gifted student continue to evolve, the following touchstones can be useful in guiding program decisions:

1. Do the program services support excellence over mediocrity?
2. Will the program offerings help students see in themselves a strength, passion, or capability that can become a highly developed talent?
3. Do the program offerings support students' varying learning needs, e.g., pace, and style?
4. Do the program offerings eliminate an artificial ceiling for learning?
5. Do the program offerings promote depth of understanding rather than just access to quantity?
6. Do the program offerings promote the gifted student's capacities for creative and critical thinking skills?
7. Do the program offerings provide a balance of curricular and co-curricular offerings including appropriate exploratory activities?
8. Do the program offerings offer opportunities to develop an understanding for relationships within and between disciples?

References

Beane, J., & Lipka, R. (1986). *Self-concept, self-esteem, and the curriculum.* New York: Teachers College Press.

Betts, G., & Neihart, M. (1988). Profiles of the gifted. *Gifted Child Quarterly, 32*(2), 248–253.

Bloom, B. (1985). Generalizations about talent development. In B. Bloom (Ed.), *Developing talent in young people* (pp. 507–549). New York: Ballantine Books.

Buescher, T. M. (1985). A framework for understanding the social and emotional development of gifted and talented adolescents. *Roeper Review, 8*, 10–15.

Buescher, T. M., & Higham, S. J. (1989). A developmental study of adjustment among gifted adolescents. In J. Van Tassel-Baska & P. Olszcwski-Kubilius (Eds.), *Patterns of influence on gifted learners: The home, the self, and the school* (pp. 102–124). New York: Teachers College Press.

Chapman, J., & McAlpine, D. (1988). Students' perceptions of ability. *Gifted Child Quarterly, 32*(1), 222–225.

Clark, B. (1988). *Growing up gifted: Developing the potential of children at home and school* (3rd ed.). Columbus, OH: Charles E. Merrill.

Clinkenbeard, P. R. (1991). Unfair expectations: A pilot study of middle school students' comparisons of gifted and regular classes. *Journal for the Education of the Gifted, 15*(1), 56–63.

Coleman, M., & Gallagher, J. (1992). *Middle school survey report: Impact on gifted students.* Chapel Hill, NC: Gifted Education Policy Studies Program, University of North Carolina at Chapel Hill.

Coleman, M. R., & Gallagher, J. (1995). The successful blending of gifted education with middle schools and cooperative learning: Two studies. *Journal for the Education of the Gifted, 18*(4), 362–384.

Coleman, M. R., Gallagher, J., & Howard, J. (1993). *Middle school site visit report: Five schools in profile.* Chapel Hill, NC: Gifted Education Policy Studies Program, University of North Carolina at Chapel Hill.

Csikszentmihalyi, M., Rathunde, K., & Whalen, S. (1993). *Talented teenagers: The roots of success and failure*. Cambridge, UK: Cambridge University Press.

Feldhusen, J. (1992). *TIDE: Talent identification and development in education*. Sarasota, FL: Center for Creative Learning.

Ford, D. (1993). An investigation of the paradox of underachievement among gifted black students. *Roeper Review, 16*(2), 78–84.

Gagne, F. (1995). From giftedness to talent: A developmental model and its impact on the language of the field. *Roeper Review, 18*(2), 103–111.

Gallagher, J., Coleman, M. R., & Nelson, S. (1995). Perceptions of educational reform by educators representing middle schools, cooperative learning, and gifted education. *Gifted Child Quarterly, 39*(2), 66–76.

Gardner, H. (1983). *Frames of mind*. New York: Basic Books.

Johnston, J. H., & Markle, G. (1986). *What research says to the middle level practitioner*. Columbus, OH: National Middle School Association.

Kulik, J. A., & Kulik, C. L. C. (1987). Effects of ability grouping on student achievement. *Equity and excellence, 23* (1&2) 22–30.

Maker, C. L. (1996). Identification of gifted minority students: A national problem, needed changes, and a promising solution. *Gifted Child Quarterly, 40*(1), 41–50.

Manaster, G. J., & Powell, P. M. (1983). A framework for understanding gifted adolescents' psychological maladjustment. *Roeper Review, 6*(2), 70–73.

McKay, J. (1995). *Schools in the middle: Developing a middle-level orientation*. Thousand Oaks, CA: Corwin Press.

Mills, C. I., & Durden, W. G. (1992). Cooperative learning and ability grouping: An issue of choice. *Gifted Child Quarterly, 36*(1), 11–16.

National Association of Secondary School Principals. (1989). *Middle level education's responsibility for intellectual development*. Reston, VA: Author.

National Association for Gifted Children. (1994). *Position paper: Middle schools*. Washington, DC: Author.

Nielsen, E., Higgins, D., Harmmond, A., & Williams, R. (1993). Gifted children with disabilities. *Gifted Child Today, 15*(5), 9–12.

Plowman, P. (1988). Elitism. *Gifted Child Today, 56*(3), 60.

Plucker, J. A., & McIntire, J. (1996). Academic survivability in high-potential middle school students. *Gifted Child Quarterly, 40*(1), 7–14.

Renzulli, J. (1994). *Schools for talent development: A practical plan for total school improvement*. Mansfield Center, CT: Creative Learning Press.

Rosselli, H. (1995). Meeting gifted students halfway in the middle school. *Schools in the Middle, 5*(3), 12–17.

Salkind, N. (1988). *Equity and excellence: The case of mandating services for the gifted child*. Unpublished document. University of Kansas.

Sicola, P. K. (1990). Where do gifted students fit? An examination of middle school philosophy as it relates to ability grouping and the gifted learner. *Journal for the Education of the Gifted, 14*(1), 37–49.

Slavin, R. E. (1990). Achievement effects of ability grouping in secondary schools: A best evidence synthesis. *Review of Educational Research, 60*(3), 471–499.

Tomlinson, C. A. (1992). Gifted education and the middle school movement: Two voices on teaching the academically talented. *Journal for the Education of the Gifted, 15*(3), 206–238.

Tomlinson, C. A. (1994). Gifted learners: The boomerang kids of middle school? *Roeper Review, 16*(3), 177–182.

Tomlinson, C. A. (1995). Deciding to differentiate instruction in middle school: One school's journey. *Gifted Child Quarterly, 39*(2), 77–87.

Treffinger, D. (1992). Programming for giftedness: Needed directions. *INNOTECH Journal, 16*(1), 54–61.

U.S. Department of Education. (1993). *National excellence: A case for developing America's talent*. Washington, DC: Author.

Wallace, D. (1985). Giftedness and the construction of a creative life. In F. Horowitz (Ed.), *The gifted and talented: Development perspectives* (pp. 361–386). Washington, DC: American Psychological Association.

Hilda C. Rosselli is the Associate Dean for Undergraduate Programs in the College of Education at the University of South Florida, Tampa. E-mail: rosselli@tempest.coedu.usf.edu

Judith L. Irvin is a professor at Florida State University, Tallahassee. E-mail: irvin@coe.fsu.edu

Originally appeared in the January 2001 issue of *Middle School Journal*, pp. 57–62. Used with permission from National Middle School Association.

UNIT 3

Exceptional and Culturally Diverse Children

Unit Selections

Key Points to Consider

- Describe the characteristics of ADHD children, and discuss the strategies teachers can use to help them.

- Who are the gifted and talented? How can knowledge of their characteristics and learning needs help to provide them with an appropriate education?

- What cultural differences exist in our society? How would multicultural education help teachers deal more effectively with these differences?

- What are some of the criticisms concerning multicultural programs?

 **Links: www.dushkin.com/online/**
These sites are annotated in the World Wide Web pages.

The Council for Exceptional Children
http://www.cec.sped.org/index.html

Global SchoolNet Foundation
http://www.gsn.org

International Project: Multicultural Pavilion
http://curry.edschool.virginia.edu/curry/centers/multicultural/papers.html

Let 1000 Flowers Bloom/Kristen Nicholson-Nelson
http://teacher.scholastic.com/professional/assessment/100flowers.htm

Multicultural Publishing and Education Catalog
http://www.mpec.org

National Attention Deficit Disorder Association
http://www.add.org

National MultiCultural Institute (NMCI)
http://www.nmci.org

The Equal Educational Opportunity Act for All Handicapped Children (Public Law 94-142) gives disabled children the right to an education in the least-restrictive environment, due process, and an individualized educational program that is specifically designed to meet their needs. Professionals and parents of exceptional children are responsible for developing and implementing an appropriate educational program for each child. The application of these ideas to classrooms across the nation at first caused great concern among educators and parents. Classroom teachers whose training did not prepare them for working with the exceptional child expressed negative attitudes about mainstreaming. Special resource teachers also expressed concern that mainstreaming would mitigate the effectiveness of special programs for the disabled and would force cuts in services. Parents feared that their children would not receive the special services they required because of governmental red tape and delays in proper diagnosis and placement.

It has been more than two decades since the implementation of P.L. 94-142, which was amended by the Individuals with Disabilities Education Act (IDEA) in 1991 and introduced the term "inclusion." Inclusion tries to assure that disabled children will be fully integrated within the classroom. Many of the above concerns have been studied by psychologists and educators, and their findings have often influenced policy. For example, research has indicated that inclusion is more effective when regular classroom teachers and special resource teachers collaborate and work cooperatively with disabled children.

The articles concerning the educationally disabled confront some of these issues. Brent Hardin and Marie Hardin present "Into the Mainstream: Practical Strategies for Teaching in Inclusive Environments" while the authors of "Mom, Will Kaelie Always Have Possibilities? discuss the realities of early childhood inclusion" and dismiss the myths surrounding the inclusion of children with disabilities. Other exceptional children are the gifted and talented. These children are rapid learners who can absorb, organize, and apply concepts more effectively than the average child. They often have IQs of 140 or more and are con-

vergent thinkers (that is, they give the correct answer to teacher or test questions). Convergent thinkers are usually models of good behavior and academic performance, and they respond to instruction easily; teachers generally value such children and often nominate them for gifted programs. There are other children, however, who do not score well on standardized tests of intelligence because their thinking is more divergent (that is, they can imagine more than one answer to teacher or test questions). These gifted divergent thinkers may not respond to traditional instruction. They may become bored, respond to questions in unique and disturbing ways, and appear uncooperative and disruptive. Many teachers do not understand these unconventional thinkers and fail to identify them as gifted. In fact, such children are sometimes labeled as emotionally disturbed or mentally retarded because of the negative impressions they make on their teachers. Because of the differences between these types of students, a great deal of controversy surrounds programs for the gifted. Such programs should enhance the self-esteem of all gifted and talented children, motivate and challenge them, and help them realize their creative potential. The two articles in the subsection on gifted children consider the characteristics of giftedness, and they explain how to identify gifted students and provide them with an appropriate education.

The third subsection of this unit concerns student diversity. Just as labeling may adversely affect the disabled child, it may also affect the child who comes from a minority ethnic background where the language and values are quite different from those of the mainstream culture. The term "disadvantaged" is often used to describe these children, but it is negative, stereotypical, and apt to result in a self-fulfilling prophecy whereby teachers perceive such children as incapable of learning. Teachers should provide academically and culturally diverse children with experiences that they might have missed in the restricted environment of their homes and neighborhoods. Leslie A. Swetnam looks at multicultural education in Australia and the United States and Hermine H. Marshall discusses strategies for positively influencing the self-concept of culturally diverse children.

'Mom, Will Kaelie Always Have Possibilities?'

The Realities of Early Childhood Inclusion

Mary Frances Hanline and Steven Daley

LEIGHA, THE 5-year-old daughter of one of the authors, recently asked, "Mom, will Kaelie always have possibilities?" Since she was just a year old, Leigha has attended a child-care program that actively includes children with disabilities. And she was trying to understand her friend Kaelie's disabilities. While she confused "possibilities" and "disabilities," Leigha innocently identified the main reasons for creating inclusive early education programs: to create normalized expectations for children with disabilities and to foster an understanding of disabilities among the nondisabled.

However, while "best practices" in early childhood education and in early childhood special education support the inclusion of children with disabilities in early childhood programs,[1] about half of all young children with disabilities receive services in settings that serve only children with disabilities.[2] Thus many preschoolers with disabilities are isolated from the learning benefits that may occur when they have daily contact with their nondisabled peers. Children who do not have disabilities are also deprived of the positive outcomes that may occur when they interact with peers who have disabilities. Moreover, family members and teachers are unable to experience the potential advantages of inclusion if young children with disabilities are educated exclusively in segregated settings.

We wish to identify here some beliefs that work to prevent the implementation of inclusive programs. These beliefs focus on the perceived needs of young children with disabilities, on the potential reactions of nondisabled children, on the anticipated demands on teachers, and on parental concerns. We have become familiar with them through our reading of the literature on inclusion, as well as through our own experiences with inclusive programs.

Belief 1. The instructional needs of young children with disabilities can't be met in an early childhood education setting, because young children with disabilities need highly structured programs.

Reality 1. Best practice in early childhood education is based on developmental theories, such as those of Jean Piaget, Lev Vygotsky, and Erik Erikson, and on a philosophy of constructivism. The primary vehicle for promoting development in these programs is child-initiated, child-directed, teacher-supported play. In contrast, the field of early childhood special education is based primarily on the behavioral theories of John Watson, Edward Thorndike, and B. F. Skinner and on the educational psychology of mastery learning. The message from these theories is that the more time the child spends in direct instruction, the more the child will learn. A further assumption is that a child with disabilities will be unable to take advantage of environmental experiences that typically promote development. Thus special education programs for young children have traditionally been more teacher-directed than typical early education programs.

These philosophical differences between the two approaches have contributed to the belief that learning opportunities in early childhood programs may not be adequate to promote the development of children with disabilities. Recently, professionals have begun to realize that there is much in common in the practice of both approaches and that polarized thinking regarding best practice may prevent children from experiencing inclusion. For example, early childhood education in general has come to recognize that teacher-directed approaches have their place, and the best practice guidelines for early childhood special education programs increasingly recognize the importance of play-oriented approaches.

Research findings indicate that inclusive settings (compared to disabled-only environments) are more stimulating and responsive to young children with disabilities. More demands for appropriate social behaviors are placed on children in inclusive settings, there are opportunities for observational learning and interactions with nondisabled peers, and children with disabilities engage in higher levels of play when they are with nondisabled children.[3]

Belief 2. Young children with disabilities can't participate in the activities of an early childhood program. Their presence has the potential of disrupting the learning activities of the other children.

Reality 2. In order to be effective, education for children with disabilities must take place within a framework that recognizes that the majority of children with disabilities progress through the same developmental stages as nondisabled children. Responsiveness to the needs of the individual child within this framework allows typical early childhood activities to be modified to meet the needs of children with disabilities without disrupting the activities for nondisabled children. For example, children can sit side-by-side with crayons and paper, each involved in learning at an individually appropriate level. One child may scribble with the crayons, while another creates the face of his mother. Or children with and without disabilities can play within a sociodramatic center together. One child may be learning to engage in simple symbolic activities, such as feeding a baby doll with a bottle, while another child may be engrossed in more elaborate play involving a scenario of planning a party, writing invitations, and going to the post office to mail the invitations.

Because most activities in early childhood settings allow for a range of developmental levels and often require fewer adaptations than are needed for older children, the needs of young children with disabilities can usually be met within the context of developmentally appropriate activities. In this way, the learning of nondisabled peers is not interrupted. However, teachers must have time to plan these adaptations, possibly in consultation with other professionals, and to evaluate their effectiveness and appropriateness.

Belief 3. Nondisabled children will tease and make fun of their peers with disabilities. Nondisabled children don't want to be friends with young children with disabilities.

Reality 3. One reason to pursue inclusion is its potential impact on the attitudes of nondisabled children toward their peers with disabilities. It is believed that nondisabled children who grow up with the opportunity to interact with children with disabilities are more likely to show greater understanding of individuals with disabilities.

While research has demonstrated that preschool children recognize the presence of disabilities, studies assessing the reactions of nondisabled children to their peers with disabilities report few rejecting behaviors. Only two studies have reported negative outcomes of inclusion.[4] Both of these studies attributed the outcomes to lack of

support for the teachers, and both highlight the importance of the availability of specialists for consultation. Studies reporting positive outcomes have demonstrated increased understanding of and sensitivity to individual differences on the part of children without disabilities as a result of direct contact with peers who have disabilities.[5] In fact, nondisabled children tend to adapt their speech to the developmental level of a listener who is disabled, suggesting that nondisabled children are responsive to the needs of peers with disabilities.[6]

Although early studies of social interactions in inclusive preschools indicated that children with and without disabilities might not play together if interactions are left to chance, more recent studies have shown that positive behaviors develop with appropriate guidance, modeling, and direction from adults.[7] When adults answer children's questions about disabilities openly and honestly and model accepting behavior, children with and without disabilities form friendships, and nondisabled children willingly assist their peers with disabilities. In fact, it has been our experience that nondisabled children frequently must be reminded not to help their friends with disabilities too much!

Belief 4. Young children with disabilities require much more teacher time, thereby taking away from the time the teacher has to interact with and instruct all the children.

Reality 4. All children require teacher time. Although studies of teacher time required for the inclusion of young children have not been reported in the early childhood literature, studies evaluating the use of teacher time in elementary and high schools indicate that additional teacher time is not needed.[8]

However, the child with disabilities may need time to adjust to a new classroom. The teacher may also spend time with the nondisabled children, demonstrating how to accommodate the needs of their new peer. In addition, when children are making the transition from one activity to another, children who are not independently mobile may need one-to-one assistance to move to the new activity, and children may need more adult assistance during those activities that present the greatest challenges. For example, a child who gets easily frustrated during a group activity may need to sit close to the teacher leading the activity, and a child who has difficulty with fine motor tasks may need one-on-one assistance when building with blocks or playing with puzzles.

However, successful inclusion is not simply a matter of more teacher time for interactions with the child who has a disability. Time is needed to consult with specialists who may be coming to support the inclusion of the child with disabilities. Early childhood teachers have indicated a need for time to participate in inservice workshops, to discuss issues with instructional assistants, and to review curriculum materials.[9] To create time for accomplishing these tasks requires flexibility in scheduling and in assigning responsibility to teachers.

Belief 5. Preschool teachers aren't able to provide for the many and varied needs of young children with disabilities.

Reality 5. Early childhood teachers have a history of accommodating the individual learning styles of young children, and so they already possess the foundation knowledge they need to effectively teach preschoolers with disabilities. However, staff development is critical, as teacher attitudes, preparation, and ongoing support are factors that contribute to the success of inclusion. Such support is essential to counter misinformation, fear, and negative attitudes.

Staff support can take a variety of forms, including in-service workshops, on-site demonstrations, direct observation with supportive feedback, discussions during staff meetings, individual consultation, and written materials. To be most effective, the support should be responsive to the needs of individual programs. Time for teachers to engage in these activities should be provided, and participation in the activities must be considered a job responsibility of individuals involved in inclusion.

Belief 6. Young children with disabilities are a burden to the preschool teacher, as they upset the optimum adult/child ratio required by high-quality early childhood programs.

Reality 6. The guidelines of the National Association for the Education of Young Children (NAEYC) may be followed when including young children with disabilities in early childhood programs. The NAEYC-recommended adult/child ratio for 4- to 5-year-olds is two adults to 20 children. While the young child with disabilities may require the assistance of a specialist or a paraprofessional, as well as one-to-one interactions with a teacher at specific times of the day, the overall adult/child ratio does not need to be different because a child with disabilities has become part of the program. For example, a child could receive occupational therapy services during lunch to improve eating skills and physical therapy during outdoor time to improve gross motor skills.

Through interagency agreements with local school systems and private agencies, the ongoing participation of specialists from multiple disciplines can be ensured, thus meeting the needs of the young child with disabilities without adding full-time staff members. For example, the school system could provide a speech and language therapist to work with the children and consult with the teachers on a regularly scheduled basis. Furthermore, in many programs, teachers have incorporated assistants, cross-age tutors, volunteers, and parents into the program routines to help provide high-quality services to all children.

Belief 7. Parents of nondisabled children don't want their children to attend inclusive programs.

Reality 7. Parental attitudes about inclusion are a critical variable. The overwhelming majority of parents of nondisabled children support the inclusion of young children with disabilities in their children's programs, and they perceive drawbacks and benefits from inclusion that are similar to those noted by parents of children with disabilities. Both groups of parents believe that inclusion allows children with disabilities to experience the real world and to be accepted by others. In addition, parents of nondisabled children generally feel that their children's sensitivity to and acceptance of differences are increased through contact with children with disabilities. Parents whose children have had a positive inclusion experience are the most accepting of inclusion, as are parents who have been involved in planning for the inclusion process.[10]

Belief 8. Parents of children with disabilities fear that their child will not receive adequate services in inclusive settings.

Reality 8. When their child with disabilities attends an inclusive program, parents want the same services they perceive to be available in specialized settings. However, once they have experienced inclusion, parents express confidence that their children's needs are met. A growing body of research indicates that providing services in inclusive settings has become one indicator of high-quality programs.[11] In support of this idea, Phillip Strain stated, "Programs that are characterized by integrated service delivery tend to be state-of-the-art in a variety of other dimensions, including extensive parental involvement; highly structured scope, sequence, and method of instruction; and attention to repeated outcome assessments."[12] Professionals in inclusive settings, however, may want to ensure that the families also receive adequate support. Linking with community agencies and promoting interactions among families of children with and without disabilities may help the families of children with disabilities feel more supported.

Inclusion is one of the major challenges facing those who work to educate young children. With creative and flexible planning, caring attitudes on the part of adults, and the wise use of community resources to provide specialized services, children with disabilities can be included successfully in early childhood education programs. Everyone involved with the inclusion process has an opportunity to be involved with a program that supports equity and acceptance as a framework for providing services to young children and their families. In this way, Leigha's question can be answered with an emphatic, "Yes, Leigha, Kaelie will always have possibilities. And Kaelie's possibilities will be greater because you are her friend."

References

1. Sue Bredekamp and Carol Copple, eds., Developmentally Appropriate Practice in Early Childhood Programs (Washington, D.C.: National Association for the Education of Young Children, 1997); and DEC Task Force on Recommended Practices, DEC Recommended Practices: Indicators of Quality Programs for Infants and Young Children with Special Needs and Their Families (Reston, Va.: Council for Exceptional Children, 1993).

2. Twentieth Annual Report to Congress on the Implementation of the Individuals with Disabilities Education Act (Washington, D.C.: U.S. Department of Education, 1998).

3. Dorothy K. Lipsky and Alan Gartner, Inclusion and School Reform: Transforming America's Classrooms (Baltimore: Paul H. Brookes, 1997); and Michael J. Guralnick, "Early Childhood Mainstreaming," Topics in Early Childhood Special Education, Summer 1990, pp. 1–17.

4. Elaine P. Simon and Andrew E. Gilman, "Mainstreaming Visually Handicapped Children," Exceptional Children, vol. 45, 1983, pp. 463–64; and Pearl E. Tait and Charles Wolfgang, "Mainstreaming a Blind Child: Problems Perceived in a Preschool Day Care Program," Early Child Development and Care, vol. 13, 1984, pp. 155–67.

5. Susan Lamorey and Diane Bricker, "Integrated Programs: Effects on Young Children and Their Parents," in Charles A. Peck, Samuel A. Odom, and Diane D. Bricker, eds., Integrating Young Children with Disabilities into Community Programs (Baltimore: Paul H. Brookes, 1993).

6. Michael J. Guralnick and Diane Paul-Brown, "Functional and Discourse Analysis of Nonhandicapped Preschool Children's Speech to Handicapped Children," American Journal of Mental Deficiency, vol. 84, 1980, pp. 444–54.

7. Samuel L. Odom, Michelle DeKlyen, and Joseph R. Jenkins, "Integrating Handicapped and Nonhandicapped Preschoolers: Developmental Impact on the Nonhandicapped Children," Exceptional Children, vol. 51, 1984, pp. 41–49.

8. Margaret C. Wang, "Serving Students with Special Needs Through Inclusive Education Approaches," in Judy Lupart, Anne Marie McKeough, and Carolyn Yewchuck, eds., Schools in Transition: Rethinking Regular and Special Education (Toronto: Thomas Nelson Canada, 1996), pp. 143–63; and Debbie Straub and Charles A. Peck, "What Are the Outcomes for Nondisabled Students?," Educational Leadership, December 1994/January 1995, pp. 36–40.

9. William D. Eiserman, Lenore Shisler, and Suzanne Healey, "A Community Assessment of Preschool Providers: Attitudes Toward Inclusion," Journal of Early Intervention, vol. 19, 1992, pp. 149–67.

10. Kim Galant and Mary Frances Hanline, "Parental Attitudes Toward Mainstreaming Young Children with Disabilities," Childhood Education, vol. 69, 1993, pp. 293–99.

11. Ibid.

12. Phillip S. Strain, "LRE for Preschool Children with Handicaps: What We Know, What We Should be Doing," Journal of Early Intervention, vol. 14, 1990, p. 294.

MARY FRANCES HANLINE is an associate professor and chair of the Department of Special Education, Florida State University, Tallahassee. STEVEN DALEY is an associate professor in the Department of Special Education, Rehabilitation, and School Psychology, California State University, Sacramento.

Into the Mainstream:
Practical Strategies for Teaching
in Inclusive Environments

Brent Hardin and Marie Hardin

Christopher, thirty-two, teaches ninth-grade English at a high school on the outskirts of Atlanta, Georgia. Although he has been a teacher for eight years and has clearly moved beyond the induction phase of his career, some classroom challenges still seem overwhelming to him.

Christopher's average day begins before 7 a.m. After he arrives at his portable classroom behind the high school, he begins his first class at 7:30. He teaches six classes throughout the day—a mix of "Technical English" and college-preparatory courses. On top of his regular teaching load, Christopher often has to substitute teach during his one planning period during the day.

Christopher's job, however, involves far more than teaching about punctuation, active voice, and sentence structure to the 115 students who visit his trailer each day. He spends much of his energy on classroom management and administrative tasks, while he struggles to work with the many special-needs students who have been integrated into his courses. During first period, for instance, an aide joins Christopher to teach a group nearly half of whom have diagnosed emotional, behavioral, or learning problems. In another class later in the day, nine of fifteen students have some type of disability. Besides making accommodations for students during his lessons, Christopher is also required to remember other details, such as the times to send some students to the office to take medication. "I can put my kids into two different categories" he says, "They're completely bouncing off the walls or they're catatonic. It's a struggle. I try to keep my energy level up."

Christopher's situation is certainly not unique. Inclusion of students with a wide range of disabilities into regular classrooms can be a daunting prospect for teachers at any career stage. However, teachers at the induction or competency-building phases can find the task of teaching students with disabilities especially challenging because they lack sufficient training and support to work with these students (Werts et al. 1996).

Teachers can, however, use a number of strategies to cope with these demands and increase their effectiveness in an inclusive environment. Using peer tutors, implementing cooperative learning, and applying reverse-inclusion techniques in the classroom can be powerful strategies to provide successful learning for all students.

Changing Demographics

The need for teachers to cope with the demands of inclusive classrooms has increased during the past several years, as the numbers of students with disabilities in public education has climbed dramatically. The Nineteenth Annual Report to Congress on the Implementation of the Individuals with Disabilities Education Act revealed that during the 1994–1995 school year there were approximately 4.7 million schoolchildren with disabilities, or almost 10 percent of the student population. At least 48 percent of students requiring special education services attend inclusive classes for most or all of the school day, a 60 percent escalation from 1994 (McLeskey, Henry, and Hodges 1998). This trend is predicted to continue. All teachers, not just special educators, should be prepared to teach students with disabilities.

Teachers' Perceptions of Competence

Thousands of teachers, at all career stages, teach students with disabilities in inclusive classrooms every day, but many do not feel competent or confident in that role. Kelly, a third-year elementary teacher in north Florida, speaks of her confidence in teaching students with disabilities in an integrated classroom:

Conceptually, I think inclusion is a great idea. But, at the same time, I don't think teachers are prepared. I know I am not. I really didn't get any experience or training teaching kids with disabilities mixed in with my regular classes. It's hard enough just handling a regular class, but throw in students with special needs and it is really overwhelming if you don't have the training or the help.

Surveys of countless teachers echo Kelly's concerns. A recent synthesis of research (Scruggs and Mastropieri 1996), based on studies dating back to 1958, indicates that approximately two-thirds of the 10,560 general educators surveyed across the years agreed with the concept of inclusion, but their degree of enthusiasm decreased when asked, "Are you prepared to teach with disabilities in your classroom?" Confidence decreased even further when questions addressed teacher readiness to make curricular or instructional modifications for identified students. When Schultz (1982) surveyed teachers to determine what specific issues were of concern, teachers said that they felt a lack of expertise in accounting for individual differences when they designed and implemented their instructional strategies.

Research indicates that educators do not feel that they have been adequately trained for inclusive environments. Lyon, Vaasen, and Toomey (1989) surveyed 440 teachers concerning their perceptions of their undergraduate and graduate training programs, questioning how such programs prepared them to address individual differences within the classroom. Sadly, the majority of the respondents reported that the training programs that they completed did not prepare them to provide effective instruction for a diverse student population. Over 93 percent of the regular educators indicated that they did not receive any hands-on experience teaching students with disabilities in their training programs.

Gallagher, Malone, Cleghorne, and Helms (1997) interviewed 115 teachers concerning their perceived training needs related to children with disabilities. Although 64 percent of the respondents reported six or more years' experience teaching students with disabilities in inclusive classrooms, they reported low confidence in several areas of basic competency. Such challenges can be daunting for inexperienced teachers trying to learn basic classroom management skills, deal with failing students, and keep track of grades and paperwork.

Practical Classroom Strategies

Educators at any career stage can, however, implement a number of simple strategies to increase their effectiveness and grow more confident in inclusive environments. Subtle changes can accommodate students with special needs without obtrusively changing the class for other students.

Peer Tutoring

Students who serve as peer tutors have been trained to assist other students in the classroom. These tutors can work with special-needs students to provide the extra attention and feedback they need in order to learn, allowing the teacher to divide his or her attention more equally among the students. Also, students with and without disabilities can work together in tutoring pairs to positively affect each other.

Greenwood, Delquadri, and Garta (1997) maintain that teachers find peer tutoring valuable because it is adaptable to any teaching style and curriculum; easy to implement; cost effective; time efficient; and effective with all ability levels. Although students can learn from each other, the teacher should carefully select the peer tutors who will work with disabled students. Not all students will be ready or able to work in a partnership with special needs students. Ellery (1995) recommends that peer tutors be (a) slightly older than their disabled counterparts, (b) emotionally mature, (c) good communicators, (d) highly skilled, and (e) volunteers.

Peer tutors may need ongoing training to become skillful helpers. The teacher should allow time to make sure that tutors understand their responsibilities for the lesson. Also, the teacher should not overlook opportunities to offer students with disabilities the chance to tutor nondisabled students. For example, a student with spina bifida who is confined to a wheelchair is perfectly capable of providing instruction, encouragement, and feedback to another student. This arrangement extends the potential for a fully inclusive learning environment.

Cooperative Learning

This strategy brings students together in groups to accomplish shared goals. The goal of cooperative learning is to ensure that all members of the group master the information at their own levels. Oftentimes individuals in the group are given specific jobs or tasks that contribute to goal attainment. Students help each other and evaluate each member's progress toward individual and group goals. For cooperative learning to be effective, students must perceive that they are positively linked to other students in their group and that each member can and must contribute. In addition, each member must understand his or her role in the cooperative group. Less-skilled students, including students with disabilities, could be perceived to be the weak links if all members perceive that they must perform the same task. This will not happen if the group understands that each member has a unique task that maximizes his or her skills and contribution to the group goal.

One example of a cooperative learning activity is a literature circle (Zemelman, Daniels, and Hyde 1993). In a literature circle, groups of four or five students choose and read the same article or book. Each student then comes to the literature circle with an assigned discussion role that accommodates skill differences, allowing for different versions of the text, including tape, film, or Braille.

Kagan (1985) recommends a cooperative learning strategy called "numbered heads," designed to actively engage all students during teacher-led instruction and discussion. Students are organized into four-member heterogeneous learning teams. After the teacher directs a question to the entire class, students are asked to put their heads together to come up with their best answer. The teacher then calls for answers from one numbered member of a group, asking, for example, "Which number 1 can answer this question?"

A substantial body of research confirms the academic and social benefits of cooperative learning approaches to instruction for students of diverse abilities. Benefits have been noted in measures of student achievement (Slavin 1990), self-esteem (Johnson and Johnson 1989), and peer relationships and interactions (Johnson, Johnson, Warring, and Maruyama 1986).

Reverse Inclusion

One way to implement reverse inclusion is to integrate several students without disabilities into a class that has several students with disabilities (Block 1994). The students without disabilities participate in the class alongside students with disabilities. Another way is to have students without disabilities role-play the disabilities of their peers during certain lessons. Examples might include having students participate in a listening exercise while blindfolded or present a poem or speech using sign language. A teacher might also invite a guest speaker to teach the students about how to use and maneuver a wheelchair. The entire class may take part in a wheelchair basketball game as a culminating event for this instructional unit. This type of instruction promotes classwide understanding and respect for all students.

Planning to Mainstream

Although awareness of these strategies is advantageous, it is important that teachers focus on the particular needs of their individual students when designing classroom lessons. The goal is to allow all students the opportunity to participate and learn in a class that is challenging and that provides opportunities for success. Thus, it is important to evaluate the effect that any lesson strategy will have on the entire class. The following criteria, adapted from suggestions by Block (1994), can be used to evaluate classroom strategies:

1. Does the plan allow students with disabilities to participate successfully, yet still be challenged? For example, a teenage student with Down's syndrome should not be given reading material at a kindergarten level to present in a cooperative learning project. The student will probably be more challenged and comfortable working with age-related material that is developmentally appropriate.

2. Does the plan adversely affect students without disabilities? It might be wise from time to time to try alternative projects or activities that allow students without disabilities to experience what it is like to be in a wheelchair or have a visual impairment. However, such changes implemented on a regular basis might negatively affect the class for students without disabilities and promote resentment toward their disabled peers.

3. Does the application cause undue burden on the teacher? For example, a student with autism may need special assistance to complete many classroom tasks. It may not be feasible for the teacher to provide the individual attention needed while also teaching the other students in the class. A better adaptation might be assisting this student for part of the class and allowing a peer tutor or classroom aide to assist at other times.

Working with students in an inclusive classroom environment is a formidable prospect for teachers at all career stages; studies indicate that teachers feel neither confident nor competent about their training or ability to work with disabled students. For new teachers this challenge can be especially troublesome. Peer tutoring, cooperative learning, and reverse inclusion are three relatively simple techniques that inexperienced teachers can implement. Although no teaching strategy works in all situations and individual learner needs must be considered, such techniques have been demonstrated as effective in inclusive environments. The merits of such applications are clear. Teacher efficacy is enhanced and confidence is ensured while students' inclusive experiences are maximized.

Key words: special education, disabilities, inclusive classrooms, teacher competence, cooperative learning

REFERENCES

Block, M. E. 1994. A teacher's guide to including students with disabilities in regular physical education. Baltimore: Brookes.

Ellery, P. J. 1995. Peer tutors work. Strategies 5:12–14.

Gallagher P., M. Malone, M. Cleghorne, and A. Helms. 1997. Perceived in-service training needs for early intervention personnel. Exceptional Children 64:19–30.

Greenwood, C. R. J. G. Delquadri, and I. J. Carta. 1997. Together we can: Class-wide peer tutoring to improve basic academic skills. Longmont, GO: Sopris West.

Johnson, D. W., and R. T. Johnson. 1989. Cooperation and competition: Theory and research. Edina, MN: Interaction Books.

Johnson, D. W., R. T. Johnson, D. Warring, and G. Maruyama. 1986. Different cooperative learning procedures and cross-handicap relationships. Exceptional Children 53(3): 247–52.

Kagan, S. 1985. Cooperative learning. Mission Viejo, CA: Resources for Teachers.

Lyon, G., M. Vaasen, and F. Toomey. 1989. Teacher's perceptions of their undergraduate and graduate preparation. Teacher Education and Special Education 12(4): 164–69.

McLeskey, J., D. Henry, and D. Hodges. 1998. Inclusion: Where is it happening? Teaching Exceptional Children 31(1): 4–10.

Office of Special Education Programs. 1997. To assure the free appropriate public education of all children with disabilities. Nineteenth annual report to Congress on the implementation of the Individuals with Disabilities Education Act. Washington, DC: Office of Special Exceptional Children.

Schultz, L. 1982. Educating the special needs student in the regular classroom. Exceptional Children 48:366–67.

Scruggs, T. E., and M. A. Mastropieri. 1996. Teacher perceptions of mainstreaming/inclusion, 1958–1995: A research synthesis. Exceptional Children 63(1): 59–74.

Werts, M. G., M. Wolery, E. D. Snyder, N. K. Caldwell, and C. L. Salisbury. 1996. Supports and resources associated with inclusive schooling: Perceptions of elementary school teachers about need and availability. Journal of Special Education 30(2): 187–203.

Zemelman, S., H. Daniels, and A. Hyde. 1993. Best practice: New standards for teaching and learning in America's schools. Portsmouth, NH: Heinemann.

Brent Hardin is an assistant professor of physical education and Marie Hardin is an assistant professor of communications, both at State University of West Georgia, in Carollton.

Challenges of Identifying and Serving Gifted Children with ADHD

Lori J. Flint

How often have we, as parents and educators, watched a story about students labeled as one thing or another on the evening news and felt it was oversimplified? Those of us who regularly work with children know that we can't oversimplify like that because, like adults, children are not always what they appear to be. Children are complicated, with a variety of factors, both positive and negative, simultaneously affecting them. Many children are labeled as gifted or learning disabled or having attention-deficit hyperactivity disorder (ADHD) as though that label explains the child, when what it really does is provide appropriate educational services to that child. But what about children who bear one label and also display other tendencies?

Take, for example, the idea of gifted children. Many people probably think of children as being identified as gifted according to a single intelligence test and don't realize that giftedness today often is measured in other ways: high motivation, exceptional creativity, outstanding achievement, and fantastic products.

Whoever these children with exceptional gifts and talents are, and however their gifts are measured, they're all really good in school, and have it made in life, right? Not necessarily. Some students identified as being gifted have other exceptionalities, as well; some have exceptionalities that preclude them from ever being identified as gifted.

This article describes the special situations and needs of three children—Tony, Mikey, and Gina. As you read the first part of the article, think about your own suggestions for interventions—how you might help them in your home or classroom. Then read the rest of the article to see what others have to say about working with children who have both giftedness and attentional difficulties.

Three Children

Tony

Nine-year-old Tony is a charmer. He has an engaging smile and knows how to turn it on and off. Tony is also a challenge to have in the classroom. He blurts out answers constantly, never stops moving, and argues with the teacher and with his peers incessantly. He is of average intelligence, displays little creativity, earns low grades on both objective and project-based work, does not like school, and typically achieves at a below-average level. Tony is disorganized and distractible and is always either talking or making other noise. He is usually missing either his work or some vital component needed to do his work. He visits the office on a regular basis because he is removed from the classroom when he is so disruptive the teacher cannot continue teaching. Tony's teacher will be happy when this school year is over, but worries about where Tony will go next year and whether his new teacher will be able to handle him—he needs a teacher who is neither too permissive nor too authoritarian. Tony carries with him two labels: He has been diagnosed with ADHD and oppositional defiant disorder (ODD). Tony is one of four children in a family headed by a single parent.

Mikey

Six-year-old Mikey was referred to the schools' student support team (SST) by his classroom teacher. Why was he referred? Mikey was distractible, inattentive, fast-moving, and talkative, to the point of not functioning well in his first-grade classroom. He also displayed some aggressive behavior and poor social skills. One member of the SST was a perceptive administrator whose experience included a 14-year stint teaching gifted children. The recommendation from the team included referring the boy for testing for the gifted program.

Exercise caution in both the identification and treatment of ADHD in children identified as being gifted.

The gifted intervention specialist in the school began evaluating Mikey, first by observing him in his classroom on several occasions, then by administering a variety of mental ability, achievement, creativity, and motivation instruments; all designed to ascertain whether Mikey was gifted according to his state's multiple criteria identification law. As he sat to take a mental ability test in a one-on-one testing situation with his school's gifted specialist, the differences this child exhibited were quickly noted. Mikey was, indeed, exceptionally active; hanging off the chair, even standing, at times, during the testing. He vocalized and was impulsive in answering nearly all questions on the tests. During the administration of a mental ability test, he rushed through the verbal and quantitative sections, performing only at the 48th percentile, and slowing only when he came to something entirely new: the matrix section of the test. He barely listened to the instructions, then dove in. As soon as he was allowed to begin, he started solving the problems rapidly and accurately; thriving on the challenge. He missed none. Unfortunately, his score on this single subtest was not adequate to place him in the gifted program, so he required additional testing. Mikey's performance on the other evaluation measures was inconsistent, ranging from the 99th percentile on some instruments designed to evaluate creativity and mental ability to the 48th on others that measured achievement and motivation. The gifted intervention specialist worked with him, using movement to set the stage for optimal performance.

After several weeks of evaluation, Mikey qualified for the gifted program, identified as creatively and cognitively gifted. Why did the gifted specialist work so hard to help this child qualify? Because she saw a child with immense potential, but who needed a great deal of help channeling that potential into constructive avenues. He was also identified, soon after this, by his family doctor as having ADHD, of both the inattentive and hyperactive types. Mikey comes from a blended family with economic difficulties. He was born when his mother was 14 years of age; his mother never finished high school, and is herself identified as having ADHD, like her mother before her.

Gina

Gina is a highly gifted fifth grader whose performance on mental ability, creativity, and achievement tests regularly place her in the 99th percentile, with scores at the ceiling of the tests. She is an award-winning artist and poet, and an academically high-achieving student who has been in gifted programs since kindergarten. Gina is easily frustrated by new tasks, cries with little or no provocation, and gloats when she figures out things the others have not. She takes great delight, outwardly at least, in all of her differences. She always wants to be first and best. Gina is in nearly constant motion: swooping into a room to announce her arrival; sitting like a frog on her chair, head hanging down and hair swinging around her face; always drawing, writing, or otherwise creating with her hands.

Most foods go untasted by her because she dislikes all but a few for various reasons: too strong, too slimy, wrong color, too disgusting. Gina will only wear clothing made of soft knits and whose tags have been removed, because everything else is either too constricting, or stiff, or makes her itch. She often has her nose turned up in distaste at environmental odors, whether they are caused by someone's lunch or the remnants of some cleaning solution.

Gina's social skills are not those of a typical fifth grader, either. Because of her emotional disability, she stands out in both her gifted and general classrooms. Her propensity toward arguing with adults amazes other students and frustrates the teachers, because she is not engaging in intellectual discourse, but rather, the sort of irrationality that comes of being opinionated and not listening to instructions, as well as an unwillingness to take academic risks. Gina comes from a family of highly gifted, highly educated people.

Attention Deficit or Overexcitability?

Though these three students display many similar behaviors, in each case the behaviors are attributable to different causes. In Tony's case, ADHD is considered the underlying problem; in Mikey's case, ADHD with psychological overintensities associated with giftedness; and in Gina's case, the psychological overintensities concomitant with giftedness alone. How can such similar behaviors be assigned such different attributions, and how can they be distinguished from one another so the correct diagnosis is made in each case?

Making a correct diagnosis is not simple; it requires that educators and other professionals make thorough evaluations for both giftedness and ADHD (Cramond, 1995; Lovecky, 1994; Ramirez-Smith, 1997). According to Webb and Latimer (1993), in recent years educators have increasingly referred gifted children for ADHD evaluation. Because characteristics and behaviors are the foundation of a diagnosis of ADHD, and they can be misleading in the case of gifted people, educators and other professionals must exercise great care when conducting such evaluation (Baum, Olenchak, & Owen, 1998), with parents and teachers working closely with the diagnosing physician.

Children with ADHD *can't* stop moving, whereas children with high psychomotor behavior *love* to move.

In children with average creative and cognitive intelligence, this diagnosis can be made by a physician well versed in the characteristics of children with attention-deficit disorder (ADD) or ADHD (see box, "What is Attention-Deficit Hyperactivity Disorder?") in a fairly straightforward manner by means of thorough psychological and physical examinations. In gifted children, however, the diagnosis may be complicated by other issues, such as psychological overexcitabilities (Dabrowski, 1972; Piechowski, 1986; Piechowski & Colangelo, 1984).

Dabrowski saw these "forms of psychic overexcitability" (OEs) as contributing to

individuals' psychological development,
so they were a measure of developmental
potential. Overexcitabilities are so often
present in creatively, academically, intellectually, or otherwise gifted people that
some educators are searching for ways to
measure overexcitabilities as a tool for
identification of gifted people. Psychological intensities are such a part of people who
are considered gifted that, for the purpose
of this article, the behaviors should be considered to be present when giftedness is
mentioned. Researchers have categorized
overexcitabilities into five main areas: psychomotor, emotional, intellectual, imaginational, and sensual, as follows:

- Those with *psychomotor overexcitabilities* are easy to spot: They are
nearly always moving. Their behavior
has been characterized as feeling
driven to move, a love of movement,
restlessness, superenergy, and a need
for a high level of activity. Rapid
speech, impulsiveness, and a need to

act are also characteristic of those who
possess this overintensity. All this
sounds remarkably like the hyperactivity of ADHD (Barkley, 1990; Hallowell & Ratey, 1995), though the
difference appears to be that children
with ADHD *can't* stop moving,
whereas children with high psychomotor behavior *love* to move.

- *Imaginational overexcitabilities* are
characterized by a facility for invention and fantasy, an ability to engage in
detailed visualization, a well-devel-
oped sense of humor, animistic and
magical thinking, and elaborate application of truth and fiction. Children
who possess imaginational OEs can
have rich and fulfilling inner experiences during the pedestrian activities
of a typical school day. What looks
like inattention could be, instead, a
rich imaginational scenario unfolding
within the child's mind. A creatively
gifted 4th-grade student described it
like this: "Social studies can be really
boring when we just read it aloud and
take notes, so I like to pretend I'm in
whatever situation we're learning
about."

- *Emotional overintensity* is one of the
more outwardly visible of the overexcitabilities. Characterized by an inten-
sity of feeling, a marked ability to
empathize with others, and somatic
expression of feelings, these children
are the ones who can see all sides of a
situation, who can find it painfully difficult to make new friends, who cry at
the smallest frustration. What appears
to be the emotional overreactivity of
ADHD could, instead, be the expression of emotional overintensity.

- *Sensual overexcitabilities* manifest
themselves as extreme sensitivity to
touch; delight with the aesthetic things
in life, such as art, music, fabric, surroundings, or words; extreme dislike
or love for certain foods due to specific
textures or tastes; sensitivity to odors
or chemicals in the environment; or
any other sensory-related experiences.
People who experience heightened
pleasure when indulging in favorite
foods or drinks are displaying this sort
of sensual overexcitability. Stopping
to feel the fabric of every item passed
in a department store, noticing the particular blue of the sky, or admiring the
shape of a flower could easily be con-

strued as distractibility, but it could
also be illustrative of being tuned in to
the beauty of one's surroundings.

**Researchers have
categorized
overexcitabilities into
five main areas:
psychomotor,
emotional, intellectual,
imaginational,
and sensual.**

Look at a classroom full of students of
any age. Some are simply there, doing as
they are told, whereas others display an absolute thirst for learning. These individuals
possess a drive to learn that knows no
boundaries—**an intellectual overintensity.**
What they learn does not seem to matter as
long as it is new and interesting. These are
the people who think and wonder, who ask
the questions instead of knowing the answers, who exhibit sustained concentration, who have excessive curiosity, and
who integrate intuition and concept. They
are naturally metacognitive thinkers, are
detailed planners, and express early concerns about values and morality. Many of
these characteristics appear only in the
child's mind, so may look, again, like inattention to the outside observer. At times,
this overexcitability also may be seen as
similar to the hyperfocusing in people with
ADHD. Intellectual OEs may also be expressed as a hyperactivity seen by outsiders as distractibility, but which may be
heightened mental arousal that never stops,
even during sleep.

Who Are They?

With all these similarities, how can we tell
the difference between a gifted child with
overexcitabilities and one with ADHD?
Both children possess exceptional mental
faculties, but one has greater availability of
resources, while the other founders in a
quagmire of disorganization and distractibility. In such cases, parents and teachers
find it difficult to distinguish between the
child who *won't* do his or her work and the
one who *can't*. Gifted children with
ADHD are usually labeled as underachiev-

ing or lazy long before they are ever labeled as ADHD.

Studies have shown that gifted children identified as having ADHD are, generally, more gifted than their non-ADHD peers (Dorry, 1994; Zentall, 1997). Because the negative behavioral manifestations of ADHD may keep these children from performing well on group tests, many educators believe diagnostic tests uncover only the children who have extremely superlative talents or gifts. Though high intelligence can help the child overcome some of the challenges of ADHD over his or her lifetime (Barkley, 1990; Phelan, 1996), it does so only to the extent that it allows the child to compensate to the point of seeming average.

These children also tend not to be nominated for gifted testing or programs. Wolfle & French, in a presentation to the National Association for Gifted Children (1990), reported the following characteristics of a typical gifted child with ADHD excluded from gifted programs:

- Makes jokes or puns at inappropriate times.
- Is bored with routine tasks and refuses to do them.
- Is self-critical, impatient with failures.
- Tends to dominate others.
- Would rather stay by oneself.
- Has difficulty moving into another topic when engrossed.
- Often disagrees vocally with others in a loud, bossy manner.
- Is emotionally sensitive—may overreact.
- Is not interested in details, often hands in messy work.
- Refuses to accept authority, nonconforming, stubborn.

This is the portrait of a child who refuses to play the school game, has his or her own ideas about how to live, and will not compromise. Teachers do not particularly tend to like these children, thus they do not generally refer them for gifted programming because, in the teacher's mind, these students do not deserve to be there. Parents find them difficult to live with, and peers reject them, so life becomes a series of negative interactions with few opportunities for self-fulfillment. The worst part is that such children are intelligent enough to realize they are different, but may be helpless to change their behaviors at their own volition.

In his work with gifted children with ADHD, Mendaglio (1995) found that these children are painfully aware of their academic failures and misbehaviors. This awareness often manifests itself outwardly as nonspecific anger. On the positive side, he reported, when such children do qualify for and are placed into programs for gifted and talented children, they and their parents report immediate, lasting, positive increases in self-esteem and attitude.

The Creativity Link

Creativity and ADHD share many, many characteristics. Indeed, both creativity and ADHD are so difficult to define precisely and can look so much alike, one might be hard pressed to define certain characteristics as one or the other. In her study of 70 gifted children, Lovecky (1994) found that almost all of these children, even those with additional learning disabilities and exceptional hyperactivity, displayed creativity. The differences between them and their gifted/non-ADHD peers was, "organizing their creative ideas into products, and sustaining enough interest and motivation to finish a project once they had gotten past the novelty of the initial idea" (p. 3).

Hallowell and Ratey (1995) found certain characteristics of the ADHD mind beneficial to the development of creativity. These included a higher tolerance for chaos and ambiguity and no firm belief that there is one proper place for ideas or images. This can lead to unusual combinations of imagery and ideas and to new ways of seeing things.

Hyper-reactivity in the minds of people with ADHD is amazing to behold. The ideas come and come, changing from one topic to another with an awesome rapidity and proliferation. With this many ideas, new ones pop up with regularity, leading to people with creative/ADHD characteristics to think of themselves as "idea people."

Educators should place the child in classrooms where expectations are high and teaching is holistic, relevant, challenging, and meaningful.

The impulsivity of ADHD can lead to a need to create—anything. This impulse is an urge that demands satisfaction. Combined with the hyperfocusing of ADHD, this impulsivity can produce impressive results in a brief period of time. Of course, there will also be many times of distractibility to balance these periods of intense concentration and productivity.

Creative production also occurs when people spontaneously bring unlike items together in unusual ways. Creative people with ADHD do this often. They see and find amusing combinations others may never have thought of. This is a strategy others have to be taught to use, usually in expensive creativity-training workshops.

Cramond (1994), in a review paper, and Piirto (1992), in her book *Understanding Those Who Create*, noted that the defining characteristics of ADHD are also key descriptors in the biographies of highly creative people. Inattention, hyperactivity, and impulsivity were frequently mentioned as characteristic of many writers, artists, authors, inventors, and composers. These characteristics transferred across disciplines and were found in every area of creativity.

How Can You Tell Whether It Is Truly ADHD?

When we see ADHD-type behaviors, in combination with giftedness of either intellect or creativity, how can we tell if we need to take action to label and treat the ADHD? This is a question asked in nearly every article on the topic. The overwhelming primary response is this: Exercise caution in both the identification and treatment of ADHD in children identified as being gifted. Beyond that, research has identified several characteristics of gifted children with ADHD—characteristics that are not generally present in the child who is gifted but not identified as having ADHD.

The first is inconsistency in performance. Non-gifted ADHD children are known for inconsistency in school performance that occurs at any time in any subject (Barkley, 1990). Being gifted does not exempt children from these sorts of academic inconsistencies (Webb & Latimer, 1993). If children are functioning at a high level in a subject one day, then failing in the same subject days later, there may be reason to suspect a problem. A thorough history of the child's performance will reveal a pattern of variability of task performance over time. These children's performance may also be linked to the teacher's characteristics and teaching style; these students will not produce quality work for a teacher they do not like or respect.

There is a movement in the field now to find a means of measuring overexcitabilities as a tool for identification of gifted people.

A visit to a gifted resource classroom, otherwise known as a gifted "pullout" program, will generally reveal a higher than normal activity level, a great deal of talkativeness, and a high level of enthusiasm and task commitment for challenging, interesting tasks. The enthusiasm, movement, talkativeness, and high activity levels are desirable, though can be exhausting for the teachers involved, because these behaviors correspond to the ways gifted children are identified today. Gifted resource classrooms generally exist to serve gifted students in elementary schools, but sometimes can be found at higher grade levels. Wherever they are found, they are often the high point of a gifted students' day or week—time away from their general education classrooms to be spent with intellectual peers. While children with ADHD tend toward inattention, and distraction in nearly every situation, gifted children with ADHD will retain the hyperactivity and problems with sustained attention, except during certain highly stimulating, novel, motivating tasks, such as those to be found in the gifted resource classroom. Those gifted children who are unresponsive to even those tasks stand out among their peers and should be investigated.

Gifted children with ADHD, like all children, not only deserve, but *require* highly stimulating and mentally and psychologically challenging environments to be successful, something few schools provide. Many gifted children have problems with school environments that provide few opportunities for creativity, provide only concrete, linear-sequential instruction, teach only at the lower levels of the taxonomy, require excessively rote and repeti-

tive work, and do not allow learners to progress at their own rate (Baum et al., 1998; Cramond, 1995; Lovecky, 1994; Zentall & Zentall, 1983). This type of learning environment can be a disaster for any child, but you can virtually guarantee it will be for the child who has characteristics of both giftedness and ADHD. These children will frequently shut down when given repetitive tasks, even knowing that unfavorable consequences are certain to follow. When one 11-year-old gifted child with ADHD was asked about this, he responded, "It actually makes me feel sick to my stomach when they make me do the same thing over and over."

When the ADHD has gone undiagnosed for many years, the student may have developed problems with self-esteem and depression.

Whereas children with ADHD tend toward not liking school and gifted children usually do, gifted children with ADHD usually have a few subjects (particularly science) they really love and may not care about the rest (Zentall, 1997). This can lead to incredible power struggles in the home and school when parents and teachers see that the child can attend in some situations but won't (or can't) in others. In children like this, underachievement begins early, with the ADHD not generally identified until at least 6th grade (Lovecky, 1994). By then the child has set up a pattern of inconsistent performance and failure to complete work, leading to frequent negative feedback, leading in turn to diminished academic self-esteem and anger. This pattern of underachievement and the negative response it generates create a cycle within the school and the family that is difficult to break.

Though gifted children frequently display mental ages and social functioning well above those of their chronological peers, they still may exhibit some discrepancies within themselves between these developmental strands, while the gifted child with ADHD may exhibit a much wider and debilitating discrepancy between intellectual age and social and emotional ages. This can cause the child to be

out of sync with everyone (Lovecky, 1993). Social skills are usually underdeveloped in these children; as a result, they may have few friends, with those few generally being younger. Again, these children are aware of their differences and lack of friends, so may become depressed or oppositional in response.

How Do We Help These Paradoxical Children Become Achievers?

Research on underachievement in general, and in gifted people with ADHD specifically, has given us ideas on how to help these children become achievers. As far back as 1959, Passow and Goldberg provided insight in their landmark study on how to reverse underachievement. Their studies revealed that if teachers wish to reverse underachievement, they should place students in a stimulating, rich environment with a teacher who is kind and accepting, who values each of them as individuals, and who maintains high expectations. In addition, the researchers found that students needed further, intensive instruction in study and organizational skills; a characteristic shared by many underachievers, and nearly all children diagnosed with ADHD (Dorry, 1994; Maxwell, 1989). In today's world, gifted children with ADHD can be taught word processing and computer skills that will allow them to compensate for their inability to write quickly or neatly, or to keep their thoughts while writing (Ramirez-Smith, 1997).

Medication works most effectively when coupled with stable parental support at home.

Teachers who have successfully worked with gifted children with ADHD recognize that cognitive therapy is helpful. It is beneficial to talk openly with students about expectations and problems and include them in developing plans of action (Mendaglio, 1995). Contracts, with student-chosen rewards, are helpful in some cases. Because gifted children tend to be primarily intrinsically motivated, external rewards and punishments have little effect unless they are selected by the children themselves. Students need to be convinced that failure is not an option, that today's work will pay off in the future, and that hard work will benefit them personally. Goal setting is another useful strategy in this area, because it helps remove the child from the impulsivity of the moment and develop focus on the future.

What About Parents?

Parenting gifted children with ADHD can be an extremely frustrating experience. There is an awareness of the child's precocity and talents that leads to higher expectations, but that, when coupled with the ADHD behaviors, leads to frustration with the child's self-destructive behaviors. Parents need to deliberately educate themselves about how to deal appropriately with these children (see box, "Tried and True Strategies for Parents") and be advocates for them, while not being rescuers available to bail the children out of every jam (Zentall, 1997). Negativity and power struggles are common in families with gifted children with ADHD. On a more positive note, a child with ADHD who is gifted, who has a supportive family, and who is taught specific ways to compensate for his or her deficits has a much greater chance of becoming a productive adult (Phelan, 1996). Though the gifted child with ADHD may for many years demand an inordinate amount of the family's re-sources, it appears that early intervention and long-term support eventually pay off.

Home-school communication is essential for the success of gifted children with ADHD (Baum et al., 1998; Ramirez-Smith, 1997; Wolfle & French, 1990). Teachers need to be informed about these children's specific needs, and most are not. How could they be? In teacher education programs, there has traditionally been little room for teaching about gifted children at all, let alone those with additional exceptionalities. Parents can be useful in providing materials that inform educators about the characteristics and needs of a gifted child with ADHD. There should be ongoing, open communication between parent and teacher, with the child included as needed.

Tried & True Strategies for Parents of Gifted Children with ADHD or Overexcitability

- **Love your children for who they are**, not for what they do or don't do; obvious, but not always easy with these extremely challenging children.
- **Set standards and *insist* they be met**. Do what it takes to communicate that failure is *not* an option, and that every action has its consequences. If there are no natural consequences, design some specific to the situation.
- **Use humor to defuse stress and anger**. An advanced sense of humor is a characteristic many gifted children share. Take advantage of it.
- **There are no quick fixes**. Know that gifted children with ADHD require intensive, long-term, interventions. Be consistent over time.
- **Communicate regularly with your child's teachers** in a positive fashion, no matter what grade your child is in, and do so *before* problems surface. Remember, your mutual goal is to help the child be successful.
- **Impose organization on your children until they prove they can do it themselves**. Find a good system and teach and reteach it. Expect backsliding from time to time, all the way through school.
- **Provide opportunities for your child to express his or her creativity**. When things get really bad, this may be his or her lifesaver.
- **Nothing breeds success like success**. Find some way to show your child that he or she can be successful at something meaningful, if only he or she tries. Provide a choice of opportunities and insist he or she chooses one and sticks with it until successful completion.
- **Make sure your child is provided with appropriate curriculum and teachers from the start**. Positively but honestly present your child and his or her needs to school administrators *before* the end of this school year for next year's placement, then trust the school personnel to do the work of placing the child appropriately.

Because of the myriad needs generated by having a gifted child with ADHD in the classroom, administrators and teachers must hold discussions about classroom placements and include both current and former teachers, administrators, and parents. Educators should place the child in classrooms where expectations are high and teaching is holistic, relevant, challenging, and meaningful (DeLisle, 1995), and where teachers are willing to teach to the child's strengths while remediating the weaknesses. Multi-modal approaches allow the gifted child with ADHD to play to his or her strengths and express creativity (Lovecky, 1994). Several successful research projects have employed talent development and attention to students' specific intelligences, talents, or gifts as means to promote academic success for at-risk students (Baum, Owen, & Oreck, 1996; Baum, Renzulli, & Hebert, 1994; Olenchak, 1994). It is clear that proper curriculums, instruction, and pacing can make a great deal of difference in the school lives of gifted children with ADHD.

In some cases, physicians may prescribe medication for students to help control the ADD/ADHD symptoms, allowing the giftedness to emerge more fully. According to many researchers, doctors should not prescribe medication unless educators, parents, and other professionals have explored all other possible avenues because medication may have some detrimental effects on creativity, imagination, and intellectual curiosity (Baum et al., 1998; Cramond, 1995). That, of course, is a question to be decided by the doctors, parents, and children; and they should make such decisions on an individual basis. Wolfle & French (1990) stated that medication works most effectively when coupled with stable parental support at home. A review of literature on the effects of stimulant medication and children with ADHD has reinforced that medication alone provides only short-term effects; people should not expect it to improve long-term adjustment in either social or academic areas (Swanson et al., 1993).

Finally, researchers have suggested counseling for some of these children, especially when the ADHD has gone undiagnosed for many years, because the child may have developed problems with self-esteem and depression. When counseling is undertaken, however, educators, parents, and others must be careful to select counselors familiar with both the social and emotional needs of gifted children and children with ADD/ADHD (Webb & Latimer, 1993).

Now What?

The literature has little to say about children doubly blessed with giftedness and ADHD, even less of the literature is research based. In a search for materials on the subject, I found no information on this topic in traditional educational literature; I found some in the social sciences literature; and the rest in the gifted literature. Because most teachers have a hard enough time keeping up with information in their own area of expertise and seldom have the opportunity to examine the gifted literature, it seems logical that this information must be disseminated into mainstream education.

Educators need to do more to improve the quality of identification of these high-potential, though terribly at-risk children and to reduce the likelihood of misdiagnosis of children who are gifted and creative and overexcitable as having ADHD. On the other hand, writers and researchers can heighten our awareness of the existence of this segment of the population so that gifted children who actually *do* have ADHD are not missed in diagnosis. Misdiagnoses can cut some students off from services that they may need. Teachers who are educated on this topic can be of immense help when it comes time to work with doctors in diagnosing possible medical conditions such as ADHD.

Finally, we must learn to value these children; they have much to offer. Though the learning environments and teaching practices discussed earlier are desirable for all children, gifted or not, these doubly-blessed students possess the creative potential to produce great ideas and make wonderful contributions to our society. With appropriate curriculums; informed teachers and administrators; and educated, involved parents working together, we can reclaim a segment of our population who currently underachieve at a high rate. Most of all, we can teach these young people that in working to show their strengths and overcome their deficits, they make themselves even better. As educators, we need to help them learn who they are, what they are capable of, and how to reach their potential.

References

American Psychiatric Association (1994). *Diagnostic and statistical manual of mental disorders* (4th ed.: DSM IV). Washington, DC: Author.

Barkley, R. (1990). *Attention deficit hyperactivity disorder: A handbook for diagnosis and treatment*. New York: Guilford Press.

Baum, S., Olenchak, F., & Owen, S. (1998). Gifted students with attention deficits: Fact or fiction? Or, can we see the forest for the trees? *Gifted Child Quarterly, 42*(2), 96–104.

Baum, S., Owen, S., & Oreck, B. (1996). Talent beyond words: Identification of potential talent in dance and music in elementary students. *Gifted Child Quarterly, 40*(2), 93–102.

Baum, S., Renzulli, J., & Hebert, T. (1994). Reversing underachievement: Stories of success. *Educational Leadership, 52*(3), 48–53.

Cramond, B. (1994). Creativity and ADHD: What is the connection? *Journal of Creative Behavior, 28*(3), 193–210.

Cramond, B. (1995). The coincidence of attention deficit hyperactivity disorder and creativity. *Monograph of the National Research Center on the Gifted and Talented, RBDM 9508, United States Government: Connecticut.* (ERIC Document Reproduction Service No. 388 016)

Dabrowski, K. (1972). *Psychoneurosis is not an illness*. London: Gryf.

DeLisle, J. (1995). ADD gifted: How many labels can one child take? *Gifted Child Today, 18*(2), 42–43.

Dorry, G. (1994). The perplexed perfectionist. *Understanding Our Gifted, 6*(5), 3, 10–12.

Hallowell, E., & Ratey, J. (1995). *Driven to distraction*. New York: Simon & Schuster.

Lovecky, D. (1993). Out of sync with everyone. *Understanding Our Gifted, 5*(5A), 3.

Lovecky, D. (1994, July/August). The hidden gifted learner. *Understanding Our Gifted, 3 & 18*.

Maxwell, V. (1989). Diagnosis and treatment of the gifted student with attention deficit disorder: A structure of intellect approach. *Reading, Writing & Learning Disabilities, 5*, 247–252.

Mendaglio, S. (1995, July/August). Children who are Gifted/ADHD., *Gifted Child Today*, 18, 37–38.

Olenchak, F. (1994). Talent development: Accommodating the social and emotional needs of secondary gifted/learning disabled students. *Journal of Secondary Gifted Education, 5*(3), 40–52.

Passow, H., & Goldberg, M. (1959). Study of underachieving gifted. *Educational Leadership, 16,* 121–125.

Phelan, T. (1996). *All about attention deficit disorder.* Minneapolis, MN: Child Management Press.

Piechowski, M. (1986). The concept of developmental potential. *Roeper Review, 8*(3), 190–197.

Piechowski, M., & Colangelo, N. (1984). Developmental potential of the gifted. *Gifted Child Quarterly, 28,* 80–88.

Piirto, J. (1992). *Understanding those who create.* Dayton: Ohio Psychology Press.

Ramirez-Smith, C. (1997). *Mistaken identity: Gifted and ADHD.* Reston, VA: The Council for Exceptional Children. (ERIC Document Reproduction No. ED413690)

Swanson, J., McBurnett, K., Wigal, T., Pfiffner, L., Lerner, M., Williams, L., Christian, D., Tamm, L., Willcutt, E., Crowley, K., Clevenger, W., Khouzam, N., Woo, C., Crinella, F., & Fisher, T. (1993). Effect of stimulant medication on children with attention deficit disorder. A "review of reviews." *Exceptional Children, 60,* 154–162.

Webb, J., & Latimer, D. (1993). *ADHD and children who are gifted (ERIC Digest No. 522).* Reston, VA: The Council for Exceptional Children.

Wolfle, J., & French, M. (1990). *Surviving gifted attention deficit disorder children in the classroom.* Paper presented at the meeting of the National Association for Gifted Children, Little Rock, AR.

Zentall, S. (1997, March). *Learning characteristics of boys with attention deficit hyperactivity disorder and/or giftedness.* Paper presented at the annual meeting of the American Educational Research Association, Chicago, IL. (ERIC Document Reproduction No. 407791)

Zentall, S., & Zentall, T. (1983). Optimal stimulation: A model of disordered activity and performance in normal and deviant children. *Psychological Bulletin, 94,* 446–471.

Lori J. Flint, *Doctoral Candidate, Department of Educational Psychology, The University of Georgia, Athens.*

Address correspondence to the author at Department of Educational Psychology, The University of Georgia, 325 Aderhold Hall, Athens, GA 30602-7143, (e-mail: LJFSTAT@AOL.COM)

Beyond the Gifted Stereotype

A new understanding of giftedness reveals many kinds of gifted learners and new ways to meet their learning needs.

Carolyn M. Callahan

How can Andy be gifted? He can't even read at grade level. And what about Sally? I saw her I.Q. score, and it was only 115!" Can a child who is a nonreader be gifted? Is an intelligence test score the only, or even the best, indicator of giftedness? Is giftedness doing what the teacher says and doing it well?

Sometimes preconceptions get in the way of understanding changes. Research has revealed new insights about giftedness and new ways to teach the wide range of gifted learners, but educational practice has not always kept up.

Unfortunately, the characteristics and needs of gifted learners receive little attention in the general education literature, often leaving teachers and administrators less able to address gifted students' needs. What are some of the myths, half-truths, and misconceptions that may still be influencing teacher and administrator decisions?

The Myths

Gifted students are a homogeneous group and need only one differentiated curriculum. The presumption is that gifted learners as a group march to the beat of a different drummer —and that they all march to the same beat of the same different drummer. Following this educationally harmful myth, school districts have created one-dimensional gifted programs and curriculums.

The old concept of giftedness, which applied to only one kind of learner, has given way to recognizing multiple talents. Some gifted students are advanced learners in multiple subjects and achieve in such traditional ways as scoring above grade level on standardized assessments. Other students may exhibit talent in a single area, such as expressive writing or advanced mathematical reasoning, but not in others.

> **The old concept of giftedness, which applied to only one kind of learner, has given way to recognizing multiple talents.**

New concepts of intelligence have provided a fresh lens for looking at talent and ability in students. The multiple intelligences described by Howard Gardner (1983, 1993) include talents in areas outside of traditional school disciplines. Robert Sternberg (1986) describes other special talents, including creative intelligence—the ability to develop innovative ideas, find new ways to extend the major ideas in a discipline, or create new paradigms that challenge traditional interpretations.

All gifted learners exhibit advanced understanding or the ability to learn at an accelerated rate, but a gifted student may not have the same level of capabilities across all areas. A student may be exceptionally advanced in one subject and need tasks that are more complex and abstract, but may not be as advanced in other subjects.

Gifted students also have different interests, learning styles, and motivations. To assume that all gifted students like to read, work for grades, or organize their efforts skillfully is a mistake. Cultural mores and behavior may mask manifestations of talent. For example, cultural background may discourage a student from demonstrating talent or from speaking unless asked a direct question.

Believing that all gifted students are alike results in the notion that schools only need to provide a single program to meet their needs. The differences among gifted students suggest that offering the same curricular options to all of them—acceleration of all gifted learners, weekly pullout programs with the same activities for all gifted learners, or occasional enrichment activities in the regular classroom—will often result in a mismatch between learner need and instructional opportunity. Instead, we need to consider multiple ways to plan appropriate instruction for gifted students.

Giftedness is determined before students come to school. Our job is to find the gifted learner and develop the giftedness that the child already has. This half-truth has resulted in the naive neglect of many gifted students and in what appear to be racially or socioeconomically discriminating services for gifted students. Many students come from homes with plentiful opportunities to learn numeracy, prereading skills, and the social and behavioral skills that ensure school success. For these students, the teacher's job is to identify extraordinary levels of learning and to differentiate the learning experience for students who have already mastered or can easily master new concepts. We can quickly spot these students, and we have done a reasonably good job of identifying them.

Many other equally able students, however, have not had opportunities to learn the skills that would have prepared them to benefit from initial school experiences. Some have not developed the traditional skills in language expression that the school culture expects for demonstrating exceptional thinking or learning ability. Others do not have a behavioral repertoire that responds to the structure of the elementary school environment. For these students, the teacher must become a developer of talent (Renzulli, 1994), creating classroom environments that use a variety of learning tasks, lessons, assignments, and assessments and providing an engaging curriculum. The teacher's challenge is to hook the learner with interesting and personally relevant learning and not underestimate the learner's potential. Students will live up to our expectations for them. Far better to err by setting high expectations and see students' talents emerge than to set low expectations and never give students the occasion to excel.

Gifted students will learn anyway. All students learn all the time. But what are they learning? Are they making the most productive use of their learning time? Are they learning anything new? Students' successes constitute the greatest reward of teaching, but it is often easier to mark success by how a student performs rather than by what the student has learned, particularly when teacher success is measured by student performance on high-stakes, grade-level assessments. Students may not be increasing their knowledge, understanding, or skill if they come to the classroom with a level of performance that exceeds what the grade-level curriculum requires.

Further, our students learn values and attitudes at school, and we should be concerned about what they learn. Is Kevin learning that school is a waste of time and teachers have

little to offer because he already learned this content before he came to school? Is Amanda learning an attitude of disrespect or contempt for other students because she can do all the tasks assigned to her group while the others struggle to complete one or two tasks or have no success at all? And is Catherine learning habits of laziness because she never exerts any mental energy to complete her assignments yet still receives *A*s on her report card?

An appropriate learning activity for gifted learners is to teach less advanced learners. Under the impression that teaching helps the gifted student learn content more thoroughly and that struggling learners benefit from peer teachers, educators often assign gifted learners to teach other students. If gifted students have not fully learned or clearly understood the material, then perhaps teaching others may be of benefit. No evidence exists, however, to show that teaching enhances understanding after a student has mastered the content or skills.

> **Research indicates that a learner is more likely to successfully model a peer who is slightly more advanced in performance level than one who differs greatly.**

To assume that the gifted student is a good teacher for struggling learners is the more egregious error. Without any training to be a teacher, the gifted student does not have the ability to diagnose learning problems, to reflect on ways that the other student might learn better, or to develop a repertoire of alternative teaching strategies. Further, the gifted student's advanced understanding of or more subtle reflections on a concept or skill could impede the less proficient learner's mastery of the subject. Some argue that the gifted learner serves as a model for other learners; however, research indicates that learners are more likely to successfully model a peer who is slightly more advanced in performance level than one whose perfor-

mance differs greatly (Schunk, 1987).

Gifted learners are always high achievers. Case studies of successful college students with learning disabilities verified that these students often go unrecognized because teachers have categorized them as below-average achievers (Reis, Neu, & McGuire, 1995). Poor reading or writing achievement—the coin of the realm in classrooms—has often stymied performance not just in language arts, but also in all subjects where information acquisition and demonstration of learning rely on the quick and masterful display of verbal skills. Because these students lacked opportunities to display achievement and learning in nontraditional formats, teachers did not notice their high levels of cognitive performance. Although teachers sometimes nominated them for gifted programs, they usually did not receive services because of low test scores—most often in verbal skills.

Even the identification of the students' learning disabilities often came late in their school careers because, ironically, they did not demonstrate sufficiently low levels of achievement. As a result, they did not receive the services or accommodations that would have allowed them to demonstrate their talents.

Bonnie Cramond (1995) has also noted the overlap in the defining characteristics of students with Attention Deficit Hyperactivity Disorder (ADHD) and those of creativity. She cautions that educators should be open-minded about the possibility that behaviors that are perceived as difficult—inattention, hyperactivity, impulsivity, difficult temperament, deficient social skills, and academic underachievement—may be indicative of creativity or giftedness, possibly in combination with ADHD. A student's inattention may be boredom with a curriculum that presents no challenge, and gifted students characteristically exhibit high energy levels that teachers may perceive as hyperactivity.

The second mask of giftedness is underachievement. These students perform well on standardized assessments or exhibit extraordinary performance outside of school, but because they fail to earn high grades in school, teachers may consider them as average or even below-average students. If students are performing at high levels in other environments, we should reflect on why the curriculum is failing to stimulate the same enthusiasm and accomplishment in the classroom. Standards are supposed to ratchet up the curriculum, but some standards and their accompanying tests may only set minimum standards that present easily cleared hurdles and do not require much effort from an advanced learner. What can we do to create a level of challenge that will raise those bars?

The gifted learner is going to do just fine without any special interventions on the teacher's part. Are all gifted students doing just fine? Many gifted learners do not receive recognition, and many others while away the day until after school when real learning can begin. That doesn't seem just fine.

Creating Classrooms of Learning: First Steps

Assess, Assess

Each student brings a different challenge to the teacher. To create responsive education experiences for many kinds of giftedness and to challenge gifted learners, teachers must assess students continually—first, to determine the students' current level of performance; then, to assess the rate at which students can learn when the learning experiences best suit their background experiences and strengths in learning style and productivity; and finally, to ensure that the students are continuing to learn throughout the year.

Use existing data from local and state assessments. Although these tests rely heavily on the ability to respond to verbal stimuli, they can provide useful information on the strengths of some students. For students who are achieving above grade level, teachers should conduct assessments throughout the year to ensure that those students are learning new content or familiar content in greater depth and complexity.

Find open-ended opportunities for performance to gauge what students already know. For example, a teacher can begin by considering, "In

what ways might I find out what my students already know about the life cycle of a plant?" Or a teacher can ask students to draw a cartoon strip that illustrates the life of a plant from birth to death, or encourage very young students to act out how a seed becomes a flower.

Rather than looking only for students whose performance is uniformly high, look for students with peaks of performance. High performance on solving problems or geometric concepts, for example, may indicate a special talent in mathematics.

Construct learning activities to engage students in a variety of ways and provide different options to demonstrate achievement. In particular, look for opportunities to assess learning strengths that do not require advanced language skills, particularly reading and writing. For example, allow students to view a film of *Hamlet* before discussing it and then look for students whose insights are reflective of deeper understanding of theme or character. Or give students the opportunity to use graphic organizers to represent the relationships among physical, cultural, social, and political geographies of a country. Reading and writing are obviously crucial skills, but students who cannot learn or demonstrate learning because of language difficulties or disabilities need recognition and an appropriate curriculum.

Learn the ways in which cultural or social differences inhibit performance among the students. For example, students in some cultural groups learn not to attempt public performance at all until they achieve complete mastery. Educators may judge these students as far less competent than they really are. In these cases, teachers should seek ways to create the opportunity for performance not inhibited by the students' cultural mores.

The first step in awakening and developing the talent of the gifted student is to move beyond our stereotypes of the gifted learner and create new ways to bring out and encourage talent. Several programs funded by the Jacob K. Javits Gifted and Talented Students Act of 1994 have been successful in creating new images of talent. For example, Project Support to Affirm Rising Talent (START), a

collaborative project on minority talent development with the Charlotte-Mecklenburg Schools, North Carolina, used Howard Gardner's model of intelligence to create specific performance assessment tasks through which students could demonstrate verbal, logical-mathematic, and spatial abilities. More important, teachers modified the curriculum to encourage students who had different styles of learning.

Create Many Kinds of Challenge

Learning the student's strengths is of little value if we do not create learning experiences that reflect an attempt to modify the learning experience of the student in light of our new knowledge.

Accommodate the complexity and creativity in students' thinking and problem solving and their knowledge in language, mathematical, spatial, musical, and artistic arenas by creating a rich variety of opportunities for performance. For a unit on tropism, for example, offer an open-ended challenge: "Show how the sun affects the way a plant grows and how other features in a plant's world may change the way it grows."

Compact the curriculum. This simple modification creates a challenging curriculum and many learning opportunities for gifted students and reduces the boredom that develops when students sit through instruction in skills and basic facts that they have already mastered. Research has found that gifted elementary school students whose teachers had eliminated 40–50 percent of the curriculum achieved as well or better on standardized tests as gifted students in a comparison group that had not had a compacted curriculum (Reis et al., 1993).

Address the curriculum at many levels of sophistication, creating high-end learning activities at increased levels of abstraction, complexity, depth, and pace of instruction while still addressing the common standards of the core curriculum. Follow Carol Ann Tomlinson's guidelines (1995) for increasing the level of challenge for gifted learners. For a science standard that requires students to identify and understand the uses of simple machines, for example, challenge gifted students to compare and evaluate the efficiency of a variety of simple machines that carry out the same task, requiring the students to define efficiency and then to create a series of tests to evaluate the machines.

Offer ways for students to become involved in individual learning activities that will motivate and challenge regardless of cultural or social backgrounds or particular learning strengths. The complex instruction model (Cohen et al., 1994) suggests ways to modify the depth and complexity of a lesson. For a history unit about the impact of the industrial revolution on society, for example, ask students to examine pictures of sweatshops, folk music of the period, muckraker literature, and historical documents. Students with varying areas of strength can all contribute to the discussion. Asking the class to compare and contrast the industrial revolution with the more recent revolution in technology offers advanced students opportunities to use abstract and complex thinking skills and also draws on all students' experiences with technology (Kaplan, 2001).

Encourage group investigation (Sharan & Sharan, 1994) to open ways for students to use their special abilities and learn the skills necessary for becoming high-level creators and problem solvers. Students in a group investigation select problems in their community, country, or the world that relate to the unit of study. Students may elect to examine evidence of the illegal use of immigrant labor, for example, and propose solutions.

By challenging the myths about giftedness and by taking these initial steps in assessment and creative instructional strategies, our classrooms can begin to address the learning needs of all students, including the many kinds of gifted learners.

References

Cohen, E. G., Lotan, R. A., Whitcomb, J. A., Balderrama, M. V., Cossey, R., & Swanson, P. E. (1994). Complex instruction: Higher order thinking in heterogeneous classrooms. In S. Sharan (Ed.), *Handbook of cooperative learning methods* (pp. 82–96). Westport, CT: Greenwood.

Cramond, B. (1995). *The coincidence of attention deficit hyperactivity disorder and creativity.* (Research-Based Decision-Making Series No. 9508). Storrs: University of Connecticut, National Research Center on the Gifted and Talented.

Gardner, H. (1983). *Frames of mind: The theory of multiple intelligences.* New York: BasicBooks.

Gardner, H. (1993). *Multiple intelligences: The theory in practice.* New York: BasicBooks.

Kaplan, S. N. (2001). Layering differentiated curriculum for the gifted and talented. In F. A. Karnes & S. M. Bean (Eds.), *Methods and materials for teaching the gifted.* (pp. 133–158). Waco, TX: Prufrock.

Reis, S. M., Neu, T. W., & McGuire, J. M. (1995). *Talents in two places: Case studies of high-ability students with learning disabilities who have achieved.* (Research Monograph 95113). Storrs: University of Connecticut, National Research Center on the Gifted and Talented.

Reis, S. M., Westberg, K. L., Kulikowich, J., Caillard, F., Hebert, T., Plucker, J., Purcell, J. H., Rogers, J. B., & Smist, J. M. (1993). *Why not let high-ability students start school in January? The curriculum compacting study.* (Research Monograph 93106). Storrs: University of Connecticut, National Research Center on the Gifted and Talented.

Renzulli, J. S. (1994). *Schools for talent development: A practical plan for school improvement.* Mansfield Center, CT: Creative Learning Press.

Schunk, D. H. (1987). Peer models and children's behavioral change. *Review of Educational Research, 57*(2), 149–174.

Sharan, Y., & Sharan, S. (1994). Group investigation in the cooperative classroom. In S. Sharan (Ed.), *Handbook of cooperative learning methods* (pp. 97–114). Westport, CT: Greenwood.

Sternberg, R. J. (1986). *A triarchic theory of giftedness.* In R. J. Sternberg & J. E. Davidson (Eds.), *Conceptions of giftedness* (pp. 223–246). New York: Cambridge University Press.

Tomlinson, C. A. (1995). *How to differentiate instruction in mixed ability classrooms.* Alexandria, VA: ASCD.

Carolyn M. Callahan is a professor in the Curry School of Education and an associate director of the National Research Center on the Gifted and Talented, P.O. Box 400265, Ruffner Hall, Rm. 262, University of Virginia, Charlottesville, VA 22904; cmc@virginia.edu.

Celebrate Diversity!

How to create a caring classroom that honors
your students' cultural backgrounds

By Mary Antón-Oldenburg, Ed.D.

"I don't want to phool around, I just want to read," writes
Olivia, a young Russian immigrant, during a reading-
reflection time. Zena, a child of African-American and
North African descent, often misses school to help her recently widowed mother care for Zena's younger siblings.
Pasha's parents, who came to the United States from India with high expectations, want their first grader to be
assigned harder work, while Susie, a middle-class white
child, has parents who want "a typical experience" for
her—she should learn to read and write, primarily
through play. Though names and some details have been
changed, these are all real children—and students of
mine.

As a teacher, juggling the expectations and experiences
of such widely diverse youngsters and their parents can
be both overwhelming and enriching. It's a challenge
more and more of us need to face. The young people who
fill our classrooms are increasingly diverse, which is a reflection of the United States as a whole. Nearly 8 million
new immigrants settled in this country between 1981 and
1990, according to the most recent figures available from
the United States Census Bureau. It is estimated that 80
percent of them came here from Latin America, the Car-
ibbean, and Asia. Experts predict that by 2020 children of
color will make up close to 46 percent of America's
school-age population.

While one of our most basic goals as teachers is to support the growth of the individual child, it can become
complicated when that child is from a very different background than our own, whatever our ethnic origin. We
need to challenge ourselves to take steps to help our students appreciate their own cultural ways, even as we help
them succeed as students.

All Learning is Culturally Constructed

The culture children bring to school can have a profound
effect on how they respond. One good example of this is
recounted in *Teaching Other People's Children: Literacy and
Learning in a Bilingual Classroom*, by Cindy Ballenger
(Teachers College Press, 1999). Puzzled by her lack of success in guiding the actions of the students in her bilingual
Haitian preschool class, Cindy noticed that her Haitian
colleagues seemed to be having an easier time with the
youngsters. These teachers used verbal patterns, she discovered, that conveyed not only a reprimand, but linked
a child's behavior to concepts of universal good and bad.
These messages were delivered with affection, but without the same attention to honoring the child's individual
feelings as is considered "best practice" for mainstream
American children. Cindy successfully learned to adapt
to this pattern of talk.

Experiences such as Cindy's suggest that we may need
to reconsider our current understanding of what is good
practice and move toward more culturally relevant teaching. Of course, that might not seem so easy when we are
faced with 25 or more students, many with different backgrounds and sets of cultural experiences. What is a
teacher to do?

Multicultural Education as a Way of Life

In caring classrooms, all children must be represented.
This means that multicultural content must be seen as a

way of life, not an add-on. Celebrate Black History Month, but take steps to make sure that representation of African-Americans—and all groups—occurs throughout the year. Regardless of your present school population, your students will benefit from a broad education that includes many diverse points of view and incorporates diverse cultural understanding. This goal can best be accomplished by seeing the teaching of multicultural content as a thread that runs through all your curricular areas.

Here are some other ways to celebrate student diverity:

- **Learn about the backgrounds of your students.** Educate yourself about unfamiliar cultures. When you have choices in curriculum, think carefully about underrepresented groups. Go beyond the obvious holidays, heroes, and foods. And remember: You have a greater potential to increase student understanding by in-depth coverage of a few cultures than you do by devoting a number of hurried days to many cultures.

With hardworking Pasha in my first-grade class, we embarked on a six-week study of the diversity of India. We were surprised to find that India has, for example, more than 100 official languages. Through exploration in film and language, culture and stories, museum visits and, yes, food, the students and I came to understand that just being from the same country does not mean that you are identical to others. We came to appreciate the multiple aspects of Indian culture, and this, in turn, helped us see that even groups that might look the same to us from their appearance have differences.

- **Encourage the teaching of multiple perspectives.** Resources abound to allow even young children to see the world from different points of view. For example, *The True Story of the Three Little Pigs,* by John Scieszka (Penguin, 1996), gives this well-worn tale a new spin by telling it from the wolf's perspective. Cut out some magazine pictures of a variety of people doing different things, and ask your students to imagine what these people are thinking. Older children will appreciate texts such as "The Bee," a poem found in *Joyful Noise: Poems for Two Voices,* by Paul Fleischman (HarperCollins, 1992), in which the points of view of a drone and a queen bee are presented.

- **Celebrate all kinds of stories.** Storytelling style can vary widely between cultures. Researchers have found that Japanese children tell shorter narratives than their white middle-class peers. In contrast, some African-American children may tell longer stories which include events and episodes that do nor appear, on the surface, to be related. They use elaborate wordplay and elicit greater participation of the audience. Latino children may tell stories in which personal relationships are emphasized rather than ones in which events are primary.

If you encounter a child whose narratives don't quite make sense to you, consider that you may be unfamiliar with that child's storytelling style. Investigate such styles and genres, in print and on audio- and videotape, and share them with your class. Audiotape the stories students tell, and look for patterns in them. Create a class library of stories told in the styles of different cultures. Ask parents for advice and suggestions.

To learn more, read *The Need for Story: Cultural Diversity in Classroom and Community,* by Anne Haas Dyson and Celia Genishi (National Council of Teachers of English, 1994), and *Chameleon Readers: Teaching Children to Appreciate All Kinds of Good Stories,* by Allyssa McCabe (McGraw-Hill, 1995).

- **Encourage the use of a child's primary language.** Research shows that children who develop strong vocabulary and concepts in their primary language will transfer these strengths to their secondary language. If two or more of your students speak in a non-English tongue, invite them to discuss among themselves a curricular topic in that language before completing an assignment or after they finish reading. Allow for journal writing in either language. Whenever possible, provide texts in a child's primary language, for reading during quiet times of the day. Encourage parents and other community members to help you provide resources in home languages to students. And most important, encourage parents to continue to discuss high-level concepts with their children in their home language.

Learn more about teaching students whose home language is not English in *Between Worlds: Access to Second Language Acquisition,* by David E. and Yvonne S. Freeman (Heinemann, 1994).

- **Be mindful of the books you read in class and the characters you choose for class study.** Pick books that portray boys and girls from diverse cultures—but first screen these books for stereotypic presentations. Ask yourself: Does this book present this group/person in a sensitive manner? Are the illustrations appropriate, or do they include exaggeration of cultural features or images? If I were a member of this culture, would I feel positive about my image in this book? Are the setting and illustrations appropriate to the time and place in which this story occurs?

- **Teach your students to actively critique the materials that they use, the media they view.** Ask students to be aware—in the books they read and the TV and videos they watch—of who is represented and how. I encourage my students to "talk back" to portrayals that they consider inaccurate. Sometimes, we create scripts based on these verbal critiques. Helping children to talk about and even rewrite texts that contain uncomfortable stereotypes or images teaches them that books can be challenged. It empowers them to view the world with a critical eye.

• **Help students create a classroom language for challenging stereotypic statements.** Model the caring but firm statements of "We don't talk about people in that manner here" and "The way that you are talking about that person [or group] is offensive to me and to many others. I don't think you mean to be so disrespectful." Help them take ownership in expressing personal views and beliefs. Include in your modeling modulators such as: "For me," "I believe," "I am wondering," and "I think."

• **Maintain high expectations for all children!** A teacher's attitude towards a student's potential is a powerful predictor for student achievement. Treat all your students as if they are the most capable. Work from the assumption that they bring great cultural resources with them—and you may just discover a treasure trove of experience and wisdom that will enrich everyone's learning.

Mary Antón-Oldenburg, Ed.D., is a teacher-researcher in Brookline, Massachusetts with 18 years' experience in grades K–8.

Lessons on Multicultural Education from Australia and the United States

LESLIE A. SWETNAM

The opportunity to compare the multicultural education practices of Australia with those in the United States occurred during my sabbatical in Melbourne, Australia. A comparison of the philosophical orientations, content and methods, and teacher preparation in multicultural education revealed some similarities in the two systems as well as some very instructive differences.

National Diversity

It is necessary first to understand the diversity of these nations. Both are relatively new countries in terms of European settlement, and both originally failed to recognize the indigenous inhabitants present at the time of their colonization. Both began their societies as colonies of England and became diverse through large influxes of immigrants.

However, comparing their diversity reveals the first major difference in philosophical orientation. In Australia the census records population diversity by asking for the nation of birth of the residents and their parents. This provides a relatively accurate description of the ethnicity of newcomers (first and second generation immigrants) to the country, although it does not accurately account for individuals born outside the nation of their ancestors; thus Chinese born in Malaysia would be counted as Malaysians. This system also makes it difficult to track racial composition because the census does not collect that information. Under this system, which is perhaps a legacy of previous assimulationist thinking, all third generation or older individuals would be considered "Australian" without reference to race or ethnicity on the census; this makes the current composition of the total population difficult to describe. However, one of the unique characteristics of diversity in Australia is that a large part of the current population (40 percent) comprises first or second generation Australians, so that for at least this proportion of the population the census contains accurate data on diversity (Allan and Hill 1995).

In the United States the census collects diversity data based on racial makeup rather than ethnicity. This also presents a challenge because individuals of mixed race are not accurately represented. In addition, race is not always a strong indicator of ethnicity (social culture) but is a physical characteristic. This method of categorization may result in less information about an individual's culture and stereotyping of individuals for many generations. The United States also categorizes Hispanic surnamed individuals into a minority group that is neither racial nor ethnic.

These two different systems, one focusing on ethnicity and the other on race, make comparison difficult. However, because of the longitudinal data collection and analysis work of Khoo and Price using categories comparable to those in the United States, a comparison is possible. According to their data 8.26 percent of the Australian population in 1999 were people of color (Aborigine, South Asian, South East Asian, North East Asian, African, etc.) (Price 2000), whereas in 2000 the population of the United States included 17.8 percent people of color (black, Asian, Native American) or 29.6 percent if Hispanics are included (Statistical Abstracts of the U.S. 2001). Although both countries have a broad range of individuals of diverse ethnicities, the United States has the greater proportion (at least double Australia's) of racial diversity.

Philosophical Orientation

The motivation for more and better multicultural education and teacher training in both countries seems to be the encouragement of cultural harmony. Australia seems to have had fewer problems with racism and discrimination. This may be due to the much smaller proportion of people of color. Moreover there is almost no history of slavery in the country or of expansion of borders into land previously claimed by another country (both nations however "conquered" lands originally held by native peoples, with those indigenous populations becoming decimated by disease and mistreatment at the hands of the colonizers). A second strong motive in the United States is the attempt to equalize academic achievement rates of the minority groups (test scores, graduation and tertiary matriculation rates, etc.) (Seeberg et al. 1998).

Improvement of student achievement is not an apparent motivation in Australia. Test scores are not routinely compared based on race or ethnicity. This may be because people of color are a relatively recent addition to the population, or because discrimination has not been as large and institutionalized a problem, or because the newest wave of immigrants are Asian, many from groups who have demonstrated high academic achievement in the United States and other countries. The achievement disparities between different racial groups in the United States, however, seems to lend urgency to the push for multicultural education there.

Lessons for Curriculum Content and Methods

In both countries progress has been made toward more inclusive curriculum content. Textbook content has been expanded to include the contributions of more cultural groups and a broader range of perspectives. However, methods remain largely unchanged in both countries. There is little evidence that teachers actually adapt their teaching methods to reach a wider range of different learning styles, including the more collectivist style of many minority cultures. They seem to continue to rely on the individualistic learning style and methods of the European-background majority population (Rothstein-Fisch, Greenfield, Trumbull 1999). This type of adaptation based on the inherent cultural learning styles of students is perhaps at a more sophisticated level of multicultural understanding and practice that necessitates more teacher training and field experience.

Inclusion of multicultural content is on a contributionist or additive level (Banks 1997). For example, bits of information and isolated art activities are highlighted or inserted into the curriculum, or separate units of study (Aboriginal studies or Black Studies) are offered. Neither nation seems to have been successful in transforming the curriculum to make diversity (methods and content) an integrated part of the ongoing curriculum while moving to more abstract levels of concept development (transformative or social action) with students. Multicultural parts of the curriculum still focus almost exclusively on the cultural recall and comprehension levels of learning.

One major difference in the multicultural programming in Australia is the emphasis on language. Whereas U.S. schools provide bilingual instruction (Spanish) as well as ESL (English as a Second Language). Australian schools provide only ESL. However, private community as well as government supported language maintenance, fluency, and literacy programs abound in Australia, and many students of non-English speaking backgrounds (defined as students who have one or more parents born in a non-English-speaking country) participate in these programs.

In addition, every elementary school chooses a LOTE (language other than English) to teach to all students in the school, with some of the most popular being Italian, Chinese, and Vietnamese. Although the effectiveness in producing students who are both fluent and literate in the LOTE can be debated, the attempt seems to increase cultural and linguistic understanding among the students, which does not seem to be present in elementary schools in the United States.

One way to strengthen multicultural education in both countries would be to institutionalize multicultural integration by embedding the content, concepts, and methods in the standard curriculum. Depending on each individual teacher to seek out content and activities to include in the curriculum results in an uneven application of the concepts. Teachers need support, training, and classroom-ready materials, not just officially stated objectives and encouragement, to effectively operationalize multicultural curriculum.

The following are widely held misconceptions among teachers about the role of multicultural education:

- Multicultural education is not as important if your student population is mainly white students born in your country.
- Language is the only major need and once students can speak the language no further multicultural inclusion is necessary.
- Encouraging cultural maintenance is divisive. (McInerney et al. 2001)

These attitudes are major obstacles to increased cultural integration of methods and materials and demonstrate the need for improved teacher training at both the preservice and inservice levels.

Lessons for Teacher Preparation

In Australia few teacher education programs require diversity training (Hill and Allan 1998). Interviews and observations in universities revealed less institutionalization of multicultural content and experience requirements for teacher candidates. Although most of the faculty in these programs try to incorporate references to and examples of cultural diversity in their lessons, the result is a variable emphasis on multicultural education dependent on the individual instructor's interests and experiences rather than intentionally embedded concepts and methods in the whole teacher education program.

In the United States multicultural education components are part of most teacher education programs. This probably stems from the desire to raise the test scores of specific racial groups in the quest for educational equality. The standards for national accreditation (NCATE) have been instrumental in incorporating multicultural education into many teacher education programs (Seeberg et al. 1998). This is not to say that this training has as yet had the desired effect in producing sensitive, skilled, and effective multicultural educators.

Both nations need to improve their diversity training for teachers to avoid just reviewing stereotypical cultural content. An effective program should incorporate preservice teachers' explorations of their own cultural values, practices, and beliefs, as well as those of other cultures so that the teacher candidates can begin to see themselves as a combination of similarities and differences in the big mosaic of human diversity.

A second very important component is instruction, activities, speakers, videos, and so forth that develop teacher candidates' sensitivity to diversity. It is much more effective to have a teacher who can seek out information about a particular culture when it is needed than one who has knowledge of only certain cultures without a sensitivity to diversity.

Finally, every teacher education program should include some focused field experiences with diverse students. Prospective teachers need to gain experience and develop a level of comfort and confidence working with students from backgrounds different than their own. The experience gained in diverse settings is invaluable to the developing teacher for future application in any classroom setting. This experience should be focused, guided, and reflected on; otherwise it may serve only to reinforce stereotypes.

Lessons for Teacher Recruitment

Because the racial and ethnic composition of the teaching force can have a real impact on the effectiveness of multicultural education, both the U.S. and Australia need to increase efforts to recruit diverse teachers. Schools of education often play a large role in this process. In both nations the percentage of racially diverse teachers is smaller than the proportion of racially diverse students. In the United States a racially diverse teaching staff is considered important for bringing a variety of viewpoints, values, experiences, and teaching styles into the school (Latham 1999). A diverse faculty also ensures that more students will at some point experience teachers from different backgrounds than their own, thus increasing the cultural diversity of their educational experience. Providing positive role models for all groups of students is important.

> Every teacher education program should include field experiences with diverse students so that prospective teachers can gain confidence working with students from backgrounds different than their own.

In both countries the majority of teachers are white, native born, middle class women who have not extensively explored their own cultural values, biases, or privilege. It is hard for them to identify and sometimes to help students whose experience of education is very different from their own.

In Australia, where the major source of diverse teachers is the pool of recent immigrants, three factors seem to contribute to the lack of diversity in the teaching force:

- Teachers who have been trained in another country and immigrate to Australia may experience discrimination based on their accents or be stereotyped into the LOTE subject area (Santoro, Kamler, and Reid 2001).
- Teachers who have been educated in another country may be uncomfortable with the teaching and classroom management styles found in this more individualistic culture (less-formal, seemingly less respectful of teachers, less-direct instruction), and this may discourage them from pursuing their former career (Donohoue-Clyne 1993).
- Many Asian teachers with children of their own are expected by their culture to stay home and raise their children rather than work outside the home as a teacher.

If the Australian educational system wants to have a diverse faculty, it must consider the following:

- Recruitment of teachers who were trained in other countries and are now living in Australia (including teachers whose families are now grown)
- Recruitment of second generation Australians of diverse backgrounds
- Teacher retraining programs that focus on English language skills as well as classroom management and curriculum content as practiced in Australia to assist teachers in their cultural transition

In the United States developing a diverse teaching force depends more on recruiting native born Americans of diverse races to enter teacher education programs. This is sometimes difficult because of competition from other professions. Recruitment programs need to focus more broadly on recruiting the following groups, all of which are rich sources of diverse teacher candidates:

- Students of color who are in the first generation of their family to attend college
- Diverse individuals already working with children, such as paraprofessionals in the schools and group leaders in daycare settings
- Individuals in occupations where retirement after twenty years leaves ample time for a second career (military personnel, police officers, fire fighters, and so forth)

Conclusion

Australia and the United States face similar challenges in teaching diverse student populations. Although recognition of the need for multicultural education is widespread in both countries, neither teaching force is consistently successful in integrating multicultural concepts and adapting methods to meet the needs of a broad population of diverse students. Adapting the existing curriculum to incorporate the multicultural content, concepts, and activities at the desired level of integration (more than bits and pieces or separate units) would be a more successful, broad-reaching strategy. A large part of the task in both countries is recruiting a more diverse teaching force and providing more effective training that develops teachers' sensitivity to diversity and provides enough experience to inform teaching behaviors to permit instructional success with all students.

Key words: multicultural education, diversity, teacher education, learning styles, recruitment

REFERENCES

Allan, R., and B. Hill. 1995. Multicultural education in Australia: Historical development and current status. In the *Handbook of research on multicultural education*. Ed. James Banks. New York: Macmillan. 763–77.

Banks, J. 1997. *Teaching strategies for ethnic studies*. 6th Edition. Boston: Allyn and Bacon. 26.

Donohoue-Clyne, I. 1993. "Children only go to school to colour in …" Overseas educated teacher's perceptions of Australian schools. *Multicultural Education* 11(3): 20–24.

Hill, B., and R. Allan. 1998. Intercultural education in Australia. In *International perspectives on intercultural education*. Ed. Kenneth Cushner. Mahwah, NJ: Lawrence Erlbaum. 15–35.

Latham, A. 1999. The teacher student mismatch. *Educational Leadership* 56(7): 84–85.

McInerney, V., D. McInerney, M. Cincotta, P. Totaro, and D. Williams. 2001. Teacher attitudes to and beliefs about multicultural education (in Australia): Have there been changes over the last 20 years? Paper presented at the annual meeting of the American Educational Research Association, Seattle, WA, April 2001.

Price, C. 2000. Australians all: Who on earth are we? Census report. Canberra: National University.

Rothstein-Fisch, C., P. Greenfield, and E. Trumbull. 1999. Bridging cultures with classroom strategies. *Educational Leadership* 56(7): 64–67.

Santoro, N., B. Kamler, and J. Reid. 2001. Teachers talking differences: Teacher education and the poetics of anti racism. *Teaching Education* 12(2): 191–212.

Seeberg, V., B. Swadener, M. Vanden-Wyngaard, and T. Rickel. 1998. Multicultural education in the United States. In *International perspectives on intercultural education*. Ed. K. Cushner. Mahwah, NJ: Lawrence Erlbaum. 257–300.

Statistical Abstracts of the United States. 2001. Washington, DC: U.S. Government Printing Office. 13.

Leslie A. Swetnam is an associate professor in the elementary licensure program at Metropolitan State College of Denver, Colorado.

From *The Clearing House*, March/April 2003. Reprinted with permission of the Helen Dwight Reid Foundation. Published by Heldref Publications, 1319 Eighteenth St. NW, Washington, DC 20036-1802. © 2003.

Cultural Influences on the Development of Self-Concept:

Updating Our Thinking

Hermine H. Marshall

Why is it that some children try new things with enthusiasm and approach peers and adults with confidence, whereas other children seem to believe that they are incapable of succeeding in many situations?... What can we learn from research that will allow us to help children approach new situations and other people with confidence?

—H. H. Marshall,
"Research in Review. The
Development of Self-Concept"

Twelve years ago I assumed along with many early childhood educators that approaching new situations with confidence indicated a child's strong self-concept; hesitation and hanging back could indicate lack of self-esteem. In my review of research on the development of self-concept written at that time, the notion that children's behavior is influenced by their cultural background had only begun to enter the research literature and thinking of early childhood educators. I pointed out briefly that cultural values can affect self-esteem and different cultures may value and encourage different behaviors. For instance, taking personal control, important in dominant American culture, might not be valued in other cultures. Yet I indicated that autonomy and initiative are behaviors to look for as reflecting positive self-concept. I implied that children who lacked these traits might have low self-esteem.

We need to increase our awareness that our perceptions, actions, and interactions and those of children derive their meanings from the cultures in which they are embedded.

The last decade has seen an increase in research on child development in different cultures. Awareness of this research has enhanced early childhood educators' sensitivity to how perspectives may vary in cultures that are different from the culture of individual educators as well as the dominant culture. Culture impacts not just which behaviors are valued and displayed but also our interpretations of these behaviors. As a result of this decade of research, it has become clear that what many of us have taken for evidence of self-esteem is influenced by our cultural perceptions. It is important, therefore, to revisit some of the issues related to self-concept development in light of a more sophisticated understanding of cultural influences. To this end, as educators we need to increase our awareness that our perceptions, actions, and interactions and those of children derive their meanings from the cultures in which they are embedded.

Constructing a view of self: independent/interdependent

Children construct their views of self "by participating in interactions that caregivers structure according to cultural values about the nature of human existence" (Raeff 1997). In Western cultures, striving toward *independence* and individuality and asserting oneself are seen as important accomplishments (Markus & Kitayama 1991). As a consequence, Westerners perceive children who are outgoing and eagerly explore new situations as demonstrating competence and having a positive self-concept, especially compared to children who do not appear to seek out and actively participate in these situations.

In contrast, Eastern cultures place greater emphasis on maintaining harmonious, *interdependent* relationships. Markus and Kitayama (1991) note that interdependent views are also characteristic of many African, Latin American, and southern European cultures. (See also Greenfield 1994.) In cultures influenced by Confucian and Taoist philosophies, self-restraint and control of emotional expressiveness is considered an indication of social maturity (Chen et al. 1998). Asserting oneself may be seen as a sign of immaturity (Markus & Kitayama 1991). Children who are shy, reticent, and quiet are likely to be considered competent and well behaved by parents and teachers in the People's Republic of China (Chen et al. 1998; Rubin 1998). These children—whom North American teachers from the dominant culture might see as inhibited and lacking in self-confidence—have a positive view of themselves and of their social relationships.

Similarly, in other cultures where interdependence or "relative enmeshment" (Garcia Coll 1990) are seen as ideal mature relationships, interdependency and interpersonal dependency are likely to be fostered between young children and their mothers. When asked about desirable child behavior, mothers from Latino cultures, such as Spanish-speaking Puerto Rican mothers, are likely to focus on respectfulness (*respecto*), a concept which assumes appropriate interrelatedness. In contrast the Anglo mothers in one study focused on autonomy and active exploration, reflecting more independent values (Harwood 1992). Moreover, some cultures such as traditional Navajo cultures expect children to observe before attempting to try things (Bacon & Carter 1991). For these children too, standing back and observing rather than exploring should not be taken as an indication of low self-esteem.

Nevertheless, although Chinese parents tend to value interdependence and cohesion and may minimize the development of individuality within the family. Taiwanese and immigrant Chinese parents seem to encourage independence so that children will be able to succeed in the larger society (Lin & Fu 1990). Likewise, some Mexican immigrant families may begin to approve of their children's independent thinking related to school topics as they become more acculturated (Delgado-Gaitan 1994).

In addition, in Eastern cultures (Markus & Kitayama 1991) and Latino cultures (Parke & Buriel 1998), primary concern centers on other people and the self-in-relationship-to-other rather than self alone. Most people in these cultures value developing empathetic understanding and attention to the needs of others. These behaviors serve to maintain harmonious relationships more than would attending to meeting one's own needs.

These contrasts should not be taken to mean that independence and interdependence are mutually exclusive (Raeff 1997). Both independent and interdependent tendencies are common to human experience. People in Western cultures value relationships and cooperation as well as independence. "Every group selects a point on the independence/ interdependence continuum as its cultural ideal" (Greenfield 1994, 4).

The impact on socialization and development

Varieties of both independence and interdependence affect socialization and development. Consequently we should be aware that how children see themselves in relationship to others is also a part of their self-concept. Educators need to expand their views of what is considered important to self-concept beyond the typical notions of autonomy, self-assertion, self-enhancement, and uniqueness and include characteristics such as empathy, sensitivity to others, modesty, cooperation, and caring as well.

We must be careful not to assume that just because children or families are from a specific ethnic or racial group that they necessarily share a common cultural experience. There are differences within cultures and within families.

Although it is important to be aware that our perceptions and interpretations of behavior are influenced by the culture(s) in which we were raised and in which we reside and that the meaning of behavior may vary for different cultures, we must be careful not to assume that just because children or families are from a specific ethnic or racial group they necessarily share a common cultural experience. There are differences within cultures and within families. Other factors impinge on how children are raised and the meanings accorded to behavior, such as the family's countries of origin, the length of time immigrant families have been in the United States, the degree of acculturation the family has experienced, educational background, and social status (Delgado-Gaitan 1994; Killen 1997; McLloyd 1999).

Some children and families experience the influence of multiple cultures. This is particularly true when parents are from different ethnic, racial, or cultural groups. In these families parents may bring values from two or more cultures to their views and practices in raising children. Regardless of children's apparent ethnic or cultural background, it is important for teachers to be sensitive to *individual* children and family members and to how a family's beliefs, attitudes, and values may affect children's behavior.

Children who are able to maintain comfort with behaviors that are valued in their home as well as those valued in the wider society may be most likely to have positive views of themselves in both cultural contexts.

Attempting to understand what each family values as important behaviors and watching for these behaviors may provide clues to the meaning of children's actions for that family and child. It is important to recognize and affirm behaviors valued by the home culture. It is also essential to provide opportunities for children to learn behaviors that are valued by the Western culture (Delpit 1988). Children who are able to maintain comfort with behaviors that are valued in their home as well as those valued in the wider society

may be most likely to have positive views of themselves in both cultural contexts.

What does this mean in practice?

My earlier research on self-concept development describes a number of ways to influence self-concept. These include helping children (1) feel they are of value, (2) believe they are competent, (3) have some control over tasks and actions, (4) learn interpersonal skills. Also noted as important is becoming aware of your expectations for children. The particular techniques for each of these recommendations remain valid today (see Marshall 1989).

Beyond these fundamentals, the following steps are based on a more sophisticated awareness of cultural and individual variations in values and behaviors. Using them as a guide will increase your sensitivity to the values and practices of the families whose children are in your care and enable you to support the development of positive self-concepts.

1. Be aware of the ways your own culture influences your expectations of children. Think about how you were raised, your family values. What behaviors were encouraged? How did your family make you feel proud? Talk to friends or other teachers about their upbringing. Within your own community, there are likely variations in what families value and in the bases for positive self-concept. This reflection and knowledge may help you begin to expand your awareness of the indications of positive self-concept.

2. Consider the cultural backgrounds of the children in your setting and their community. Observe how children approach new tasks, relate to other people, and react to praise. This may raise some questions. Be a good listener. If you teach at the primary level, chat with the children before and after school or at lunchtime. Be careful that surface appearances

do not influence your perceptions or interactions. Gather more information about the cultural and ethnic groups represented in your class (as noted below).

3. Learn about the cultures from which the children in your program or school may come. Read about the values and child rearing practices of these cultures. (See the "For further reading" list.) Talk to community leaders or people you know who have greater knowledge of these cultures.

Contact community-based organizations, such as the National Council of La Raza (NCLR). Inviting representatives of such organizations to talk to teachers in your setting may be helpful. Still, do not assume that this general information is sufficient. Further understanding of the cultural background of *particular* children in your class will be necessary since, in every cultural and ethnic group, individual and generational differences are likely.

4. Use your basic knowledge of the culture to talk with each family about its values and practices. Learn what families think is important to consider for their children. You might share with them what you have been learning about their culture or cultures. Explain that you recognize that every family is different and that you would like to know what they think and what they value as important. Asking about the families' methods for teaching and learning may be useful. Discuss what happens if children raise questions or explore on their own and how children and adults show respect. It is important to accept what family members say as valuable information to consider and avoid letting your own values and methods stifle communication.

5. Build on what you have learned from each family. Provide opportunities for children to learn in a variety of ways. For example, children might learn by observing first, trying things out on their own, or by doing tasks with a partner or group of peers. Children need opportunities to demonstrate caring and cooperating.

All children will benefit from enhanced opportunities to learn and interact in a variety of ways. Enlarge your repertoire of responses; some children will find more comfort in nonverbal acceptance—a smile or nod—than praise. In all cases, showing respect for ways of interacting that derive from the home culture is critical to the support and development of a child's self-concept. Practices that are clearly harmful to the child, of course, should not be supported. In such a case, being able to discuss with the family why the practice is detrimental is important (see Gonzalez-Mena & Bhavnagri 2000).

6. *Infuse the curriculum and classroom environment with a rich variety of materials from the cultures of your children as well as other cultures.* Parents may be able to share songs or stories or bring in something special representing their home culture. Find books and posters that represent the children in your class. Introduce as snacks special treats from the children's cultures. Seeing their ethnic groups and cultures of origin valued will enhance children's self-concepts.

Conclusion

It is not enough to assume that affirming young children's assertiveness, confidence, and independence suffices to support self-concept development. Such qualities as show-ing respect for and being sensitive to others, learning by observing, and exhibiting humility may also evidence positive self-concept and should be nourished. Acknowledging the contributions and values of all the families whose children are in our care while also supporting children's development of necessary skills to succeed in mainstream America is most likely to enhance the development of children's self-esteem.

Hermine H. Marshall, Ph.D., is emerita professor at San Francisco State University, at which she was coordinator of the early childhood and master's degree programs. She has conducted research on self-concept, self-evaluation, and classroom processes. She thanks Elsie Gee for critical comments on an earlier version of this article.

From *Young Children*, November 2001, pp. 19-22. © 2001 by the National Association for the Education of Young Children. Reprinted by permission.

UNIT 4
Learning and Instruction

Unit Selections

Key Points to Consider

- Compare and contrast the different approaches to learning. What approach do you think is best, and why? What factors are important to your answer (for example, objectives, types of students, setting, personality of the teacher)?

- What are some principles for effective teaching that derive directly from brain research and different conceptualizations of intelligence?

- What teaching strategies could you use to promote greater student retention of material? What are good ways to attract and keep students' attention? Must a teacher be an "entertainer"? Why or why not?

- How can a teacher promote positive self-esteem, values, character, caring, and attitudes? How are they related to cognitive learning? How much emphasis should be put on cultivating character or positive student interactions? How would you create a "caring" classroom? Discuss whether this would interfere with achievement of cognitive learning targets.

- If you wanted to create a constructivist classroom in the subject area and/or grade in which you want to teach, what would the classroom look like? What would you emphasize, and how would your actions reflect constructivist principles and research on intelligence? How would technology be used in an effective manner with constructivist approaches?

- How can teaching for standards be integrated with differentiation? How is it possible to use different instructional strategies to help all students obtain high standards? What kinds of test preparation are appropriate?

 **Links: www.dushkin.com/online/**
These sites are annotated in the World Wide Web pages.

Education Week on the Web
http://www.edweek.org
Online Internet Institute
http://www.oii.org
Teachers Helping Teachers
http://www.pacificnet.net/~mandel/
The Teachers' Network
http://www.teachers.net/

Learning can be broadly defined as a relatively permanent change in behavior or thinking due to experience. Learning is not a result of change due to maturation or temporary influences. Changes in the behavior and thinking of students result from complex interactions between their individual characteristics and environmental factors. A continuing challenge in education is understanding these interactions so that learning can be enhanced. This unit focuses on approaches within educational psychology that represent different ways of viewing the learning process and related instructional strategies. Each approach to learning emphasizes a different set of personal and environmental factors that influence certain behaviors. While no one approach can fully explain learning, each is a valuable contribution to our knowledge about the process and the improvement of student performance.

The discussion of each learning approach includes suggestions for specific techniques and methods of teaching to guide teachers in understanding student behavior and in making decisions about how to teach. The articles in this section reflect a recent emphasis on applied research conducted in schools, research on the brain, and on constructivist theories.

Researchers have recently made significant advances in understanding the way our brain works. Information processing refers to the way that the mind receives sensory information, stores it as memory, and recalls it for later use. This procedure is basic to all learning, no matter what teaching approach is taken, and we know that the method used in processing information determines to some extent how much and what we remember. The first two articles in the Learning and Cognition subsection present some of the fundamental principles of brain functioning, information processing and cognition. The third and fourth articles focus on human intelligences.

In the past, behaviorism was the best-known theory of learning. Most practicing and prospective teachers are familiar with concepts such as classical conditioning, reinforcement, and punishment, and there is no question that behaviorism has made significant contributions to understanding learning. But behaviorism has also been subject to much misinterpretation, in part because it seems so simple. In fact, the effective use of behavioristic principles is complex and demanding, as the fifth article on praise points out.

Constructivist learning theory is currently the predominant theory of learning that is recognized by educational psychologists. According to constructivists, it is important for students to actively create and reorganize knowledge. There is a need for students to interpret within meaningful contexts so that what is learned is well connected with existing knowledge. Two articles are devoted to constructivist learning. Constructivism is illustrated with the use of cognitive maps called *webs of skills*.

Social psychological learning emphasizes the affective, social, moral, and personal development of students. Social psychology is the study of the nature of interpersonal relationships in social situations. In education, this approach looks at teacher-pupil relationships and group processes to derive principles of interaction that affect learning. Two articles in this section examine the application of social psychological principles to learning. In the first, the importance of recognizing and inviting such needs as affirmation, contribution, purpose, and power is stressed. In the second article, healthy self-esteem is suggested to be developed not by focusing on oneself but by being involved in externally oriented, meaningful activities.

Instructional strategies are the teacher behaviors and methods of conveying information that affect learning. Teaching methods or techniques can vary greatly, depending on objectives, group size, types of students, and personality of the teacher. For example, discussion classes are generally more effective for enhancing thinking skills than are individualized sessions or lectures. For the Instructional Strategies subsection, four articles have been selected that show how teachers can use principles of cognitive psychology and intelligence in their teaching within the current standards-based environment. The first article emphasizes the importance of concept mapping to encourage and support students' thinking. In the second article implications of using a constructivist approach are summarized, with an emphasis on collaboration and cooperative inquiry. In the third article the importance of properly aligning standards, student learning styles, and multiple intelligences is stressed.

Technology is also becoming a pervasive opportunity for teaching and learning. The fourth article in this section summarizes effective applications of technology in the classroom. Differentiated instruction is addressed in the last article as a teaching method that can accommodate learning for all students.

ASK THE COGNITIVE SCIENTIST

Students Remember...
What They Think About

How does the mind work—and especially how does it learn? Teachers make assumptions all day long about how students best comprehend, remember, and create. These assumptions—and the teaching decisions that result—are based on a mix of theories learned in teacher education, trial and error, craft knowledge, and gut instinct. Such gut knowledge often serves us well. But is there anything sturdier to rely on?

Cognitive science is an interdisciplinary field of researchers from psychology, neuroscience, linguistics, philosophy, computer science, and anthropology who seek to understand the mind. In this regular American Educator *column, we will consider findings from this field that are strong and clear enough to merit classroom application.*

By Daniel T. Willingham

Issue: The teacher presents a strong, coherent lesson in which a set of significant facts is clearly connected to a reasonable conclusion. But, at test time, the students show no understanding of the connections. Some students parrot back the conclusion, but no facts. Others spit back memorized facts, but don't see how they fit together. Though the lesson wasn't taught in a rote way, it seems like rote knowledge is what the students took in. Why do well-integrated, coherent lessons often come back to us in a less meaningful, fragmented form? Can cognitive science help explain why this result is so common—and offer ideas about how to avoid it?

Response: Rote knowledge is devoid of all meaning (as discussed in my last column, Winter 2002). The knowledge that these students appear to be regurgitating is probably not rote knowledge. It is probably "shallow" knowledge: The students' knowledge has meaning (unlike rote knowledge), in that the students understand each isolated part, but their knowledge lacks the deeper meaning that comes from understanding the relationship among the parts. For reasons noted below, this is a common problem in the early stages of learning about a new topic. But it also has another remediable source, which is the focus of this column.

Cognitive science has shown that what ends up in a learner's memory is not simply the material presented—it is the product of what the learner thought about when he or she encountered the material. This principle illuminates one important origin of shallow knowledge and also suggests how to help students develop deep and interconnected knowledge.

Let's start with an example of shallow knowledge. Suppose that you are teaching a high school class unit on World War II and

develop a lesson on the Japanese attack on Pearl Harbor. Many facts might be included in such a lesson: (a) Japan had aspirations to be a regional power; (b) Japan was engaged in a protracted war with China; (c) because they were at war, European countries could not protect their colonies in the South Pacific; and (d) the attack on Pearl Harbor resulted in a declaration of war on Japan by the United States. The overarching point of this lesson might be to show that the attack on Pearl Harbor was a strategic mistake for the Japanese, given their war aims. (See Figure 1 for a diagram of the lesson.)

We can see two ways that this meaningful lesson might end up as shallow knowledge in the student's mind. The student might commit to memory some or all of these four facts. But knowing these facts without understanding how they relate to one another and can be integrated to support the conclusion leaves the facts isolated; they are not without meaning, but neither are they as rich as they might be. The student has the trees, but no view of the forest.

Alternatively, the student might commit to memory the conclusion, "The attack on Pearl Harbor, although militarily a successful battle for Japan, was ultimately detrimental to its long-range war plans." But memorizing this conclusion without understanding the reasoning behind it and knowing the supporting facts is empty. It isn't rote—the student knows Japan initiated and won a battle at the place called Pearl Harbor. But the knowledge certainly is "shallow"—it has no connections.*

We have all had students memorize phrases from class or a textbook more or less word-for-word, and although what the student says is accurate, we can't help but wonder whether he or she really understands the ideas those words represent. Let's dig deeper.

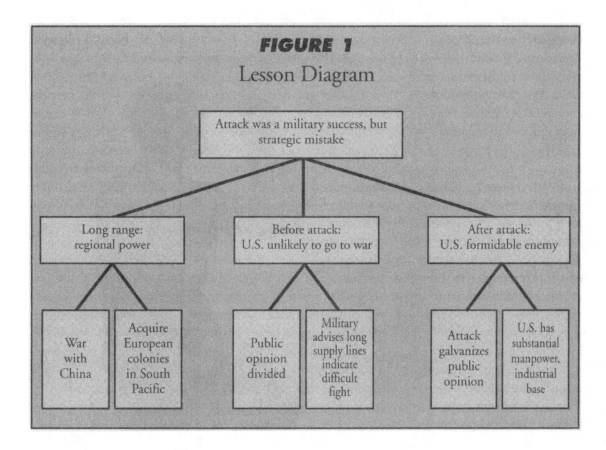

FIGURE 1

Lesson Diagram

Attack was a military success, but strategic mistake

Long range: regional power

Before attack: U.S. unlikely to go to war

After attack: U.S. formidable enemy

War with China

Acquire European colonies in South Pacific

Public opinion divided

Military advises long supply lines indicate difficult fight

Attack galvanizes public opinion

U.S. has substantial manpower, industrial base

Memory Is as Thinking Does

When students parrot back a teacher's or the textbook's words, they are, of course, drawing on memory. Thus, the question of why students end up with shallow knowledge is really a question about the workings of memory. Needless to say, determining what ends up in memory and in what form is a complex question, but *there is one factor that trumps most others in determining what is remembered: what you think about when you encounter the material.* The fact that the material you are dealing with has meaning does not guarantee that the meaning *will* be remembered. If you think about that meaning, the meaning will reside in memory. If you don't, it won't. For example, if I teach about Pearl Harbor, some sailing enthusiasts may start thinking about the ships of the era and pay minimal attention to the rest of the class—just a few minutes after the bell rings they won't remember much about the causes and consequences of Pearl Harbor. Memory is as thinking does.

A classic experiment illustrating this principle was conducted by Thomas Hyde and James Jenkins in 1969. It examined how one thinks about material and the effect of that thinking on memory. Subjects in their experiment listened to a list of words at a rate of one word every two seconds. Different groups of subjects were to perform different tasks upon hearing each word. Some were to rate each word as to whether it made them think of pleasant or unpleasant things, whereas others were asked to count the number of times the letter *E* appeared in the word. Rating the pleasantness forces the subject to think about the word's meaning; the word *garbage* is unpleasant because of what it means—what it is associated with in one's memory. Counting *E*s, on the other hand, forces one to think about the spelling of the word, but not its meaning. Thus, the experimenters manipulated what subjects thought about when they encountered each word. Subjects were not told that their memory for the words would later be tested; they thought they were merely to make the pleasantness or the *E*-counting judgment.

One other detail of the experiment is especially important. The word list actually consisted of 12 pairs of very highly associated words, such as *doctor–nurse*, although this fact was not pointed out to any of the subjects. The order in which the words were read was random (except that related words were not allowed to be next to one another in the list).

The results are shown in Figure 2. First look at the left side of the chart, which shows the mean number of words recalled. Memory was much better when subjects made the pleasantness ratings. Thinking about the meaning of material is especially helpful to memory. This finding is consistent across hundreds of other experiments.

The right side of the figure shows a measure of clustering—the extent to which subjects paired the associated words as they tried to remember them. When a subject recalled a word (e.g., *doctor*), what percentage of the time was the next word recalled the highly associated one (*nurse*)? As the figure shows, subjects who thought about the word's meaning (i.e., rated pleasantness) not only remembered more words, they tended to remember the related words together, even though the related words did not appear together in the list. The subjects who counted *E*s did not tend to remember related words together.

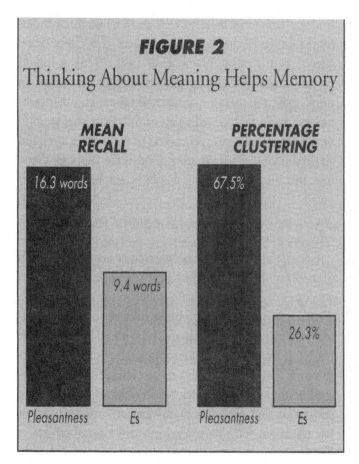

FIGURE 2
Thinking About Meaning Helps Memory

MEAN RECALL
16.3 words — Pleasantness
9.4 words — Es

PERCENTAGE CLUSTERING
67.5% — Pleasantness
26.3% — Es

These results forcefully make the point that meaningful structure that is in the environment may or may not end up being stored in memory. In the Hyde and Jenkins experiment, the fact that some of the words were related in meaning was largely lost on the subjects who counted *E*s because thinking about *E*s did not encourage the subjects to process meaning. Subjects who made the pleasantness ratings tended to group the words together by meaning as they recalled them. Whatever subjects thought about when they heard the words (which, teachers will note, depends on what they were *asked* to think about) was what ended up in memory.

In the Hyde and Jenkins experiment, the "what they think about" principle is divided into thinking about meaning versus not thinking about meaning. Other experiments show that even if one thinks about meaning, the particular *aspect* of the meaning that one considers will be stored in memory, and other aspects of meaning will not. For example, in one experiment (Barclay et al., 1974), subjects were presented with words to remember in the context of a sentence. The sentence biased subjects to think of one or another feature of the to-be-remembered word: For example, some subjects read "The man lifted the *piano*," which encouraged thinking about the fact that pianos are heavy. Other subjects read "The man tuned the *piano*," which encouraged considering that pianos produce music. In the next phase of the experiment subjects were told that their memory for some of the nouns in the sentences would be tested and that for each sentence they would get a hint. For *piano*,

some subjects were given the hint, "something heavy." If they had read the sentence about lifting the piano, this hint matched the feature they had thought about, but if they read the sentence about tuning the piano, the hint didn't match. (Other subjects saw a hint that matched the piano tuning sentence; that hint was "something with a nice sound.")

The results showed that subjects remembered about three times as many words when the hint for the test matched what subjects had thought about when they first read the word. Again, the point is that what is stored in memory is quite specific to what you think about when you encounter the material. It is not the case that if you think about *piano*, then *piano* and all of its features are stored in memory. You might think about its music-producing qualities, its weight, its cost, and so on. Or you might not focus on the referent at all, but rather on the physical properties of the word itself, as when Hyde and Jenkins asked subjects to count *E*s. In each case, what you think about is what you remember.

So what does this have to do with shallow knowledge? It shows where shallow knowledge might come from. Meaning that is in the environment won't end up in memory if students don't think about it. Students with shallow knowledge have apparently thought about the material in a shallow way. This conclusion reframes the question we might ask: Why would students think about the material in a shallow way, given that we didn't present it to them that way? Obviously, a student would learn only isolated facts or unsupported conclusions if that is what the teacher taught, but I find it difficult to believe that this is a common practice. The notion that education should emphasize meaning is deeply ingrained in our system and has been for a generation or more. There cannot be many teachers who ask their students to learn facts without concern for a larger picture. So how do students end up with shallow knowledge? There are several possible answers.

1. As noted at the beginning of this article, in one form, shallow knowledge is simply a step on the way to deep knowledge. Consider again the hierarchical diagram shown in Figure 1. I argued that shallow knowledge could either be memorization of the conclusion (top of the hierarchy) without knowing the facts that back it up (bottom of the hierarchy), or memorization of the facts without integrating them into a conclusion. Clearly the sort of deep knowledge we want our students to have is objectively harder to obtain than shallow knowledge, because knowledge of the facts *and* knowledge of the conclusion *and* knowledge of their interrelationships are prerequisite to it. We want students to know how the different levels of hierarchy relate to one another; it's not enough to have memorized each level in isolation of the others. That connected knowledge will inevitably be the last thing that the student acquires. Thus, some students' knowledge will be shallow simply because they are not far enough along yet.

2. Other students may effectively quit learning before they reach the deep understanding that is our goal for them. A student may learn the facts about Pearl Harbor and think

"All right, I've learned a lot about this stuff." The student is correct (so far as it goes) and simply doesn't realize that there is yet more to do.

3. Students' perception of what they are supposed to learn—and what it means to learn—may contribute to shallow knowledge. A student may seek to memorize definitions and pat phrases word-for-word from the book because the student *knows* that this information is correct and cannot be contested. When I was in eighth grade, we were given a list of vocabulary terms that we were to define and then study in preparation for a weekly test. A friend defined "cherub" as "an angel of the second order." My friends and I teased him because his definition missed what we thought was the key aspect of the word—that a cherub is small, chubby, and rosy-cheeked. He was unmoved and kept repeating "that's what the dictionary said." He liked the fact that his answer was uncontestable. Students may memorize exactly what the teacher or textbook says in order to be certain that they are *correct*, and worry less about the extent to which they understand.

4. Despite what was offered to students in the teacher's lesson, the students attended to (thought about) something different—and that's what they remembered.

What Does This Mean for Teachers?

This fundamental principle of memory—memory is as thinking does—yields a clear strategy to encourage deep, meaningful knowledge. If students think about the meaning of material, meaning will end up in memory. How can teachers be sure that students are thinking about meaning?

Obviously there is no one way to ensure that students think about the meaning of material. A compelling story may be appropriate for one lesson, whereas a carefully designed laboratory project works for a second, and a well-structured group discussion for a third. One possible common misconception is that learners can only understand meaning if they themselves construct the meaning in a physically active way. A moment's reflection should tell us that "listening" does not imply passivity or shallowness. We have all been to "active, participatory" workshops that felt like a waste of time, and we have been to lectures where we "just listened" that were gripping and informative. Constructing meaning is a matter of being *mentally* engaged; being physically engaged might help at times, but it is not necessary.

How can we ensure that students are mentally engaged? While there is still more to learn about applying this research on thinking and memory to teaching, several key principles have emerged to guide teachers in developing assignments, classroom activities, and assessments.

• **Anticipate what your lesson will lead students to think about**. The direct relationship between thought and memory is so important that it could be used as a self-check for a teacher preparing virtually any assignment: *Always try to anticipate what students will be thinking when they are doing the assignment*. Doing so may make it clear that some assignments de-signed with one purpose in mind will achieve another. For example, a teacher once told me that, as part of a unit on the Underground Railroad, he had his students bake biscuits so that they would appreciate what escaped slaves ate most nights. He asked what I thought of the assignment and my reply was that his students will remember baking biscuits. In other words, his students probably thought for 30 seconds about the relation of the baking to the course material, and then spent 30 minutes thinking about measuring flour, mixing dough, and so on.

Another example comes from my recent observation of my nephew as he completed a book report. The teacher asked the students to draw a poster that depicted all of the events of the book. The purpose of the assignment was to have students think of the book as a whole, and to consider how the separate events related to one another. This purpose got lost in the execution. My nephew spent a lot more time thinking about how to draw a good castle than he did about the plot of the book.

• **Use discovery learning carefully**. The principle above—anticipate the students' thoughts—also illuminates the use and misuse of discovery learning. There is little doubt that students remember material they generate themselves better than material that is handed to them. This "generation effect," as it is called (Slamecka & Graf, 1978), is indeed powerful, and it is due, in part, to forcing the learner to think about the meaning of material (although other techniques can do that as well). Part of the effect does seem to be unique to the actual generation of the answer, over and above thinking about meaning. One might suppose, therefore, that discovery learning should be employed whenever possible. However, given that memory follows thought, one thing is clear: *Students will remember incorrect "discoveries" just as well as correct ones*.

Considerable care must be taken to ensure that the path of students' thoughts will be a profitable one. For example, advocates of discovery learning often point out that children learn to use some computer software rapidly and effectively merely by "playing around with it." That may be true, but that learning environment is also quite structured in that profitless actions are immediately discouraged by the system not working. In effect, the system is so structured that profitless discoveries are impossible; but few classroom activities can achieve this kind of structure. How much anatomy will students learn by "playing around" with frog dissection? Can one anticipate the thoughts of students who dissect frogs with little direction? Although discovery learning may be powerful in highly structured contexts that make the correct discovery virtually inevitable, in others it is likely to prove unproductive.

Constructing meaning is a matter of being mentally engaged.

• **Design reading assignments that require students to actively process the text**. Many concrete strategies have been suggested for helping students to get more out of reading that likely have some or all of their effect by making readers think about the meaning of what they are reading. *Techniques such as writing outlines, self-examination during learning, review* *questions, and previews can encourage or require students to integrate the material and to thereby process (i.e., think about) the meaning.* These different techniques are more or less effective in different situations, perhaps due to the specific materials being studied (e.g., McDaniel & Einstein, 1989); general principles guiding when each technique should be used have not been forthcoming. Nevertheless, although one technique or another may be more effective for a given lesson or group of students, using any strategy that encourages the processing of meaning is almost always better than not using one.

• **Design lessons so that students can't avoid thinking about the lesson's goal**. On a more positive note, the "memory is as thinking does" principle can yield steps teachers can take to help students develop deep, interconnected knowledge: *Lessons should be directed so that students are very likely to think (or can't help but think) about the goal of the lesson.* The goal of the Underground Railroad lesson was not really about biscuits—it was to encourage students to consider the experience of escaped slaves. Therefore, a more effective starting point for that lesson would be to ask students leading questions that encourage consideration of what escaped slaves' experiences would be like, which might include questions of how they would obtain food, and what the constraints were on the food they could get (inexpensive, cooked rapidly, etc.). My nephew would have gotten more out of his book report project if it had emphasized what the teacher was really interested in (the connection among the book's events), perhaps by having the students label the events and connections among them (e.g., this event moves the character towards his goal; this event causes that event) and de-emphasizing the students' artistic contribution by having them use clip art or simply writing the events in words.

• **Design tests that lead students to think about and integrate the most important material**. The "memory is as thinking does" principle may also be applied to methods of assessing student knowledge: *Like lessons, study guides for texts should be developed that force students to think about the goals of the lessons being assessed.* For better or worse, some students expend their greatest effort to understand material as they prepare for an examination. Even if you would rather see such students motivated by a passion to learn, you can use the students' motivation to earn a good grade to ensure that they are getting the most out of your lessons. Announcing the general topics to be covered on an exam leaves the specifics of what to learn up to the student. Even if the teacher emphasizes that deep understanding will be tested, the student may misconstrue what is deep or, as noted earlier, the student may quit once some facts have been memorized, believing that he or she has already done quite a bit of studying. Suppose, however, that the teacher provides a list of integrative questions for the students to study from, such as "Describe why the attack on Pearl Harbor was a strategic mistake by Japan, given its war aims." Suppose further that the students know that the examination will consist of five questions from the 30-question list that they have been given, with an essay to be written on each of the five questions. Students will very likely restrict their studying to the 30 question list, but that might be just fine with the teacher if he or she feels that any student who can answer those 30 questions has mastered the material. This method of testing has the advantage of ensuring that while students are highly motivated, they think about the deepest meaning of the material that the teacher intended.

In summary, in the early stages of learning, students may display "shallow" learning. These students have acquired bits of knowledge that aren't well-integrated into a larger picture. Research tells us that deep, connected knowledge can be encouraged by getting students to think about the interrelation of the various pieces of knowledge that they have acquired. Cognitive science has not progressed to the point that it can issue prescriptions of exactly how that can be achieved—that job is very much in the hands of experienced teachers. But in considering how to encourage students to acquire meaningful knowledge, teachers will do well to keep the "memory is as thinking does" principle in mind.

References

Barclay, J. R., Bransford, J. D., Franks, J. J., McCarrel, N. S., & Nitsch, K. (1974). Comprehension and semantic flexibility. *Journal of Verbal Learning & Verbal Behavior, 13*, 471–481.

Hyde, T. S. & Jenkins, J. J. (1969). Differential effects of incidental tasks on the organization of recall of a list of highly associated words. *Journal of Experimental Psychology, 82*, 472–481.

McDaniel, M. A. & Einstein, G. O. (1989). Material-appropriate processing: A contextualist approach to reading and studying strategies. *Educational Psychology Review, 1*, 113–145.

Slamecka, N. J. & Graf, P. (1978). The generation effect: Delineation of a phenomenon. *Journal of Experimental Psychology: Human Learning & Memory, 4*, 592–604.

Readers can pose specific questions to "Ask the Cognitive Scientist," American Educator, *555 New Jersey Ave. N.W., Washington, DC 20001 or to **amerend@aft.org***

*My last column (Winter 2002, available at **www.aft.org/ american_educator/winter2002/CogSci.html**) discussed another common problem for students: inflexible knowledge. Like shallow knowledge, inflexible knowledge is meaningful—the catch is that it doesn't translate well to other relevant situations. To extend our World War II example, a student with inflexible knowledge may learn the conclusion and an adequate number of supporting facts, developing a real understanding of Japan's mistake. But, when the history class moved on to study another war, the student may not recognize an analogous strategic mistake. Developing flexible knowledge, such as being able to track strategic mistakes as a theme throughout military history (or to generalize, for example, to corporate history) requires much further study.

Daniel T. Willingham is associate professor of cognitive psychology and neuroscience at the University of Virginia and author of Cognition: The Thinking Animal. *His research focuses on the role of consciousness in learning.*

Beyond Learning By Doing: The Brain Compatible Approach

The current position of the field of experiential education within mainstream education places at a premium attempts to significantly broaden and deepen experiential pedagogy beyond mere "learning by doing." This article will explore one such attempt—the Brain Compatible Approach—and its potential linkages with experiential education. An overview of the Brain Compatible Approach will be outlined, followed by a discussion of several key principles. Linkages between these principles and experiential education will be discussed, as well as several "Quick Tips" on possible practical applications of the research. Finally, the benefits of aligning experiential education with the Brain Compatible Approach will be explored.

Keywords: Education, Brain Compatible, Pedagogy

Jay W. Roberts

Over the last ten years, experiential education has made many in-roads with the mainstream educational establishment. The success of programs such as Project Adventure and Outward Bound working within schools has been well documented. Additionally, ropes course, environmental, and outdoor education programs have become prevalent in many school districts across the country. Yet, with all these advances, there are still many barriers between our pedagogy and traditional schooling. We remain literally, and figuratively, "outside" the educational establishment. Recent initiatives toward accountability and standards have placed experiential education in the crosshairs of reform-minded politicians and school consultants. "Learning by doing" is often described as "process heavy," devoid of content, and a hold-out from 1960s progressivists' approaches. One researcher has gone so far as to say "recent history of American education and controlled observations have shown that learning by doing and its adaptations are among the least effective pedagogies available to the teacher" (Hirsch, 1996, p. 257).

The current position of the field within mainstream education places at a premium attempts to significantly broaden and deepen experiential pedagogy beyond mere "learning by doing." This paper will explore one such attempt—the Brain Compatible Approach—and its potential linkages with experiential education. An overview of the Brain Compatible Approach will be outlined, followed by a discussion of several key principles. Linkages between these principles and experiential education will be discussed as well as several "Quick Tips" on possible practical applications of the research. Finally, the benefits of aligning experiential education with the Brain Compatible Approach will be explored.

The Brain Compatible Approach

In July of 1989, President George Bush declared the 1990s the "Decade of the Brain." What followed was a revolution in research, articles, books, and television specials on what we know about how the brain functions and learns. The medical advances in particular have been many and remarkable. We have learned more about the brain in the past five years than the previous one hundred. Additionally, nearly 90 percent of all neuroscientists who have ever lived are alive today (Brandt & Wolfe, 1998).

While still relatively new as a field of inquiry, the Brain Compatible Approach has yielded several intriguing findings:

- *Neuroplasticity:* The brain changes physiologically as a result of experience and it happens much quicker than originally thought. The environment in which the brain operates determines to a large degree the functioning ability of the brain (Brandt & Wolfe, 1998).

- *The brain is complex and interconnected:* Just as a city or jazz quartet has many levels of interaction and connectedness, the brain has an infinite number of possible interconnections. In essence, there are no isolated, specialized areas but rather the brain is simultaneously processing a wide variety of information all at once (Caine & Caine, 1994).

- *Every brain is unique:* Our brains are far more individualized in terms of physiology, neural wiring, bio-chemical balance, and developmental stage than previously thought (Jensen, 2000).

Each of these findings suggests re-consideration of the way we currently educate. Caution must also be practiced. Much of the current research is new, and steps from research to application are inherently complex and difficult. Already, several researchers have questioned the validity of educational applications of brain research (Bruer, 1997). If nothing else, the sheer volume of new information about how the brain functions and learns forces us to question what we truly "know" about learning and educational practice.

Principles of Brain Based Learning

Drawing from the findings above, several intriguing principles and practical implications have emerged. The following principles are of particular interest to experiential educators as they support some long-standing practices within experiential education and also push the envelope of what may be possible in the future.

Principle #1: Pattern and Meaning Making

Research supports the claim that the search for meaning is innate and occurs through patterning (Caine & Caine, 1994). Patterning refers to the meaningful organization and categorization of information (Nummela & Rosengren, 1986). The brain is designed to search for and integrate new information into existing structures and actively resists "meaningless" patterns (Caine & Caine). The process is constant and does not stop—regardless of whether or not we have stopped teaching! This principle reinforces many of the practices we attribute to experiential learning including emphasis on context and framing, learner involvement in the teaching of the material, alternating between details and big picture (whole/part), reflection components, and relevancy (i.e., relating information to students' previous experience and learning).

> **Quick Tip #1:** Chunking can be an effective tool for presenting the learner with information in an organized, meaningful way. Look at the following list of letters: IBFVTNOJBLKFJ. Try to memorize them as presented. Now look at the next list of letters: JFK, LBJ, ON, TV, FBI. The second list is much easier to memorize even though they are the same letters. They have simply been chunked and arranged in a meaningful way that draws on previous experience and information. Consider how you might chunk small activities (lessons or even directions) and large, multi-day experiences. How can you arrange the information in a more meaningful, patterned way?

> **Quick Tip #2:** Use a "Big Picture." Remember that your students do not have the same view of the course, lesson, or program that you do. Provide them with a big picture as soon as possible at the beginning of the experience. Rather than an exhaustive outline or itinerary, the big picture gives your students a taste of what's coming and allows them to begin making pat-

terns, connections, and frames for the experience. Revisit the big picture a few times throughout the experience to further solidify the link. In this regard, it is helpful to have it on a flip chart or other visual aid. Try using a "you are here" map with a movable arrow.

Principle #2: The Brain as a Parallel Processor

The human brain is the ultimate, multi-tasking machine, constantly doing many things at once. This is because the brain is geared toward survival and is, in actuality, poorly designed for linear, lock-step instruction (Jensen, 2000). Consider how you learned to ride a bicycle. Did you learn through reading a book or hearing a lecture on the separate topics of bike parts, safety, and operation? No. It is more likely you learned through a more dynamic and complex series of experiences. Current research supports the notion that the brain learns best through rich, complex, and multi-sensory environments (Jensen). In this sense, the teacher is seen more as an *orchestrator* of learning environments rather than an instructor of linear lesson plans or even a facilitator of experiences (Deporter, Reardon, & Singer-Nourie, 1999). Practical applications for parallel processing include the use of multi-modal instructional techniques (visual, auditory, kinesthetic) and multiple intelligence activities (Gardner, 1985). Simulations and role-plays mimic our natural learning environment and encourage complex processing. Lastly, enriched learning environments can be orchestrated through the components of challenge, novelty, choice, high feedback, social interaction, and active participation (Diamond & Hopson, 1998). If the benefits of enriched, multi-sensory, complex learning environments continue to be supported by the research, experiential theory and practice can and must play a larger role in the classroom of the future.

> **Quick Tip #3:** Use the EELDRC (Enroll, Experience, Label, Demonstrate, Review, Celebrate) design frame (Deporter et al., 1999) to create a dynamic, complex, multi-sensory lesson plan. In the *Enroll* segment, seek to engage students in the material through intrigue and answering the learner question "What's In It For Me?" Give them a brief *Experience* to immerse students in the new information. Use the *Label* segment to punctuate the most salient points with a "lecturette" or debrief. Provide an opportunity for the participants to *Demonstrate* with the new information to encourage connections and personalization of the material. *Review* the material to cement the big picture and, finally, find a way to *Celebrate* the experience to reinforce positive associations with the learning.

Principle #3: Stress and Threat

Learning is enhanced by challenge and inhibited by threat (Jensen, 2000). Paul MacLean offers a model for considering this principle through his Triune Brain theory (1978). MacLean categorizes the brain into three main regions or separate brains—the Reptilian (or R-complex), the Mammalian (or Limbic), and the Neo-Mammalian (or Neo-Cortex). The reptilian brain controls physical survival and basic needs (flight or fight responses). This is our most primitive "brain." The second brain—the Mammalian—houses both the hippocampus and amygdala—the primary centers for emotion and memory. Lastly, the most advanced part of our brains, according to MacLean, is our Neo-Cortex. It is here where we use higher order thinking skills—synthesizing, logical and operational thinking, speech, and planning for the future (Caine & Caine, 1994).

In this model, the brain has the capacity to "shift" up or down depending on perception of the immediate environment. Perceived threat an force the brain to "downshift" to lower order thinking (Hart, 1983). Yet, heightened challenge and stress, referred to as eustress, can invite an up-shift response into higher order thinking skills in the neo-cortex. Recent research has suggested that the chemical and physiological responses to stress and threat are radically different (Caine & Caine, 1994). Psychological models also support a difference between perceived challenge and threat (Csikszentmihalyi, 1991). This idea is expressed in experiential pedagogy through the concepts of adaptive dissonance and the "comfort zone." In both cases, the felicitator or teacher intentionally places the learner in stressful situations to encourage and invite new adaptive behaviors and mental models that may be more successful or effective for the learner.

Caine and Caine (1994), suggest that specific learning conditions can create situations of up-shifting or downshifting. Downshifting can occur when "pre-specified 'correct' outcomes have been established by an external agent; personal meaning is limited; rewards and punishments are externally controlled; restrictive time lines are given; and the work to be done is relatively unfamiliar with little support available" (Caine & Caine, p. 84). By contrast, to create up-shifting conditions "outcomes should be relatively open ended; personal meaning should be maximized; emphasis should be on intrinsic motivation; tasks should have relatively open-ended time lines; and should be manageable and supported" (Caine & Caine, p. 85). Emotions also play a critical role in both memory encoding and threat perception (LeDoux, 1996). Too little emotion and the brain has a difficult time "tagging" the material for long term memory. Too much emotion and the situation may be perceived as threatening, causing a downshift in mental functions (Brandt & Wolfe, 1998).

Practical applications of the stress/threat principle are numerous and exciting for the experiential field. Experiential pedagogy, with its emphasis on novelty, interpersonal interaction, challenge by choice, and the use of emotions such as play, fear, and humor, is uniquely suited to address stress/threat balances. Understanding how these brain compatible principles can be strengthened by experiential learning opens the possibility for meaningful dialogue with mainstream education.

Quick Tip #4: To lower threat levels early in your program, make a strong emphasis on relationship building both peer-peer and teacher-student. Work the group from the "inside-out" by making a conscious effort to spend personal time with as many students as possible, either on the trail or at water breaks. Work the group "outside-in" by facilitating highly interactive experiences like paired shares, new games, or trust activities.

Quick Tip #5: Use the 60/40 rule for planning your lesson plans. Sixty percent of your experiences should be ritual based activities that are repetitive (like morning check-ins, skill progressions, warm-ups, or post-activity debriefs) to allow your participants to experience known activities in an unknown environment. But be sure to make approximately 40 percent of activities novel. The introduction of elements of suspense, surprise, and disorder keep learners engaged and can be an effective way to manage attention spans. Instead of circling up every time, "rhombus-up" with your group every so often. Mix-up de-briefs by using paired shares, group reports, or silent journaling instead of large group discussion. Introduce skill sections playfully with characters and costumes (knots with Ivana Climbalot, or baking with Chef Boyarentyouhungry).

Conclusion

Evidence and theories from the Brain Compatible Approach support much of what we do. Understanding the human brain's tendency toward pattern and "meaning-making" reinforces the intentional use of reflection and synthesis in experiential education. Viewing the brain as a parallel processor encourages the creation of enriched environments for learners. Experiential methodology facilitates such enriched environments through challenge, social interaction, feedback, and active participation. Finally, the differences between stress and threat responses support our pedagogical approach including the effective use of emotion and the importance of novelty and choice. Recent developments in brain research should also push us toward new questions and research queries. What is the role of emotion in experiential education? How do we define, operationally, the differences between stressful and threatening experiences and responses? How is the mind-body connection supported in current brain research? What part can experiential methodology play in the creation of enriched classroom environments?

We must move beyond mere "learning by doing" for our fields' philosophical underpinnings and practical approaches to become more influential in mainstream education. Using only the learning by doing definition, experiential education becomes nothing more than activities and events with little to no significance beyond the initial experience. One educator recently told me she calls this the "Inoculation Effect" (shoot 'em up; hope it takes). This was not John Dewey's vision and it cannot be our lasting legacy. Many of us entered this field after becoming disenchanted or burned-out on mainstream educational practice. We have also seen the remarkable changes and results that can occur through experiential learning. We believe very strongly that it works. Yet, as a field, we remain long on practice and short on theory and research. The Brain Compatible Approach is one avenue for helping experiential educators articulate how and why the methodology is effective.

How can we achieve more legitimacy while holding fast to our principles? Moves toward identifying the philosophical approaches of experiential education should be encouraged (Itin, 1999). Efforts must be made to increase both qualitative and quantitative research that cross into mainstream education. As educators, we also have a responsibility to learn about our field. At a recent AEE conference, I was surprised to learn how few experiential education practitioners knew of E.D. Hirsch—one of the strongest critics of progressive approaches and a major figure in the standards-based movement. Hirsch defines learning by doing as "a phrase once used to characterize the progressivist movement but little used today, possibly because the formulation has been the object of much criticism and even ridicule" (Hirsch, 1996, p. 256). With critics like this and few legitimate platforms from which to respond, it is not surprising that experiential education remains largely locked out of our schools. Knowing some of the latest trends and movements within the fields of education, psychology, and sociology will strengthen our voice and message.

While there is value in experiential education's subversive, outside-the-mainstream persona, we must also seek ways to come in from the "outside," invite dialogue, and encourage interaction across disciplines. The Brain Compatible Approach, as a promising new area of research and study, offers an excellent opportunity to do just that. In the next 20 years, will experiential education be a program (like field trips, ropes courses, and character education) to be implemented in schools or, will it be a broader, pedagogical foundation from which to work? The future depends on how we live that question.

References

Brandt, R., & Wolfe, P. (1998). What do we know from brain research? *Educational Leadership, 56*(3), 8–13.

Bruer, J. T. (1997). Education and the brain: A bridge too far. *Educational Researcher, 26*(8), 4–16.

Caine, G., & Caine, R. (1994). *Making connections: Teaching and the human brain.* New York: Addison Wesley.

Csikszentmihalyi, M. (1991). *Flow: The psychology of optimal experience.* New York: Harper Perrenial.

Deporter, B., Reardon, M., & Singer-Nourie, S. (1999). *Quantum teaching.* Needham Heights, MA: Allyn & Bacon.

Diamond, M., & Hopson, J. (1998). *Magic trees of the mind.* New York: Penguin Putnam.

Gardner, H. (1985). *Frames of mind: The theory of multiple intelligences.* New York: Basic Books.

Hart, L. (1983). *Human brain, human learning.* New York: Longman.

Hirsch, E. G. (1996). *The schools we need and why we don't have them.* New York: Doubleday.

Itin, C. (1999). Reasserting the philosophy of experiential education as a vehicle for change in the 21st century. *Journal of Experiential Education, 229*(2), 91–98.

Jensen, E. (2000). *Brain-based learning.* San Diego, CA: The Brain Store.

LeDoux, J. (1996). *The emotional brain: The mysterious underpinnings of emotional life.* New York: Simon & Schuster.

MacLean, P. D. (1978). A mind of three Minds: Educating the triune brain. In J. Chall, & A. Mirsky (Eds.), *Education and the brain* (pp. 308–342). Chicago: University of Chicago Press.

Nummela, R., & Rosengren, T. (1986). What's happening in students' brains may redefine teaching. *Educational Leadership 43*(8), 49–53.

Jay Roberts, M.Ed., *is the Director of Wilderness Programs at Earlham College in Richmond, Indiana and teaches in the Education program. He also spent seven years working as a facilitator for Learning Forum Supercamp, an internationally recognized brain compatible learning program. He can be reached at roberja@earlham.edu*

ABILITY AND EXPERTISE

It's Time to Replace the Current Model of Intelligence

BY ROBERT J. STERNBERG

BILLY HAS an IQ of 121 on a standardized individual intelligence test, and Jimmy has an IQ of 94 on the same test. What do these scores, and the difference between them, mean? The conventional answer to this question is that they represent a kind of intellectual predestination: The two children possess inborn gifts that are relatively fixed and will, to a large extent, predict their future achievement. So no one will be surprised if Billy goes on to do well in high school and gets into a good college—or if Jimmy barely gets through school and ends up with a minimum-wage job—because that's what this familiar and widely accepted model of human intelligence would lead us to expect.

But a scientific model is just a way of fitting together pieces of information and things we have observed into a pattern that makes sense. It does not represent the certain or only way of arranging the pieces, and models can be and often are modified or even discarded when we make new discoveries or look at what we know in new ways. This happened, for example, in the early seventeenth century, when the Ptolemaic model of the solar system, in which all the heavenly bodies were said to revolve around the earth, was replaced by the Copernican, sun-centered, model of the solar system.

Many psychologists now question the simple identification of IQ with ability, which the old model of human intelligence posits. They believe that abilities are too broad and too complex to be measured by the kind of IQ test that Billy and Jimmy took. They also believe that environment and genetics play a part and, furthermore, that abilities are not a fixed quantity: They can be modified by education and experience. I'd like to propose a further, and important, building block for this new model of human intelligence—namely that the difference in Billy's

and Jimmy's IQ scores simply means that the two children are at a different stage in developing the expertise measured by the IQ test. Furthermore, I suggest that people who study abilities and those who study expertise are really talking about the same thing. What we are measuring when we administer a Wechsler Intelligence Scale for Children (WISC) or an Iowa Test of Basic Skills (ITBS) or an SAT are the same. They are not different in kind but only in the point at which we are measuring them.

In the Eye of the Beholder

When we give an achievement test, we accept the idea that we are testing a form of expertise, but this is equally true when we administer an IQ test. What differs is the level of expertise we measure and, probably more important, the way we perceive what we are measuring. The familiar IQ/ability model creates a certain expectation: that one kind of accomplishment (IQ test scores) will predict—and, in fact, lead to—another kind of accomplishment (grades or scores on achievement tests). And of course we also use different words to describe the two kinds of accomplishment.

But this way of looking at the two kinds of test scores is a familiar convenience rather than a psychological reality. Solving problems on a verbal-analogies test or a test of mathematical problem solving, which are supposed to test a child's abilities, calls for expertise just the way so-called achievement tests do: You can't do well on these so-called tests of ability without knowing the vocabulary or having some familiarity with problem-solving techniques. The chief difference between ability and achievement tests is not what they measure but the point at which they measure it. IQ and other tests of ability are, typically, administered early in a child's school career, whereas various indications about school performance, such as grades or achievement test scores, are collected later. However, all of the various kinds of assessments are of the same kind, psychologically. They all test—to some extent—what you know and how well you can use it. What distinguishes ability tests from the other kinds of assessments is how the ability tests are used (usually, predictively), rather than what they measure. There is no qualitative distinction.

But if the distinction between what these tests measure does not exist, how do we come to make it? The answer is a complicated story, but the principal reason is historical accident. Briefly, the two kinds of testing were developed separately and used on different groups of people. IQ/ability testing, which originated in Alfred Binet's testing of young children, focused on exceptionally low levels of performance and came to be viewed primarily as predictive. Early studies of expertise were done with adults. They focused on exceptionally high levels of performance and came to be viewed as measures of achievement.

The Traditional Model

According to the traditional model of fixed individual differences, the capabilities that a child inherits interact with the child's environment to produce, at an early age, a relatively fixed potential for achievement. Children fulfill this potential to a greater or lesser degree. Thus, if a child who scores well on ability tests does well in school, we say he is living up to his potential. If, as sometimes happens, his achievement does not match his test scores, we call him an *underachiever*—or if the kid confounds expectations by working hard and doing well, he gets the label of *overachiever*. Ironically, ability test scores are considered a better indicator of what a child can achieve (or should achieve) than what the child actually does. A test of verbal analogies, in this view, might actually tell us more about a person's verbal abilities than the person's comprehension of the reading he or she does in everyday life; or a test of mathematical problem-solving skills might be viewed as more informative than the mathematical problem solving the person does on the job.

According to this model, the more intelligent students (that is, the ones with higher IQs) do better in school. As a result, they are likely to attend selective colleges, go on to professional schools, and eventually get well-paying jobs and enjoy other forms of success. The less intelligent do worse in school and may drop out. At best, they probably have to be satisfied with low-status credentials that reflect hard work rather than ability, and their role in the labor market is to fill the jobs that the more intelligent people don't want to do.

This is the view Richard Herrnstein and Charles Murray present in *The Bell Curve* (1994), and as people who have read the book will remember, it assigns African Americans as a group to the status of an underclass, based on the average "potential" of group members displayed in IQ and other ability tests. Herrnstein and Murray's use of the traditional model has occasioned a great deal of controversy. However, the view of IQ as fixed and determinant is, unfortunately, consistent with many current educational practices and common views about intellectual competence.

Developing Expertise

The idea that abilities are a form of developing expertise offers a more flexible and optimistic view of human capabilities, and one that is more in line with what we are discovering about human intelligence. Children become experts in the skills needed for success on ability tests in much the same ways that they become experts in doing anything else—through a combination of genetic endowment and experience (Ericsson, 1996). To do well on a test, a child needs to acquire, store, and learn how to use at least two kinds of knowledge: explicit knowledge of a domain and implicit or tacit knowledge of a field. Knowledge of a domain is subject-matter knowledge: In American history, for example, it would be the facts, trends, and major ideas about the political, economic, and social development of our country. Implicit knowledge is the kind of knowledge one needs to be successful in a field but which is not part of the subject matter and often is not even talked about. For example, in American history, the role of the Federalist Papers in the shaping of the U.S. Constitution would be explicit knowledge; how to use the library or Internet to research an essay about the Federalist Papers and how to take and organize notes and carry the paper through successive drafts to completion would be implicit knowledge.

Tests measure both explicit and implicit knowledge: knowledge of the subject matter and knowledge about how to take a test. This is as true of ability tests as it is of achievement tests. A verbal-analogies test, for example, measures explicit knowledge of vocabulary and a student's ability to reason with this knowledge, but the test also measures implicit knowledge of how to take a test. Thus, the student has to work within certain time limits and choose the best answer from a list of answers no one of which is exactly right.

To translate the gaining of expertise on test-taking into procedural terms, students need

- direct instruction in how to solve test-like problems—usually this takes place in school;
- practice in solving such problems, again usually in academic contexts;
- an opportunity to watch others, such as teachers or other students, solve test-like problems;

- practice thinking about such problems, sometimes mentally simulating what to do when confronting them;
- rewards for successful solutions (good grades, praise from teachers, other kinds of recognition), thereby reinforcing such behavior.

The difference between Billy's score of 121 and Jimmy's 94 also reflects a number of personal and cultural factors, and they do not all pertain to what we usually consider expertise. For example, the two boys may possess different degrees of "test-wiseness," that is, understanding the tricks of taking tests (Millman, Bishop, and Ebel, 1965; Bond and Harman, 1994). They may feel differing levels of anxiety and/or alertness on the day they are tested, and this would probably show itself in their scores. Cultural differences between them may lead to different attitudes about the importance of doing well on a test, particularly one that clearly does not "count." Most important of all, the boys may be at different levels of developing expertise in the skills that the test measures.

Individual Differences

But saying that IQ tests and other assessments of ability are testing the same thing as achievement tests and that the expertise revealed is not fixed should not be taken to mean that everybody has the same intellectual capacity. The difference in expertise that Billy and Jimmy reveal on their IQ tests may indicate an underlying difference in their capacities. However, IQ tests do not directly measure these differences and neither do any of the other ways in which we currently seek to measure ability (see, for example, Vygotsky, 1978). Individual differences in developing expertise result in much the same way as in most kinds of learning: from (a) the rate of learning (which can be caused by the amount of direct instruction received, the amount of problem solving done, the amount of time and effort spent in thinking about problems, and so on); and from (b) the asymptote of learning—that is, the limit set by ability to what a student can ultimately achieve, given unlimited training. This limit, or asymptote, can be caused by differences in numbers of schemas—the networks of information on various subjects stored in our memories—the organization of schemas, efficiency in using schemas, and so on (see Atkinson, Bower, and Crothers, 1965). For example, children can learn how to solve the various kinds of mathematical problems found in tests of mathematical abilities, whether through regular schooling, a special course, or through assimilation of everyday experience. When they learn, they will learn at different rates, and reach different asymptotes. Ultimately the differences represent genetic and environmental factors that are interacting in ways that we cannot now measure.

Various Kinds of Expertise

As I've already noted, the so-called ability tests typically come earlier in a student's school career than the various types of achievement tests, but what IQ tests measure is not psychologically prior. Achievement tests might just as well be used to predict scores on ability tests—and sometimes they are, as for instance, when school officials try to predict a student's college admissions test scores on the basis of the student's grades. When we look at the test of abilities as though they are psychologically prior, we are confusing the order in which students usually take these tests with some kind of psychological ordering. But in fact, our temporal ordering implies no psychological ordering at all. The recent change in the meaning of the acronym *SAT* (from Scholastic Aptitude Test to Scholastic Assessment Test) reflects the recognition that what was called an aptitude test measures more than just "aptitude"—indeed, it hints at the interchangeability of the two kinds of tests. Nevertheless, the SAT is still widely used as an ability test, and the SAT-II, which more directly measures subject-matter knowledge, as a set of achievement tests.

Tests that claim to measure ability through questions employing vocabulary, reading comprehension, verbal analogies, arithmetic problem solving, and the like are all, in part, tests of achievement. Even abstract-reasoning tests measure achievement in dealing with geometric symbols, which is a skill taught in Western schools (Laboratory of Comparative Human Cognition, 1982). Indeed, if we examine the content of ability tests, it is clear that they measure achievement that the students taking the test should have accomplished several years back. We could just as well use academic performance to predict ability-test scores. The problem with the traditional model is not that it proposes a correlation between ability tests and other forms of achievement. That undoubtedly exists. It is rather the traditional model's proposing that the capacities measured by the tests *cause* later success—or failure—instead of merely preceding it.

An Illusion of Causality

The notion that success on ability tests predicts success in many other areas gains credibility from the fact that some of the skills or qualities that make people more expert at taking tests are also likely to make them successful in other aspects of life in our culture. Taking a test, say, of verbal or figural analogies, or of mathematical problem solving, typically requires skills such as (a) puzzling out what someone else wants (here, the person who wrote the test), (b) command of English vocabulary, (c) reading comprehension, (d) allocation of limited time, (e) sustained concentration, (f) abstract reasoning, (g) quick thinking, (h) symbol manipulation, and (i) suppression of anxiety and other emotions that can interfere with test performance. These skills are also part of what is required for successful performance in school and in many kinds of job performance. Thus, an expert test-taker is likely also to have skills that will be involved in other kinds of expertise as well, such as expertise in getting high grades in school.

To the extent that the expertise required for one kind of performance overlaps with the expertise required for another kind of performance, there will be a correlation between performances. However, the expertise that ability tests measure is not the cause of school or job expertise; it is itself an expertise that overlaps with school or job expertise. Differences in test scores, academic performance, and job performance are all effects of different levels of expertise.

The New Model

The notion of *developing* expertise means that people are constantly in the process of developing expertise when they work within a given domain. Individuals can differ in rate and asymptote of development. However, the main constraint in achieving expertise is not some fixed prior level of capacity, of the kind measured by IQ tests. It is the degree to which students are purposefully engaged in working and teachers in helping them. This involves direct instruction, active participation, role modeling, and reward.

The model of developing expertise has five key elements: metacognitive skills, learning skills, thinking skills, knowledge, and motivation. The elements all influence one another, both directly and indirectly. For example, learning leads to knowledge, but knowledge facilitates further learning.

1. Metacognitive skills. Metacognitive skills refer to students' understanding and control of their own learning. These skills would include what a student knows about writing papers or solving arithmetic word problems, both in regard to the steps that are involved and how these steps can be executed effectively (Sternberg 1985, 1986, 1988; Sternberg and Swerling, 1996).

2. Learning skills. Learning skills are sometimes divided into explicit learning, which occurs when we make an effort to learn, and implicit learning, which occurs when we simply pick up information without any particular effort. Examples of learning skills are distinguishing relevant from irrelevant information; putting together the relevant information; and relating new information to information already stored in memory (Sternberg, 1985, 1986).

3. Thinking skills. There are three main sets of thinking skills. Critical (analytical) thinking skills include analyzing, critiquing, judging, evaluating, comparing and contrasting, and assessing. Creative thinking skills include creating, discovering, inventing, imagining, supposing, and hypothesizing. Practical thinking skills include applying, using, and practicing (Sternberg, 1985, 1986, 1994, 1997). They are the first step in translating thought into real-world action.

4. Knowledge. There are two main kinds of knowledge that are relevant in academic learning. Declarative knowledge is of facts, concepts, principles, laws, and the like. It is "knowing that." Procedure knowledge is of procedures and strategies. It is "knowing how." Of particular importance is procedural tacit knowledge, which involves knowing how the system in which one is operating functions (Sternberg, Wagner, Williams & Horvath, 1995).

5. Motivation. There are a number of different kinds of motivation, and in one or another of its forms, motivation is probably indispensable for school success. Without it, the student never even tries to learn (McClelland, 1985; McClelland, Atkinson, Clark, and Lowell, 1976; Bandura, 1977, 1996; Amabile, 1996; Sternberg and Lubart, 1996).

6. Context. All of the elements discussed above are characteristics of the learner. However, it is a mistake to assume, as conventional tests usually do, that factors external to the student's mastery of the material play no part in how well the student does on a test. Such contextual factors include whether the student is taking the test in his or her native language, whether the test emphasizes speedy performance, the importance to the student of success on the test, and the student's familiarity with the kinds of material on the test.

Novices—beginning learners—work toward expertise through deliberate practice. But this practice requires an interaction of all five of the key elements in the model. At the center, driving the elements, is motivation. Without it, nothing happens. Motivation drives metacognitive skills, which in turn activate learning and thinking skills, which then provide feedback to the metacognitive skills, enabling the student's level of expertise to increase (see also Sternberg, 1985). The declarative and procedural knowledge acquired through the extension of the thinking and learning skills also results in these skills being used more effectively in the future.

All of these processes are affected by, and can in turn affect, the context in which they operate. For example, if a learning experience is in English but the learner has only limited English proficiency, his or her learning will be inferior to that of someone with more advanced English language skills. Or if material is presented orally to someone who is a better visual learner, that individual's performance will be reduced.

Eventually, as the five elements influence one another, the student reaches a kind of expertise at which he or she becomes a reflective practitioner who is able to consciously use a certain set of skills. But expertise occurs at many levels. The expert first-year graduate or law student, for example, is still a far cry from the expert professional. People thus cycle through many times, on the way to successively higher levels of expertise.

Implications for the Classroom

The model of abilities as a form of developing expertise has a number of immediate implications for education, in general, and classroom practice, in particular.

First, teachers and all who use ability and achievement tests should stop distinguishing between what the two kinds of tests assess. The measurements are not different in kind but only in the point at which they are being made.

Second, tests measure *achieved* levels of developing expertise. No test—of abilities or anything else—can specify the highest level a student can achieve.

Third, different kinds of assessments—multiple-choice, short answer, performance-based, portfolio—complement one another in assessing multiple aspects of developing expertise. There is no one "right" kind of assessment.

Fourth, instruction should be geared not just toward imparting a knowledge base, but toward developing reflective analytical, creative, and practical thinking with a knowledge base. Students learn better when they think to learn, even when their learning is assessed with straightforward multiple-choice memory assessments (Sternberg, Torff, and Grigorenko, 1998).

The model I've proposed here views students as novices who are capable of becoming experts in a variety of areas. The traditional model, which posits fixed individual differences—and typically bases the kind of instruction a student gets on these differences—holds many students back from attaining the expertise they are capable of. It is true that for various reasons (including, perhaps, genetic as well as environmentally based differences), not all individuals will reach the same ultimate level of expertise. But they should all be given the opportunity to reach new levels of competence well beyond what they, and in some cases, others may think possible. The fact that Billy and Jimmy have different IQs tells us something about differences in what they now do. It does not tell us anything about what ultimately they will be able to achieve.

References

Amabile, T. M. (1996). *Creativity in context*. Boulder, CO: Westview.

Atkinson, R. C., Bower, G. H., & Crothers, E. J. (1965). *An introduction to mathematical learning theory*. New York: John Wiley & Sons.

Bandura, A. (1977). Self-efficacy: Toward a unifying theory of behavioral change. *Psychological Review*, 84, 181–215.

Bandura, A. (1996). *Self-efficacy: The exercise of control*. New York: Freeman.

Bond, L., & Harman, A. E. (1994). Test-taking strategies. In R. J. Sternberg (Ed.), *Encyclopedia of human intelligence* (Vol. 2, pp. 1073–1077). New York: Macmillan.

Ericsson, A. (Ed.) (1996). *The road to excellence*. Mahwah, NJ: Erlbaum.

Herrnstein, R. J., & Murray, C. (1994). *The bell curve*. New York: Free Press.

Laboratory of Comparative Human Cognition (1982). Culture and intelligence. In R. J. Sternberg (Ed.), *Handbook of human intelligence* (pp. 642–719). New York: Cambridge University Press.

McClelland, D. C. (1985). *Human motivation*. New York: Scott Foresman.

McClelland, D. C., Atkinson, J. W., Clark, R. A., & Lowell, E. L. (1976). *The achievement motive*. New York: Irvington.

Millman, J., Bishop, H., & Ebel, R. (1965). An analysis of test-wiseness. *Educational and Psychological Measurement*, 25, 707–726.

Sternberg, R. J. (1985). *Beyond IQ: A triarchic theory of human intelligence*. New York: Cambridge University Press.

Sternberg, R. J. (1986). *Intelligence applied*. Orlando, FL: Harcourt Brace College Publishers.

Sternberg, R. J. (1988). *The triarchic mind: A new theory of human intelligence*. New York: Viking-Penguin.

Sternberg, R. J. (1994). Diversifying instruction and assessment. *The Educational Forum*, 59(1), 47–53.

Sternberg, R. J. (1997). *Successful intelligence*. New York: Plume.

Sternberg, R. J., & Lubart, T. I. (1995). *Defying the crowd: Cultivating creativity in a culture of conformity*. New York: Free Press.

Sternberg, R. J., & Lubart, T. I. (1996). Investing in creativity. *American Psychologist*, 51, 677–688.

Sternberg, R. J., & Spear-Swerling, L. (1996). *Teaching for thinking*. Washington, DC: APA Books.

Sternberg, R. J., Torff, B., & Grigorenko, E. L. (1998). Teaching triarchically improves school achievement. *Journal of Educational Psychology*, 90, 374–384.

Sternberg, R. J., Wagner, R. K., Williams, W. M., & Horvath, J. (1995). Testing common sense. *American Psychologist*, 50, 912–927.

Vygotsky, L. S. (1978). *Mind in society: The development of higher psychological processes*. Cambridge, MA: Harvard University Press.

This work was supported by the U.S. Office of Educational Research and Improvement (Grant R206R50001), but this support does not imply endorsement of positions taken or conclusions reached.

Robert J. Sternberg is IBM Professor of Psychology in the Department of Psychology at Yale University. His areas of specialization are human abilities and cognition. A long version of this article appeared in **Educational Researcher,** *April 1998.*

It's No Fad: Fifteen Years of Implementing Multiple Intelligences

by Thomas R. Hoerr

Educators do a great job of identifying winners and losers in the classroom. Regardless of how sensitively academic hierarchies are designed, everyone recognizes the pecking order they create. Is it any wonder, then, that students who aren't considered smart often lose interest in school? How many of us, after all, continue to engage in activities at which we repeatedly fail?

Granted, not all children are equally smart, and failure can sometimes be even more enlightening than the smooth road of success. What makes the theory of multiple intelligences (MI) significant is its acknowledgment that children demonstrate intelligence in many different ways. The job of an educator, then, becomes identifying the ways in which children exhibit intelligence and using their particular strengths to help them learn.

In *Frames of Mind* (1983), Howard Gardner challenged the general perception of intelligence by suggesting that there are eight different ways to learn (see Table 1). Gardner was speaking mainly to an audience of psychologists, but the realization that there are many ways to demonstrate intelligence resonated with educators. MI revealed a way to help more students learn and to help students learn more.

Table 1
THE THEORY OF MULTIPLE INTELLIGENCES

Intelligence	Definition	Examples of persons who evidence this intelligence
LINGUISTIC	sensitivity to the meaning and order of words	Winston Churchill Mario Cuomo Barbara Jordan
LOGICAL-MATHEMATICAL	the ability to handle chains of reasoning and to recognize patterns and order	Benjamin Banneker Bill Gates Stephen Jay Gould
MUSICAL	sensitivity to pitch, melody, rhythm, and tone	Louis Armstrong George Gershwin Yo Yo Ma
BODILY-KINESTHETIC	ability to use the body skillfully and handle objects adroitly	Mia Hamm Harry Houdini Michael Jordan
SPATIAL	ability to perceive the world accurately and to re-create or transform aspects of that world	Maya Lin Peter Max Frank Lloyd Wright
NATURALIST	ability to recognize and classify numerous flora and fauna of an environment	Charles Darwin Jane Goodall John Muir
INTERPERSONAL	ability to understand people and relationships	Martin Luther King, Jr. Ronald Reagan Oprah Winfrey
INTRAPERSONAL	access to one's emotional life for understanding oneself and others	Bill Cosby Anne Frank Eleanor Roosevelt

The faculty of New City School has been implementing MI since 1988. Before 1988, New City was considered a creative and diverse school, but there was no organizing framework, no intellectual or pedagogical model that guided our efforts. *Frames of Mind* seemed to support our faculty's extant beliefs: All children have strengths; the arts are important; and who you are is more important than what you know. I convened a voluntary faculty committee at New City, and we spent several months discussing the practicalities of implementing MI.

MI gave us a model and a vocabulary to talk about how curriculum, instruction, and assessment could be designed to enable more students to succeed. Not only did MI expand our conception of academics; it changed how we communicate with parents. For us, MI has become a philosophy of education that affects our relationships with students, administrators, parents, and each other.

Despite our grounding in MI, New City still administers standardized tests each spring (Hoerr 2000). Our students' scores on these tests, consistently several years above grade level, illustrate that high test scores can be achieved through non-traditional teaching techniques.

MI has made our curriculum and instruction far more inclusive of varied learning styles. Rather than simply relying on the linguistic approach to teaching, we have found ways to incorporate other intelligences into our instruction. One first-grade teacher introduces the *th* sound by having her students *th*read yarn into a piece of fabric. A third-grade teacher at New City demonstrates ratios by having her students lie on the floor inside a full-size shape of a buffalo made with masking tape so they can compare the length of their limbs to the buffalo's. A fifth-grade teacher has his students explore the American Civil War period through visual art. Students learn that through clothing, facial expressions, jewelry, and even calluses on hands, they can make inferences about how people lived and what they believed.

At New City, solid assessment is intertwined with curriculum and instruction; here, too, MI provides the foundation. In one class, kindergartners demonstrate how the systems of the human body function using everyday objects to create a model. The children then explain the life-size bodies they have created: a juice box serves as the heart and, as it contracts, forces air into plastic bags that serve as lungs. There is a spine of popsicle sticks and a brain of pasta. Veins and arteries, made of yarn, are respectively red and blue. Second-graders show their understanding of the challenges that faced Lewis and Clark by creating frontier stores to sell the provisions needed for the journey across the uncharted West. Fourth-graders dress as famous figures they have studied to demonstrate an understanding of the concept of biography. As Rosa Parks or Albert Einstein, the students are encouraged to embrace the characteristics that made the individual famous. Sixth-graders reflect on identity and the future by creating multi-volume biographies that include writings, drawings, family photos, survey results, charts, graphs, and information obtained from interviews with relatives.

These examples capture only part of what happens at New City School each day. Rather than fitting kids to curriculum, predetermining scholastic winners and losers, MI allows educators to help develop kids' strengths. Some of the core differences between traditional teaching and teaching in an MI school are shown in Table 2.

Educators at New City believe that who you are is more important than what you know. Success in most of life's endeavors is dependent upon knowing oneself, capitalizing on personal strengths, and working well with others. As a result, we explicitly teach the interpersonal and intrapersonal intelligences. Our report card, for example, begins with *Intrapersonal Intelligence* and addresses areas such as motivation, confidence, problem-solving, responsibility, effort, and work habits. *Interpersonal Intelligence* follows and focuses on appreciation for diversity and teamwork. At each parent-teacher conference, we begin by talking about the qualities—the intelligences—that we feel are most important.

Table 2
DIFFERENCES BETWEEN TRADITIONAL AND MI CLASSROOMS

In a traditional classroom	In an MI classroom
The kids with strong scholastic intelligences are smart and the other kids are not.	Everyone has a different profile of intelligences; we are all smart in different ways.
Teachers create a hierarchy of intellect.	Teachers use all students' intelligences to help them learn.
The classroom is curriculum-centered.	The classroom is child centered.
Teachers help students acquire information and facts.	Teachers help students create meaning in a constructivist way.
The focus is on the scholastic intelligences, the 3 R's.	The Personal Intelligences are valued: Who you are is more important than what you know.
Teachers work from texts.	Teachers create curriculum—lessons, units, themes.
Teachers assess students by paper and pencil "objective" measures.	Teachers create assessment tools—Projects, Exhibitions, Portfolios (PEPs)—which incorporate MI.
Teachers close the door and work in isolation.	Teachers work with colleagues in using MI, developing collegiality.

Our pursuit of MI has transformed our faculty relations as well. Roland Barth's notion of "collegiality" (1990)—adults learning with and from one another—has become the norm. Our faculty committees, framed around our professional growth, examine various aspects of MI implementation, from the garden committee for exploring the naturalist intelligence, to the assessment committee incorporating MI in determining what students know, to the diversity committee for helping us better appreciate one another. Our frequent educator visitors and our MI conferences have helped us become reflective practitioners, aware of what we are doing and why we are doing it.

Implementing MI requires a creative and energetic faculty willing to work together to find strategies that help kids grow. Rather than just presenting information in a test-retest format, teachers develop curriculum and design assessment tools. Both students and teachers flourish in this kind of setting. Clearly, based on the fifteen-year experiment with multiple intelligences at New City School, MI is no fad, but a proven approach to education for the twenty-first century.

References

Barth, R. 1990. *Improving Schools from Within*. Jossey-Bass: San Francisco.

Gardner, H. 1983. *Frames of Mind: The Theory of Multiple Intelligences*. New York: Basic Books.

Hoerr, T. 2002. *Becoming a Multiple Intelligences School*. Alexandria, Va.: ASCD Press.

Thomas R. Hoerr is the head of the New City School in St. Louis

CAUTION— PRAISE CAN BE DANGEROUS

By Carol S. Dweck

THE SELF-ESTEEM movement, which was flourishing just a few years ago, is in a state of decline. Although many educators believed that boosting students' self-esteem would boost their academic achievement, this did not happen. But the failure of the self-esteem movement does not mean that we should stop being concerned with what students think of themselves and just concentrate on improving their achievement. Every time teachers give feedback to students, they convey messages that affect students' opinion of themselves, their motivation, and their achievement. And I believe that teachers can and should help students become high achievers who also feel good about themselves. But how, exactly, should teachers go about doing this?

In fact, the self-esteem people were on to something extremely important. Praise, the chief weapon in their armory, is a powerful tool. Used correctly it can help students become adults who delight in intellectual challenge, understand the value of effort, and are able to deal with setbacks. Praise can help students make the most of the gifts they have. But if praise is not handled properly, it can become a negative force, a kind of drug that, rather than strengthening students, makes them passive and dependent on the opinion of others. What teachers—and parents—need is a framework that enables them to use praise wisely and well.

Where Did Things Go Wrong?

I believe the self-esteem movement faltered because of the way in which educators tried to instill self-esteem. Many people held an intuitively appealing theory of self-esteem, which went something like this: Giving students many opportunities to experience success and then prais-

ing them for their successes will indicate to them that they are intelligent. If they feel good about their intelligence, they will achieve. They will love learning and be confident and successful learners.

Much research now shows that this idea is wrong. Giving students easy tasks and praising their success tells students that you think they're dumb.[1] It's not hard to see why. Imagine being lavishly praised for something you think is pretty Mickey Mouse. Wouldn't you feel that the person thought you weren't capable of more and was trying to make you feel good about your limited ability?

But what about praising students' ability when they perform well on challenging tasks? In such cases, there would be no question of students' thinking you were just trying to make them feel good. Melissa Kamins, Claudia Mueller, and I decided to put this idea to the test.

Mueller and I had already found, in a study of the relationship between parents' beliefs and their children's expectations, that 85 percent of parents thought they needed to praise their children's intelligence in order to assure them that they were smart.[2] We also knew that many educators and psychologists thought that praising children for being intelligent was of great benefit. Yet in almost 30 years of research, I had seen over and over that children who had maladaptive achievement patterns were already obsessed with their intelligence—and with proving it to others. The children worried about how smart they looked and feared that failing at some task— even a relatively unimportant one—meant they were dumb. They also worried that having to work hard in order to succeed at a task showed they were dumb. Intelligence seemed to be a label to these kids, a feather in their caps, rather than a tool that, with effort, they could become more skillful in using.

In contrast, the more adaptive students focused on the process of learning and achieving. They weren't worried about their intelligence and didn't consider every task a measure of it. Instead, these students were more likely to concern themselves with the effort and strategies they needed in order to master the task. We wondered if praising children for being intelligent, though it seemed like a positive thing to do, could hook them into becoming dependent on praise.

Praise for Intelligence

Claudia Mueller and I conducted six studies, with more than 400 fifth-grade students, to examine the effects of praising children for being intelligent.[3] The students were from different parts of the country (a Midwestern town and a large Eastern city) and came from varied ethnic, racial, and socioeconomic backgrounds. Each of the studies involved several tasks, and all began with the students working, one at a time, on a puzzle task that was challenging but easy enough for all of them to do quite well. After this first set, we praised one-third of the children for their *intelligence*. They were told: "Wow, you got *x* number correct. That's a really good score. You must be smart at this." One-third of the children were also told that they got a very good score, but they were praised for their *effort*: "You must have worked really hard." The final third were simply praised for their *performance*, with no comment on why they were successful. Then, we looked to see the effects of these different types of praise across all six studies.

We found that after the first trial (in which all of the students were successful) the three groups responded similarly to questions we asked them. They enjoyed the task equally, were equally eager to take the problems home to practice, and were equally confident about their future performance.

In several of the studies, as a followup to the first trial, we gave students a choice of different tasks to work on next. We asked whether they wanted to try a challenging task from which they could learn a lot (but at which they might not succeed) or an easier task (on which they were sure to do well and look smart).

The majority of the students who had received praise for being intelligent the first time around went for the task that would allow them to keep on looking smart. Most of the students who had received praise for their effort (in some studies, as many as 90 percent) wanted the challenging learning task. (The third group, the students who had not been praised for intelligence or effort, were right in the middle and I will not focus on them.)

These findings suggest that when we praise children for their intelligence, we are telling them that this is the name of the game: Look smart; don't risk making mistakes. On the other hand, when we praise children for the effort and hard work that leads to achievement, they want to keep engaging in that process. They are not diverted from the task of learning by a concern with how smart they might—or might not—look.

The Impact of Difficulty

Next, we gave students a set of problems that were harder and on which they didn't do as well. Afterwards, we repeated the questions we had asked after the first task: How much had they enjoyed the task? Did they want to take the problems home to practice? And how smart did they feel? We found that the students who had been praised for being intelligent did not like this second task and were no longer interested in taking the problems home to practice. What's more, their difficulties led them to question their intelligence. In other words, the same students who had been told they were smart when they succeeded now felt dumb because they had encountered a setback. They had learned to measure themselves from what people said about their performance, and they were dependent on continuing praise in order to maintain their confidence.

In contrast, the students who had received praise for their effort on the easier task liked the more difficult task just as much even though they missed some of the problems. In fact, many of them said they liked the harder problems even more than the easier ones, and they were even more eager to take them home to practice. It was wonderful to see.

Moreover, these youngsters did not think that the difficulty of the task (and their relative lack of success) reflected on their intelligence. They thought, simply, that they had to make a greater effort in order to succeed. Their interest in taking problems home with them to practice on presumably reflected one way they planned to do this.

Thus, the students praised for effort were able to keep their intellectual self-esteem in the face of setbacks. They still thought they were smart; they still enjoyed the challenge; and they planned to work toward future success. The students who had been praised for their intelligence received an initial boost to their egos, but their view of themselves was quickly shaken when the going got rough. As a final test, we gave students a third set of problems that were equal in difficulty to the first set—the one on which all the students had been successful. The results were striking. Although all three groups had performed equally well on the first trial, the students who had received praise for their intelligence (and who had been discouraged by their poor showing on the second trial) now registered the worst performance of the three groups. Indeed, they did significantly worse than they had on the first trial. In contrast, students who were praised for working hard performed the best of the three groups and significantly better than they had originally. So the different kinds of praise apparently affected not just what students thought and felt, but also how well they were able to perform.

Given what we had already seen, we reasoned that when students see their performance as a measure of their intelligence, they are likely to feel stigmatized when they perform poorly and may even try to hide the fact. If, however, students consider a poor performance a temporary setback, which merely reflects how much effort they have put in or their current level of skill, then it will not be a stigma. To test this idea, we gave students the opportunity to tell a student at another school about the task they had just completed by writing a brief description on a prepared form. The form also asked them to report their score on the second, more difficult trial.

More than 40 percent of the students who had been praised for their intelligence lied about their score (to improve it, of course). They did this even though they were reporting their performance to an anonymous peer whom they would never meet. Very few of the students in the other groups exaggerated their performance. This suggests that when we praise students for their intelligence, failure becomes more personal and therefore more of a disgrace. As a result, students become less able to face and therefore deal with their setbacks.

The Messages We Send

Finally, we found that following their experiences with the different kinds of praise, the students believed different things about their intelligence. Students who had received praise for being intelligent told us they thought of intelligence as something innate—a capacity that you just had or didn't have. Students who had been praised for effort told us they thought of intelligence more in terms of their skills, knowledge, and motivation—things over which they had some control and might be able to enhance.

And these negative effects of praising for intelligence were just as strong (and sometimes stronger) for the high-achieving students as for their less successful peers. Perhaps it is even easier to get these youngsters invested in looking smart to others. Maybe they are even more attuned to messages from us that tell them we value them for their intellects.

How can one sentence of praise have such powerful and pervasive effects? In my research, I have been amazed over and over again at how quickly students of all ages pick up on messages about themselves—at how sensitive they are to suggestions about their personal qualities or about the meaning of their actions and experiences. The kinds of praise (and criticism) students receive from their teachers and parents tell them how to think about what they do—and what they are.

This is why we cannot simply forget about students' feelings, their ideas about themselves and their motivation, and just teach them the "facts." No matter how objective we try to be, our feedback conveys messages about what we think is important, what we think of them, and how they should think of themselves. These messages, as

we have seen, can have powerful effects on many things including performance. And it should surprise no one that this susceptibility starts very early.

Melissa Kamins and I found it in kindergarten children.[4] Praise or criticism that focused on children's personal traits (like being smart or good) created a real vulnerability when children hit setbacks. They saw setbacks as showing that they were bad or incompetent—and they were unable to respond constructively. In contrast, praise or criticism that focused on children's strategies or the efforts they made to succeed left them hardy, confident, and in control when they confronted setbacks. A setback did not mean anything bad about them or their personal qualities. It simply meant that something needed to be done, and they set about doing it. Again, a focus on process allowed these young children to maintain their self-esteem and to respond constructively when things went wrong.

Ways of Praising

There are many groups whose achievement is of particular interest to us: minorities, females, the gifted, the underachieving, to name a few. The findings of these studies will tell you why I am so concerned that we not try to encourage the achievement of our students by praising their intelligence. When we worry about low-achieving or vulnerable students, we may want to reassure them they're smart. When we want to motivate high-achieving students, we may want to spur them on by telling them they're gifted. Our research says: Don't do that. Don't get students so invested in these labels that they care more about keeping the label than about learning. Instead of empowering students, praise is likely to render students passive and dependent on something they believe they can't control. And it can hook them into a system in which setbacks signify incompetence and effort is recognized as a sign of weakness rather than a key to success.

This is not to say that we shouldn't praise students. We can praise as much as we please when they learn or do well, but should wax enthusiastic about their strategies, not about how their performance reveals an attribute they are likely to view as innate and beyond their control. We can rave about their effort, their concentration, the effectiveness of their study strategies, the interesting ideas they came up with, the way they followed through. We can ask them questions that show an intelligent appreciation of their work and what they put into it. We can enthusiastically discuss with them what they learned. This, of course, requires more from us than simply telling them that they are smart, but it is much more appreciative of their work, much more constructive, and it does not carry with it the dangers I've been describing.

What about the times a student really impresses us by doing something quickly, easily—and perfectly? Isn't it appropriate to show our admiration for the child's ability? My honest opinion is that we should not. We should not be giving students the impression that we place a high value on their doing perfect work on tasks that are easy for them. A better approach would be to apologize for wasting their time with something that was too easy, and move them to something that is more challenging. When students make progress in or master that more challenging work, that's when our admiration—for their efforts—should come through.

A Challenging Academic Transition

The studies I have been talking about were carried out in a research setting. Two other studies[5] tracked students with these different viewpoints in a real-life situation, as they were making the transition to junior high school and during their first two years of junior high. This is a point at which academic work generally becomes more demanding than it was in elementary school, and many students stumble. The studies compared the attitudes and achievement of students who believed that intelligence is a fixed quantity with students who believed that they could develop their intellectual potential. We were especially interested in any changes in the degree of success students experienced in junior high school and how they dealt with these changes. For the sake of simplicity, I will combine the results from the two studies, for they showed basically the same thing.

First, the students who believed that intelligence is fixed did indeed feel that poor performance meant they were dumb. Furthermore, they reported, in significantly greater numbers than their peers, that if they did badly on a test, they would seriously consider cheating the next time. This was true even for students who were highly skilled and who had a past record of high achievement.

Perhaps even worse, these students believed that having to make an effort meant they were dumb—hardly an attitude to foster good work habits. In fact, these students reported that even though school achievement was very important to them, one of their prime goals in school was to exert as little effort as possible.

In contrast to the hopelessly counterproductive attitude of the first group, the second group of students, those who believed that intellectual potential can be developed, felt that poor performance was often due to a lack of effort, and it called for more studying. They saw effort as worthwhile and important—something necessary even for geniuses if they are to realize their potential.

So once again, for those who are focused on their fixed intelligence and its adequacy, setbacks and even effort bring a loss of face and self-esteem. But challenges, setbacks, and effort are not threatening to the self-esteem of those who are concerned with developing their potential; they represent opportunities to learn. In fact, many of these students told us that they felt smartest when things were difficult; they gained self-esteem when they applied themselves to meeting challenges.

What about the academic achievement of the two groups making the transition to junior high school? In both studies, we saw that students who believed that intelligence was fixed and was manifest in their performance did more poorly than they had in elementary school. Even many who had been high achievers did much less well. Included among them were many students who entered junior high with high intellectual self-esteem. On the other hand, the students who believed that intellectual potential could be developed showed, as a group, clear gains in their class standing, and many blossomed intellectually. The demands of their new environment, instead of causing them to wilt because they doubted themselves, encouraged them to roll up their sleeves and get to work.

These patterns seem to continue with students entering college. Research with students at highly selective universities found that, although they may enter a situation with equal self-esteem, optimism, and past achievement, students respond to the challenge of college differently: Students in one group by measuring themselves and losing confidence; the others by figuring out what it takes and doing it.[6]

Believing and Achieving

Some of the research my colleagues and I have carried out suggests that it is relatively easy to modify the views of young children in regard to intelligence and effort in a research setting. But is it possible to influence student attitudes in a real-life setting? And do students become set in their beliefs as they grow older? Some exciting new research shows that even college students' views about intelligence and effort can be modified—and that these changes will affect their level of academic achievement.[7] In their study, Aronson and Fried taught minority students at a prestigious university to view their intelligence as a potentiality that could be developed through hard work. For example, they created and showed a film that explained the neural changes that took place in the brain every time students confronted difficulty by exerting effort. The students who were instructed about the relationship between intelligence and effort went on to earn significantly higher grades than their peers who were not. This study, like our intelligence praise studies, shows that (1) students' ideas about their intelligence can be influenced by the messages they receive, and (2) when these ideas change, changes in performance can follow.

But simply getting back to basics and enforcing rigorous standards—which some students will meet and some will not—won't eliminate the pitfalls I have been describing. This approach may convey, even more forcefully, the idea that intelligence is a gift only certain students possess. And it will not, in itself, teach students to value learning and focus on the *process* of achievement or how to deal with obstacles. These students may, more than ever, fear failure because it takes the measure of their intelligence.

A Different Framework

Our research suggests another approach. Instead of trying to convince our students that they are smart or simply enforcing rigorous standards in the hopes that doing so will create high motivation and achievement, teachers should take the following steps: first, get students to focus on their potential to learn; second, teach them to value challenge and learning over looking smart; and third, teach them to concentrate on effort and learning processes in the face of obstacles.

This can be done while holding students to rigorous standards. Within the framework I have outlined, tasks are challenging and effort is highly valued, required, and rewarded. Moreover, we can (and must) give students frank evaluations of their work and their level of skill, but we must make clear that these are evaluations of their current level of performance and skill, not an assessment of their intelligence or their innate ability. In this framework, we do not arrange easy work or constant successes, thinking that we are doing students a favor. We do not lie to students who are doing poorly so they will feel smart: That would rob them of the information they need to work harder and improve. Nor do we just give students hard work that many can't do, thus making them into casualties of the system.

I am not encouraging high-effort situations in which students stay up studying until all hours every night, fearing they will displease their parents or disgrace themselves if they don't get the top test scores. Pushing students to do that is not about valuing learning or about orienting students toward developing their potential. It is about pressuring students to prove their worth through their test scores.

It is also not sufficient to give students piles of homework and say we are teaching them about the importance of effort. We are not talking about quantity here but about teaching students to seek challenging tasks and to engage in an active learning process.

However, we as educators must then be prepared to do our share. We must help students acquire the skills they need for learning, and we must be available as constant resources for learning. It is not enough to keep harping on and praising effort, for this may soon wear thin. And it will not be effective if students don't know *how* to apply their effort appropriately. It is necessary that we as educators understand and teach students how to engage in processes that foster learning, things like task analysis and study skills.[8]

When we focus students on their potential to learn and give them the message that effort is the key to learning, we give them responsibility for and control over their achievement—and over their self-esteem. We ac-knowledge that learning is not something that someone gives students; nor can they expect to feel good about themselves because teachers tell them they are smart. Both learning and self-esteem are things that students achieve as they tackle challenges and work to master new material.

Students who value learning and effort know how to make and sustain a commitment to valued goals. Unlike some of their peers, they are not afraid to work hard; they know that meaningful tasks involve setbacks; and they know how to bounce back from failure. These are lessons that cannot help but serve them well in life as well as in school.

These are lessons I have learned from my research on students' motivation and achievement, and they are things I wish I had known as a student. There is no reason that every student can't know them now.

Endnotes

1. Meyer, W. U. (1982). Indirect communications about perceived ability estimates. *Journal of Educational Psychology*, 74, 888–897.
2. Mueller, C. M., & Dweck, C. S. (1996). Implicit theories of intelligence: Relation of parental beliefs to children's expectations. Paper presented at the Third National Research Convention of Head Start, Washington, D.C.
3. Mueller, C. M., & Dweck, C. S. (1998). Intelligence praise can undermine motivation and performance. *Journal of Personality and Social Psychology;* 75, 33–52.
4. Kamins, M., & Dweck, C. S. (1999). Person vs. process praise and criticism: Implications for contingent self-worth and coping. *Developmental Psychology*.
5. Henderson, V., & Dweck, C. S. (1990). Achievement and motivation in adolescence: A new model and data. In S. Feldman and G. Elliott (Eds.), *At the threshold: The developing adolescent.* Cambridge, MA: Harvard University Press; *and* Dweck, C. S., & Sorich, L. (1999). Mastery-oriented thinking. In C. R. Snyder (Ed.). *Coping.* New York: Oxford University Press.
6. Robins, R. W. & Pals, J. (1998). Implicit self-theories of ability in the academic domain: A test of Dweck's model. Unpublished manuscript, University of California at Davis; *and* Zhao, W., Dweck, C. S., & Mueller, C. (1998). Implicit theories and depression-like responses to failure. Unpublished manuscript, Columbia University.
7. Aronson, J., & Fried, C. (1998). Reducing stereotype threat and boosting academic achievement of African Americans: The role of conceptions of intelligence. Unpublished manuscript, University of Texas.
8. Brown, A. L. (1997). Transforming schools into communities of thinking and learning about serious matters. *American Psychologist, 52,* 399–413.

Carol S. Dweck is a professor of psychology at Columbia University, who has carried out research on self-esteem, motivation, and academic achievement for thirty years. Her new book, Self-Theories: Their Role in Motivation, Personality, and Development, *was just published by The Psychology Press.*

From the *American Educator*, Spring 1999, pp. 4-9. © 1999 by Carol S. Dweck. Reprinted by permission.

Webs of Skill:
How Students Learn

Identifying the complex and variable ways that students learn and develop can help educators provide differentiated instruction.

Kurt W. Fischer and L. Todd Rose

Two bright, energetic 7-year-olds, Clara and Scott, want to read well, but they differ greatly in their patterns of skills. Clara can read the words "dog," "black," and "waffle" (as well as many others), and she can make rhymes with them and sound out the letters to pronounce the word. Scott can read those words, too, but he struggles with the rhyming and sounding out, especially for "black" and "waffle." Scott's performance changes dramatically when his teacher helps him. She provides a choice of words that rhyme with "black" or shows Scott how to sound out the word, and he performs perfectly for a while. Then, after a few minutes without her support, he again struggles with the rhyming and sounding out.

To understand and explain these variations in learning and development, we must detect the patterns behind Clara's and Scott's actions. When faced with the task of explaining such complexity, scientists and educators have typically retreated into oversimplifications. Most focus on a single factor to explain variation—typically, intelligence, developmental stage, or developmental norm. "Clara is smarter than Scott," or "Clara is at a higher stage than Scott," or "Scott is below grade norm, and Clara is at norm." But why can Scott perform the tasks correctly with his teacher? There is more to the differences than can be explained by a one-factor ladder of increasing competence, knowledge, or intelligence.

As researchers, educators, and parents, we are keenly aware, and often painfully reminded, that students do not all climb the same ladder. Their individual academic and social skills do not develop at the same time or in the same manner but in much more interesting and complex ways. A dynamic analysis of how students construct their skills offers a richer understanding of their learning dif-

ferences—both the diverse pathways of different children, such as Clara and Scott, and the large variations in skills of an individual child that occur as a function of context and emotional state, as in Scott's activities with his teacher.

Each student constructs distinct pathways in every important learning domain, including reading, mathematics, and social interaction. At the same time, each student possesses a different level of skill in the learning domains; these variations in performance are a function of the student's emotional state and how much immediate support the student receives.

Constructive Webs of Development

An alternative framework for understanding learning and development is a dynamic approach that moves beyond the static one-dimensional ladder and builds on the concept of a constructive web of skills (Fischer & Bidell, 1998). Seeing learning as a dynamic construction of webs facilitates understanding the complex patterns of development and learning. Figure 1 depicts a small-scale version of this web; the strands represent potential skills that are developing in a domain, and the points of connection among the strands represent the integration of these skills. To read words, for example, the student needs to develop two different learning domains: visual-graphic skills, such as reading written letters and words; and sound analysis, such as rhyming and sounding out words. The idea of constructive webs explains how students can vary yet remain stable in development and leads to a recognition of patterns of variability that have eluded the classical models in the ladder framework.

Students continually construct multiple strands in their webs, such as sight and sound strands for reading words, with each skill contributing to the emergence of more complex skills along a strand. For example, identifying the letters of the alphabet helps students build the skills of reading and spelling individual words. A strand considered by itself is like a ladder of skills in a domain; however, it branches and connects with other strands—and there are many strands, not just one. In reading an alphabetic language such as English, the reader connects strands for visual-graphic and sound analysis to read effectively.

Students do not all learn in the same cookie-cutter fashion, and a dynamic analysis of learning and development provides powerful new tools for understanding their variations.

The development of a given skill involves diverse strands, branches, and connections, with one student showing a web like that in Figure 1 for reading and another student showing a different web. Unlike the rigid steps of a ladder, the sequence and order of the strands in a constructive web are not predetermined, nor is there one universal sequence.

FIGURE 1

A Constructive Web of Development

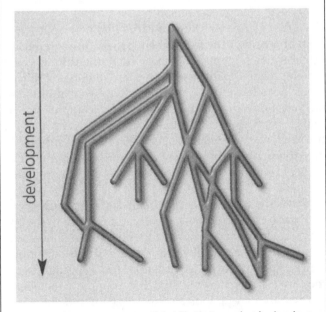

The strands represent potential skills that are developing in a learning domain, and the points of connection among the strands represent the intergration of these skills.

FIGURE 2

Pathway A: A Common Web for Reading Words

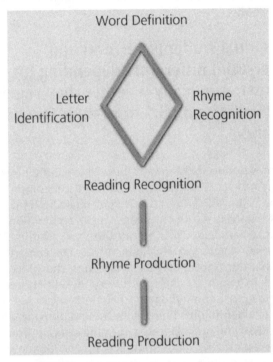

In this illustration of the constructive web for the standard theory of reading alphabetic languages, the sight (letter indentification) and sound (rhyme recognition) domains are at first independent but then come together as students integrate sight and sound skills to read words.

At the same time, webs often demonstrate a great deal of order. Students commonly show similar strands, branches, and connections, as well as similar start and end points. These components are completely lost in the one-dimensional image of a ladder, which forces all students into one rigid model. Uncovering the orderly patterns through dynamic analysis of constructive webs creates powerful tools to help educators move beyond normative approaches and build effective individualized instruction. Two students in the same classroom may look similar in test performance, but their strengths and problems can be different because they are progressing through distinct developmental webs.

Early development of reading illustrates this type of ordered variability. In one study by our research group, the Dynamic Development Research Group at Harvard University (Knight & Fischer, 1992), 120 students in 1st, 2nd, and 3rd grades, ages 6-8, performed a series of six tasks with familiar words from their scholastic reading series in school. The six tasks all related to reading individual words: word definition, letter identification, rhyme recognition, rhyme production, reading recognition, and reading production. Examining these tasks allowed us to identify for each individual student the webs of skill development for learning to read single words (Fischer, Knight, & Van Parys, 1993). The webs from the study are far simpler than the one in Figure 1 because of the small number of tasks that we included in the study. With more tasks, the webs would show more strands and connections.

Individual students perform and understand differently depending on context, especially whether they receive high or low support from their teachers or others.

According to the standard theory of reading development, proficient reading comes from the integration of visual-graphic skills, such as letter identification, with sound-analysis skills, such as rhyme recognition (LaBerge & Samuels, 1974; Snow, Burns, & Griffin, 1998; Torgesen, Wagner, & Rashotte, 1994). The constructive web that illustrates this standard theory, shown as Pathway A in Figure 2, starts with word definition because students must know the word before they can use it appropriately. Initially, the sight and sound domains are independent and not integrated, forming separate branches for the early tasks: letter identification and rhyme recognition. Later, the two branches come together as students integrate sight and sound skills to read words and become proficient readers.

In our study, most normal readers, like Clara, demonstrated this developmental pathway and fit the standard theory. Clara's rhyming and reading tasks connected closely for each word that she read, so the sight and sound tasks in her constructive web integrated to form reading skills.

At the same time, a number of students performed the tasks differently and constructed two distinctive alternative webs that did not indicate integration (see fig. 3). Scott had difficulty with rhyming and sounding out words such as "black" and "waffle," even though he could read them. He was developing along one of the alternative webs, in which sight and sound tasks were not integrated. In Pathway B, the two strands remain separate and unintegrated. The web begins like the others, with word definition and then letter identification, but the remaining tasks develop along independent branches for reading and rhyming and do not achieve full integration. Rhyming tasks typically develop later than reading tasks, as with Scott.

The third web, Pathway C, shows even less integration, with three separate branches for letter identification, rhyming, and reading, as well as slow development of both reading and rhyming skills. The students who produced Pathway C all showed serious reading problems, and some of those developing along Pathway B had prob-

lems, too. These alternative webs illustrate the difficulty that poor readers have in integrating skills across strands.

Focusing only on deficits in the alternative webs is a mistake, however. The students producing these webs could read many of the words in the study, and some performed normally on standardized reading tests. They were developing along alternative pathways, learning to read without integrating the sights and sounds of words in the "normal" way. Learning to read is more difficult for most students following alternative pathways, but eventually many students with severe reading problems become skilled readers and writers by developing along distinctive pathways. In a study of highly successful adults who were dyslexic as students, Rosalie Fink (1995) found that they had become powerfully literate readers and writers, even though they still retained their difficulties with reading individual words, especially integrating the sights and sounds of novel words. These successful adults had found their own independent pathways to literacy.

Developmental Range

Although a student develops along an individual web for reading, no individual acts consistently at a specific level on a strand; instead, he or she acts within a range of levels. Initially, Scott could not rhyme or sound out the words, but when his teacher provided support, he moved temporarily to a higher level, rhyming and sounding out successfully for several minutes. All students show similar variations in developmental range. They never remain fixed at one stage, even for a specific domain, such as reading words in the class curriculum, but instead vary across several stages or levels. Teachers know intuitively about this variation and are wary of claims that students operate at a fixed level of ability.

At first glance, this kind of variability may appear random or chaotic, especially when viewed through the lens of classic developmental theory. Like the differences in developmental pathways, however, there is order in what looks like chaos. An especially powerful influence on variation is contextual support for complex performance. Scott showed his ability to rhyme and sound out the harder words when his teacher provided support by prompting rhyming and sounding out, but this high-level ability disappeared in a few minutes after her support stopped.

The same variation occurs in all skills. A youth's competence at chess improves greatly in response to support from a mentor, and it varies with other factors: new situations, different challengers, and varying emotional states. Adults show this variation, too, especially when they are learning new material. For example, a member of our research group took a course about neural networks. In class, he demonstrated good use of network concepts with the support of the teacher's instruction, but when he went home and tried to explain neural networks to his

FIGURE 3

Two Alternative Webs for Reading Words

Pathway B: Independence of reading and rhyming

Pathway C: Independence of reading, letter identification, and rhyming

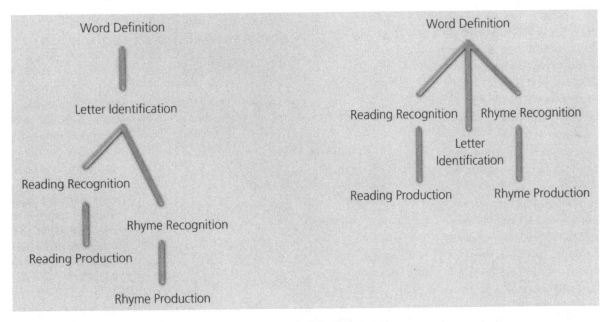

All pathways of reading development begin with word definition skills (see figure 2), but these alternate pathways to reading show different skills developing independently. Learning to read is more difficult for most students following alternative pathways, but eventually many become skilled readers.

wife, his level of understanding plummeted to much simpler, less sophisticated concepts.

Extensive research has shown that each learner's range of development is defined by two upper limits of performance—the functional and optimal levels (Fischer & Bidell, 1998; Fischer, Knight, & Van Parys, 1993). Under low-support conditions, students function less skillfully, and their highest competence is their functional level, which is their best performance in most everyday functioning. When they receive high support, their highest competence is their optimal level, their best performance when a person or the context prompts the key components of the task for them. The optimal level develops in spurts during certain age periods, which are related to growth in neural networks in the brain (Fischer & Rose, 1998), but the functional level develops more slowly and continuously and varies greatly across domains.

Jill, 15, illustrates optimal and functional levels as she learns the mathematical relation between addition and multiplication for positive whole numbers. Addition and multiplication both involve combining numbers to get bigger numbers, with addition combining single numbers and multiplication combining groups of numbers (Fischer, Hand, & Russell, 1984). Explaining this conceptual relation between addition and multiplication eludes most adoles-

cents, but when they turn 15 or 16, they can explain it with high contextual support. When Jill's teacher or friend prompts her with key ideas, Jill can explain this relation coherently for several specific arithmetic problems (such as $8 + 8 + 8 + 8 + 8 = 40$ and $5 \times 8 = 40$) and exhibit competence at her optimal level. Within a few minutes after the prompting ends, however, her level of performance drops abruptly, and she cannot successfully explain the same relation that she dealt with cogently with support. Her level of performance on a test will depend similarly on whether the test question prompts the key components or not. In the classroom, students demonstrate this kind of fluctuation in understanding every day.

A primary goal of education is to improve the functional-level performance of students so that they can then produce the skill on their own.

The range between optimal and functional levels is large, as shown in the graph for skill growth in Figure 4. The graph shows only the levels that emerge during the

FIGURE 4

Developmental Range: Optimal and Functional Levels

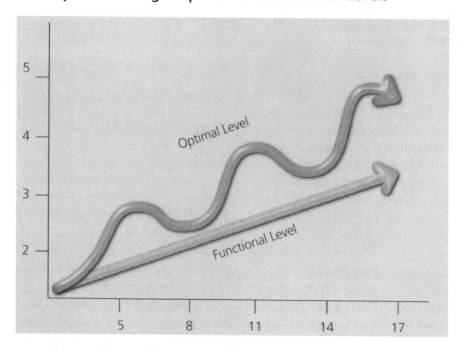

The optimal level of skill is the level that a student can reach when he or she receives support. The functional level of skill is the level the student demonstrates independently, without help from context or teachers.

school years; 13 developmental levels emerge between birth and age 30. Jill is in the midst of the spurt in optimal understanding that occurs at about age 15, but several years will pass before she can sustain the same understanding in ordinary performance and without high support. Variation of this kind occurs in almost all types of skills—not only reading, mathematics, and science, but also sports, social interaction, planning, and self- organization.

Dynamic Development

Students do not all learn in the same cookie-cutter fashion, and a dynamic analysis of learning and development provides powerful new tools for understanding their variations. The multiple webs of development capture the natural variability among students, and developmental range demonstrates how the variability occurs within each student.

Identifying common alternative webs provides a useful tool for educators because the webs illuminate the different ways that students learn important skills and show that students learn in multiple ways. Even individual students perform and understand differently depending on context, especially whether they receive high or low support. A primary goal of education is to improve the func-

tional-level performance of students so that they can then produce the skill on their own. At the same time, an optimal-level skill is a target that students experience as realistic because they can achieve it if given high support.

When educational assessments distinguish alternative developmental webs for learning and note the differences between functional and optional levels of skill, educators can teach better, write more effective curricular materials, and improve the quality of their students' learning.

References

Fink, R. (1995). Successful dyslexics: A constructivist study of passionate-interest reading. *Journal of Adolescent and Adult Literacy*, 39, 268–280.

Fischer, K. W., & Bidell, T. R. (1998). Dynamic development of psychological structures in action and thought. In R. M. Lerner (Ed.), *Handbook of child psychology: Vol. 1. Theoretical models of human development* (5th ed., pp. 467-561). New York: Wiley.

Fischer, K. W., Hand, H. H., & Russell, S. L. (1984). The development of abstractions in adolescence and adulthood. In M. Commons, F. A. Richards, & C. Armon (Eds.), *Beyond formal operations* (pp. 43–73). New York: Praeger.

Fischer, K. W., Knight, C. C., & Van Parys, M. (1993). Analyzing diversity in developmental pathways: Methods and concepts. In R. Case & W. Edelstein (Eds.), *Contributions to human development: Vol. 23. The new structuralism in cognitive development: Theory and research on individual pathways* (pp. 33–56). Basel, Switzerland: Karger.

Fischer, K. W., & Rose, S. P. (1998). Growth cycles of brain and mind. *Educational Leadership, 56*(3), 56–60.

Knight, C. C., & Fischer, K. W. (1992). Learning to read words: Individual differences in developmental sequences. *Journal of Applied Developmental Psychology, 13,* 377–404.

LaBerge, D., & Samuels, S. J. (1974). Toward a theory of automatic information processing in reading. *Cognitive Psychology, 6,* 293–323.

Snow, C. E., Burns, M. S., & Griffin, P. (Eds.). (1998). *Preventing reading difficulties in young children.* Washington, DC: National Academy Press.

Torgesen, J., Wagner, R., & Rashotte, C. (1994). Longitudinal studies of phonological processes of reading. *Journal of Learning Disabilities, 27,* 276–286.

Authors' note: Thomas Bidell, Jeanne Chall, Rosalie Fink, Jane Haltiwanger, Catherine Knight, Samuel P. Rose, and Robert Thatcher contributed to the arguments and evidence in this paper. Preparation of this article was supported by grants from Mr. and Mrs. Frederick P. Rose, Harvard University, and NICHD grant #HD32371.

Kurt W. Fischer is Charles Bigelow Professor and Director of the Mind, Brain, and Education Concentration, Harvard Graduate School of Education, Larsen Hall 702, Appian Way, Cambridge, MA 02138; kurt_fischer@email.msn.com. **L. Todd Rose** is a doctoral student, Harvard Graduate School of Education, Human Development and Psychology, Larsen Hall 103, Appian Way, Cambridge, MA 02138; rosela @gse.harvard.edu.

Invitations to Learn

Students care deeply about learning when their teachers meet their need for affirmation, contribution, purpose, power, and challenge.

Carol Ann Tomlinson

Do students care about learning? The answer is, of course, that "it depends." At 4 years old, David asked his teacher a question as a lesson began: "Is this going to be a 'learning experience'? Because if it is, I don't want to do it." That same 4-year-old had the patience of Job in trying to figure out how to navigate a new computer program at home.

In 10th grade, Kenisha did what she had to do to pass her classes. By 11th grade, she was part of an AVID group[1] and was proud of the high grades she was making in advanced classes.

Josh was often reduced to tears by homework. Yet, the best part of his day was the discussions and debates on such topics as ethics and philosophy that he shared with his family over dinner each evening.

Until this year, Bethany was convinced that students who did well in class were either smarter than she was, or luckier, or just better liked by the teacher. She drifted through school and the principal's office, alternating between anger and resignation. Now she loves parent-teacher conference days, when she can share with her mother her learning goals and evidence of her growth.

The students in Ms. Larrick's 6th period English class began the year by skipping class whenever they could. They hated English. By the end of the year, they refused to miss class discussions of *Antigone*.

Early in the year, Jana was skeptical about math. Her teacher told the students that he expected them to work like mathematicians. They would learn math as a language—a way of thinking. They would have to decide which tools to use to be effective with a range of problems that would crop up in school, in town, or in the news. Jana wasn't sure that she could do math that way. It seemed less predictable than math had always been in the past. In June, she wrote her teacher a note saying that she thought that she might like to be a math teacher, or maybe an engineer.

Javier was angry last year that his family had moved to a place where he knew no one and no one understood him when he spoke. This year, he works hard at spelling and math. His teacher asked him to tutor a Spanish-speaking boy three years younger than he is. The boy looks forward to sessions with Javier, and Javier can't let him down. Javier's teacher also helps him find books about Mexican culture and Mexican Americans that he can share with his young friend as they work together on reading.

Jessica and Dane had always found history boring. Ms. Brittle asked them to go on a personal odyssey in their community as they read Homer's *Odyssey* and studied the history of ancient Greece and Rome. They found possibilities in themselves and their town that they had never considered. They also saw a purpose in history that they hadn't seen before.

Do students care about learning? Absolutely—when they are invited to learn.

What Is Invitational Learning?

Few students are drawn to lists of facts. Not many find computations, theorems, and proofs inherently interesting. Worksheets evoke little satisfaction in the young.

The impetus to learn generally does not come first from content itself, but rather because a teacher has learned to make the content inviting.

Although there are students who dutifully learn the facts, perform the computations, and complete the worksheets, it would be hard to argue that such activities lead even these students to be eager learners. At best, such tasks promote intellectual compliance and a hunger for stars and *A*s—not an insatiable desire to learn. The impetus to learn generally does not come first from content itself, but rather because a teacher has learned to make the content inviting.

What invites students to learn? Because students vary, what is inviting will vary as well. In general, however, students have at least five needs that teachers can address to make learning irresistible: affirmation, contribution, purpose, power, and challenge. Sometimes, teachers find that the learning environment is key to meeting student needs. Sometimes the mode of instruction is key. Generally, environment and instruction work in tandem to invite, inspire, and sustain student learning. Together, they make the content important.

Affirmation

Many young people seek first an affirmation that they are significant in the classroom. Perhaps more and more young people are uncertain of their significance in the world at large, or perhaps the young have always been on a quest for significance. Whatever the reason, students come to school needing to know that

- I am accepted and acceptable here just as I am.
- I am safe here—physically, emotionally, and intellectually.
- People here care about me.
- People here listen to me.
- People know how I'm doing, and it matters to them that I do well.
- People acknowledge my interests and perspectives and act upon them.

Initially, Javier did not feel accepted and acceptable in his class as he was. The class did not feel safe, either emotionally or academically. Javier felt as though his lack of English was an inconvenience for his teacher. He did not feel listened to. No one seemed to know his interests or perspectives.

Kenisha also lacked a sense of affirmation in her 10th grade classes. She was often the only African American student in advanced classes. No links existed between her community and the content of her classes. When she didn't complete her work, teachers generally "let it slide."

Josh does not feel affirmed in his class. He has a learning disability, and despite his best efforts, he cannot keep up with the written tasks.

Homework is especially problematic because there is so much of it and he is already exhausted from the effort of the day. He believes that he is a poor student and that he is not smart. The work that his teacher assigns is not designed for him; it makes him feel like a misfit.

Teachers issue a crucial invitation to learning when young learners feel an abiding sense of affirmation from teacher and peers in a class. When that sense of affirmation is lacking, learning is at risk.

Contribution

To make a difference in any sort of community, one must contribute. Many students come to school looking for a way to contribute to their world. They need to feel that

- I make a difference in this place.
- I bring unique and valuable perspectives and abilities to this place.
- I help other students and the entire class to succeed.
- I am connected to others through mutual work on common goals.

Javier's new teacher understood the power of contribution to promote learning. Even when Javier's language skills were at their most tentative, she found someone to whom Javier's contribution was crucial. Because Javier knew someone else was counting on him, he was able to accept the inevitable frustrations that stem from acclimating to a new language and culture.

Twelve-year-old Toby awoke one Monday feeling ill. When Toby's mother realized that he wasn't feeling well, she suggested that he stay in bed. Toby's response surprised her: "I can't stay home, Mom," he said with conviction. "What would Mrs. Lind do if I weren't in class today? And how could my writing group get its work done?" This would be a remarkable story in any case. It's more potent perhaps because Toby has Down's syndrome. In his mixed-ability English class, his role was clear and important to him. He made a difference there, and he needed to be there.

The child who can remain mute in class discussions for days, weeks, and months does not feel like a contributor. The student who is always "the taught" during group work—and never "the teacher"—does not feel like a contributor. By contrast, teachers invite students to learn when students feel that their presence makes a positive, tangible difference in the work of the class.

Purpose

Students come to school in search of purpose. They need to know that

- I understand what we do here.
- I see significance in what we do.
- What we do reflects me and my world.
- The work we do makes a difference in the world.
- The work absorbs me.

At 4, David saw no purpose in most of his kindergarten "learning experiences." But the computer was another story: The programs gave him access to things he cared about—ideas and activities that seemed important to him.

Ms. Larrick's 6th period students had a long history of seeing literature as unrelated to their lives. The language in their books seemed so unlike the language they spoke. They were uninterested in dissecting plot, setting, protagonist, antagonist, and conflict. Ms. Larrick changed all that when she asked them, "Have you ever felt like a victim?" They talked about what it meant to be a victim, whether people have to be victims, what people can change in their lives, and what they can do when they can't change circumstances. Hand-waving discussions ensued. Then she asked the students, "Want to read a book about a victim and see if your ideas hold up?" *Antigone* became their favorite book—at least until they discovered themselves in the next book.

For Javier, decoding words, writing, and spelling remain arduous. His work feels more purposeful to him when he reads and writes about the country he left behind and about other young people who learned to make a new life in a new place.

Teachers invite their students to learn when they demonstrate that student learning has purpose—when students discover meaning and relevance implicit in books, ideas, and tasks. Without meaning, schoolwork is purposeless for students.

Power

From infancy, the young seek increasing dominion over their world. Turning over in the crib, learning to open the refrigerator door, crossing the street, deciding what to wear to school, and spending the night at a friend's house are important milestones, in part because they signal growing independence and power. Teachers who purposefully assist young learners to develop a sense of power invite their students to learn. To feel powerful in the classroom, students need to believe that

- What I learn here is useful to me now.
- I make choices that contribute to my success.
- I know what quality looks like and how to create quality work here.
- Dependable support for my journey exists in this classroom.

Jessica and Dane saw history as a parade of data to be memorized to satisfy adults—until this year. This year, the teacher showed them how to find themselves in the past and how to use history as a tool for thinking. As one student explained, "Other teachers told us *what* to think. This one is different because she showed us *how* to think and that we *can* think."

Kenisha found AVID to be an important part of her life because the program empowered her to achieve academic success. Through AVID, she learned how to take notes, use her time wisely, select crucial courses, study with peers, prepare for exams, apply to college, and more. The program also placed her in the company of peers and teachers who overtly supported her journey as a student.

Bethany is also having a better year because she has found a sort of power in the classroom. This year, her teacher works with students to set learning goals for each topic and skills area. Some goals are common to the class; others indicate an individual's need for continued growth. Students keep records of their progress on the goals. Rubrics and work samples help students understand the hallmarks of quality work. For the first time, the route to success is not a mystery to Bethany. She feels in control of her fate as she participates in parent-teacher conferences, presenting to her mother both her goals and evidence of her growth during the marking period.

A teacher invites students to learn when the classroom is a place that consistently builds students' capacity to be at the helm of their fate. By contrast, when students feel powerless in the classroom, learning loses its appeal.

Challenge

Something deep inside humans seeks challenge despite fears. Students feel challenged in the classroom when they perceive that

- The work here complements my ability.
- The work stretches me.
- I work hard in this classroom.
- When I work hard, I generally succeed.
- I am accountable for my own growth, and I contribute to the growth of others.
- I accomplish things here that I didn't believe were possible.

Josh did not feel challenged by the work in his class—he felt defeated. Rather than complementing his abilities, the work ran counter to his strengths. No matter how much effort he expended, he experienced little success—just the promise of more work. In his classroom, he didn't accomplish the impossible. Instead, he became more convinced that school was impossible for him.

Jana had been successful in past math classes. This year, she wasn't so sure of herself. The teacher abandoned math as solely algorithmic and instead challenged students to be math thinkers. At first, the new approach was frightening to Jana. In the end, she found herself stretched. Not only was she successful, but she had a new sense of herself as a mathematician.

What constitutes a challenge for one student may feel like defeat to another. When teachers design routes to learning that push individual students into a bit of discomfort—and when they then support student success at that new level—they invite students to learn.

Issuing Invitations to Learn

Teachers extend learning invitations in many ways. Such invitations exist in the way that a teacher addresses students, in the learning environment, in classroom procedures, and in student work that provokes both engagement and understanding.

The message of learning invitations may take a variety of forms: I want to know you. I have time for you. I try to see things through your eyes. This classroom is ours, not mine.

The message of such invitations may take many forms: I have respect for who you are and who you can become. I want to know you. I have time for you. I try to see things through your eyes. This classroom is ours, not mine. There is room for what you care about in what we learn. Your peers and I need you here as a partner in learning. I will help you understand yourself and your world through what we learn. What we do here today will open up all sorts of possibilities for you. You have essential roles here that help us all be more effective and efficient. I enjoy thinking about what we do here. Your success is central in this classroom. There is a clear roadmap to success here, and I will share it with you. When one route to learning doesn't work, we'll find another. I am your partner in growth. We are on a mission to learn. There is great support for you here but no room for excuses. I watch you and listen to you carefully. I make sure that I use what I learn to help you learn better. You're growing, but you're not finished growing. There is no finish line in learning.

In fact, what teachers actually say to students is less important to invitational learning than are students' collective experiences in the classroom. Excellent teachers may speak the invitations to learn, but students respond because the actions of those excellent teachers consistently convey invitation.

Do students care about learning? One of the most satisfying discoveries in the teacher's life is that when teaching is genuinely invitational, there exists no "off switch" to student engagement in learning.

Note

1. AVID (Advancement Via Individual Determination) provides academic and social support to ensure that students—particularly the least-served students with desire and academic potential—will succeed in the most rigorous curriculum and enroll in 4-year colleges.

AVID serves more than 65,000 middle and high school students at 1,275 schools in 21 states and 15 countries.

Carol Ann Tomlinson is Professor of Educational Leadership, Foundations, and Policy at the University of Virginia, Charlottesville, VA 22903; cat3y@virginia.edu. She is author of *How to Differentiate Instruction in Mixed-Ability Classrooms* (ASCD, 2001).

The Tyranny of Self-Oriented Self-Esteem

by James H. McMillan, Judy Singh, and Leo G. Simonetta

In Ryann's second-grade classroom there was a poster on one wall to celebrate each individual student. For one week during the year each student was the "special child" of the class, and the space on the poster indicated unique and valued things about the child, such as a favorite color, hobbies, or family. Students put up pictures and other items to announce publicly what they thought was good about themselves. (Ryann, daughter of one of the authors, liked being a "special child" for a week, but the parent was not as enthusiastic.)

Activities for this type are common in elementary schools, all seeking to boost the self-esteem of the students. They assume that self-esteem is the key to achievement, and in fact much evidence, both anecdotal and research-based, shows that students achieve more with self-esteem. Teachers also seem to accept self-esteem as critical for intellectual development and necessary for students to excel or even achieve needed competence in academic tasks. According to Barbara Lerner, "Teachers generally seem to accept the modern dogma that self-esteem is the critical variable for intellectual development—the master key to learning. Children... cannot achieve excellence, or even competence, until their self-esteem is raised."[1]

Linking self-esteem to success and overall well-being is so well accepted that there are many institutes, foundations, task forces, and centers dedicated to promoting self-esteem programs. For example, there is the California Task Force to Promote Self-Esteem and Personal and Social Responsibility, the Center for Self-Esteem, the National Council for Self-Esteem.[2] In addition, an increasing number of books, monographs, audiocassettes, and videocassettes stress developing self-esteem, as well as "how to" programs for teachers at all levels. The fundamental idea is that once educators focus on improving students' self-esteem, not only will behavior and achievement improve, but students also will be more satisfied, better adjusted, and happier. The assumption is that concentrating on enhancing self-esteem will produce these positive outcomes.

But is it possible, with the best of intentions, to overemphasize self-esteem with self-oriented activities?

What are we teaching our children by encouraging and reinforcing a self-focus, and what are its long-term consequences? Since the mid-'60s, psychology has transformed our way of thinking about explanations for people's behaviors, shifting from outside the self (behaviorism) to within the self. The psychologist Martin Seligman terms our current culture one of "maximal selfs," in which the individual should be gratified,

fulfilled, self-actualized, and in control.[3] Seligman argues that this revolutionary change has caused increased depression, hopelessness, and other personal difficulties because of the dual burden of high expectations and self-control. Since the focus is on ourselves as being responsible, and on an expectation that we will be most content and happy if we concentrate on what is best for us, coping with failure to reach our expectations becomes difficult. If Seligman is correct, many facets of current self-esteem programs may be based on fundamentally flawed and misdirected theory. In this article the theory of self-oriented self-esteem programs will be reviewed, with illustrations of suggested practices based on this theory and the results that can be expected from this approach. An alternative theory will be recommended, with suggested practices.

Self-Oriented Self-Esteem

Many self-esteem programs fundamentally encourage students to think more about themselves, to be more introspective and self-oriented. The idea is that the self can be enhanced by focusing on it positively. Barbara Lerner refers to this as "feel-good-now self-esteem."[4] Jack Canfield, a well-known advocate of self-esteem enhancement, has suggested several strategies for the classroom that emphasize introspection: 1) assume an attitude of 100 percent responsibility by getting students to think about what they are saying to themselves; 2) focus on the positive—"I spend a lot of my time having students recall, write about, draw, and share their past experiences"; 3) learn to monitor your self-talk by replacing negative thoughts with positive—"I can learn to do anything I want, I am smart, I love and accept myself the way I am"; and 4) identify your strengths and weaknesses.[5]

A popular self-esteem book for educators suggests enhancing self-esteem with one or more of the following: improving self-evaluation skills; developing a sense of personal worth; reflecting on self-esteem; thinking of oneself in positive terms; discovering reasons the individual is unhappy; or examining sources of and influences on self-esteem. Their emphasis is on enhancing students' positive self-perceptions.[6] Such ideas are often implemented in classroom activities that teach students introspective thinking: for example, keeping a journal about themselves and indicating "what I like best about myself",[7] teaching a unit entitled "I Am Great" that emphasizes their individuality through self-portraits, silhouettes of themselves, "who am I," and "coat of arms" exercises,[8] and programs such as Developing Understanding of Self and Others (DUSO), Toward Affective Development, and Dimensions of Personality. Some less-complex programs simply encourage student self-talk with phrases such as "I'm terrific" or "I'm great." All these activities or programs are designed to promote self-acceptance and self-awareness, to help students become aware of their unique characteristics, and to "put children in touch with themselves."[9]

Accomplishment means that self-esteem is enhanced as children work hard to meet externally set, reasonable standards of achievement.

Although these are well-intentional programs, their encouragement of self-introspection may distort a normal, healthy perspective about oneself into self-importance, self-gratification, and ultimately selfishness. If the message is that "me" is most important, will selfishness be viewed as normal and expected? Are we making a virtue of self-preoccupation? If so, such "selfism" may have negative consequences. As William Damon points out, "A young mind might too readily interpret a blanket incantation toward self-esteem as a lure toward self-centeredness."[10] Damon believes that placing the child at the center of the universe is psychologically dangerous because "… it draws the child's attention away from the social realities to which the child must adapt for proper character development."[11] Children taught to place themselves first care most for their own personal experiences, and in doing so they do not learn how to develop respect for others. According to Lerner, the feel-good-now variety of self-esteem eventually leads to unhappiness, restlessness, and dissatisfaction.[12] Finally, Seligman argues that our obsession with self is responsible for an alarming increase in depression and other mental difficulties.[13] It is well-documented that such problems result from rumination and obsessive thinking about oneself.[14]

There are other negative consequences of overemphasizing self-oriented self-esteem. For most students, and surely young children, the idea of self-esteem is abstract and hard to understand. Generalized statements such as "you're valued," or "you're great," or "you're special" have no objective reality. They are simply holistic messages that, untied to something tangible and real, have little meaning.[15] Teachers making such statements will lose credibility because children are adept at discerning valid feedback from such vague generalizations. Students may develop a skepticism toward and distrust of adults, or even worse may learn to tune them out entirely, as the teacher "shades the truth [with] empty rhetoric, transparent flattery, bland distortions of reality."[16] By trying to bolster self-esteem with messages that are not "entirely" true, teachers inadvertently undermine the trust of the child. For students who already have low self-esteem, such statements reinforce a noncaring attitude from adults. From the perspective of children, caring adults

"tell it like it is" and don't hide the truth—they don't cover up or make things up that aren't true.

In contrast, there is ample evidence that our mental health improves as we forget ourselves and focus on activities that are not self-oriented. Often we are most happy when we are so involved in outside pursuits that we don't think about ourselves. This leads us to an alternative theoretical foundation for self-esteem: the notion that healthy self-esteem results not from self-preoccupation and analysis but just the opposite—from not being self-oriented but being occupied by interests and pursuits external to self. Indeed, many self-esteem enhancement programs appear to be based on this idea.

Accomplishment and External-to-Self-Oriented Self-Esteem

As an alternative to the self-orientation approach, we suggest that a healthy esteem results not from self-preoccupation and analysis but from activities that result in meaningful accomplishment or have an external-to-self orientation. Accomplishment means that self-esteem is enhanced as children work hard to meet externally set, reasonable standards of achievement. Lerner calls this "earned" self-esteem: "Earned self-esteem is based on success in meeting the tests of reality—measuring up to standards—at home and in school. It is necessarily hard-won, and develops slowly, but is stable and long-lasting, and provides a secure foundation for further growth and development. It is not a precondition for learning but a product of it."[17]

Achieving meaningful success in schoolwork enhances self-esteem after many years of meeting standards and demands. A foundation for self-esteem based on tangible evidence is internalized by students because it makes sense to them in their social environment. Internally meaningful performance and accomplishment can be attributed to ability and effort. Such internal attributions underlie a sense of self-efficacy so that the child becomes confident in being a capable learner. Striving for achievement also directs children's thinking off themselves and on something external to themselves. This change in thinking orientation determines self-esteem programs that theoretically are diametrically opposed to self-oriented programs.

Recently there have been signs that psychologists may be changing their views about the emphasis on selfism to enhance self-esteem. Seligman maintains that many have lost a sense of commitment to larger entities outside themselves—country, church, community, family, God, or a purpose that transcends themselves. Without these connections people are left to find meaning and fulfillment in themselves.[18] The negative consequences of de-emphasizing other people, groups, community, and the larger society include vandalism, violence, racial tensions, high divorce rates, and drug abuse. Some psychologists attribute the growth of the "me" generation and selfish behavior to the emphasis on individuality and related themes.[19] Others argue that schools should promote selflessness by emphasizing group welfare over individuals, involvement rather than isolation, and self-denial rather than self-centeredness.[20]

These authors suggest that student well-being is best enhanced by pursuits that take attention away from self, in which one gets "lost." Such pursuits could include a hobby; a concern for helping others; having a purpose or cause bigger than oneself; submitting to duty or to a role in community; or academic success following meaningful effort. The hypothesis is that self-esteem is a byproduct of successful external-to-self experiences. The more success a student has in such activities, the stronger his or her own self-esteem will be.

From a social-psychological perspective, participating constructively with others is necessary for positive self-esteem. As stated by Damon:

> Growing up in large part means learning to participate constructively in the social world. This in turn means developing real skills, getting along with others, acquiring respect for social rules and legitimate authority, caring about those in need, and assuming social responsibility in a host of ways. All of these efforts necessarily bring children out of themselves. They require children to orient themselves toward other people and other people's standards.[21]

By focusing outside themselves children learn respect for others and an objective reference for acquiring a stable and meaningful sense of themselves.

It is the outward focus that forms the foundation for self-esteem.

Some examples of self-esteem programs appear to be based on this external-to-self hypothesis. One is a successful program in which students are involved in an art project structured to enhance a feeling of belonging and accomplishment. Self-esteem is improved by involving students in meaningful group activity; not by self-introspection.[22] Another program reports that children acquire self-esteem from successful experiences and appropriate feedback in motor skill development.[23] Several other programs also stress successful achievement in affecting self-esteem.[24] In each case the program involves students in some meaningful activity, rather than focusing on themselves.

Conclusion

Clearly, educators need to concentrate their efforts on improving students' self-esteem. The important question is: how should this be done? We have suggested that approaches emphasizing meaningful achievement and external-to-self pursuits will result in more healthy self-esteem than programs that are self-oriented.

Teachers and administrators need to design programs directing student attention away from the self, not toward it. Paradoxically, positive self-esteem develops as students forget about self-esteem, focus on external pursuits, and obtain positive feedback following meaningful involvement and effort.

Notes

1. Barbara Lerner, "Self-esteem and Excellence: The Choice and the Paradox," *American Educator* 9 (1985): 10–16.
2. Jack Canfield, "Improving Students' Self-esteem," *Educational Leadership* 48 (1990): 48–50.
3. Martin E. P. Seligman, "Boomer Blues: With Too Great Expectations, the Baby-Boomers Are Sliding into Individualistic Melancholy," *Psychology Today* 22 (1988): 50–55.
4. Lerner, "Self-esteem and Excellence."
5. Canfield, "Improving Students' Self-esteem."
6. James A. Beane and Richard P. Lipka, *Self-concept, Self-esteem, and the Curriculum* (Boston: Allyn and Bacon, 1984).
7. Anne E. Gottsdanker-Willenkens and Patricia Y. Leonard, "All about Me: Language Arts Strategies to Enhance Self-Concept," *Reading Teacher* 37 (1984): 801–802.
8. Richard L. Papenfuss, John D. Curtis, Barbara J. Beier, and Joseph D. Menze, "Teaching Positive Self-concepts in the Classroom," *Journal of School Health* 53 (1983): 618–620.
9. Frederic J. Medway and Robert C. Smith, Jr., "An Examination of Contemporary Elementary School Affective Education Programs," *Psychology in the Schools* 15 (1978): 266.
10. William Damon, "Putting Substance into Self-Esteem: A Focus on Academic and Moral Values," *Educational Horizons* (Fall 1991): 13.
11. Ibid., 17.
12. Lerner, "Self-esteem and Excellence."
13. Seligman, "Boomer Blues."
14. Thomas J. Lasley and John Bregenzer, "Toward Selflessness," *Journal of Human Behavior and Learning* 3 (1986): 20–27.
15. Damon, "Putting Substance into Self-esteem."
16. Ibid., 15.
17. Lerner, "Self-esteem and Excellence," 13.
18. Martin E. P. Seligman, *Learned Optimism: The Skill to Conquer Life's Obstacles, Large and Small* (New York: Random House, 1990).
19. Sami I. Boulos, "The Anatomy of the 'Me' Generation," *Education* 102 (1982): 238–242.
20. Lasley and Bregenzer, "Toward Selflessness."
21. William Damon, "Putting Substance into Self-esteem," 16–17.
22. Marilee M. Cowan and Faith M. Clover, "Enhancement of Self-concept through Discipline-based Art Education," *Art Education* 44 (1991): 38–45.
23. Linda K. Bunker, "The Role of Play and Motor Skill Development in Building Children's Self-confidence and Self-esteem," *Elementary School Journal* 91 (1991): 467–471.
24. David L. Silvernail, *Developing Positive Student Self-concept* (Washington, D.C.: National Education Association, 1987).

From *Educational Horizons*, Winter 2001, pp. 92-95. © 2001 by Educational Horizons. Reprinted with permission of the author.

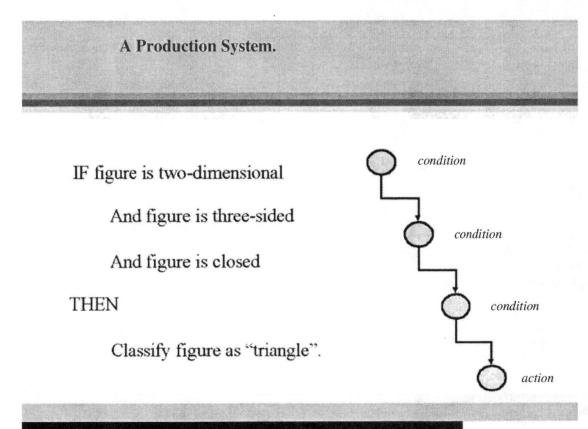

A Production System.

IF figure is two-dimensional

And figure is three-sided

And figure is closed

THEN

Classify figure as "triangle".

condition

condition

condition

action

Figure 2: A production sequence based on contingency statements

ies later emerged employing the use of this new visual tool or spatial representation of knowledge, some challenging Piaget's developmental theory in asserting that primary-grade children are capable of understanding abstract concepts by developing very thoughtful concept maps which they can explain intelligently to others (Symington & Novak, 1982). Other studies by Novak et al. demonstrated that graduate students found that concept maps helped them *learn how to learn* and were useful as a tool to represent changes in their knowledge structures over time. These same graduate students also indicated that concept maps were useful for representing knowledge in any discipline and that concept maps were helpful in organizing and understanding new subject matter (Novak, 1990). Another study conducted by Dagher and Cossman (1990) aimed at analyzing science teaching in schools found that verbal explanations of science concepts are not well-suited for helping students construct concept maps. The study suggested that some categories of propositions that are analogical, functional, and mechanical in nature would be more appropriate for developing concept maps. Such categories would enable more *conceptually transparent* concept maps (Wandersee, 1990) making it possible to better evaluate students' understandings, changes in understandings and misconceptions in understandings of science concepts. Concept mapping techniques began as paper-based and evolved to computer-based tools with the innovation of visual de-

sign software. This article discusses the use of two computer-based concept mapping tools, Inspiration® and Semnet®, in an educational setting to foster meaningful learning and understanding.

Computer-Based Concept Mapping Tools

Inspiration® and Semnet® are computer-based visual thinking environments that allow users to create concept maps (also known as semantic networks or nets), webs, outlines, and graphic organizers. They are easy-to-use, multiplatform, and Web-enabled (can be ported to the Web). The basic elements of concept mapping software are *nodes* and *links*. Learners use nodes to represent ideas and links to represent relationships that connect ideas. Applying these elements to our earlier example of the schema for the concept "school," *students* and *teachers* would each be a node in the concept map and *students learn from teachers* would be a link. As the nodes and links become interrelated, a structural knowledge representation emerges paving the way for a meaningful understanding of the knowledge domain depicted. In order to build a concept map, the learner must "transform the knowledge to be mapped from its current linear form to a context-dependent form" (Wandersee, 1990, p. 927). This process forces the learner to interact with the knowledge domain, identify the key concepts, and relate them to

LEARNING STRATEGY	CATEGORY	EDUCATIONAL EXAMPLE
Planning	Organization strategy for basic learning tasks	Preparing advance organizers for learning
Organizing	Organizational strategy for basic learning tasks	Grouping or ordering to-be-learned items from a list or a section of prose
Outlining	Organizational strategy for complextasks	Outlining a passage or creating a hierarchy
Webbing	Organizational strategy for complex tasks	Creating a diagram to show the relationship among facts and concepts
Writing	Elaboration strategies for complex tasks	Paraphrasing, summarizing, or describing how new information relates to existing knowledge
Knowledge mapping Brainstorming Concept mapping	Elaboration strategies for complex tasks	Creating analogies, metaphors, and other structures that describe how new or more complex information relates to existing information
Reflection Exploration	Comprehension monitoring strategies	Checking for comprehension failures using self-questioning and other methods that help students find the main ideas and elaborate on important information

Table 1

each other in a meaningful way. Prior knowledge and personal experience play an important role in this learning task ultimately creating a reorganization of existing schemata into a new knowledge structure that is useful and pertinent.

The main advantage to the utilization of computer-based concept mapping tools such as Inspiration® and Semnet® is that they remove the drudgery and mess of revising paper-based concept maps (Anderson-Inman & Zeitz, 1993). Computer-based concept maps can be modified dynamically making it possible for learners to reflect their improved understanding of a content domain over time by revising their concept maps quickly and easily. Revisions can also be initiated or guided by teachers, which makes concept mapping effective as a means of assessing student learning (McClure, Sonak, & Suen, 1999). Computer-based concept maps can also be used as planning tools to organize a project or a learning activity. In essence, concept mapping can be used as a learning strategy, an instructional strategy, a strategy for planning a curriculum, and a means of assessing students' understanding of abstract concepts (Novak, 1990). Although the focus of this article is primarily on the use of computer-based concept mapping as a learning strategy, other uses will be briefly explored.

Concept Mapping as a Learning Strategy

Inspiration® supports the following learning strategies that according to Weinstein and Mayer (1986) fall under four categories: organizational strategies for basic learning tasks, organizational strategies for complex learning tasks, elaboration strategies for complex learning tasks, and comprehension monitoring skills. Table 1 displays the strategies, the associated category, and an educational context.

It is evident from the above associations that Inspiration® can have extensive classroom uses that support students in *learning how to learn*. Students can use this mindtool as an organizational strategy to identify important concepts of a content domain and the interrelationships between them. This process serves the same purpose as outlining a chapter but requires a more thorough analysis of the content (Jonassen, 1996). Students are engaged in generating a semantic network that mirrors their understanding of the content under study. This spatial representation of ideas and relationships becomes a scaffold for acquiring new knowledge (Spoehr, 1994). As students progress in the learning process, they can revisit their concept maps and modify the content by adding new ideas, formalizing undeveloped ideas and reorganizing relationships between ideas based on new understandings. This exploratory and reflective process serves as a comprehension monitoring strategy that helps students move through the three stages of knowledge acquisition proposed by schema theorists (e.g., accretion, restructuring, and tuning) proposed by Norman (1978). The following is an example to illustrate the above.

In EDIT 704, a graduate course at George Mason University that addresses learning theory and instructional

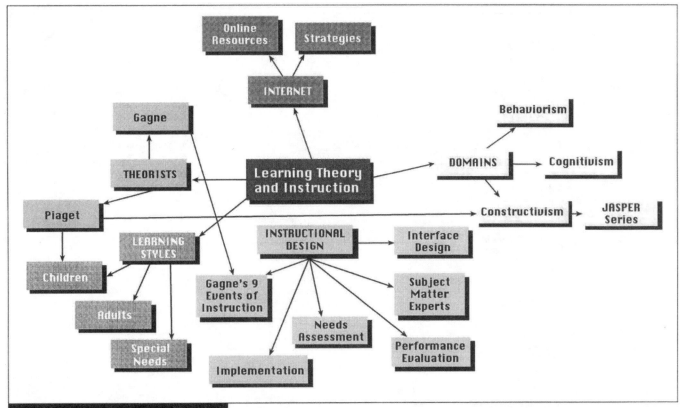

Figure 3: First iteration of a concept map

technology, students used Inspiration® to construct concept maps to represent their understanding of the various learning theories and their relationship to instruction in preparation for a research paper on learning theory. Beginning with propositional networks that largely depicted the acquisition of declarative knowledge, students revised their concept maps every couple of weeks ending with elaborate semantic networks that reflected a deeper and more meaningful understanding of the content (structural knowledge), based on new readings and instructional activities conducted throughout the course. The semantic network provided a rich information base guiding students in their end semester writing task. In this example, students used concept mapping both as an organizing tool and a comprehension monitoring tool. [Shown] is an example of a student's propositional network (first iteration) and its evolution into a semantic network (fourth iteration). The first iteration (Figure 3) supports the organizational strategy for basic learning tasks and the knowledge acquisition phase of accretion. The learner is organizing concepts in clusters based on the readings and prior knowledge. The structure is incomplete; however, it acts as a prototype module for the construction of a new knowledge module (Norman, 1978). The concept map relates the following five concepts to the main concept of learning theory and instructional design: theorists, the Internet, domains, instructional design, and learning styles. The learner has provided further groupings for each of these concepts

however no relationships or elaborations have yet been identified.

The fourth iteration (Figure 4) supports the organizational strategy for complex learning tasks (webbing) and the knowledge-acquisition phase of restructuring. The learner has achieved new insight into the structure of the topic and is making elaborations by creating relationships between the concepts in the diagram. The concept map shows evidence in "jumps in understanding" specifically as it relates to the concept of "theorists."

The learner is recognizing deficiencies in previous concept maps and restructuring the knowledge base by making inferences and adding analogies (Norman, 1978). A noticeable inference in this concept map is the finding of similarities between Ausubel's meaningful reception learning and schema theory.

Inspiration® also supports nonvisual thinkers by allowing users to toggle between the diagram view (the visual representation of the concept map) and an outline view. At any time during the creation of a concept map, a user can toggle to the outline view to view the concept map in an outline form. The outline view provides a hierarchical structure of the concept map based on the links between nodes. Users can use this view to add new topics, insert subtopics, and rearrange the organizational structure of the concept map. Users can also type notes in outline view under each topic or subtopic to help convert the concept map into a document in preparation of a writing assignment. All changes performed in the *outline view*

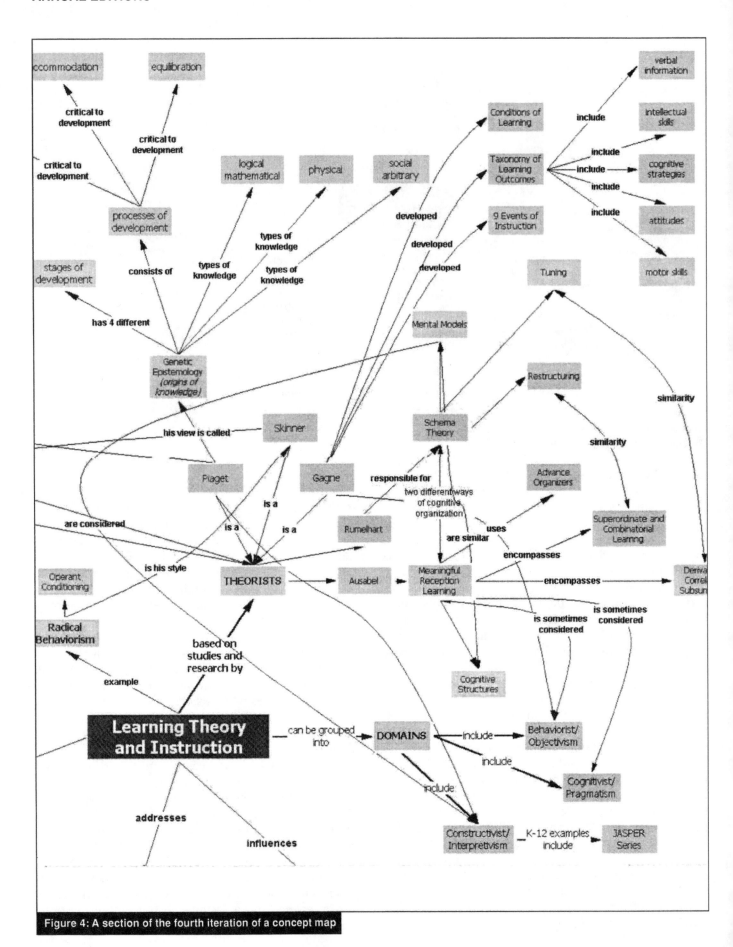

Figure 4: A section of the fourth iteration of a concept map

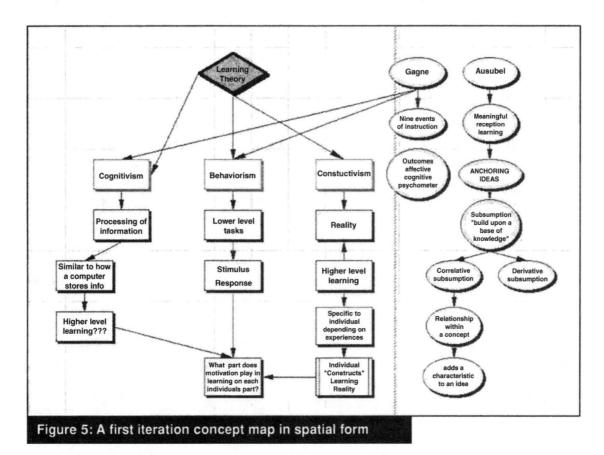

Figure 5: A first iteration concept map in spatial form

are reflected in the *diagram view* and vice versa. Figure 5 shows a diagram view of a concept map on learning theory created in Inspiration® in EDIT 704, and Figure 6 shows the corresponding outline view. The intuitiveness of the software in converting the concepts and links to an outline view (and vice versa) makes it easier for the linear thinker (or the visual thinker) to fine tune the structure when viewing it in a more familiar form.

Concept Mapping as an Instructional Strategy

Inspiration® also has a *rapid fire* feature that allows users to get down their ideas as fast as they can think of them without having to create new symbols each time. This feature can support brainstorming as a learning strategy and can be used by teachers as a tool to generate an organized structure for new or complex content, based on student input. For example, teachers can pose questions during class that encourage students to generate analogies and metaphors to help them relate new content to existing knowledge, and they can capture student responses by entering them instantaneously into Inspiration® using the rapid fire feature. At the end of such a brainstorming session, a student-generated concept map emerges that can serve as an advance organizer for future class discussions. This example can also be perceived as a preinstruc-

tion or assessment exercise, allowing teachers to inspect students' existing knowledge structures to identify misconceptions and adapt instruction to facilitate new learning (McClure, Sonak, & Suen, 1999). Other features of Inspiration® include a library of symbols that range from pictures of animals to geometric shapes allowing users to contextualize their concept maps. Users can also create their own symbols to illustrate concepts and use colors and other drawing tools to highlight and accentuate the main ideas and interrelationships.

It is not difficult from the above discussion to visualize the effectiveness of this computer-based concept mapping tool in facilitating student learning. Students can use it as a study aid to organize thoughts, create outlines, plan research papers, and examine content domains by extracting main concepts and ideas and realizing the interconnectedness of those ideas. Teachers can use this tool as a planning aid to actively generate graphic organizers for content, create lesson plans, and adapt instruction to students' needs by monitoring students' use of concept mapping to develop key concepts of a content domain.

Concept Mapping as a Collaborative Thinking Tool

The other visual learning tool discussed in this paper is Semnet®. SemNet® software can be used to represent knowledge domains much in the same way Inspiration®

```
+ Learning Theory
   I. + Constructivism
      A. = Reality
   II. + Behaviorism
      A. + Lower level tasks
         1. + Stimulus
            Response
            a) - What part does motivation play in learning on each individuals
               part?
   III. + Cognitivism
      A. + Processing of information
         1. + Similar to how a computer stores info
            a) - Higher level learning???
   IV. + Miscellaneous Thoughts
      A. + Specific to individual depending on experiences
         1. - Individual "Constructs" Learning Reality
      B. - Higher level learning
      C. + Gagne
         1. - Name events of instruction
      D. - Outcomes
         affective
         cognitive
         psychomotor
      E. Ausubel
         1. + Meaningful reception learning
            a) + ANCHORING IDEAS
               (1) - Subsumption
               "build upon a base of knowledge"
               (a) - Correlative subsumtion
                  1) + Relationship within a concept
                  (1) - adds a characteristic to an idea
               (b) Derivative subsumtion
```

Figure 6: The same concept map in outline form

does. It allows users to organize ideas about any topic in the form of a semantic network linked by named relations. However, the main difference between Semnet® and Inspiration® is that Semnet® creates a hypertext environment that allows the user to navigate between concepts through the named relations by emphasizing the concept-relation-concept in the construction of the knowledge map. This is based on the principle that concepts are ideas that can usually be described by a word or a phrase and that concepts can be understood through their relations to other concepts. Thus Semnet® "preserves the subject-verb-object relationship between two concepts to show the core concept, relationship, and related concepts as a 'web' or knowledge to which other illustrative material may be linked and attached" (Semnet Research Group, 1991). For example, the concept music can be understood through the word "music" and also through its relations to other concepts (Figure 7).

Those relations are elaborated using the subject-verb-object, which is the basis for normal sentence construction, as can be seen in Figure 7. A concept-relation-concept is known as an instance. In Figure 7, there are seven instances. By providing this structure, Semnet® forces

students to elaborate on the linkages between nodes (concepts) in a concept map promoting the interdependence between declarative and procedural knowledge right from the start and eliminating the propositional stage. While students are constructing semantic networks or knowledge maps, they are actively seeking information to describe concepts by naming them and naming relationships that link two or more concepts together. In the process, they are creating an information map of their knowledge structure and this is much more useful than rote memorization. According to Weinstein and Mayer (1986), this supports elaboration strategies of complex tasks. The dots appearing next to the related concepts—emotion, balance, life, style, form, rhythm, melody, harmony, and so on—imply that the user has created an individual net or knowledge structure for each of those concepts. By clicking on a related concept, Semnet® will show the user the individual net in which the related concept becomes the central or core concept.

This cascading metaphor of connecting *instances* through active links to other instances is a unique feature of Semnet® software that makes it ideal for use as a collaborative thinking tool. Different users can create individual concept maps (or nets) that can be merged together to create a larger and more encompassing net through a social knowledge construction process that involves collaboration. Collaboration in this context implies the clarification of ideas through the use of concept maps. According to the Semnet® Research Group (1991), Semnet® software "can support collaborative endeavors such as curriculum development by teams of professionals." Curriculum developers can form a community of practice and communicate their expertise by constructing individual concept maps to represent a model curriculum and then use these maps as a shared resource to initiate a discussion aimed at synthesizing ideas. Novak (1990) emphasized how this process can facilitate building a science curriculum, for example, around the *major conceptual schemes* of science (reflecting the psychological structure of knowledge) instead of the traditional topical (logical) arrangement of the science curriculum currently in place. He further elaborates (referencing Wandersee, 1990) by stating that "concept maps can be used to present both a global view of a K–12 science curriculum built around basic science concepts, and varying degrees of magnification to the level of a specific science lesson with each map showing key concepts and concept relationships necessary to understand the larger or the more explicit domain of science" (p. 944). Semnet® software provides the technological potential of dynamically linking individual maps to construct a larger map, making it possible to "telescope from a macro to a microscopic concept map for the domain to be studied" (Novak, 1990, p. 944). Using Semnet® software as a tool to engage in curriculum building supports the process of social negotiation that is a fundamental principle of communities of practice and what

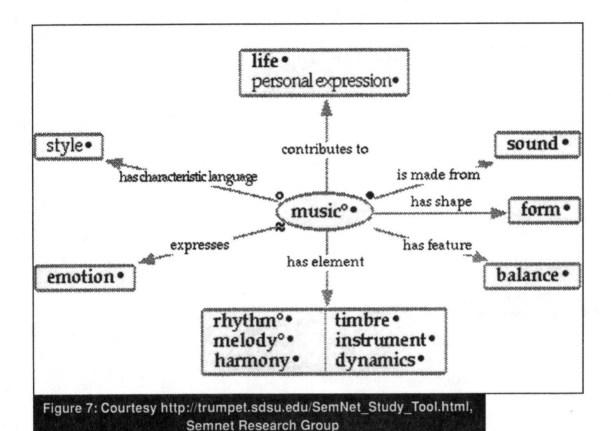

Figure 7: Courtesy http://trumpet.sdsu.edu/SemNet_Study_Tool.html, Semnet Research Group

makes this exercise truly collaborative. This process can have major implications for classroom use. Teachers can engage students in collaborative activities that require the construction of individual computer-based concept maps to be used as blueprints for the realization of a larger task (project) that requires the integration of these maps into a single comprehensive structure.

To summarize, Table 2 outlines the three concept mapping strategies discussed above (concept mapping as a learning strategy, concept mapping as an instructional strategy, and concept mapping as a collaborative thinking tool) and their implications for instruction and classroom use.

Conclusion

Concept mapping is a powerful and effective cognitive tool that encourages students to organize their knowledge about a content domain and to be explicit about the nature of relationships between ideas (Spoehr, 1994). Concept mapping forces students to think meaningfully about the content domain in order to identify and verify important concepts, classify concepts, describe the relationship between concepts and assess its meaning, analyze the nature of the relationship, and form the link or connection which engages the most critical thinking (Jonassen, 1996). Depending on how concept mapping is utilized in an instructional context, it can alter the en-

coding process that in turn affects the learning outcome and performance of students. As a learning strategy, concept mapping can support organizational strategies, elaboration strategies, and comprehension monitoring strategies in varying degrees of complexity. Computer-based concept mapping tools such as Inspiration® and Semnet® can facilitate these learning strategies by helping students create propositional and semantic networks to articulate and communicate their meaningful understanding and hence structural representation of a knowledge domain and by providing rich information structures that can synthesis, and evaluation of knowledge.

As an instructional strategy, teachers can use computer-based concept mapping to engage students in a generative, preinstructional dialogue about concepts and principles of a knowledge domain and subsequently capture this dialogue in a concept map to create an advance organizer of the content to be studied based on students' input. Teachers can also use this advance organizer as a diagnostic tool to create appropriate lesson plans aimed at clarifying misconceptions that students may have about the knowledge domain under study. Finally, computer-based concept mapping can be used as a collaborative tool to foster teamwork and facilitate project-based activities by encouraging the sharing, discussion, and integration of spatial representations of content in order to construct a more cohesive and comprehensive knowledge structure.

CONCEPT MAPPING CAN BE USED AS A:	SPECIFIC ACTIVITIES INCLUDE:	THESE ACTIVITIES CAN FACILITATE THE FOLLOWING CLASSROOM APPLICATION:
Learning strategy or a study tool	Planning, organizing, outlining, webbing, knowledge mapping, reflection, exploration	Writing a paper Conducting research Designing a science experiment Outlining a chapter Creating story Webs
Instructional strategy or a teaching tool	Planning, organizing, brainstorming, preinstruction assessment exercise	Preparing an advance organizer Preparing a lesson plan Organizing assessment Supporting generative learning activities
Collaborative thinking tool	Curriculum planning, project planning, collaboration, exploration, reflection, knowledge building	Creating communities of practice Facilitating interdisciplinary projects Collecting and organizing information and resources

Table 2

REFERENCES

Anderson-Inman, L., & Zeitz, L. (1993). Computer-based concept mapping: Active studying for active learners. *The Computer Teacher, 21*(1), 6–8, 10–11.

Dagher, Z., & Crossman, G. W. (1990, April). *The nature of verbal explanations given by science teachers.* Paper presented at the annual meeting of the National Association for Research in Science Teaching, Atlanta, GA.

Gagne, E. D., Yekovich, C. W., & Yekovich, F. R. (1993). *The cognitive psychology of school learning.* New York: HarperCollins College Publishers.

Hannafin, M. J. (1992). Emerging technologies, ISD, and learning environments: Critical perspectives. *Educational Technology Research & Development, 40*(1), 49–63.

Inspiration® Software, Inc. www.inspiration.com.

Jonassen, D. H., & Tessmer, M. (1997). An outcomes-based taxonomy for instructional systems design, evaluation, and research. *Training Research Journal, 2,* 11–46.

Jonassen, D. H. (1996). *Computers in the Classroom: Mindtools for Critical Thinking.* Englewood Cliffs, NJ: Prentice Hall Inc.

Jonassen, D. H. (1988). Designing structured hypertext and structuring access to hypertext. *Educational Technology, 28*(11), 13–16.

Norman, D. (1978) Notes toward a theory of complex learning. In A. M. Lesgold, J. W. Pelligrino, S. D. Fokkema, & R. Glaser (Eds.), *Cognitive psychology and education.* Norwell, MA: Plenum Publishers.

Novak, J. D. (1990). Concept mapping: A useful tool for science education. *Journal of Research in Science Teaching, 27*(10), 937–949.

Parsons, J. J., & Oja, D. (1996). *Computer concepts.* CTI, Cambridge, MA.

Semnet Research Group, Inc. (1991). *Semnet study tool.* http://trumpet.sdsu.edu/semnet.html

McClure J., Sonak, B., & Suen, H. (1995). Concept map assessment of classroom learning: Reliability, validity, and logistical practicality. *Journal of Research in Science Teaching, 36*(4), 475–492.

Spoehr, K. T. (1994). Enhancing the acquisition of conceptual structures through hypermedia. In K. McGilly (Ed.), *Classroom lessons: Integrating cognitive theory and classroom practice.* Cambridge, MA: MIT Press.

Symington, D. & Novak, J. D. (1982). Teaching children how to learn. *Educational magazine, 39*(5), 13–16.

Wandersee, J. H. (1990). Concept Mapping and the Cartography of Cognition. *Journal of Research in Science Teaching, 27*(10), 923–936.

Weinstein, C. E., & Mayer, R. E. (1986). The Teaching of Learning Strategies. In Wittrock (Ed.), *Handbook of research on teaching.* New York: Macmillan Publishing.

Nada Dabbagh is an assistant professor in the instructional technology program at George Mason University. She teaches graduate courses in instructional design, Web-based instruction, and learning theory. She is currently working on a book that examines the pedagogical implications of the use of Web-based course management tools in designing and developing online learning environments.

Dr. Nada Dabbagh Assistant Professor Instructional Design and Development MS-5D6, Commerce II Building Graduate School of Education George Mason University Fairfax, VA 22030 ndabbagh@gmu.edu

From *Journal of Computing in Teacher Education,* Winter 2001, pp. 16-23. © 2001 by International Society for Technology in Education. Reprinted by permission.

Teachers Bridge to Constructivism

Kathryn Alesandrini and Linda Larson

People learn while doing," says the constructivist update of an old adage. Teachers, however, often learn without doing when it comes to learning about constructivism and related teaching methods. Many teachers have not participated in a constructivist-type classroom or even seen it modeled, so they tend to teach as they were taught. Until teachers experience constructivism themselves, they may not be equipped to plan and facilitate constructivist activities by their students. In this article, we discuss and illustrate the value of using a constructivist bridge-building activity to help teachers make the transition to constructivist classrooms.

What Teachers Need to Know about Constructivism

Constructivism has become a popular term that can refer to many things, including the way teachers teach and the way students learn. Some have dubbed the constructivist approach that we describe "radical constructivism" (Spiro et al. 1991), but we refer to it simply as "constructivism." Indeed, the constructivist approach posits a radical departure from traditional teaching practices (Brooks and Brooks 1993; Jonassen, Peck, and Wilson 1999; Kafai and Resnick 1996; Lambert 1995) as the following basic tenets of constructivism illustrate:

Learning results from exploration and discovery. Constructivists see learning as a process of actively exploring new information and constructing meaning from the new information by linking it to previous knowledge and experience. Throughout the learning experience, meaning is constructed and reconstructed based on the previous experiences of the learner. In the constructivist paradigm, the teacher's role is not to lecture or provide structured activities that guide students, step by step, to mastery of some teacher-imposed goal. Instead, teachers in a constructivist classroom are called to function as facilitators who coach learners as they blaze their own paths toward personally meaningful goals.

Learning is a community activity facilitated by shared inquiry. Collaboration and cooperative inquiry have proved to be effective educational strategies, yet conventional methods often limit interactivity to cooperative discussion groups. Constructivism favors collaborative work groups that actually work together interactively to accomplish shared goals. Collaboration goes beyond cooperation, because it requires learners to reflect upon and share their insights with the group (cf. Henderson 1996; Driscoll 1994). Collaboration facilitates each member's ability to see problems from multiple perspectives or different points of view. Group members constantly "negotiate meaning" during the constructivist activity to adjust to the developing solution of the problem. The product evolves and changes as a result of the interaction between group members.

Learning occurs during the constructivist process. Rather than requiring an understanding *before* applying that understanding to the construction of something, students in a constructivist classroom learn concepts *while* exploring their application. During this application process, students explore various solutions and learn through discovery. Learners play an ongoing, active, and critical role in assessment. Teachers evaluate end products in traditional assessment, but the constructivist approach to evaluation emphasizes self-assessment. In constructivist classrooms, learners articulate what they have learned as it relates to their prior knowledge. In fact, it is through the self-assessment activities of reflection and verbalization that learners actually realize the meaning of what they have experienced.

Another major difference from the traditional approach is that assessment is done throughout the entire learning process, not just at the end. Formative evaluation (assessment that occurs throughout the learning process) therefore plays a key role in helping learners as they experiment during the constructivist activity. To the constructivist, the process of evaluation is as important, if not more important, than the outcomes of evaluation.

Learning results from participation in authentic activities. Constructivists believe that learning should be based on activities and problems that students might encounter in the "real world." In traditional classrooms, however, activities often are decontexualized to the point that they bear little resemblance to meaningful, authentic activities.

Outcomes of constructivist activities are unique and varied. A traditional hands-on activity that is teacher guided often results in student products that essentially "all look alike." In contrast, constructivism posits that learners create knowledge from new information in light of their previous experiences. Since each learner brings a distinct background of experience, results of constructivist projects will differ. Typically, no two products from a constructivist activity look anything alike.

Constructivism clearly represents a fundamental change in all aspects of the teaching and learning process. Teachers cannot be expected to embrace these changes without adequate preparation involving hands-on experience and modeling in the adoption of these new methods.

Why Bridge Building for Teachers?

Based on the premise that the best way to learn about constructivism is to experience it firsthand, we devised a simple constructivist activity—building a paper bridge—that teachers could experience to learn the basics about constructivism. A follow-up authentic activity allowed the teachers to take the next step and develop a constructivist activity for their own classrooms.

In the bridge-building activity, teachers work in small groups to plan, construct, and reflect on building a paper bridge (figures 1-3). The challenge is for each group to create, using only newspaper, tape, and rubber bands, a unique structure strong enough to hold at least a 16-ounce bottle of water. Prior to actually building the bridge, each group specifies several additional objectives and develops a scoring rubric.

The bridge-building activity consists of a 10-step "constructivist activity" process closely related to the design technology process (Dunn and Larson 1998). The constructivist activity process entails five major components: investigation, invention, implementation, evaluation, and celebration. Investigation includes the development of context, clarification of the task, and inquiry through questioning and research. Invention consists of planning and realizing or building a model. Implementation sometimes overlaps with invention and occurs through the process of realizing or building a model and later modifying it as needed. Evaluation refers to the activities of testing, interpreting, and reflecting on the experience. The last major component, celebration, is described below along with the preceding nine steps illustrated with comments from several teams of teachers.

1. *Contextualizing.* Working in small groups, teachers draw on their past experiences in deciding how the team will proceed. "Bridges are normally sturdy; they have support poles. We integrated multiculturalism in our design by designing human figures as the support base" (Team A).

2. *Clarifying.* Teams determine what they needed to know to build the bridge. "We need to know how bridges are structured, how weight is held by a bridge" (Team A).

3. *Inquiring.* Teachers conduct research by posing relevant questions and searching credible sources for answers. "One member of our group found a Web site that outlined all components and typical designs of bridges. From our research we have concluded that our bridge will consist of vertical and horizontal beams" (Team B).

4. *Planning.* Teachers sketch their plans on paper and may even build a test-case model. "Since we decided to create the bridge using beams, we used pencils, pens, and tape to create our premodel. Our premodel proved that our bridge would be easy to construct, functional, and sturdy" (Team B).

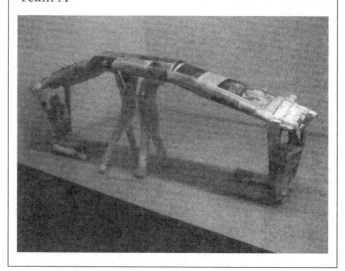

Team A

5. *Realizing.* Using only newspaper, tape, and rubber bands, teachers construct bridges to achieve their objectives. No two bridges look alike since groups are not following a cookbook-type recipe for the project. Each group produces a unique creation to achieve its own objectives. "Once we knew how to assemble the bridge from our premodel, we started the construction process" (Team B).

6. *Testing.* Teachers test the model bridge and record observations. "We tested our model by placing a 20-ounce water bottle on top, and it held up fine as long as the dolls' legs were in the right position. But there was not enough diagonal support" (Team A). "Our bridge did not hold the bottle of water. We decided to create a frame for our bridge" (Team C).

7. *Modifying.* Teachers make necessary modifications to achieve stated objectives. "We repositioned the two center supports to face a different direction and better support the bridge" (Team A). "We added the frame which worked" (Team C).

8. *Interpreting.* Teachers interpret the results of their tests. "This is a great model for building a bridge out of newspaper. This bridge was easy to construct, sturdy, and structurally sound, fast to construct, and looked very much like a bridge" (Team B).

9. *Reflecting.* Teachers evaluate their bridges by applying the rubrics they created earlier. "I felt our bridge represented our group, because we had a Latina, an Asian, a Caucasian, and an African American. We used newspapers in English, Spanish, Japanese, and Chinese. I really felt passionate and proud of our bridge. I felt that its main purpose, which was to represent different cultures coming together, was clear" (Team A).

Team C

constructivism. Of the four teams cited here, 82 percent found the activity "very or extremely useful." Over 90 percent of the participants say they enjoyed the social interaction of the activity.

Assessment within a Constructivist Framework

Teachers actively engage in the assessment process from the beginning, when they specify objectives and write rubrics to score the results of the constructivist activity. As stated, the only imposed requirement is that the bridges be strong enough to hold at least a 16-ounce bottle of water. In addition to the strength criterion, each group specifies three other objectives and related criteria for their rubrics. Often the criteria reflect the values, experiences, and backgrounds of group members. For example, Team A selected multiculturalism as one of their criteria to reflect the cultural diversity of the group. Their bridge looked like a parade float, with an arch supported by human figures from different cultures. Other criteria have included design creativity, design simplicity, bridge span, conservation of resources, and a host of other factors. Each group of teachers uses the rubric they initially create to score their final product. Not surprisingly, each group generally achieves a perfect or near-perfect score. After scoring their own team's bridge, teams participate in a "gallery walk" in which each team uses both their own and the other teams' rubrics to score the bridges produced by others. Teachers realize that their "excellent" work would likely receive a poor or failing grade when held to a different standard. For example, Team B's more traditional bridge structure with beams did not adhere to the multicultural or creativity criteria of Team A and would therefore be graded down if Team A's rubric were used to score it. The experience helps teachers appreciate the limitations of traditional grading practices in a constructivist classroom.

Team B

10. *Celebration.* Teachers in the small groups share their accomplishments by presenting results to the larger group. "We shared our rubric with the group, explaining our criteria for a [top] score of 4. The group agreed that we earned a 4" (Team A). Another teacher wrote, "Celebration and sharing was the best! It gave us a sense of pride and accomplishment."

Most teachers who participate in this 10-step bridge-building activity report that it helps them learn about

Taking the Next Step: Constructivism in the Classroom

In the follow-up activity to bridge building, teachers prepare an authentic constructivist activity for their own students on any topic of their choosing. The only requirements are that the activity be authentic and that it address one or more skills in the subject matter frameworks. Teachers work individually to structure an activity according to the same 10-step process they used to build the paper bridge. They begin by setting objectives and creating a scoring rubric that both they and their students may use to assess the final products. They then plan the activity, create a model, and reflect upon their respective projects. Finally, they try out the activity with their own students.

Prior to the bridge-building activity, a common misconception among teachers is that a hands-on activity is synonymous with a constructivist activity. Many hands-on activities, of course, don't allow for multiple solutions and outcomes—students are expected to follow the teacher's directions and create a copy-cat product rather than generating their own unique productions. While less than one-third of teachers surveyed felt confident that they could create constructivist activities for their students prior to the bridge-building activity, over 90 percent successfully created a true constructivist activity on the first try after it. We believe that this success results from the modeling they experienced during the bridge-building activity.

The benefits of constructivism are reinforced as teachers observe the impact of their authentic constructivist projects on their students. A high school math teacher, for example, devised a geometry activity that requires students to construct 3-D scenes or objects from three-dimensional polygons. The teacher's model consisted of a small paper-flower garden. Students used paper pyramids, cubes, decahedrons, and more to construct a wide array of unique characters: a dinosaur, clown, rat, puppy, flower, turtle, and so forth. In another project, a sixth grade teacher created a phonogram chart to help students understand hieroglyphics used by the ancient Egyptians. Her students worked in teams to create unique charts, which they used to code their own names and common words. These teachers reported that their students enjoyed the constructivist project, just as they had, and gained a sense of accomplishment in what they created.

Most teachers find it difficult to create a truly constructivist activity for their students. As one participant explained, "The activity that we created was very difficult. It really makes you examine your subject thoroughly and understand how difficult these concepts are for students to master. The inclusion of constructivist activities greatly increases a student's involvement in the topic."

The bridge-building activity helps teachers literally see the unique productions that result when team members bring their own background and experience to bear on the creative process. They witness that constructivism goes beyond the typical hands-on activity. They also learn that assessment is relative—grades result from applying a rubric that relates to specified criteria or objectives. Perhaps most important, teachers appreciate the pure enjoyment joined with a sense of pride and accomplishment that result from constructivist activities.

Key words: constructivism, classroom activities, assessment, teaching process, facilitation

REFERENCES

Brooks, J. G., and M. C. Brooks. 1993. *The case for constructivist classrooms.* Alexandria, VA: Association for Supervision and Curriculum Development.

Driscoll, M. P. 1994. *Psychology of learning for instruction.* Boston, MA: Allyn & Bacon.

Dunn, S., and R. Larson. 1998. *Design technology: Children's engineering.* Philadelphia: The Palmer Press.

Henderson, J. G. 1996. *Reflective teaching.* 2nd ed. Englewood Cliffs, NJ: Merrill.

Jonassen, D. H., K. L. Peck, and B. G. Wilson. 1999. *Learning with technology: A constructivist approach.* Columbus, OH: Prentice Hall.

Kafai, Y. B., and M. Resnick. 1996. *Constructionism in practice: Designing, thinking and learning in a digital world.* Mahwah, NJ: Lawrence Erlbaum Associates.

Lambert, L. 1995. *The constructivist leader.* New York: Teachers College Press.

Spiro, R., P. Feltovich, M. Jacobson, and R. Coulson. 1991. Knowledge representation, content specification, and the development of skill in situation-specific knowledge assembly: Some constructivist issues as they relate to cognitive flexibility and hypertext. *Educational Technology* 31 (9): 22–25.

Kathryn Alesandrini is a professor of instructional design and technology at California State University, Los Angeles. Linda Larson is a full-time lecturer in the Department of Educational Psychology at California State University, in Long Beach.

From *The Clearing House*, January/February 2002, pp. 118-121. Reprinted with permission of the Helen Dwight Reid Educational Foundation. Published by Heldref Publications, 1319 Eighteenth St., NW, Washington, DC 20036-1802. © 2002.

Making Students as Important as Standards

Educators can align curriculum, instruction, and assessment with both standards and students in mind so that standards serve teaching and learning—instead of the other way around.

Richard W. Strong, Harvey F. Silver, and Matthew J. Perini

The Geneva, New York, school district, which serves more than 95 percent of its county's low-income families, is celebrating its recent awards: the U.S. Department of Education's Model Professional Development Award and an Outstanding Title I School award for Geneva's North Street Elementary School.

In LaGrange, Georgia, 6th graders at Long Cane Middle School have achieved gains of 20.5 percent on state tests in reading, 18.6 percent in math, and 15.1 percent in language arts.

And in Bossier Parish, a mid-sized city in northwest Louisiana, the district's high school students have just tied for the lowest failure rate on the state's LEAP 21 test—Louisiana's newest and most rigorous standards-based test.

> **Stop writing curriculum documents and start writing curriculum that students want to learn.**

A similar pattern involving the recent success of students whose performance had been average and below average is emerging in Illinois, Oregon, Delaware, New Jersey, New York, and Georgia, where schools have organized their work in improving student performance around the concept of double alignment—the idea that curriculum, instruction,

and assessment need to be aligned to both students and standards.

Why Double Alignment?

For almost 25 years, alignment has meant organizing teaching around goals, aims, objectives, and, now, standards. When state tests began to appear, teachers and administrators became more focused than ever, making sure that curriculum, instruction, and assessment were tied closely to the new standards and test items. Although standards have helped educators forge a common vision, they have also left some students believing that schools only care about their test scores. If we hope to see the kinds of improvement that tests and standards call for, then educators need to put students—their differences, interests, struggles, and successes—at the center of education. But how are educators to accomplish this double alignment? Our current work in schools suggests five guidelines:

- Make standards simple and deep.
- Use models of difference like learning styles and multiple intelligences to help all students succeed.
- Increase the role of assessment and conversation to help students identify and overcome difficulties.

- Stop writing curriculum documents and start writing curriculum that students want to learn.
- Collaborate with colleagues to determine what kinds of work are easy and difficult for students.

Standards: Simple and Deep

This is not a call to dispense with standards. Rather, standards can serve teaching and learning—instead of the other way around—when educators develop a clear and manageable vision of what they want students to understand and be able to do. In short, schools need standards that keep educators focused on achievement but that leave them the time and flexibility they need to pay attention to the individuals in their classrooms. Through six years of research into state tests and standards, we have found that no matter the content area, almost all states' test items assess a relatively small, but important, skill set. We call these core skills the Hidden Skills of Academic Literacy.

Reading and study skills include the abilities to

- Collect and organize ideas and information through note taking;
- Use abstract vocabulary; and
- Read and interpret visual data.

FIGURE 1

The Strategic Index

Strategy	Purpose and Description	Learning Style	Multiple Intelligences
Etch-A-Sketch	A note-taking device using symbols and discussion of key ideas and important details	Interpersonal Self-expressive Mastery	Verbal-linguistic Spatial Interpersonal Intrapersonal
Four-Way Reporting and Recording	A strategy that uses a jigsaw structure and a variety of note-taking devices for collecting and sharing information	Self-expressive Mastery Understanding Interpersonal	Verbal-linguistic Interpersonal Spatial Logical-mathematical
Power Notes	A note-taking device for organizing information according to the power of the ideas recorded	Mastery Understanding	Verbal-linguistic Logical-mathematical

*Adapted with permission from *So Each May Learn: Integrating Learning Styles and Multiple Intelligences* (p. 109) by H. F. Silver, R. W. Strong, and M. J. Perini, 2000. Alexandria, VA: ASCD. Copyright © 2000 by Silver Strong & Associates, L.L.C.

Reflective skills include the abilities to

- Plan effectively;
- Critique performance against set criteria; and
- Persevere when work becomes difficult or complex.

Thinking skills include the abilities to

- Make reasonable inferences, form hypotheses, and test those hypotheses;
- Analyze and apply models and concepts; and
- Conduct a comparative analysis.

Communication skills include the abilities to

- Construct well-formed explanations;
- Write effectively in the following genres: personal, narrative, comparison, problem and solution, and argument; and
- Write effectively about two or more readings.

When schools focused their instruction around this simple but deep set of skills, teachers found that these standards gave them increased freedom to select the content, texts, and projects that would best produce new learning for their students.

Models of Difference

Schools have at their disposal two powerful models for understanding learning differences and developing student potential: learning styles and multiple intelligences. The concept of learning styles stems from the work of Carl Jung (1923) and, later, that of Katharine Briggs and Isabel Briggs Myers (1962/1998). Learning styles models provide educators with a map of how different students learn best. For example, our learning style model (Silver & Hanson, 1998) documents four learning styles: a mastery style described as realistic, practical, and results-oriented; an understanding style that tends to be theoretical, logical, and knowledge-oriented; a self-expressive style characterized as imaginative, insightful, and future-oriented; and an interpersonal style that seeks learning that is personal, experiential, and socially oriented.

Howard Gardner's (1983, 1999) multiple intelligences model describes eight ways in which humans can be smart. Unlike the learning styles model, the multiple intelligences model focuses on the content of learning (language, math and logic, music, spatial relations, bodily/kinesthetic, social interaction, self-understanding, and the world of nature) and its relationship to the various disciplines.

By tapping into the power of these models and using them to guide decisions about teaching and learning,

educators have succeeded in reaching all students. Consider the following examples:

Getting to know students systemically. Most of the schools we work with really know their students. At the beginning of the year, teachers ask students to reflect on and answer five simple questions:

- What are you good at?
- What do you do for fun?
- What interests you?
- When school is hard, what makes it hard?
- Five years from now, what do you want to be like?

After students have reflected on their learning strengths, interests, difficulties, and goals, schools use learning style instruments like the Learning Preference Inventory (Hanson & Silver, 2000) and multiple intelligences instruments like the Multiple Intelligences Indicator (Silver, Strong, & Perini, 2001) to develop a learning profile for each student. Schools keep all this information—each student's self-reflection, learning style profile, and multiple intelligences profile—in a permanent record so that teachers can determine how to engage students who are particularly difficult to reach. The information is especially valuable when working with underachievers. Teachers use students' style and intelligence profiles to determine why specific types of

FIGURE 2

Task Rotation on Fossil Evidence

Mastery	Interpersonal
What can we learn about the past by studying fossils?	Some animals are omnivores; they eat both meat and plants. Observe yourself as you eat a strawberry and a slice of steak. How did you chew differently? What teeth did you use? How did your jaw move? Describe the differences you observed. Explain the differences and tell why they might exist.

Understanding	Self-Expressive
Compare pictures of dinosaurs. Explain how the creatures are alike/different in structure (head, body, teeth, eyes, etc.). Explain how these differences helped the animal survive and adapt.	You have been on an archaeological dig and have discovered the bones of a new dinosaur. A. Draw a picture of the dinosaur. B. Write a riddle or set of clues so that other scientists may properly classify the creature by its characteristics.

learning prove difficult for particular students and to develop effective prescriptions that accommodate students' preferences and strengths. For example, knowing that mastery-style learners focus on facts and details but often have trouble making inferences when reading makes prescription both easier and more effective: Capitalize on the mastery-style learner's strengths (thrives on modeling and practice, looks for regular feedback, and likes direct instruction) to help the student develop the needed inference skills.

Using styles and intelligences to select appropriate strategies. When Carl Carrozza, a middle school science teacher in Catskill, New York, plans the next week's lessons on ecosystems, he doesn't just think about content and he doesn't just think about academic skills; he thinks about his students as well. Carrozza knows that he has students with diverse learning styles and intelligence profiles. For example, one student prefers to learn step-by-step and has a strong predilection toward all things visual, whereas another student is more interpersonal and learns best through conversation. Meanwhile, a third student loves numbers and likes to figure things out for himself. A fourth student is a dreamer with a strong ethical or intrapersonal twist. For him, everything needs to be connected to values and imagination.

Because Carrozza knows that his class includes a blend of learning

styles and multiple intelligences, and because he knows the importance of note taking for student achievement, he uses a strategic index (see fig. 1). The strategic index helps him select the note-taking strategies that he will use throughout the week to help his students learn about both note taking and biomes, while he also demonstrates his interest in the different styles and intelligences within his classroom.

> **Teachers can use students' learning styles and multiple intelligences profiles to develop effective learning prescriptions that accommodate students' preferences and strengths.**

Giving all learners the chance to succeed. Joyce Jackson, an educator who works for the Kentucky Department of Education, makes it her business to help all students in low-achieving schools succeed on the state tests. Jackson knows that the tests and standards are challenging; for example, one standard states that students should understand scientific ways of thinking and working and use those methods to solve real-life problems. Core content associated with the standard include knowing

(1) that each plant or animal has structures that serve different functions in growth and survival, (2) that scientists develop explanations using observations and what they already know about the world, and (3) that reasonable explanations are based on evidence from investigations.

> **Using conversation as an assessment tool demonstrates an interest in students—how they think and why they struggle.**

Jackson also understands that classrooms are diverse places and that different students process and apply information differently. In response, Jackson and a group of science teachers developed a set of task rotations (Silver, Hanson, Strong, & Schwartz, 1996) associated with the standards and test items. The task rotations allow students with different learning styles to acquire the content and skills in the ways that best match their needs and strengths as learners (see fig. 2). Teachers can use task rotations in various ways; for example, to build the deepest level of comprehension, they may ask students to complete all four tasks. Alternatively, teachers may ask struggling learners to choose from the rotation those tasks with which

FIGURE 3

Questions Tied to Factors in Student Motivation: *To Kill a Mockingbird*

Success What are my standards?	**Ideas** Prejudice Courage	**Skills** Persuasive writing Character description
Curiosity What questions and problems will I use to organize my unit?	• Where does prejudice come from and what can we do to overcome it? • What makes a great persuader and how can you become one? • How can an author create living characters with only a pen and some paper?	
Relationships What contexts can I create to make learning meaningful?	• Improving teaching • Newspaper reporting • Legal argument	
Originality What products can my students create to help them learn my standard (persuasive writing about character and prejudice)?	• A letter to Miss Caroline on how to be a better teacher. • A summation to the jury. • An editorial arguing that Tom Robinson be found not guilty.	

they feel most comfortable. Then teachers can use these tasks as bridges to help learners develop their thinking in other, less-preferred styles.

Assessment and Conversation

When Jerry Huels, a high-school mathematics teacher in Ladue, Missouri, became frustrated with the quality of his students' mathematical explanations, he discussed the issue with them. He learned that his students were equally frustrated and found their own explanations confused, confusing, and downright boring. This gave Huels an idea. Tapping into his math library, he found a selection of general audience math books that explain math problems, puzzles, and solutions in clear and compelling language. Huels and his students examined samples of the authors' writings and kept track of the techniques that the authors used to achieve clarity and maintain readers' interest. His students then used these models and their analyses of them to improve and revise their own explanations.

Huels is not curtailing his commitment to standards by using conversation as an assessment tool. Rather, a simple review of his lesson shows that students are building four of the Hidden Skills of Academic Literacy, including the ability to use abstract vocabulary, critique and revise performance against set criteria, analyze and apply models and con-

cepts, and communicate effectively within key genres (mathematical explanations).

Just as important as standards, however, are students. Unlike purely cognitive models of instruction, Huels's work demonstrates his interest in students—how they think and why they struggle.

Curriculum for Student Engagement

Educators have mapped, benchmarked, and analyzed gaps in their schools' curriculums for years—valuable work, to be sure. The time has come, however, to pay attention to what motivates students when we design curriculum. When we conducted research on what motivates students in the classroom (Strong, Silver, & Robinson, 1995), we discovered that four factors play a significant part in student motivation and that each of these factors tells us something important about curriculum design.

Success. Students want to feel competent and believe that their efforts pay off and are recognized, so standards should be clear. To achieve this clarity, educators can organize curriculum around a few powerful content ideas and teach to the Hidden Skills of Academic Literacy.

Curiosity. Students want to feel engaged by meaningful questions, enigmas, mysteries, and conundrums. Educators should provide

students with thoughtful questions and interesting problems to explore.

Originality. Students want to create unique products. Educators should design assessments that allow students to enunciate their own visions and points of view on the subjects that they study.

Relationships. Students want to see the relationships between what they are studying and their own experiences and futures. Educators should connect standards to students' lives, concerns, and futures as workers and citizens.

Thus, designing curriculum that engages students means addressing the factors that contribute to student motivation. Figure 3 illustrates one teacher's efforts to address these factors in a unit on Harper Lee's novel, *To Kill a Mockingbird* (1960).

By focusing on student motivation as well as on standards, teachers have created units that have not only increased student engagement but that have also positively influenced student performance on state tests.

Collaborating on Double Alignment

In many of the schools we work with, teachers on grade level or department teams meet once each marking period to negotiate assessment contracts—agreements on the kinds of work that are most crucial to helping students meet the standards. For example, a team of 4th grade teachers agreed that students should produce the following work for English language arts:

- At least one retelling each week,
- At least one explanation of a character's actions each month,
- At least one story each month,
- At least one personal narrative written about a memory each month.

Once teachers create these contracts, they select four students at various levels of achievement (high, high-average, low-average, low) as case studies. The students' work serves as the basis for collaborative decision making about how to revise instruction to meet various students' needs.

Double alignment requires school leaders who provide teachers with the time and resources to assess and plan for student differences.

Assessment contracts are not for teachers only. Administrators also get involved, helping teachers construct realistic time lines and secure adequate planning time for reaching the systemwide goal of helping all students succeed. Indeed, as Carol Ann Tomlinson and Susan Demirsky Allan show in *Leadership for Differentiating Schools and Classrooms*

(2000), administrators play a crucial role in responding to students' differences and needs. Double alignment requires school leaders who use such models as the Hidden Skills of Academic Literacy to provide focus for instruction and a results-centered approach to assessment, ongoing professional development linked to differentiation, and the time and resources teachers need to assess and plan for student differences.

When leaders provide sufficient support, schools change for the better. Good teaching flourishes. Rich dialogue about improvement emerges. Structures such as assessment contracts foster buildingwide discussion about students and their needs. Curriculum does more than cover—it motivates. And, even as test scores improve, students no longer harbor the suspicion that tests are the only things that their schools care about.

References

Briggs, K. C., & Myers, I. B. (1962/1998). *Myers-Briggs type indicator* (form M). Palo Alto, CA: Consulting Psychologists Press. (Original work published 1962)

Gardner, H. (1983). *Frames of mind: The theory of multiple intelligences*. New York: BasicBooks.

Gardner, H. (1999). *Intelligence reframed: Multiple intelligences for the 21st century*. New York: Simon & Schuster.

Hanson, J. R., & Silver, H. F. (2000). *The Hanson-Silver learning preference inventory*. Trenton, NJ: Thoughtful Education Press.

Jung, C. (1923). *Psychological types* (H. G. Baynes, Trans.). New York: Harcourt, Brace.

Silver, H. F., & Hanson, J. R. (1998). *Learning styles and strategies* (3rd ed.). Woodbridge, NJ: Thoughtful Education Press.

Silver, H. F., Hanson, J. R., Strong, R. W., & Schwartz, P. B. (1996). *Teaching styles and strategies* (3rd ed.). Woodbridge, NJ: Thoughtful Education Press.

Silver, H. F., Strong, R. W., & Perini, M. J. (2001). *The multiple intelligences indicator*. Trenton, NJ: Thoughtful Education Press.

Strong, R. W., Silver, H. F., & Robinson, A. (1995, September). What do students want (and what really motivates them)? *Educational Leadership, 53*(1), 8–12.

Tomlinson, C. A., & Allan, S. D. (2000). *Leadership for differentiating schools and classrooms*. Alexandria, VA: ASCD.

Richard W. Strong is Vice President and **Harvey F. Silver** is President, Silver Strong & Associates, Crestwood Professional Building, 941 Whitehorse Ave., Ste. 24, Trenton, NJ 08610; (800) 962-4432; questions@silverstrong.com.
Matthew J. Perini is Director of Publishing, Thoughtful Education Press, 334 Kinderkamack Rd., 2nd Fl., Oradell, NJ 07649; mperini@ silverstrong.com.

From *Educational Leadership*, November 2001, pp. 56-61. Reprinted with permission of the Association for Supervision and Curriculum Development. © 2001 by ASCD. All rights reserved.

The Integration of Instructional Technology into Public Education: Promises and Challenges

Rodney S. Earle
Contributing Editor

Introduction

Will instructional technology (IT) ever be integrated into public schools? An interesting question—or rather a series of related questions of interest to educators and parents: What do we mean by "instructional technology"? What is integration? What is the current status of IT in classrooms? Are there constraints or barriers to integration? What are the effects of preservice teacher preparation and inservice professional development? How does one proceed with technology integration? How do we apply the lessons learned from "older" technologies to the "newer" technologies of the last two decades?

This article will address each of these questions in order to help us to grasp the prospects for the integration of instructional technology into public education as well as to consider the promises and challenges of such a venture.

Instructional Technology Defined

What is "instructional technology"? Is it merely a synonym for computers, or does its meaning transcend hardware and software to include both physical and intellectual facets in its domain?

Let us start with trying to understand the concept of technology. Although *Webster's New Collegiate Dictionary* takes a sociological perspective in its definition of technology as "… the totality of the means employed to provide objects necessary for human sustenance and comfort" and "a technical method of achieving a practical purpose," the prevailing public definition based on current usage is "technology equals machinery." This limited focus on machinery at the expense of process ignores the true sense of technology as "the systematic application of scientific and other organized knowledge to practical tasks" (Galbraith, 1967, p. 12) and thus as a problem-solving process using human and other resources to seek solutions to human problems.

Within this broader sociological framework of technology, we find the terms "educational technology" and "instructional technology." Often used interchangeably, both share a common interest in the processes of human learning and teaching, with some variations in definitions and levels of complexity, depending upon one's personal viewpoint. For convenience and consistency, we will most likely blend elements of the two terms, but use "instructional technology" as our primary focus in this article.

Instructional technology may best be understood by reviewing several definitions culled from the writings of several scholars in the field:

[Instructional technology] is concerned with improving the effectiveness and efficiency of learning in educational contexts, regardless of the nature or substance of that learning.... Solutions to instructional problems might entail social as well as machine technologies. (Cassidy, 1982, p. 1)

The systemic and systematic application of strategies and techniques derived from behavioral and physical sciences concepts and other knowledge to the solution of instructional problems. (Gentry, 1995, p. 7)

... the media born of the communications revolution which can be used for instructional purposes along side the teacher, textbook, and blackboard... [as well as]... a systematic way of designing, carrying out, and evaluating the total process of learning and teaching in terms of specific objectives, based on research in human learning and communications, and employing a combination of human and nonhuman resources to bring about more effective instructions. (Commission on Instructional Technology, 1970, p. 19)

... the application of our scientific knowledge about human learning to the practical tasks of teaching and learning. (Heinich *et al.*, 1993, p. 16)

... a complex, integrated process involving people, procedures, ideas, devices, and organizations for analyzing problems, and devising, implementing, evaluating, and managing solutions to those problems involved in all aspects of human learning. (AECT, 1977, p. 1)

Instructional technology is the theory and practice of design, development, utilization, management, and evaluation processes and resources for learning. (Seels & Richey, 1994, p. 9)

Despite these more comprehensive viewpoints from the literature that instructional technology encompasses the broader processes of teaching and learning, the prevailing public perspective incorporates instructional technology as a synonym for computer technology. In other words, as noted above, technology means computers in the minds of many. That myopic view has generated some of the problems related to integration, in particular, the focus on access to hardware at the expense of effective pedagogy, as if one particular medium is the panacea for the challenges facing education. Isn't this a *déjà vu* experience for the field of educational technology? Haven't most technological innovations in our past concentrated on hardware rather than the process? Think back forty years, if, like me, you've been involved in the field that long. Remember instructional television? Federal and state funding loaded schools with television sets, with very little attention to pedagogical processes and professional development for teachers. We

cannot assume that, just because adequate resources have been obtained, integration would naturally follow.

However, since the challenges of integrating instructional design and other *technological processes* into teacher practices have been addressed adequately elsewhere (Branch, 1994; Driscoll, Klein, & Sherman, 1994; Earle, 1994, 1998; Reiser, 1994), the focus of our discussion here will be on aspects of the integration of new computer and communications technologies into schools.

The Current Status of Classroom Technology

A nationwide survey of teachers and superintendents commissioned by Jostens Learning Corporation (1997) indicated that the computer revolution has had a tremendous impact in the classroom. Surprisingly, however, the emphasis was on student access to information outside the classroom and improved student motivation, not on specific academic achievement. In fact, fewer than half of the teachers used computers for instructional purposes, rather than word-processing, spreadsheets, or graphics for personal productivity only. Differing priorities showed that teachers would rather see additional funding used to increase the number of computers in classrooms, while superintendents felt that teacher training would best improve computer effectiveness. A variety of other surveys (Bosch, 1993; Niess, 1991; Trotter, 1997), while reporting strong computer usage by teachers, actually indicated a lack of integrated use with the curriculum. In many instances, it has been a case of fitting the curriculum to the computer rather than the computer to the curriculum.

Let us begin with a comprehensive look at school technology in a series of articles by *Education Week* (1997), which shared several interesting facts about the state of computer technology in public education:

- "The dividends that educators can expect from this... unprecedented support for school technology... are not yet clear.... There is no guarantee that technology improves student achievement." (Trotter, 1997, p. 6)
- 43% of respondents in a survey felt that the introduction of computers into public schools was not happening fast enough. (Trotter, 1997, p. 7)
- Despite the lack of research evidence, 74% of the public and 93% of educators agreed that computers had indeed improved the quality of education, teaching, and learning. (Trotter, 1997, p. 8)
- Research on the effects of technology on student achievement offers mixed results. (Viadero, 1997, p. 12)
- Placing computers and software in classrooms is not enough. Discovering whether technology "works" is not the point. The real issue is when and under what circumstances. Like any other tool, teachers have to

come up with a strategy or pedagogy to make it work. (Viadero, 1997, p. 16)

- Wise use of technology takes adequate training time, planning, support, and teacher ownership (Viadero, 1997, p. 16)

- Money spent on school technology is wasted without an equal effort to help teachers with its use and integration into the curriculum. (Zero, 1997, p. 24)

Is it possible that blasphemies are beginning to be heard outside the church of technology? Bronner (1997) posed this question and, in describing an "intellectual backlash" and feelings of skepticism about technology use, cited several educational sources to criticize the use of "glitzy toys" and "bogus stuff" in the middle of an "educational catastrophe" where children cannot read or write. Such a backlash will be productive if it makes us re-examine how we use technology in the classroom (Pool, 1997). Bronner's comment that "schools may be overwired and children undertaught" is cause for reflection for those who feel that "new media tools offer a great promise for a new model of learning—one based on discovery, participation…, learning partnerships, and learning cultures" (p. 4).

The promise is indeed real—as illustrated by recent studies showing that new technologies have indeed transformed classrooms for K–12 students and teachers. "Around the nation teachers are using technology to create exciting and creative learning environments where students teach and learn from each other, solve problems, and collaborate on projects that put learning in a real-world context" (*GLEF Blast Newsletter*, 2001, p. 1). In a meta-analysis of the value and use of technology in K–12 education (Valdez *et al.*, 2000), the North Central Regional Laboratory found that "technology innovations are increasing the demand for reforms in teaching and learning approaches that, in turn, are having a significant impact on technology use expectations" (p. iii). The report also found a very strong connection between appropriate teacher use of technology and increased student achievement.

> Technology offers opportunities for learner-control, increased motivation, connections to the real world, and data-driven assessments tied to content standards that, when implemented systematically, enhance student achievement as measured in a variety of ways, including but not limited to standardized achievement tests. (p. iii)

Working in an appropriately designed technology-rich environment has the potential of producing a variety of positive outcomes (Tiene & Luft, 2001): improved patterns of social interaction, changes in teaching styles, more effective teaching, increased student (and perhaps, teacher) motivation, and enhanced student learning. Achieving this potential, however, is the challenge, and it requires the correct vision of technology and its integration.

A Closer Look at Technology Integration

Definitions of both terms (technology and integration), whether broad or limited, drive the problem. Computer technology is merely *one* possibility in the selection of media and the delivery mode—part of the instructional design process—not *the* end but merely one of several means to the end. Integration does not just mean placement of hardware in classrooms. If computers are merely add-on activities or fancy work sheets, where is the value (Hadley & Sheingold, 1993)? Technologies must be pedagogically sound. They must go beyond information retrieval to problem solving; allow new instructional and learning experiences not possible without them; promote deep processing of ideas; increase student interaction with subject matter; promote faculty and student enthusiasm for teaching and learning; and free up time for quality classroom interaction—in sum, improve the pedagogy. Wager (1992) argued that "the educational technology that can make the biggest difference to schools and students is not the hardware, but the process of designing effective instruction" (p. 454), which incorporates computer technology and other media appropriately.

Integrating technology is not about technology—it is primarily about content and effective instructional practices. Technology involves the tools with which we deliver content and implement practices in better ways. Its focus must be on curriculum and learning. Integration is defined not by the amount or type of technology used, but by how and why it is used.

Successful technology adoption/integration requires concerted focus on the mission of improving education for all students. It grows from the mission. As an add-on or fad, it soon withers. It must be seen as an ongoing innovative process designed to meet instructional/learning needs (Robey, 1992). Bernauer (1995) captured a significant insight when he stated that "it is not technology *per se* that has resulted in improved student outcomes, but rather how the technology was used and integrated into instructional processes" (p. 1). While noting increased student proficiency in using technology for learning rather than as technology for its own sake, he also attributed such achievements to teacher planning and expertise, recognizing that true success must be measured in terms of improvement in teaching and learning, not merely in the placement of computers in classrooms. Munoz (1993), who described herself as a technophile, emphasized the prudent, ethical use of technology and warned us to "resist the seductive force of technology to replace rather than enhance" (p. 49). She stressed that very human elements such as intuition, judgment, imagination, and creativity cannot be replaced and that technology may fail if it is viewed as change for the sake of change.

Dede (1997) reinforced this perspective by stressing that "unless other simultaneous innovations occur in pedagogy, curriculum, assessment, and school organization, the time and effort expended on instructional technology produce few improvements in educational outcomes—a result that reinforces many educators' cynicism about fads based on magical machines" (p. 13).

Fullan (2000), in a review of educational reform, reminds us that, since technology is ubiquitous, the issue is not whether, but *how* we contend with it. He stresses that as technology becomes more powerful, good teachers become more indispensable.

> Technology generates a glut of information, but it has no particular pedagogical wisdom—especially regarding new breakthroughs in cognitive science about how learners must construct their own meaning for deep understanding to occur. This means that teachers must become experts in pedagogical design. It also means that teachers must use the powers of technology, both in the classroom and in sharing with other teachers what they are learning. (p. 582)

Initially, the real power of technology probably lies in the way its use causes teachers to develop different perspectives through rethinking teaching and learning (Riedl, 1995; Ritchie & Wilburg, 1994). Teaching with technology causes teachers to confront their established beliefs about instruction and their traditional roles as classroom teachers.

Forces of Change

Kurt Lewin's (1951) force field analysis theory illustrates the dynamics at work in the change process. Movement from the present level of performance to a desired level is facilitated by driving or encouraging forces, while at the same time, it is hindered by restraining (or resisting, discouraging) forces. The present situation usually represents a state of equilibrium or balance between these driving and restraining forces.

Driving forces for technology integration might include the power and potential of new developments, rapid availability, creativity, Internet access, ease of communication, or the promise of impact on learning. Restraining forces might include barriers and constraints such as technical support, teacher expertise, time for planning, or pedagogical applications.

So, how do we make changes? Do we increase the driving forces or decrease the restraining forces? The former, by far the easiest because of our control over such forces, proves to be the less effective, since all that results is an increase in tension with a quick return to the status quo. Senge (1990) has stressed that when innovators change one part of a system, the system almost always works to change itself back again unless those solutions move from a symptomatic to a fundamental change in the system. For technology to become an integral aspect of classrooms and curricula, the changes in teacher and student behaviors must, of necessity, be fundamental to the system rather than quick fix or Bandaid solutions which merely focus on the surface symptoms. Reiser and Salisbury (1995) have referred to this phenomenon as "straighten[ing] the deck chairs [while] the structure of the ship we are traveling on remains the same" (p. 232).

Covey's (1990) analogy provides a useful strategy for addressing change through the responses to driving and restraining forces:

> The question of whether to increase driving or decrease restraining forces is analogous to the question, "If I'm driving a car and see the emergency brake is partly on, should I release the brake or put on more gas?" Accelerating may increase the speed, but it may also burn up the engine. Releasing the brake, on the other hand, would allow you to attain high speeds more efficiently. (p. 223)

Hence, focusing on reducing restraining forces would appear to be a more productive use of our energy. So let us attempt to identify these forces and consider their nature.

Constraints and Barriers: Identification of Restraining Forces

Despite the general sense that the computer revolution of the last decade has had a major impact in schools, the nature of this impact seems to be limited to access and information retrieval rather than improved teaching methods or revitalized school and classroom structures (Hativa & Lesgold, 1996). Did we over-promise and fail to deliver? Was it a matter of unfulfilled expectations? Were there unexpected outcomes, constraints, barriers, or contextual considerations which were overlooked or underestimated?

What are the restraining, resisting, or discouraging forces that affect change efforts in teacher practices, especially related to technology? The following constraints and barriers have been acknowledged by a number of scholars (Pelgrum, 2001). What would it take to convert these barriers to facilitating factors in technology integration? Often it seems to be a fine line between the two perspectives. It is in this arena that we should expend the bulk of our energy.

- Access to hardware and software as well as funding (Hope, 1997; Lan, 2000; Leggett & Persichitte, 1998; Lumley & Bailey, 1993).
- Time for planning, personal exploration, online access, and skill development (Duffield, 1997; Hope, 1997; Lan, 2000; Leggett & Persichitte, 1998; Sheingold & Hadley, 1990).
- Technical and administrative support and resources (Leggett & Persichitte, 1998; Schrum, 1995).
- Training and expertise (Cafolla & Knee, 1995; Hope, 1997; Shelton & Jones, 1996).

- Resistance, passivity, school cultures, and traditions of teaching (Beacham, 1994; Cafolla & Knee, 1995; Cohen, 1987; Cuban, 1986; Ertmer, 1999; Hope, 1997; Lumley & Bailey, 1993).
- Vision and leadership (Cafolla & Knee, 1995; Ely, 1995; Hope, 1997; Lan, 2000; Lumley & Bailey, 1993).
- Support for integration of technologies into instruction and the curriculum (Cuban, 1986; Hancock & Betts, 1994).

Ertmer (1999) grouped these barriers into two categories: first-order barriers extrinsic to teachers (access, time, support, resources, training) and second-order barriers intrinsic to teachers (attitudes, beliefs, practices, resistance). She asserted that "even if every first-order barrier were removed, teachers would not automatically use technology" (p. 51) and in fact, rather than being eliminated completely, such barriers will "continue to ebb and flow throughout the evolutionary integration process" (p. 52).

Teachers and Technology

Tucker (1992) advocated "unleashing the full potential of technology" by "letting the genie out of the bottle" (p. 50)—as if, by allowing this powerful force to roam into schools, something magical will automatically happen and all our wishes will be granted. Although many of us strongly believe in the great promise that technology holds for both learners and teachers, we also need to remember that, first and foremost, technology is a communication tool. "It is not the silver bullet that will solve all of our education problems, but it is certainly a useful tool that enables us to link various learning communities together in new and different ways" (Taylor, 2000, p. 4). It is not about what technology by itself can do, but what teachers and learners may be able to accomplish using these tools.

In labeling technology as the "great siren song of education," Kearsley (1998) argued that "educational technology [has become] primarily, if ironically, a distraction (on a grand scale) from what matters most— effective learning and good teaching" (p. 47). By focusing merely on how to use computers, technology training has failed and has caused us to miss the forest for the trees by not addressing how to teach students more effectively using a variety of technological tools. Kearsley further lamented the lack of technology preparation for teachers (too little and too late), stressing the realistic need for extensive and sustained practice over years, not one-day workshops (p. 49). What teachers need to know most is how to teach content more effectively. Because of our quick fix mindset in education, we myopically "teach people how to use specific types of technology [rather than] how to solve educational problems using technology when needed and appropriate" (p. 50). A recent survey by Jostens Learning Corporation (1997) and the American Association of School Administrators reported that teacher training, while readily available, focuses merely on basic computer operation and fails to address helping teachers use technology to teach more effectively.

Even though Gardner (1991) has expressed the view that "a well-trained and effective teacher is still preferable to the most advanced technology, and that even excellent hardware and software are to little avail in the absence of appropriate curricula, pedagogy, and assessment" (p. 223), he nevertheless admitted that "immersing oneself in a problem using the latest technology… can make a significant contribution to student learning" (p. 223). For him, the most important question is "whether such technological prosthetics actually improve classroom performance and lead to deeper understandings" (p. 223) and become "helpful handmaidens in the [learning] process" (p. 233).

Postman (1992) has warned us that new technologies alter "the things we think about…, the things we think with…, and the arena in which thoughts develop" (p. 20). Hence, technology has become a serious arena for academic work (Mollgaard & Sides-Gonzales, 1995). This is the promise and the potential. It is also the challenge. The questions to be addressed are: "Who is in charge? Who is the driving force?" The answer should be the teachers who use the technology well. It cannot be the technology in and of itself.

A review of research studies and reports compiled in the early years of the past decade (Sivin-Kachala & Bialo, 1995) demonstrated the value of technology in enhancing student achievement, improving students' attitudes about themselves and about learning, and changing the learning environment. However, these authors emphasized that "the decisions made by well-trained educators [necessarily] determine the computer's ultimate instructional effectiveness" (p. 17) and that "the most important determinant of student attitudes when using technology is the teacher" (p. 24).

Lessons from Our Technological Past

The future belongs to those who respect the past, acknowledge the present, and grasp the future (Gustafson, 1993, p. 31).

In our past attempts at educational reform we have always looked for *new* solutions to old problems, equating "change" with "newness," and "ineffective" with "old." People just like the idea of newness. That's what grabs their attention. New for old. Not effective for ineffective. Not efficient for inefficient (Earle, 1992).

Focusing exclusively upon the newness of computer technology alone, independent of teaching and learning processes, may cause us to repeat technological history without reaping the potential benefits of this remarkable technology. We may unintentionally succumb to the malady of "data, data everywhere, but not a thought to think" (Theodore Roszak, in Rhee, 2000).

Our infatuation with the promises and possibilities of technology as hardware at the expense of technology as a process has overshadowed key lessons which we have learned from prior experiences in the field of educational technology: There is no one best medium; the medium is the means, not the ends; and the medium is not the message. Snider (1992) reminds us that focusing exclusively on technology as a panacea for improving schools has been somewhat fruitless across decades of technological innovations. "From lantern slides to language labs, from closed-circuit television to microcomputers, attempts to improve American schools with modern machines have been something less than a resounding success. Beginning with the magic lantern and the stereoscope of 1900, machines in the classroom have generated some promise, a fair amount of controversy, and a great deal of hype. During these 90-plus years, however, the basic acts of classroom teaching have changed very little despite sporadic efforts at research and reform—with and without machines" (p. 316).

Callister (1992) has added his own historical insights to our current dilemma in order to remind us of yet another lesson from the past: the power of the teacher in technology integration.

Inventions from Edison's phonograph and the blackboard to audiotape and instructional television have all been pressed into service to make up for the perceived deficiencies of the ordinary classroom teacher. But efforts to replace teachers with technology have uniformly failed. Inventions intended to take over teaching come and (mostly) go; what happens in classrooms looks pretty much the same.

Why? Because technology enthusiasts continue to forget a basic fact: Machines are tools, valuable only when a human intelligence organizes their use in a productive way. In the classroom, that human is the teacher, who controls the nature of the environment and what happens there. Good classroom tools extend the teacher's power to create a rich learning environment. If the teacher does not know what to make of the tool, or fears it, or misconstrues its uses, it will be used badly or not at all. If the teacher perceives the machine as a master, not as a servant, its potential will never be realized. (pp. 324–325)

Principles of Integration

Instructional technology does, indeed, hold a remarkable promise for changing the quality of teaching and learning in our schools. It is the catalyst for transformation—but this does not mean that we merely need more computers in our classrooms. Technology also involves *process*. Too often our efforts to improve education have resulted in our unrealistic isolation of technological processes. Remember my earlier reference to our experiences with educational television? We expended our resources on installing equipment, which soon began to gather dust because we neglected the process components—learning, teaching practices, and curricula. Technologies are valuable resources, but only when used in a systematic process for developing human competence (Earle, 1992).

Questions about technology integration often center around schools and classrooms. Such questions fall short of the target. It is relatively easy to "place" technology in physical locations. The real question must focus on integration into teaching practices, learning experiences, and the curriculum. Integration (from the Latin *integrare*, to make whole) includes a sense of completeness or wholeness and incorporates the need to overcome artificial separations by bringing together all essential elements in the teaching and learning process—including technology (as *one* of the elements, not the sole element).

Change starts with the individual teacher, who, upon catching the vision, is willing to take risks, to experience Christopherian confrontations or encounters (Gardner, 1991) in rethinking teaching and learning, and to model for and be a mentor to peers. Just as Christopher Columbus confronted the intuitive impression that the earth is flat with the conception of a spherical earth, so teachers must grasp the opportunity to reconsider established practices and rethink teaching and learning. Conversion to a theory, practice, process, or approach, such as technology integration, is a very personal process. It involves *preparation* of the teacher (building relationships of trust, helping teachers feel and recognize the power of teaching with technology, personalizing training, and finding out teacher needs, interests, and concerns), *commitment* by the teacher, *following-up* on that commitment by the support team, and *resolving teacher concerns* arising during the change process. Teachers move through at least three levels—confidence, competence, and creativity. It is a process of gradualness as they progress from learner to adopter to leader. At first they utilize existing practices, then adapt to their own needs, and finally design their own integrated experiences. Such teachers "face their own fears and struggles with technology and change by taking the time to reflect on their own role and professional practice in this process of integration" (Norum *et al.*, 1999, p. 202).

It is important to remember that technology is not a subject (Duffield, 1997). The focus of integration is on pedagogy—effective practices for teaching and learning. Teachers need to be able to make choices about technology integration without becoming technocentric by placing undue emphasis on the technology for its own sake without connections to learning and the curriculum. For both preservice preparation and inservice professional development, this means providing experiences, primarily in instructional design, media selection, modeling exemplary technology practices, clinical activities, resource sharing, and extensive and sustained training and practice. Ertmer (1999) explains that "teachers need opportunities to observe *models* of integrated technology use, to *reflect* on and discuss their evolving ideas with mentors and peers, and to *collaborate* with others on meaningful projects as they try out their new ideas about teaching and learning with technology" (p. 54).

The curriculum must be the vehicle for technology integration. Just as reading is content-free (i.e., incorporates all subject areas), so is technology. We must weave technology into the fabric of learning, or as Cuban (1986) admonished: Fit the computer to the curriculum, not the curriculum to the computer.

Exemplary practices reported in professional journals such as *Educational Technology, Tech Trends, Technology and Learning, Educational Leadership,* and *Learning and Leading with Technology* have showcased individuals, programs, and schools that have successfully taken on the restraining forces listed above. Such efforts show us that reducing these forces is the key to overcoming the obstacles and breaking down the barriers to the meaningful integration of technology into teaching and learning. Converting these restraining forces to facilitating factors is essential. Take any of the restraining forces listed above—access, time, support, training, leadership, or resistance—and one can see that it is much easier to remove the barrier by resolving and reducing concerns than to attempt to use additional force to plow through the barrier—the former approach is facilitative and constructive while the latter is divisive and destructive. The solutions are many and varied depending on local conditions (Leggett & Persichitte, 1998; Lumley & Bailey, 1993).

Final Reflections

Any innovation is fraught with promises and challenges. Involving key stakeholders is often the way to achieve the potential promises while addressing and overcoming the related challenges (Waddoups *et al.,* 2001). Hence the need to focus on the teacher and the learner and not the technology—through the curricula and practices which bring teachers and learners together. Contrary to critical comments about the sparseness and poor quality of technology research, Margaret Honey at the Education Development Center recently testified before the U.S. Senate that one can find ample empirical evidence that technology does have a positive impact *when the right conditions are in place* (Honey, 2001). She concluded that, if technologies are to be used to support real gains in educational outcomes, six factors must be in place: leadership, solid educational objectives, professional development, adequate technology resources, time, and evaluation (Honey, Culp, & Carrigg, 2000). Additionally, Norris, Smolka, and Soloway (2000), in a convergent analysis of technology studies, have identified their set of critical conditions as access to technology and time on task, adequate teacher preparation, effective curriculum,

supportive school/district administration, and supportive family. In other words, establish appropriate conditions by converting restraining forces to facilitating factors.

Such remarkable interactive technologies deserve the opportunity to deliver on their promises and meet (or even exceed) their potential. Let us truly learn from our technological past and grasp the future by addressing today's realities so that we can reap tomorrow's possibilities.

References

Association for Educational Communications and Technology (1977). *The definition of educational technology.* Washington, DC: AECT.

Beacham, B. (1994). Making connections: Transforming ivory towers and little red school houses. In J. Willis, B. Robin, & D. A. Willis (Eds.). *Technology and Teacher Education Annual 1994* (pp. 742–744). Charlottesville, VA: Association for Advancement of Computing in Education.

Bernauer, J. A. (1995). *Integrating technology into the curriculum: First year evaluation.* A paper presented at the annual meeting of the American Educational Research Association, San Francisco, CA, (ED 385-224).

Bosch, K. A. (1993). Is there a computer crisis in the classroom? *Schools in the Middle, 2*(4), 7–9.

Branch, R. M. (1994). Common instructional design practices employed by secondary school teachers. *Educational Technology, 34*(3), 25–33.

Bronner, E. (November 10, 1997). High-tech teaching is losing its gloss. *New York Times,* p. 4.

Cafolla, R., & Knee, R. (1995). Factors limiting technology integration in education: The leadership gap. *Technology and Teacher Education Annual 1995* (pp. 556–559). Charlottesville, VA: Association for Advancement of Computing in Education.

Callister, T. A. (1992). The computer as doorstep: Technology as disempowerment. *Phi Delta Kappan, 74*(4), 324–329.

Cassidy, M. F. (1982). Toward integration: Education, instructional technology, and semiotics. *Educational Communications and Technology Journal, 20*(2), 75–89.

Cohen, D. (1987). Educational technology, policy, and practice. *Educational Evaluation and Policy Analysis, 9,* 153–170.

Commission on Instructional Technology. (1970). *To improve learning: A report to the President and the Congress of the United States.* Washington, DC: Commission on Instructional Technology.

Covey, S. R. (1990). *Principle-centered leadership.* New York: Simon & Schuster.

Cuban, L. (1986). *Teachers and machines: The classroom use of technology since 1920.* New York: Teachers College Press.

Dede, C. (1997). Rethinking how to invest in technology. *Educational Leadership, 55*(3), 12–16.

Driscoll, M. P., Klein, J. D., & Sherman, G. P. (1994). Perspectives on instructional planning: How do teachers and instructional designers conceive of ISD planning practices? *Educational Technology, 34*(3), 34–42.

Duffield, J. A. (1997). Trials, tribulations, and minor successes: Integrating technology into a preservice preparation program. *Tech Trends, 42*(4), 22–26.

Earle, R. S. (1992). Talk about teaching: New lamps for old. *Educational Technology, 32*(3), 35–37.

Earle, R. S. (1994). Instructional design and the classroom teacher: Looking back and moving ahead. *Educational Technology, 34*(3), 610.

Earle, R. S. (1998). Instructional design and teacher planning: Reflections and perspectives. In R. M. Branch & M. A. Fitzgerald (Eds.), *Educational Media and Technology Yearbook* (Volume 23, pp. 29–41). Englewood, CO: Libraries Unlimited.

Education Week (1999, Nov. 10). Schools and reform in the information age, *17*(11).

Ely, D. (1995). *Technology is the answer! But what was the question?* Capstone College of Education Society, University of Alabama, (ERIC Document Reproduction Service No. ED 381 152).

Ertmer, P. (1999). Addressing first- and second-order barriers to change: Strategies for technology implementation. *Educational Technology Research and Development, 47*(4), 47–61.

Fullan, M. (2000). The three stories of education reform. *Phi Delta Kappan, 81*(8), 581–584.

Galbraith, J. K. (1967). *The new industrial state.* Boston, MA: Houghton Mifflin.

Gardner, H. K. (1991). *The unschooled mind: How children think and how schools should teach.* New York: Basic Books.

Gentry, C. G. (1995). Educational technology: A question of meaning. In G. Anglin (Ed.), *Instructional technology: Past, present, and future.* Englewood, CO: Libraries Unlimited.

GLEF Blast Newsletter. (2001, August 2), San Francisco CA: The George Lucas Educational Foundation.

Gustafson, K. L. (1993). Instructional design fundamentals: Clouds on the horizon. *Educational Technology, 33*(2), 27–32.

Hadley, M., & Sheingold, K. (1993). Commonalities and distinctive patterns in teachers' integration of computers. *American Journal of Education, 101*, 261–315.

Hancock, V., & Betts, J. (1994). From the lagging to the leading edge. *Educational Leadership, 51*(7), 24–29.

Hativa, N., & Lesgold, A. (1996). Situational effects in classroom technology implementations: Unfulfilled expectations and unexpected outcomes. In S. J. Kerr (Ed.), *Technology and the future of schooling: Ninety-fifth yearbook of the National Society for the Study of Education,* part 2 (pp. 131–171). Chicago: University of Chicago Press.

Heinich, R., Molenda, M., & Russell, J. D. (1993). *Instructional media and the new technologies of instruction.* New York: Macmillan.

Honey, M. (2001, July 25). Technology's effectiveness as a teaching and learning tool. Testimony and statement for the record before the Labor, HHS, and Education Appropriations Subcommittee of the U.S. Senate. Education Development Center, Inc. Available: http://www.edc.org/spotlight/Tech/mhtestimony.htm

Honey, M., Culp, K. M., & Carrigg, F. (2000). Perspectives on technology and education research: Lessons from the past and present. *Educational Computing Research, 23*(1), 5–14.

Hope, W. C. (1997). Why technology has not realized its potential in schools. *American Secondary Education, 25*(4), 29.

Jostens Learning Corporation. (1997, April 7). Survey analysis by Global Strategy Group. San Diego: Jostens Learning Corporation.

Kearsley, G. (1998). Educational technology: A critique. *Educational Technology, 38*(2), 47–51.

Lan, J. (2000). Leading teacher educators to a new paradigm: Observations on technology integration. *AACTE Briefs 21*(10), 4–6.

Leggett, W. P., & Persichitte, K. A. (1998). Blood, sweat, and TEARS: 50 years of technology implementation obstacles. *Tech Trends, 43*(3), 33–36.

Lewin, K. (1951). *Field theory in social science.* New York: Harper.

Lumley, D., & Bailey, G. D. (1993). *Planning for technology: A guidebook for school administrators.* New York: Scholastic.

Mollgaard, T., & Sides-Gonzales, K. (1995). Stockbroker of the technological curriculum: Leadership and technology. *Tech Trends, 40*(5), 28–30.

Munoz, Z. C. (1993). A technophile looks at technology, education, and art. *Art Education, 46*(6), 48–49.

Niess, N. L. (1991). Computer-using teachers in a new decade. *Education and Computing, 7,* (3–4), 151–156.

Norris, C., Smolka, J., & Soloway, E. (2000). Extracting value from research: A guide for the perplexed. *Technology & Learning, 20*(11), 45–48.

Norum, K. E., Grabinger, R. S., & Duffield, J. A. (1999). Healing the universe is an inside job: Teachers' views on integrating technology. *Journal of Technology and Teacher Education, 7*(3), 187–203.

Pelgrum, W. J. (2001). Obstacles to the integration of ICT in education: Results from a worldwide educational assessment. *Computers and Education, 37*(2), 163–178.

Pool, C. R. (1997). A new digital literacy: A conversation with Paul Gilster. *Educational Leadership, 55*(3), 6–11.

Postman, N. (1992). *Technopoly: The surrender of culture to technology* New York: Vintage Books.

Reiser, R. A. (1994). Examining the planning practices of teachers: Reflections on three years of research. *Educational Technology, 34*(3), 11–16.

Reiser, R., & Salisbury, D. (1995). Instructional technology and public education in the United States: The next decade. In G. Anglin (Ed.), *Instructional technology: Past, present, and future* (pp. 227–235). Englewood, CO: Libraries Unlimited.

Rhee, R. (2,000, July 8). Quantity vs. quality. *Korea Herald,* p. 1.

Riedl, J. (1995). *The integrated technology classroom: Building self-reliant learners.* Boston: Allyn and Bacon.

Ritchie, D., & Wilburg, K. (1994). Educational variables influencing technology integration *Journal of Technology and Teacher Education, 2*(2), 143–153.

Robey, E. (Ed.) (1992). *Opening the doors: Using technology to improve education for students with disabilities.* Macro International Inc.

Schrum, L. M. (1995). *Telecommunications for personal and professional uses: A case study.* Paper presented at the annual meeting of the American Educational Research Association, San Francisco, CA (ERIC Document Reproduction Service No. ED 385 230).

Seels, B. B., & Richey, R. C. (1994). *Instructional technology: The definition and domains of the field.* Washington, DC. AECT.

Senge, P. M. (1990). *The fifth discipline: The art & practice of the learning organization.* New York: Doubleday/Currency.

Sheingold, K. & Hadley, M. (1990). *Accomplished teachers: Integrating computers into classroom practice.* New York: Bank Street College of Education, Center for Technology in Education.

Shelton, M., & Jones, M. (1996). Staff development that works! A tale of four t's. *NAASP Bulletin, 80*(582), 99–105.

Sivin-Kachala, J., & Bialo, E. R. (1995). *Report on the effectiveness of technology in schools 1990–1994.* Washington, DC: Software Publishers Association.

Snider, R. C. (1992). The machine in the classroom. *Phi Delta Kappan, 74*(4), 316–323.

Taylor, D. R. (2000). Developing powerful learning communities using technology. *AACTE Briefs, 21*(14), 4–5.

Tiene, D., & Luft, P. (2001). Teaching in a technology-rich classroom. *Educational Technology, 41*(4), 23–31.

Trotter, A. (1997). Taking technology's measure. In *Technology counts: Schools and reform in the information age.* (Vol. 17, Issue 11, pp. 6–11), *Education Week.*

Tucker, M. (1992). The genie in the bottle. *Electronic Learning, 12*(3), 50.

Valdez, G., McNabb, M., Foertsch, M., Anderson, M., Hawkes, M., & Raack, L. (2000). *Computer-based technology and learning: Evolving uses and expectations.* Oak Brook, IL: North Central Regional Laboratory.

Viadero, D. (1997). A tool for learning. In *Technology Counts: Schools and reform in the information age* (Vol. 17, Issue 11, pp. 12–18), *Education Week.*

Waddoups, G. L., Wentworth, N. M., & Earle, R. S. (2001, in press). Faculty learning to use technology: PT3 supported systemic reform initiatives in teacher education. *Tech Trends.*

Wager, W. (1992). Educational technology: A broader vision. *Educational and Urban Society, 24*(4), 454–465.

Zehr, M. A. (1997). Teaching the teachers. In *Technology Counts: Schools and reform in the information age* (Vol. 17, Issue 11, pp. 24–29). *Education Week.*

Rodney S. Earle is Professor of Teacher Education at Brigham Young University, Provo, Utah (e-mail: rodney_earle@byu.edu).

From *Educational Technology*, January/February 2002, pp. 5-13. © 2002 by Educational Technology Publications, Inc. Reprinted by permission.

Using Data to Differentiate Instruction

In an age of standards, using assessment data to differentiate instruction is essential.

Kay Brimijoin, Ede Marquissee, and Carol Ann Tomlinson

At Redlands Elementary School, Ms. Martez's 5th graders are studying the math concept of greatest common factor.[1] Following an interactive lesson, students participate in a self-assessment procedure that Ms. Martez has created. Using a car windshield metaphor, she asks,

> How many [of you] are clear as glass about how greatest common factor works? How many have bugs on your windshield? How many have windshields covered with mud? (Brimijoin, 2002)

On the basis of their spontaneous self-assessment of "glass, bugs, and mud" and their earlier work on greatest common factor, Ms. Martez assigns students to three follow-up activities. With only a few exceptions, the students' self-assessment matches what Ms. Martez had determined from her pre-assessment.

Because the group of students who are as "clear as glass" understands and can apply greatest common factor at both the conceptual and skill levels, she has these students use a Euclidean algorithm to find the greatest common factor in a series of exercises. A group of "buggy" students—who understand the basic concept of greatest common factor, but still need to build their confidence through application—play a greatest common factor game that Ms. Martez has created. And she sends the "muddy" group to sort factors in a giant Venn diagram constructed of two hula-hoops. This oversized graphic organizer provides a kinesthetic and interpersonal learning experience for those who need ad-

ditional practice to master the basic concept and skills.

During this time, Ms. Martez offers support and answers questions using a red-yellow-green cup system to prioritize student requests for assistance. A student sets a red cup on his or her desk to say "I can't go on without help." A yellow cup means that the student has questions but isn't completely blocked, and a green cup means that the student understands what he or she is doing. Two students tell Ms. Martez they are "really buggy *and* muddy," and she immediately announces the opening of a "math clinic" where she works on intensive, explicit instruction.

Because Ms. Martez had devoted time at the beginning of the year to talk with her students about the importance of gathering assessment data directly from them, students engage in their tasks smoothly and do not question groupings or complain about assignments. She had modeled the windshield strategy and together she and her class had created a generic rubric for each degree of understanding. Teaching students this self-assessment technique helped accustom them to instruction differentiated by readiness and structures that support student-centered learning (Tomlinson, 1999).

Three-Dimensional Data Collection

For Ms. Martez, informal and formal data about student learning not only shape in-

struction but also determine its effectiveness. She uses multiple methods of data collection and views the process as dynamic and continuous. She sees her role as data collector in three dimensions: to determine students' prior understanding and achievement, to track their responses to moderate challenges, and to measure their outcomes against expected performance goals (Brimijoin, 2002; Bruner, 1963; Tomlinson, 1995).

Pre-Assessment

Ms. Martez uses a wide array of pre-assessments when teaching new content. During a math lesson introducing basic algebra concepts, for instance, she asks students,

> What do you suppose it means to think algebraically? Take out your math logs and write, even if you write that you don't know.

Oral questioning, written journal prompts, objective tests, webbing, K-W-L (What do you *know*? What do you still *want* to know? What did you *learn*?) charts, group discussions, and brainstorming sessions provide rich data about students' existing schema, including critical misconceptions (Bransford, Brown, & Cocking, 2000).

Moderate Challenges

Ms. Martez believes that because students differ in their grasp of key concepts, she must modify her instruction to help them build knowledge, refine skills, and apply understandings on increasingly sophisticated tasks (Wiggins & McTighe, 1998). Assessment helps her modify instruction so that each student is appropriately challenged. She uses paper-and-pencil or performance-based formative assessments, including objective tests or quizzes, quick-writes, essays, and open-ended problems, varying the type according to the content being studied. She also develops a clear sense of what the culminating assessment will be when she first lays out the lesson or unit.

Rather than seeing assessment as an end-of-lesson or end-of-unit phenomenon, Ms. Martez incorporates it at the beginning, at the end, and everywhere in between.

Ms. Martez gives her students "task cards," which specify the steps in a learning process or experience. These cards include a set of directions for a task in order to facilitate independent learning and nurture autonomy. For example, each of Ms. Martez's learning groups had task cards with step-by-step directions to guide them through their assignments on greatest common factor. The task cards also frequently include rubrics that spell out performance expectations on assignments.

At the end of a lesson, students write in their journal a one-line description or an answer to a question about what they have learned in the lesson. Their responses are "exit tickets" for formative or ongoing assessment to help the teacher evaluate the effectiveness of a lesson design and keep instruction focused on key learning goals and individual needs.

Standards Testing

Teaching in a grade that requires state standardized assessments forces Ms. Martez to reconcile her "gotta get it covered and memorized by testing time" mentality and her belief in concept-centered differentiated instruction. She confesses to feeling conflicted about working wholeheartedly in two seemingly contradictory worlds of teaching and learning.

Three weeks before state standards testing, Ms. Martez asks students to go through their math books and select topics that they have mastered and those that need more work. She reflects on the results and decides to set up centers on such topics as

fractions, place value, geometry, and statistics, cycling students through centers related to their areas of need, and assigning "experts" to assist their peers.

Using Assessment to Target Learner Needs

Ms. Martez uses questioning and observing to differentiate instruction and ensure that her instruction is a good match for the varied needs of her students (Brimijoin, 2002). She adjusts questions or performance tasks to be more structured for those who are struggling with a concept and more abstract for those who have mastered the concept. Rather than seeing assessment as an end-of-lesson or end-of-unit phenomenon, Ms. Martez incorporates it at the beginning, at the end, and everywhere in between.

Ms. Martez invests much time and energy in mapping the "start and finish" by first constructing a big picture of assessment results that students bring with them. By the 5th grade at Redlands Elementary, students have one set of state standards test scores from 3rd grade and one set of nationally standardized scores from 4th grade. Ms. Martez enters all these scores on a spreadsheet. During individual conferences, Ms. Martez guides students in setting target goals for their progress and areas of emphasis for her instruction. At the end of the year, she enters all 5th grade scores from state standardized tests and calculates the percentage gains for each student and for the class overall.

Informal and formal data about student learning not only shape instruction but also determine its effectiveness.

At the end of this past year, 74 percent of her students passed the reading assessment, an overall gain of 27 percentage points over their 3rd grade test results; 58 percent passed math, a gain of 5 percentage points; 58 percent passed social studies, a gain of 24 percentage points; and 74 percent passed the science assessment, a gain of 32 percentage points (Brimijoin, 2002). Ms. Martez attributes the improvement in test score results chiefly to her use of pre-assessment, self-assessment, and ongoing assessment to differentiate instruction for individual learning needs:

The facts stuck because they were scaffolded into existing information, taught at the students' readiness levels, hooked in with interests, and nailed down with instruction targeted to the students' strongest learning styles.... Differentiation works in a standardized testing world.... We can't afford not to do it and expect to meet state standards, especially in low socioeconomic areas like Redlands. (Brimijoin, 2002, p. 263)

Ms. Martez uses the results of test score analysis to reflect on her teaching, comparing her curriculum design and instruction from one year to the next, noting strengths as well as weaknesses, and identifying questions that still need answering in order to refine her practice (Zeichner & Liston, 1996).

The students are also data collectors. They accept responsibility for monitoring their own progress and see that they have a role in shaping instruction. Ms. Martez weaves information gleaned from journal responses with formative quiz and test results. She sees assessment as a powerful tool to be used through the whole process of teaching and learning; one that demands the same kind of evaluation skills that good teachers use for effective management.

Ms. Martez advises other teachers that carefully articulated, continuous assessment that drives curriculum design "maximizes teaching time, streamlines instruction, and facilitates learning for all students." She insists that assessment is not "just another plate added to the 12-piece service," but a means of enhancing student and teacher performance.

Note

1. This article uses pseudonyms for the teacher and school.

References

Bransford, J., Brown, A., & Cocking, R. (Eds.). (2000). *How people learn: Brain, mind, experience, and school.* Washington, DC: National Academy Press.

Brimijoin, K. (2002). *A journey toward expertise in differentiation: A preservice and inservice teacher make their way.* Unpublished doctoral dissertation. University of Virginia, Charlottesville.

Bruner, J. (1963). *The process of education.* New York: Vintage Books.

Tomlinson, C. (1995). *Differentiating instruction for mixed-ability classrooms.* Alexandria, VA: ASCD.

Tomlinson, C. (1999). *The differentiated classroom: Responding to the needs of all learners.* Alexandria, VA: ASCD.

Wiggins, G., & McTighe, J. (1998). *Understanding by design.* Alexandria, VA: ASCD.

Zeichner, K., & Liston, D. (1996). *Reflective teaching: An introduction.* Mahwah, NJ: Lawrence Erlbaum Associates.

Kay Brimijoin is an assistant professor at Sweet Briar College, Sweet Briar, VA 24595; brimijoin@sbc.edu. **Ede Marquissee** teaches 6th grade at Summit Middle School, 4509 Homestead Road, Fort Wayne, IN 46814; emarquissee@sacs.k12.in.us. **Carol Ann Tomlinson** is a professor at the Curry School of Education, University of Virginia, Ruffner Hall, Charlottesville, VA 22904; cat3y@virginia.edu

UNIT 5

Motivation and Classroom Management

Unit Selections

Key Points to Consider

• Discuss several ways to motivate both at-risk and typical students. What difference is there?

• Why should motivational style be consistent with instructional techniques?

• How are motivation and classroom management related?

• Discuss several ways to discipline both typical students and those with exceptionalities.

• How are classroom management and discipline different? Discuss whether discipline can be developed within students or whether it must be imposed by teachers, supporting your argument with data derived from your reading.

 **Links: www.dushkin.com/online/**
These sites are annotated in the World Wide Web pages.

Canada's Schoolnet Staff Room
http://www.schoolnet.ca/home/e/

The term *motivation* is used by educators to describe the processes of initiating, directing, and sustaining goal-oriented behavior. Motivation is a complex phenomenon, involving many factors that affect an individual's choice of action and perseverance in completing tasks. Furthermore, the reasons why people engage in particular behaviors can only be inferred; motivation cannot be directly measured.

Several theories of motivation, each highlighting different reasons for sustained goal-oriented behavior, have been proposed. We will discuss three of them: behavioral, humanistic, and cognitive. The behavioral theory of motivation suggests that an important reason for engaging in behavior is that reinforcement follows the action. If the reinforcement is controlled by someone else and is arbitrarily related to the behavior (such as money, a token, or a smile), then the motivation is extrinsic. In contrast, behavior may also be initiated and sustained for intrinsic reasons such as curiosity or mastery.

Humanistic approaches to motivation are concerned with the social and psychological needs of individuals. Humans are motivated to engage in behavior to meet these needs. Abraham Maslow, a founder of humanistic psychology, proposes that there is a hierarchy of needs that directs behavior, beginning with physiological and safety needs and progressing to self-actualization. Some other important needs that influence motivation are affiliation and belonging with others, love, self-esteem, influence with others, recognition, status, competence, achievement, and autonomy.

The dominant view of motivation in the educational psychology literature is the cognitive approach. This set of theories proposes that our beliefs about our successes and failures affect our expectations and goals concerning future performance. Students who believe that their success is due to their abilities and efforts are motivated toward mastery of skills. Students who blame their failures on inadequate abilities have low self-efficacy and tend to set ability and performance goals that protect their self-image.

In the unit's first selection, Martin Covington addresses the classic distinctions between intrinsic and extrinsic reinforcement. He attempts to reconcile the two motivations in his discussion of the ways in which student interest, criterion-referenced grading, and recognition for learning can lesson the negative effects of extrinsic reinforcers. In the second article, Marge Sherer focuses on how to encourage a love of learning. She reflects on a conversation with Mihaly Csikszentmihalyi and his concept of "flow" in which a high level of challenge is met with the skills to meet the challenge. In the final article about motivation, Mike Muir invites us to consider how underachieving students become academically engaged. It is fascinating to see that the seventh graders that he interviews value the same motivating factors that are recommended by researchers who study learning goals. Both students and researchers advocate meaningful, authentic tasks, differentiated assignments, and support for student autonomy through choice in activities.

No matter how effectively students are motivated, teachers always need to exercise management of behavior in the classroom. Classroom management is more than controlling the behavior of students or disciplining them following misbehavior. Instead, teachers need to initiate and maintain a classroom environment that supports successful teaching and learning. The skills that effective teachers use include preplanning, deliberate introduction of rules and procedures, immediate assertiveness, continual monitoring, consistent feedback to students, and specific consequences.

The first article in this subsection describes the most current thinking about classroom management techniques that best meet the needs of learner-centered classrooms. Mary McCaslin and Thomas Good believe that teachers who value teaching for understanding need to help students internalize a commitment to certain standards of behavior, rather than settle for compliance. They suggest that this can be accomplished by teaching students to coordinate their multiple academic and social goals.

The next four articles address issues of classroom management facing teachers today. The first article, "When Children Make Rules," shows how students can be engaged in the constructivist process. The next article focuses on a proactive approach, creating a positive middle school learning environment that is a developmentally appropriate strategy. The third article by Robert and Jana Marzano emphasizes the importance of quality student-teacher relationships as a basis for classroom management. The final article in this section speaks to the subject of corporal punishment in the classroom as a means of discipline, and how children's rights must be protected.

Intrinsic Versus Extrinsic Motivation in Schools: A Reconciliation

Abstract

This article explores the nature of the relationships between intrinsic and extrinsic motivation in schools, and in particular examines critically the assertion that these processes are necessarily antagonistic. The weight of evidence suggests that rewards in the form of school grades and the focus of many students on doing well, gradewise, need not necessarily interfere with learning for its own sake. Educational implications of these findings are considered. One such implication is that focusing on students' interests can be a valuable motivational strategy.

Keywords:
   motivation; achievement; appreciation

Martin V. Covington[1]
Department of Psychology, University of California at Berkeley, Berkeley, California

When psychologists speak of motivation, they typically refer to the reasons that individuals are aroused to action. Over the past 50 years, two quite different kinds of reasons have emerged in the thinking of psychologists: intrinsic and extrinsic reasons. Individuals are said to be driven to act for extrinsic reasons when they anticipate some kind of tangible payoff, such as good grades, recognition, or gold stars. These rewards are said to be extrinsic because they are unrelated to the action. In effect, the activity becomes a means to an end. By contrast, individuals are said to be intrinsically motivated when they engage in activities for their own sake. In this instance, the rewards reside in the actions themselves; that is, the actions are their own reinforcement. Put differently, in the case of intrinsic motivation, the repetition of an action does not depend as much

on some external inducement as on the satisfaction derived from overcoming a personal challenge, learning something new, or discovering things of personal interest.

For generations, observers have extolled the virtues of learning for its own sake, not only because of the benefits of personal growth or enhanced well-being, but also because intrinsically based learning is the handmaiden to better, more efficient learning. For example, intrinsically engaged students are more likely than extrinsically driven students to employ deep-level, sophisticated study strategies in their work (Ames & Archer, 1988). Perhaps most noteworthy for establishing causal, not merely correlational, relationships are studies (e.g., Schunk, 1996) in which students were randomly assigned to varying achievement conditions. Those students who were

directed to work for the goals of mastery, exploration, and appreciation demonstrated greater task involvement and used more effective learning strategies than children who were directed to focus on their performance alone.

At the same time, experts also lament the prospects of encouraging intrinsic engagement in a world controlled by extrinsic rewards (e.g., Kohn, 1993). My purpose here is to explore briefly the nature of the relationship between intrinsic and extrinsic motivation in schools, and in particular to examine critically the assertion that these processes are necessarily antagonistic, such that the will to learn for its own sake is inhibited or even destroyed by the offering of extrinsic rewards and incentives like school grades.

It is important to be clear about what the issue is. The issue is not that offering tangible rewards will necessarily interfere with learning. To the contrary, offering students tangible rewards sometimes actually increases learning, especially if the assignment is seen as a chore or boring. Rather, the issue is whether offering rewards focuses undue attention on the tangible payoffs, thereby decreasing students' appreciation of what they are learning.

OBSTACLES TO INTRINSIC ENGAGEMENT

The potentially destructive impact of tangible rewards on the will to learn for its own sake has been documented in several ways. First, there is the prospect that once these rewards are no longer available, students will show little or no inclination to continue in their studies (Covington, 1998). Second, there is the possibility that offering rewards to students for doing what already interests them may also undercut personal task involvement. For example, if a teacher tries to encourage intrinsic values directly, say, by praising students for pursuing a hobby, then, paradoxically, these interests may actually be discouraged. This phenomenon is the so-called overjustification effect (Lepper, Greene, & Nisbett, 1973). According to one interpretation, such discouragement occurs because the value of an already justifiable activity becomes suspect by the promise of additional rewards—hence the term overjustification—so that the individual reasons, "If someone has to pay me to do this, then it must not be worth doing for its own sake."

The goal of fostering a love of learning is complicated not only by offering or withholding tangible rewards, but also by the scarcity of these rewards. In many classrooms, an inadequate supply of rewards (e.g., good grades) is distributed by teachers unequally, with the greatest number of rewards going to the best performers or to the fastest learners. This arrangement is based on the false assumption that achievement is maximized when students compete for a limited number of rewards. Although this may maximize motivation, students are aroused for the wrong reasons—to win over others and to avoid losing—and these reasons eventually lead to failure and resentment (Covington, 1998). In this competitive context, grades stand as a mark of worthiness, because it is widely assumed in our society that one is only as worthy as one's ability to achieve competitively.

If high grades not only are important for the tangible future benefits they bestow—being the gateway to prestigious occupations—but also serve as an indication of one's personal worth, then what becomes of the valuing of learning in the scramble for grades? Is not the valuing and appreciation of learning marginalized? No, apparently not. There can be little doubt that students also value learning, irrespective of the grades they receive (see Covington, 1999).

A RECONCILIATION

How can we resolve this apparent contradiction? The observations of students themselves provide some answers (Covington, 1999; Covington & Wiedenhaupt, 1997).

First, students readily acknowledge that they strive for the highest grades possible, but—and this is the important point—different students have different reasons for a grade focus. It is these reasons that in turn determine the degree to which students become intrinsically engaged. For instance, when students strive for high grades as a mark of approval, to impress other people, or to avoid failure, they will value learning only to the extent that it serves to aggrandize their ability status, not for any inherent attraction of the material itself. If, by contrast, students have a task-oriented purpose in striving for high grades (e.g., if they use grades as feedback for how they can improve and learn more), then they will appreciate their accomplishments for their positive proper-ties. In effect, it is not necessarily the presence of grades per se, or even a dominant grade focus, that influences the degree to which learning is appreciated. Rather, students' valuing of what they learn depends on their initial reasons for learning and the meaning they attach to their grades. This implies that striving for good grades and caring for learning are not necessarily incompatible goals. The degree of compatibility of these goals is influenced by the reasons for learning.

Second, the degree to which students become intrinsically engaged in their schoolwork depends in part on whether they are achieving their grade goals, that is, whether they feel successful. On the one hand, being successful in one's studies promotes an appreciation for what one is learning. On the other hand, falling short of one's grade goals may intensify one's concentration on doing better (to the point that appreciation of the subject matter is excluded), divert attention to protecting one's sense of worth, or cause feelings of hopelessness about ever succeeding, feelings that bode ill for both the goal of appreciation and the goal of achievement. Thus, the degree of goal compatibility is also influenced by experiences of success and failure.

Third, students also indicate that they often manipulate academic circumstances to create a tolerable balance between grades and caring. The most frequent strategies involve making school more interesting by deliberately seeking out what is of interest to them, even in the case of boring assignments, or arranging a course of study, or even a college major, around personal interests. Thus, the compatibility of grades and caring is also influenced by personal interests.

From these observations, we can conclude that students are more likely to value what they are learning, and to enjoy the process, (a) when they are achieving their grade goals; (b) when the dominant reasons for learning are task-oriented reasons, not self-aggrandizing or failure-avoiding reasons; and (c) when what they are studying is of personal interest.

The role of personal interest in this equation is especially noteworthy. Although it is not surprising that people enjoy learning more about what already interests them, what is intriguing is the extent to which pursuing one's own interests offsets the potentially negative effects of receiving a disappointing grade. In fact, the evidence suggests that a student's appreciation for what he or she is learning is far greater when the student is failing but interested in the task than when the same student is succeeding, gradewise, but has little interest in the subject-matter content.

A related point concerning this equation also deserves comment. Receiving a good grade, especially for interesting work, increases, not decreases, intrinsic engagement. This finding seems to contradict the previously mentioned expectation that providing people with tangible payoffs for pursuing what already interests them will dampen their enthusiasm. Students themselves offer several plausible explanations for why these worries may be exaggerated, if not groundless. Based on their experiences, some students report anecdotally that doing well causes positive feelings like pride, which in turn increases their enthusiasm for learning. Other anecdotal observations suggest that doing well reduces worry about failing, so that students are freer to explore what is most interesting. And, according to yet other students, being successful stimulates them to study more, and the more they learn, the more interesting the material is likely to become. Whatever the explanation, it seems that the effects of tangible payoffs on intrinsic processes are far from simple.

EDUCATIONAL IMPLICATIONS

What practical steps do these findings suggest for how schools can serve both the goal of disseminating knowledge and the goal of promoting an appreciation of what is learned in the face of an ever-present grade focus?

First, the most obvious implication is that a major instructional goal should be to arrange schooling around the personal interests of students. Second, obviously learning cannot always be arranged around personal preferences, nor can students always succeed. Nonetheless, instructional practices can alter the meaning of failure when it occurs. Basically, this step involves eliminating the climate of scarcity of rewards by defining success not in the relative sense of outperforming others, but rather absolutely, that is, in terms of whether students measure up to a given standard of performance, irrespective of how many other students do well or poorly (Covington & Teel, 1996). When well-defined standards of performance are provided, the failure to achieve them tends to motivate students to try harder because failure implies falling short of a goal, not falling short as a person.

Third, in addition to creating grading systems that encourage intrinsic reasons for learning, teachers should provide payoffs that actively strengthen and reward these positive reasons. Although students focus primarily on the prospects of getting a good grade, they are also more likely to invest greater time and energy (beyond what is necessary for the grade) in those tasks for which there are additional tangible, yet intrinsically oriented payoffs. These payoffs include the opportunity to share the results of their work with others, or the chance to explain more deeply and personally why what they learned was important to them. This suggestion implies that, far from being incompatible, intrinsic and extrinsic reasons for learning are both encouraged by tangible rewards, but by different kinds of tangible rewards. This proposition sheds an entirely new light on the concerns raised by many experts regarding the overjustification effect. It is not the offering of tangible rewards that undercuts personal task engagement so much as it is the absence of those kinds of payoffs that encourage and recognize the importance of being involved in and caring about what one is learning.

Finally, students are the first to acknowledge a conflict between the goals of striving for high grades and enjoying learning. However, the conflict arises, they say, not out of any incompatibility of goals. Rather, the demands of school leave little room to pursue either goal fully, let alone to pursue the two goals together. As a result, students must prioritize these objectives, a process that typically favors the goal of striving for grades, and they lament what they forfeit. But prioritizing is not the same as incompatibility. The recommendations made in this review can act to balance these priorities more in favor of intrinsic engagement and a love of learning.

Recommended Reading

Cameron, J., & Pierce, W. D. (1994). Reinforcement, reward and intrinsic motivation: A meta-analysis. *Review of Educational Research, 64,* 363–423.

Condry, J., & Koslowski, B. (1979). Can education be made "intrinsically interesting" to children? In D. Katz (Ed.), *Current topics in early childhood education* (Vol. II, pp. 227–260). Norwood, NJ: Ablex.

Cordova, D. I., & Lepper, M. R. (1996). Intrinsic motivation and the process of learning: Beneficial effects of contextualization, personalization and choice. *Journal of Educational Psychology, 88,* 715–730.

Covington, M. V. (1992). *Making the grade: A self-worth perspective on motivation and school reform.* New York: Cambridge University Press.

Elliot, A. J., & Harackiewicz, J. M. (1996). Approach and avoidance achievement goals and intrinsic motivation: A mediational analysis. *Journal of Personality and Social Psychology, 70,* 461–475.

Note

1. Address correspondence to Martin V. Covington, Department of Psychology, 3210 Tolman Hall, University of California at Berkeley, Berkeley, CA 94720-1650.

References

Ames, C., & Archer, J. (1988). Achievement goals in the classroom: Student learning strategies and motivation processes. *Journal of Educational Psychology, 80*, 260–267.

Covington, M. V. (1998). *The will to learn: A guide for motivating young people.* New York: Cambridge University Press.

Covington, M. V. (1999). Caring about learning: The nature and nurturing of subject-matter appreciation. *Educational Researchers, 34*, 127–136.

Covington, M. V., & Teel, K. M. (1996). *Overcoming student failure: Changing motives and incentives for learning.* Washington, DC: American Psychological Association.

Covington, M. V., & Wiedenhaupt, S. (1997). Turning work into play: The nature and nurturing of intrinsic task engagement. In R. Perry & J. C. Smart (Eds.), *Effective teaching in higher education: Research and practice, special edition* (pp. 101–114). New York: Agathon Press.

Kohn, A. (1993). *Punished by rewards.* New York: Houghton Mifflin.

Lepper, M. R., Greene, D., & Nisbett, R. E. (1973). Undermining children's intrinsic interest with extrinsic rewards: A test of the "overjustification" hypothesis. *Journal of Personality and Social Psychology, 28*, 129–137.

Schunk, D. H. (1996). Goal and self-evaluative influences during children's cognitive skill learning. *American Educational Research Journal, 33*, 359–382.

From *Current Directions in Psychological Science,* February 2000, pp. 22-25. © 2000 by Blackwell Publishing Ltd., Oxford, UK. Reprinted by permission.

Do Students Care About Learning?

A Conversation with Mihaly Csikszentmihalyi

Learning to enjoy the intrinsic rewards of hard work is essential to successful human development, Mihaly Csikszentmihalyi, author of Becoming Adult: How Teenagers Prepare for the World of Work, *tells us. Here he talks with* Educational Leadership *about how to help students seek out the challenging and engaging activities that will propel them on their way toward becoming productive adults.*

Marge Scherer

In your study, you identified students who stood out from the crowd because they, more than their peers, could find enjoyment in both work and play. You also found students who were disengaged and passive about most of the activities they participated in. What was the context of your longitudinal study?

With the help from a grant from the Alfred P. Sloan Foundation, we identified 1,000 children who were in 6th, 8th, 10th, and 12th grades in 12 school districts from Orlando, Florida, to Long Beach, California, and everywhere in between. Nine years later, we are still following some of the participants as young adults, although a much smaller group of them.

We selected students randomly. We were not looking for children who enjoyed school or did not enjoy school. We just tried to get as much of a cross-section as possible. We developed questionnaires and interviewed these students, but we obtained most of our data through giving each student a programmable pager for a week. This pager would go off eight times a day, early morning to 11 P.M., at random moments. Whenever the pager signaled, the students would take out a little booklet and write where they were, what they were doing, what they were thinking about, their level of concentration, how happy they were, and how creative they felt when doing different activities.

They reported about 30 times during the week, so we received about 30,000 reports. And that allowed us to begin to see these children's experiences, the feelings and thoughts they had during the day, both at school and out of school. For instance, every time the pager went off, they had to say whether what they were doing was more like play, more like work, or like neither work nor play.

Was life more like work or play for these teenagers?

About 30 percent of the time they stated that it was like work; 30 percent of the time, they said that what they were doing was like play; 30 percent neither; and they reported that for 10 percent of their time, what they were doing was like both work and play.

In your follow-up studies, you concluded that students who often say that what they are doing is like both work and play are more likely to go on to college or make a successful transition to work.

Those students who say that whatever they do is more like work seem to do well in high school. Although they say that what they are doing is work and they don't enjoy it at the moment, they record on the response sheet that the activity is important to their future. So they understand that, "Okay. This is work. It's not pleasant. But it will profit me in the future."

It's when they are participating in extracurricular activities that students most often say that they are both working and playing.

Those kids who say that what they do is mostly play enjoy their activities, but they don't think of them as being important for the future. But the best situation is when a person sees a life activity as both work and play. Unfortunately, only about 10 percent of the time do students report this experience. Some kids never report that they have this experience. The worst thing is to frequently feel that what you do is neither enjoyable right now nor good preparation for the future.

You say affluent students are more likely to say they are enjoying their activities than poorer students. Did you see any differences in attitudes among other groups of students?

Males much more than females say that what they do is play. Caucasian students play more than Asians, Hispanics, or African Americans. The survey has a lot of markers in terms of ethnicity, class, and gender. We found that those who see what they do as play get into better colleges after they leave high school. College selection procedures favor kids who do well academically but who also are engaged in original or interesting extracurricular activities.

It's when they are participating in extracurricular activities that students most often say that they are both working and playing.

What is it about extracurricular activities that makes them engaging to students?

Students say that they are doing something that is important to them. The activity is voluntary to a large extent. Kids can choose to do things that match their own interests and skills. So they are doing something fun. But at the same time they are doing work to adult specifications. If you work on the high school newspaper, you have to observe the deadlines and you produce something that is real.

Our youngest son, for instance, was uninterested in school until he began to hang out with the theater group and started building sets, doing the lighting and sound effects, painting the scenery, doing carpentry, and so forth. Once he did that, he became more able to focus on everything. And now he's teaching at MIT.

Flow describes the spontaneous, effortless experience you achieve when you have a close match between a high level of challenge and the skills to meet the challenge.

His academic classes did not offer him an opportunity to meet serious adult standards, but the extracurricular activity did.

Explain what you mean by the flow experience, the title of your earlier book.

Flow describes the spontaneous, effortless experience you achieve when you have a close match between a high level of challenge and the skills you need to meet the challenge. Flow happens when a person is completely involved in the task, is concentrating very deeply, and knows moment by moment what the next steps should be. If you're playing music, you know what note will come next, and you know how to play that note. You have a goal and you are getting feedback. The experience is almost addictive and very rewarding.

Small children are in flow most of the time as they learn to walk and talk and other new things. They choose what to do and they match their skills with challenges. Unfortunately, they begin to lose this feeling once they go to school because they can't choose their goals and they can't choose the level at which they operate. They become increasingly passive. We find that in Europe and the United States, about 15 percent of adults really can't remember any experience that seems like flow. A similar proportion, about 15 percent, claim that they have the flow experience several times a day.

We've published many articles on multiple intelligences and learning styles. Do you think people of a certain kind of intelligence are more likely to have the flow experience?

It depends on whether there are opportunities for your particular skill or intelligence. If you are musically inclined, for instance, and there is no opportunity to play music at your school and no other place to get the experience of playing, then you are at a disadvantage. In some cultures, there will be opportunities for one kind of intelligence more than for another.

The learning disability that may be an obstacle to experiencing flow is the inability to concentrate. Concentration is one of the hallmarks of the flow experience. If you have, for instance, an attention deficit, it may be difficult to get focused enough.

Have you found that any curriculum subjects lend themselves to more engagement than others?

Yes. There have been quite a few dissertations on this topic. Typically, students rate history the worst subject for engagement, whereas they rate anything having to do with computers high. And vocational subjects seem to be better than academic subjects for encouraging engagement.

Students get flow from group work, from individual tasks, and from quizzes much more often than they do from listening to the teacher or from watching audiovisuals.

We're in a testing culture now, with much emphasis on standards and high-stakes assessments. Is this new priority deflating students' love of learning, or is it beneficial because it offers challenges?

To the extent that the results of the tests are taken seriously, testing worries me. If a test

is fair and not above the heads of most of the kids, then students can take the test as a game and a challenge. Flow is easiest to experience when you are challenged, have clear goals, and get clear feedback. Now, if you're listening to a teacher, all of those things are missing. There's nothing to keep your attention focused. Whereas in a test, you have to pay attention. There is a challenge. The goals are clear. You can lose yourself in the activity. Unless it's way too difficult or way too easy, you can enjoy taking a test. But that doesn't mean that one should take any test very seriously because test results don't correlate much with anything.

Not with higher achievement or success in life?

Not that I know of. I would be interested in seeing the evidence that scores on tests correlate with happiness or success in life.

What recommendations do you have for teachers who want to structure instructional activities to achieve more flow or more engagement for students?

The more they can show the relevance of what they're doing to the life of the student, the better. That's the first and most obvious requirement. You also have to make clear the goal of every lesson. The student must know what he or she is supposed to achieve at the end. And teachers need a way to find out how well the students are learning. Computer-assisted teaching can be quite useful because there you can see your progress and you can change and correct your work as you move along. The fact that students feel positive about group activities suggests the need for more group work. There's too little group activity in high school except in science labs where two or three kids have to solve a problem or learn something together. There are many things that adults could do to make learning more engaging to students.

On the other hand, sometimes it seems to me that the best thing would be to forbid children to go to school until they can demonstrate that they have a real interest in something. Of course, such a system would be fair only if we had preschools for all children, where they could be exposed to a stimulating environment in a playful setting.

Education should be available to everyone, obviously. But education should not be an obligation, but rather a privilege that you earn by showing that you're curious about some part of the world. You get your education through that curiosity. The role of the teacher would then be to find the material that would allow the student to explore his or her curiosity. Because no matter what you're curious about, if you are really curious, you will have to learn everything else.

Whether the topic is bugs or stars or singing, there are connections. There is mathematics behind the music and chemistry behind the animals. Once the students are hooked on their interest, the teacher should be the gatekeeper to the enormous richness of information in the world. The role of the teacher is not to convey the same content to a captive audience, which becomes almost immediately aversive to most children.

I'm interested in how you became interested in the idea of flow. Was it an experience of your own that led you to find out more about it?

Essentially, I was interested in psychology. At the time, you couldn't get a degree in psychology by studying happiness or well-being, but creativity was something you could study.

So I studied creativity in artists. And I was struck by how these artists would get completely lost in what they were doing for long periods of time. And yet, once they finished the canvas, they never looked at it again. Most of them weren't trying to sell their art. The finished painting was an excuse for them to paint. The process of painting was the reward that motivated them.

So I started wondering, Does this happen in other aspects of life? It turned out that people play music for the same reason. They play music to go on the journey, not to reach the destination. In sports, it is the same. I thought that the experience that made the activity so rewarding would be different in music or chess or rock climbing. Instead, what was so surprising was how similarly everyone described how they felt, even though what they were doing was so different.

And for yourself, what are the activities that give you the experience of flow?

When I was in high school, I played chess competitively. I used to paint. I did serious rock climbing. Later, I wrote fiction for *The New Yorker*. All of these are wonderful flow activities. Now I get creative enjoyment mostly from work and from hiking here in Montana with the family.

What family characteristics are most conducive to inspiring a love of learning?

Modeling is the best strategy. If the kid grows up seeing that his parents and other adults have no interest in anything except making money, it's unlikely that he or she will learn that it's fun to study or learn new things.

It boils down to the essentials: support and challenge. By challenge I mean high expectations, high standards, allowing the child a lot of independence, exposing students to new opportunities whenever possible. Support means simply that the child feels that the family as a whole is interested in every member's welfare. If the mother comes home tired, the kids will notice it and try to help her and so forth.

When their families give them both support and challenge, children are more likely to choose harder subjects in high school, get better grades, end up in better colleges, and have higher self-esteem in college or after college. If they receive support only, the kids tend to be happy and feel better about themselves, but they're not necessarily ambitious. They don't try to advance in school. They don't take harder classes.

If the family offers a lot of challenges but does not provide support, then the kids tend to do well in school, but they're not very happy. And if they have neither support nor challenge from the family, then it's bad all around. Support and challenge impart different strengths. Challenge gives children vision and direction, focus and perseverance. Support gives the serenity that allows them freedom from worry and fear.

I was struck by how these artists would get completely lost in what they were doing for long periods of time.

Teenagers often have a great deal of anxiety that gets in their way when they tackle a challenge. What's the antidote to anxiety?

Well, there are several. One is tutoring or help in the subjects that provide the most anxiety; another is building up students' strengths. It's often the case that once the students find something that they are really good at, then the anxiety disappears in the other situations. The parents should monitor what the child is interested in and give opportunities to excel at those subjects.

Going back to our youngest son, we weren't the ones who helped him. Once he found that he was as good as or better than others at something, it gave him the feeling that he could do other things, too.

We have an idea in education that we have to work on our weaknesses. To a certain extent, that makes sense. But it makes even more sense to work on the strengths. Because once someone has developed strengths, then everything else becomes easier. Second, if you feel miserable studying mathematics and you spend all your time learning mathematics, chances are you will never be very good at it anyway. If the child is good at photography, allow him or her to explore and develop those strengths.

So you wouldn't be a fan of the core curriculum that requires all students to master certain culturally important content?

No, I think that's kind of silly. Look at our presidents. President Bush was a low *C* student all his life, and so was Clinton until he got to be a Rhodes scholar. It's kind of hypocritical to expect that all children should be good across the board when most adults aren't successful at everything.

The important thing is to stimulate the curiosity, reinforce the curiosity, and build on the strengths of the child. And then you have a vibrant, lively community instead of people who have been stuffed with information that they don't care about.

Of all the students you interviewed, do any stand out as special examples?

Hundreds. One could write a shelf of novels on the lives of these kids.

There was a boy from Kansas City who, at age 12, was really in bad shape. He hated school. He had nothing that he liked. His self-esteem was low. He was in trouble with the school. We thought he would end up having serious trouble.

Then, in his senior year, when we looked at his booklet, we noticed that he had completely changed. He was happy. He felt strong self-esteem. He'd write that he was especially happy when he was looking for a valve or pipes at the hardware store or when he was carrying some rocks to his truck. When he was doing these things, he felt really positive. And we couldn't understand what he was talking about.

Challenge gives children vision and direction, focus and perseverance. Support give the serenity that allows them freedom from worry and fear.

In the interviews, we asked him, What is this about looking for a valve or carrying rocks? He told us that he had a business building koi ponds. At some time in his junior year, he saw one of these Japanese fishponds in somebody's garden, and he became so fascinated that he built one in his own yard and one for his neighbor. And then he started building ponds commercially. At age 18, he bought a panel truck for his koi pond business. And he felt tremendous. He had to learn everything from plumbing to biology: how the fish live and what to feed them. He learned chemistry. He learned mathematics to understand water pressure and volume. Senior year he did great in school. He ended up going to a community college and taking technical courses. That is what can happen when a kid makes a connection between something inside and an opportunity outside. To me, that's how education should be. To educate means to lead out. And we don't lead kids out. We kind of stop them. To educate is to expose kids to many possibilities until they find a connection between what's really important to them and the world out there. And then we must nurture and cultivate that connection.

Did the act of writing the journals help the students in your study become more active in their pursuit of learning?

Definitely. Some psychologists use journal writing as therapy. Once you really have an idea of what you're doing, you have a chance to take charge of your behavior. Often kids are put in a dependent state in school; they are not supposed to take any initiative except in what the teachers want them to do. Television puts them in another kind of dependent state. Many come to tacitly believe that they have no say over their own development as human beings.

Writing things down and reflecting on them is one of those things that makes a person ask, Why am I doing these things when I feel so bad when I do them? Why don't I do more of those things that make me happy?

Mihaly Csikszentmihalyi is the D.J. and C.S. Davidson Professor of Psychology at the Drucker School of Management, Claremont Graduate University in Claremont, California. He is the author or coauthor of 15 books, among them *Flow: The Psychology of Optimal Experience* (Harper & Row, 1990) and, with Barbara Schneider, *Becoming Adult: How Teenagers Prepare for the World of Work* (BasicBooks, 2000). **Marge Scherer** is Editor in Chief of *Educational Leadership*; el@ascd.org.

Curriculum Integration in the Era of Disciplinary Standards

What Engages Underachieving Middle School Students in Learning?

Underachieving students provide insights to help teachers select teaching strategies that more closely match how students learn. Relationships, trust, and respect emerge as critical motivators.

By Mike Muir

Ben, Doris, Eric, Cathy, Mike, and Andy are probably just like some of the students you have. Ben does well when he turns in his work, but often misplaces, loses, and forgets papers and books. Doris' teachers feel that they do not know her well, because she is frequently absent and very quiet when in school. Eric does not do much of his work despite the fact that he is bright, garrulous, and personable. Cathy is the kind of friendly student you would like to have in class, but her mom often keeps her home to care for her six younger siblings. Mike wants to be a pilot or work with computers but does not see how school is preparing him for his future. Andy is an extraordinary artist whose learning style does not seem to match his schoolwork.

One of the most persistent questions facing individual teachers is, "How do I motivate *all* children to learn?"

These six students are all underachievers. Their teachers identified each of them as such and they readily recognize themselves as being bright but not doing well in school or not liking school much. They happily identify with this characterization, rather than being offended by it. They also each agreed to be interviewed, so that I might gain some insight into what they believe motivates them to learn.

The Challenge

Public education faces a difficult challenge: educating every youth in the country. In the face of this challenge is the fact that there are many children who are undermoti-

vated, disengaged, and underachieving. Even early in the 20th century, there was concern that many students had dropped out physically or mentally (Kaminsky, 1992). In the 1915 book, *All The Children of All The People,* Smith's exploration into the challenge of educating all students, begins:

> However reluctant one may be to acknowledge the fact, it is nonetheless certain that the task of trying to educate everybody, which our public schools are engaged in, has proved to be far more difficult than the originators of the idea of such a possibility thought it would be when they set out upon the undertaking. (Smith, 1915, p. v)

Teachers are challenged daily by students who do not seem interested in learning. Teachers struggle with discipline issues and with meeting the needs of students at widely differing ability and achievement levels. One of the most persistent questions facing individual teachers is, "How do I motivate *all* children to learn?" The real problem facing educators is helping all students achieve optimal learning (conceptual understanding and the ability to apply knowledge to new problems, learning, and creations) with high quality content (from the students' own interests, from state and local curricula, and national standards). If we are serious about educating every child, we must include every child in meaningful, engaged learning. That means using teaching techniques that match what we know about how kids learn.

I decided to ask underachieving students what they thought about how they learn well. There is a lot written about how experts think students learn well. Although these studies and theories can be very helpful to teachers, there is much less written about how *students* think they learn well, especially from the point of view of underachieving students. I asked my underachieving students a series of questions. The first set included open ended questions such as the following:

- Think of a good learning experience. What made that a good learning experience?
- Describe a good class or teacher that you have now or have had in the past. What made them good?
- Imagine that the State Department of Education came to you and asked you how to design courses and units so that you could really learn well. What would you tell them?
- What is the one thing you would change about how your classes are taught or how your teachers teach that would help you to learn better?

These questions did not suggest any factors which might help them learn better, but solicited the students' own ideas. The second set of questions was based on what research advises might help students learn. This set of questions included:

- How do your teachers try to make school interesting to you?
- How do your teachers give you choices and let you help in class decision-making?
- How do your teachers try to help you see how course content is useful or important?
- How is school preparing you for your future?

There are two things that you, the reader, should keep in mind as you read this study. The first is that the sample is small and narrow: There are only six students in the study. This sample includes only middle school students not those in elementary or high school, and it includes students from rural, central New England, rather from other possible demographic regions.

The second is that this is a "theory building" study designed to explore what students think. Because it is a theory building study, and not a theory testing study, I do not have achievement data on these students. While the stories and conclusions are presented to help you build your own theories about what motivates underachieving students to learn, it will not "prove" that any particular motivator will help students. What I have done below, however, is point out where the students' ideas connect with the professional literature on learning.

Keep in mind that with this kind of study, it is up to you to decide if these students' opinions and my conclusions match your own experience base, theories, and beliefs about motivating underachievers.

You do not have to accept my results. This study can be a model for your own action research, and I enthusiastically invite readers to ask your underachieving students questions about how they think they learn well. All six students had clear ideas of how they learn well, what they liked and disliked about how their teachers teach, and what recom-

Figure 1
Components of Meaningful Engaged Learning

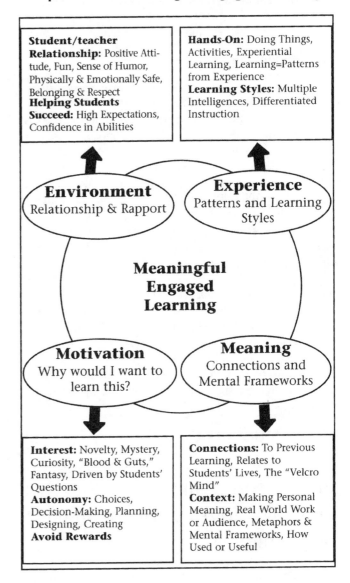

mendations they would make about changing schools in ways that would help them learn better. This leads me to think that you will find the same when you ask your students.

The six students were seventh graders attending one of two middle schools in rural, western Maine. Both schools are approximately the same size, serving about 500 students in grades seven and eight. Both schools divide students into five academic teams of four teachers (math, science, social studies, and language arts) and about 100 students each. Both are consolidated schools located in their respective county seats. They bring in students from a wide surrounding area, creating a diverse student demographic. For example, there are students who live in town and students who live in the woods; there are students of lawyers and doctors and students of farmers, woodsmen, and factory workers.

To add more credibility to the findings from the student interviews, I also interviewed four of their teachers, and conducted classroom observations. Synthesizing these findings with the literature on learning and motivation, a theory for meaningful, engaged learning begins to emerge. There are four key components: the learning environment, experience, motivation, and meaning making.

Environment

I had expected students to focus on intrinsic motivators closely related to content, including hands-on activities, choice, curiosity, pace, and alignment with personal goals. Those were validated by the students, but not as strongly as the importance of relationship, trust, and respect in the classroom. Andy talked about how teachers who nag turn him off to learning and Mike said that he would not learn from a teacher who did not like him. Eric and Ben both feel they learn better from teachers who joke around and create an environment where it is safe to ask questions and make mistakes. Eric says he does not learn well from teachers who are grumpy and Ben equates boring classes with teachers who are too serious and not having much fun. Ben said he would tell the Department of Education that students are not having enough fun in school and that they should have more. Cathy likes caring teachers who give her one-on-one assistance and attention. Doris likes teachers who know her capabilities and push and challenge her, but are not authoritarian. Dowty (1997) and Emerick (1992) also report that the student/teacher relationship is key to improving achievement.

All six students thought they learned best from experiential work such as projects, especially when they had input into project design or in selecting a topic.

A teacher having clear expectations was especially important to Doris. She wanted teachers to use a lot of repetition so that she would be sure to know what they wanted from her. Interviews and observations revealed numerous strategies that teachers used to help students succeed: giving students personal attention, using a variety of teaching strategies, making sure students start with success before moving on to more challenging work, working from student strengths rather than focusing on their weaknesses, having peers explain a difficult concept, giving students a second chance, creating an environment where mistakes are viewed as a learning opportunity, and using questions to guide students.

Teachers should create a respectful environment within their classrooms. They should get to know their students well, including their interests and aspirations, and personal histories and contexts. This might be facilitated by long term relationships with students, achieved through looping, multiage classrooms, or multiyear classrooms. Teachers

should treat students as if they genuinely like and respect them, even when disciplining them.

Experience

Educators should remember that most learning is finding patterns in experiences (Schank & Cleary, 1995). These patterns become schema and help define how a person perceives and understands her world. Experience provides students with rich sensory data, furnishing multiple cues for memory and recall (Rumelhart, 1980; Bruning, Schraw, & Ronning 1995). It is not surprising, then, that all six students thought they learned best from experiential work such as projects and hands-on activities, especially when they had input into project design or in selecting a topic.

Doris thought that hands-on activities were the best part of school. Eric's favorite classes were the ones that were taught in an active way. Cathy equated "fun" with doing group projects that allowed for individual student input. Ben sees hands-on activities and projects as a way to make school interesting and fun for all students. Eric recommends that more teachers be active and fun, and Cathy recommends less book work in exchange for more activities. Andy talked about how math class was one of his favorites because they did hands-on work. Doris says that fun schoolwork is "doing something," not just reading or studying, and Cathy does not mind reading and writing assignments, as long as the teacher combines it with hands-on activities.

Andy and Doris say that part of what they liked about hands-on activities was that there was often more than one solution, and not everyone had to do the work the same way or at the same pace. They disliked lockstep teaching. Many of the students went on to complain that they did not learn well from too much bookwork. Eric and Cathy said it was because there was too much sitting and they wanted to be more active. The recommendations that several of the students would make to the Department of Education focused on reducing the amount of bookwork and increasing the amount of hands-on work. Nearly all the students liked project-based teaching and thought they learned well from it.

Despite their interest in doing things and hands-on work, none of the students wanted to forgo all bookwork. Their descriptions of hands-on activities and project work were full of references to researching, reading, and writing. Cathy was specific about not minding bookwork as long as there were some more active components to the work, as well.

Much of the talk about active hands-on learning revolved around discussions of respecting and providing for students' diverse learning styles. Both Doris and Ben commented on how different students learn differently and that students sometimes might be placed into groups according to how they learn best. Doris saw differentiated assignments as a form of fairness. Ben recommended that teachers help students discover how they best learn. Only Eric thought he learned well with traditional schoolwork, although his math teacher reports that he is doing best in math with the nontraditional activities. Educators should keep in mind that people perceive and process experiences differently (Sternberg, 1997; Gardner, 1983, 1998, 1999; Fairhurst & Fairhurst, 1995; Papert, 1996). Teachers can meet students' diverse needs by using a variety of teaching strategies from learning style or Multiple Intelligence theories. Teachers can also provide assignments, such as projects, that are flexible enough that different students can complete the task in different ways.

Teachers' responsiveness to students' individual learning differences was very important to the six participants. All the students and all the teachers interviewed agreed with Papert (1996) that most failure to learn is a result of instruction not matching the individual's learning style. Further, despite the common motivators (teacher relationship, hands-on work, and choices), there were individual differences between how the students felt they learned well.

Motivation

Motivation is the next key factor. This does not refer to why teachers might want students to learn material, but why students themselves might want to learn it. Subconsciously, students decide every day what they will learn and what they will not. Teachers can increase the likelihood that students will learn when they try to motivate the students intrinsically or extrinsically. Intrinsic motivation is very powerful. Teachers can invoke it by relating learning to student interests and goals, or finding ways to make learning interesting, perhaps by using novelty, mystery, curiosity, "blood and guts," or fantasy.

Each student had typical adolescent interests: playing sports, socializing with friends, toying with computers and video games, and listening to music. So, it may not be surprising that teachers struggle to tie their academics into these fairly non-academic interests and hobbies. Even though much of the work did not tie in with these interests, the students did find some of the work interesting. Much of it was dependent on the individual. Doris liked teachers sharing stories from their past. Cathy liked lessons related to government and books such as *The Outsiders* and *Huck Finn* that related to the South, where she used to live. Ben thought his fourth grade teacher, who dressed up as story characters, was interesting. One of his teachers reports that Ben likes blood and guts and anything that's gory, "books that have gory stuff things in them. He loved Edgar Allan Poe." Of the work that students agreed is interesting, projects and hands-on work giving students choices and limited autonomy headed the list.

Despite their interest in doing things and hands-on work, none of the students wanted to forgo all bookwork.

Extrinsic motivation can either improve learning or shut it down. A focus on punishments and rewards can be counterproductive to learning (Kohn, 1993, 1994). Autonomous supportive strategies (such as providing students

choices and giving them opportunities for decision making, planning, designing, and creating), on the other hand, can make extrinsically required learning as powerful as intrinsically motivated learning (Deci & Ryan, 1985; Deci, Spiegel, Ryan, Koestner, & Kauffman, 1982; Deci, Vallerand, Pelletier, & Ryan, 1991).

The student participants liked having choices and input into their learning. Choice was one of the key attractions of hands-on and project work. Students also described being given choices among class assignments and required readings, setting schedules, and being flexible in how they meet content requirements. Choice was also one of the teachers' key strategies for meeting students' different learning styles, and several teachers believed that choice is a way to spark student interest or to engage students.

Choices and input were important components of project work for Ben, Doris, and Cathy. Doris said she wanted to do class projects and assignments her own way. Cathy wanted input into the kinds of work she does; she does not mind parameters, but does not want to be told exactly what to do. Ben thinks he learns best when he is doing hands-on activities that students have more control over. Design projects, by definition, involve students in deciding how to solve a problem. In other projects, students were given choices about how to represent their work, and project topics were often student selected.

Meaning

Meaning is the fourth component. People do not compile knowledge in some objective data retrieval system. Memory works primarily to make meaning of experience and functions as a connection machine, making associations between different memories, facts, skills, and attitudes (Anderson, Reynolds, Schallert, & Goetz, 1977; Anderson, Spiro, & Anderson, 1978; Schank & Cleary, 1995; Rumelhart, 1980; Bruning, et. al., 1995). By providing contexts for learning and mental frameworks for new knowledge, teachers can help students learn material better by helping them develop associations, connections, and contexts for understanding and meaning making.

Seeing connections and believing that content is useful is important to these students. Both Eric's and Ben's good learning experiences involved learning something they perceived as being useful to them. Eric says he sees how language arts might be useful to him as a businessman and that he can see how math would be useful in everyday life. Cathy says she likes social studies, mostly because of the connections the teacher makes between ancient societies and today's. Ben says his math teacher shows how content and skills are useful through application projects, like building bridges and boats. Eric says that some of his teachers explain how course content might be useful to careers he is interested in.

Teachers say they use a variety of strategies to help students connect to content and understand its usefulness. Eric's and Cathy's math teacher uses problems and projects related to real world problems, and their language arts teacher says she tries to connect her teaching to the students' lives and tries to teach writing skills as the need arises from the students' own writing. Ben's and Doris' science teacher mostly tries to make interdisciplinary connections or connections to lessons the students have had previously. Their social studies teacher shared a variety of ways she tries to connect her teaching to students' lives:

> I guess it's really easy with the geography to connect in their own lives, because you can always compare people and customs. As far as U.S. History connecting to their lives, I guess I would do that more with what is going on now in the world, using topics like gun control, the death penalty, as well as laws and amendments. You can bring it right to their personal life.

Teachers need to find ways to relate learning to students' lives, whether that is showing how new knowledge and skills are useful to them or by connecting it to their own lives. Involving students in work for an audience beyond the teacher and other students, giving them real world work to complete, or using metaphors while presenting new information are strategies that help students make meaning of what they are learning.

Conclusion

It is not surprising that improved instruction, which involves students in meaningful, engaged learning, is viewed as a remedy to the growing concern over the high social and economic cost of large numbers of disengaged and at-risk youth (North Central Regional Educational Laboratory, 1997; Williams, 1996). Identifying practices which help these diverse populations learn well is a step toward creating an educational system serving all students.

Mike, Andy, Ben, Doris, Eric, and Cathy allowed me insights into how they think they learn well, in a hope that I can select teaching strategies that more closely match how students learn. You may wish to follow up with your own action research into how your underachieving students learn well. Finding out what motivates our underachieving students will help inform and equip teachers in the struggle to lead all students to academic achievement.

References

Anderson, R., Reynolds, R., Schallert, D., & Goetz, E. (1977). Frameworks for comprehending discourse. *American Education Research Journal, 14*, 367–381.

Anderson, R., Spiro, R., & Anderson, M. (1978). Schemata as scaffolding for the representation of information in connected discourse. *American Education Research Journal, 15*, 433–440.

Bruning, R. H., Schraw, G. J., & Ronning, R. R. (1995). *Cognitive psychology and instruction.* Englewood Cliffs, NJ: Merrill.

Deci, E. L., & Ryan, R. M. (1985). *Intrinsic motivation and self-determination in human behavior.* New York: Plenum.

Deci, E. L., Spiegel, N. H., Ryan, R. M., Koestner, R., & Kauffman, M. (1982). The effects of performance standards on teaching styles: The behavior of controlling teachers. *Journal of Educational Psychology, 74*, 852–859.

Deci, E., Vallerand, R., Pelletier, L., & Ryan, R. (1991). Motivation and education: The self-determination perspective. *Educational Psychologist, 26* (3 & 4), 325–346.

Dowty, G. (1997). *The development of at-risk children's self-efficacy for social functioning and interpersonal relationships: A review of the literature and implications for residential interventions.* Unpublished paper. University of Main, Orono, Maine.

Emerick, L. J. (1992). Academic underachievement among the gifted: Students' perceptions of factors that reverse the pattern. *Gifted Child Quarterly, 36*(3), 140–146.

Fairhurst, A., & Fairhurst, L. (1995). *Effective teaching effective learning: Making the personality connection in your classroom.* Palo Alto, CA: Davies-Black Publishing.

Gardner, H. (1983). *Frames of mind.* New York: Basic Books.

Gardner, H. (1998). A multiplicity of intelligences. *Scientific American Presents: Exploring Intelligence, 9*(4), 18–23.

Gardner, H. (1999). *The disciplined mind.* New York: Simon & Schuster.

Kaminsky, J. (1992). A pre-history of educational philosophy in the United States. *Harvard Educational Review, 62*(2), 179–198.

Kohn, A. (1993). *Punished by rewards: The trouble with gold stars, incentive plans, A's, praise, and other bribes.* Boston: Houghton Mifflin.

Kohn, A. (1994). *The risks of rewards.* ERIC digest (EDO-PS-94-14). Urbana, IL: ERIC Clearinghouse on Elementary and Early Childhood Education.

North Central Regional Educational Laboratory. (1997). *At risk children and youth.* Retrieved December 11, 1997, from http://www.ncrel.org/sdrs/areas/at0cont.htm

Papert, S. (1996). *The connected family: Bridging the digital generation gap.* Marietta, GA: Longstreet Press.

Rumelhart, D. (1980). Schemata: The building blocks of cognition. In R. Spiro, B. Bruce, & W. Brewer (Eds.), *Theoretical issues in reading comprehension* (pp. 33–58). Hillsdale, NJ: Erlbaum.

Schank, R., & Cleary, C. (1995). *Engines for education.* Hillsdale, NJ: Lawrence Erlbaum.

Smith, W. H. (1915). *All the children of all the people: A study of the attempt to educate everybody.* New York: Macmillan.

Sternberg, R. (1997). What does it mean to be smart? *Educational Leadership, 54*(6), 20–24.

Williams, B. (Ed.). (1996). *Closing the achievement gap: A vision for changing beliefs and practices.* Alexandria, VA: Association for Supervision and Curriculum Development.

Mike Muir is an Assistant Professor of Education at the University of Maine at Farmington and Director of the Maine Center for Meaningful Engaged Learning (www.mcmel.org). E-mail: mmuir@maine.edu.

From *Middle School Journal,* November 2001, pp. 37-43. © 2001 by the National Middle School Association. Reprinted by permission.

When Children Make Rules

In constructivist classrooms, young children's participation in rule making promotes their moral development.

Rheta DeVries and Betty Zan

Sherice Hetrick-Ortman's kindergartners were passionate about block building. These children at the Freeburg Early Childhood Program in Waterloo, Iowa, lavished care on their complex structures and felt justly proud of their creations. Some of the children were concerned, however, about problems in the block area. They discussed the matter at group time and came up with some new rules to post in the block-building area:

- Keep hands off other people's structures.
- No knocking people's structures down.
- Four friends in the block area at one time.

When children care about a classroom problem such as this one and take part in solving it, they are more likely to view the resulting rules as fair. Having *made* the rules, they are more likely to observe them. Just as important, participating in the process of rule making supports children's growth as moral, self-regulating human beings.

Rules in schools have traditionally been made by teachers and given to children. Today, many teachers see the benefits of allowing children to have a voice in developing classroom rules. But if we are not careful, this involvement can be superficial and meaningless. How can we best involve children in making classroom rules?

Morality and Adult-Child Relationships

We speak from a constructivist point of view, inspired by the research and theory of Jean Piaget. In constructivist education, rule making is part of the general atmosphere of mutual respect, and the goal is children's moral and intellectual development (DeVries & Zan, 1994).

Piaget (19832/1965) identified two types of morality that parallel two types of adult-child relationships: one that promotes optimal moral and intellectual development, and one that retards it. *Heteronomous* morality consists of conformity to external rules without question. Overly coercive relationships with adults foster this type of morality and can impede children's development of self-regulation. *Autonomous* morality, by contrast, derives from an internal need to relate to other people in moral ways. Cooperative relationships with adults foster this type of morality and help children develop high levels of self-regulation.

Obviously, children and adults are not equals. However, when the adult respects the child as a person with a right to exercise his or her will, their relationship has a certain psychological equality that promotes autonomy.

Piaget, of course, did not advocate complete freedom, and neither do we. Although constructivist teachers minimize the exercise of adult authority or coercion in relation to children, *minimize* does not mean *eliminate* (DeVries, 1999; DeVries & Edmiaston, 1999; DeVries & Kohlberg, 1987/1990). Rather, we strive for a balance that steadily builds the child's regulation of his or her own behavior.

Norms and Rules in Constructivist Classrooms

To investigate how constructivist teachers use external control and how they develop classroom norms and rules, we interviewed the teachers at the Freeburg Early Childhood Program, a laboratory school serving children ages 3–7 in a predominantly low-income neighborhood. The school's aim is to demonstrate constructivist practices.

Norms Established by Teachers

We define *norms* as specific expectations that teachers establish for children's behavior—ways of behaving that everyone takes for granted as part of the culture of the classroom. A norm is usually unwritten and sometimes unspoken until someone violates it and the teacher takes corrective action. The Freeburg teachers' reflections revealed three kinds of norms that existed in their classrooms:

- *Safety and health norms* ensure children's well-being. Our teachers articulated these as non-negotiables. Examples include "No hurting others," "Lie down at rest time," "Keep shoes on outside," "No crashing trikes or other vehicles," and "Don't throw sand."
- *Moral norms* pertain to respect for people and animals. They often relate to fair treatment or distribution of goods. Examples of these are "Take fair turns," "Talk through a conflict until there is a resolution," "If you bring a live animal into the classroom, try to make it comfortable," and "No hurting animals."
- *Discretionary norms* consist of routines and procedures to make the classroom run smoothly and make learning possible. Kathy Morris, the teacher in the 3-year-olds' class, pointed out that

young children do not like chaos, and they need adults to figure out routines that work so that events run smoothly. Discretionary norms also include societal norms for politeness and individual responsibility that children need to know. Examples include "Sit with the group at group time," "Wait until all are seated at lunch before eating," and "Clean up your place after lunch."

All teachers must sometimes exert external control.

All teachers have safety and health norms, moral norms, and discretionary norms. These norms are acceptable and necessary uses of external authority in a constructivist classroom. But constructivist teachers carefully evaluate their reasons for norms and attempt to minimize the use of external control as much as possible.

Rules Made by Children

We define rules as formal agreements among teachers and children. Constructivist teachers often conduct discussions of problems that relate to their norms and engage children in making classroom rules that arise from these norms.

When teachers first suggest that children make rules, children often parrot such adult admonitions as "Never talk to strangers" or "Raise your hand and wait to be called on." This occurs especially when children are unaccustomed to a sociomoral atmosphere in which they feel free to express their honest opinions. Children may view rule making as another exercise in trying to figure out the right answer or say what they think the teacher wants to hear. The rules that they suggest may not reflect a real understanding of the need to treat others in moral ways. When children only mindlessly restate adults' rules, they have not engaged in true rule making.

Children who engage in true rule making sometimes reinvent rules that elaborate on already established norms. Although these elaborations are not entirely original, they still give the children feelings of autonomy in their power to create rules. For example, Gwen Harmon's 4-year-olds, working within the classroom norm "Don't hurt animals," developed the following practical and concrete rules regarding the chicks that they hatched in the classroom:

- Pick them up safely.
- Don't push them.

- Don't squeeze them.
- Don't put things in their box.
- Don't punch them.
- Don't put them on the light bulb.
- Don't drop them.
- Don't throw them.
- Don't pick them up by their wings.
- Don't color on them.
- Don't pull their heads off.

Reinvented rules demonstrate children's understanding of the moral norm because they translate the norm into children's own words and provide elaborations that make sense to them. Sometimes the elaborations are novel, dealing with situations that the teacher had not considered discussing. For example, in Beth Van Meeteren's 1st grade classroom, where the norm is to treat others with respect, children made the rule, "When people pass gas, do not laugh, or they will be upset or embarrassed."

Sometimes children develop entirely original rules. Unlike reinvented rules, invented rules reflect children's power to make decisions in the classroom. For example, Dora Chen's class of 4-year-olds invented a new rule in response to a problem they saw during one of their classroom routines. One day during clean-up, a child saw another child finishing a snack and felt that no one should eat snacks during clean-up time. He told the teacher, who raised the issue at group time. She asked, "What should our rule be?" After a 17-minute discussion in which the children suggested various possibilities, the teacher clarified the choice between "No snack during clean-up: throw it away" or "Finish snack before going outdoors." The children voted to throw away their unfinished snacks when clean-up started.

The new rule, driven by children's interest and concern, went beyond the teacher's concerns. Although the teacher preferred giving the children more time to finish their snacks, she believed that the children's solution was fair given the one-hour activity time in which to eat snacks.

Guidelines for Exerting External Control

Some people have the misconception that constructivist teachers are permissive and that external control never occurs in constructivist classrooms. In fact, all teachers must exert external control sometimes. From our discussions with teachers and our understanding of research and theory,

we have derived four general guidelines for the use of external control.

Provide a general and pervasive context of warmth, cooperation, and community. We draw inspiration for this guideline from the work of Jean Piaget, especially from *The Moral Judgment of the Child* (1932/1965). Many others, however, have come to this same conclusion starting from different theoretical perspectives (Nelson, 1996; Watson, 2003). In fact, almost all of the recent classroom management programs on the market, with the exception of Assertive Discipline, stress the importance of cooperation and community (Charles, 2002).

Act with the goal of students' self-regulation. A developmental perspective leads us to focus on the long term. We want to contribute to the development of autonomous, self-regulating human beings who can make decisions based on the perspectives of all involved. Therefore, compliance is not our primary goal. Of course, we all wish sometimes that children would be more compliant. But we constantly remind ourselves and one another that developing self-regulation takes time, and we celebrate significant events, such as when an aggressive child actually uses words for the first time to tell another child what he wants instead of slugging him.

Minimize unnecessary external control as much as is possible and practical. Constructivist teachers do use external control; in fact, they use it quite a bit. As Piaget states, "However delicately one may put the matter, there have to be commands and therefore duties" (1932/1965, p. 180). Teachers in constructivist classrooms, however, use external control of children consciously and deliberately, not impulsively or automatically. The teachers with whom we work constantly ask themselves whether the external regulation is absolutely necessary.

Through discussions with teachers Gwen Harmon, Shari McGhee, and Christie Sales, we have identified several situations that can lead to unnecessary control of children. Avoidable control-inducing situations occur when

- The classroom arrangement invites rowdy behavior.
- Children do not know the classroom routine.
- Too many transitions lead to too much waiting time.
- Crowding in a part of the classroom leads to conflicts.

- Group time goes on for too long; children become restless, and some act out.
- Activities are not sufficiently engaging to appeal to children's purposes, and children become aimless.
- The classroom does not contain enough materials, and children compete for what is available.
- Clean-up is poorly organized, and children resist cleaning up after activity time.
- A mismatch exists between the teacher's expectations and the children's competencies.
- The teacher attributes a character flaw to a child who misbehaves.

When external control is necessary, use the least amount necessary to secure compliance. Ideally, the constructivist teacher uses external control judiciously to make sure that the child's experience overall is a mixture increasingly in favor of the child's self-regulation. When external regulation becomes necessary, the teacher must preserve the child's dignity and autonomy—for example, by giving the child a choice and thus returning a degree of autonomy as soon as possible.

Meaningful Rule Making

For many years, we have advocated allowing young children to make classroom rules, arguing that such opportunities are part and parcel of a constructivist, democratic classroom. By encouraging children to make classroom rules, the teacher minimizes unnecessary external control and promotes the development of children's moral and intellectual autonomy.

To genuinely think for themselves and exercise autonomy, children must be given the power to make rules and decisions that both elaborate on classroom norms and break new ground. By actively seeking out appropriate opportunities and recognizing them when they arise in the daily life of the classroom, teachers can create classrooms that are fair and democratic.

References

Charles, C. (2002). *Building classroom discipline* (7th ed.). Boston: Allyn and Bacon.

DeVries, R. (1999). Implications of Piaget's constructivist theory for character education. In M. Williams & E. Schaps (Eds.), *Character education.* Washington, DC: Character Education Partnership.

DeVries, R., & Edmiaston, R. (1999). Misconceptions about constructivist education. *The Constructivist, 13*(3), 12–19.

DeVries, R., & Kohlberg, L. (1987/1990). *Constructivist early education.* Washington, DC: National Association for the Education of Young Children.

DeVries, R., & Zan, B. (1994). *Moral classrooms, moral children: Creating a constructivist atmosphere in early education.* New York: Teachers College Press.

Nelson, J. (1996). *Positive discipline.* New York: Ballantine Books.

Piaget, J. (1932/1965). *The moral judgment of the child.* London: Free Press.

Watson, M. (2003). *Learning to trust.* San Francisco: Jossey-Bass.

Rheta DeVries is a professor and Director of the Regents' Center for Early Developmental Education, University of Northern Iowa, 107 Schindler Education Center, Cedar Falls, IA 50701; (391) 273–2101; rheta.devries@uni.edu. **Betty Zan** is an assistant professor and Research Fellow at the Regents' Center for Early Developmental Education; (319) 273–2101; betty.zan@uni.edu.

A Positive Learning Environment Approach to Middle School Instruction

School personnel need to reconsider young adolescents' needs and create a learning environment that contributes to positive behavior as well as academic achievement.

Peggy Hester, Robert A. Gable, and M. Lee Manning

Middle school teachers must be prepared to educate an increasingly diverse population of young adolescents (Manning, 1999/2000). Most of these students will respond positively to instruction, and will interact appropriately with both peers and adults. However, some students have persistent behavioral problems that, if unchecked, can intensify and become more complicated. It is critical to intervene early with these students; failure to do so puts the student at increased risk for conflicts with classmates, teachers, and family members (Asher & Coie, 1990; Patterson, Capaldi, & Bank, 1989; Webster-Stratton, 2000). That risk, in turn, is associated with academic problems. Indeed, mounting evidence indicates that a strong relationship exists between student academic performance and classroom conduct (e.g., Cantwell & Baker, 1987; Delaney & Kaiser, 2001; Kaiser & Hester, 1997). Research also demonstrates that students who do not perform well in class often have an increased incidence of discipline problems (Nelson, Scott, & Polsgrove, 1999). Other classroom factors, such as improper curricular placement, negative management styles, and ineffective instruction, can exacerbate an already difficult situation (Kauffman, 2001). Given these circumstances, it follows that school personnel need to reconsider young adolescents' needs and create a learning environment that contributes to positive behavior as well as academic achievement.

In recent years, various researchers (e.g., Dodge, 1993; Kaiser & Hester, 1997) have underscored the critical role that early intervention plays in preventing behavior problems in schools. While few persons would argue against the idea of prevention, educators sometimes unwittingly hinder efforts to address student learning/behavior problems (e.g., by withholding specialized supports until a student fails) (Kauffman, 2001). Prevention/ intervention is neither simple nor easy, and it often requires collaboration among various school personnel. It is important to recognize that the concept of "early intervention" is independent of a student's chronological age or grade level. Successful preventive intervention hinges on establishing a learning environment that supports students' positive and adaptive behaviors, identifying students who require more individualized programs, and determining ways to better serve all students. In the following discussion, the authors examine some common behavior problems in middle schools and then explore research-based implications for establishing a positive and supportive learning environment. Finally, they discuss the emergent role that school personnel play in promoting positive academic and behavioral outcomes for all students.

Understanding Young Adolescents' Behaviors

The current education scene in the United States is marked by changing demographics, declining resources, and increasing pressure to produce positive student outcomes. Despite these challenges, many schools have reported improvements in student performance. Yet, we know that some students suffer disproportionally from the consequences of these forces—academically, emotionally/behaviorally, or both.

What responses do young adolescents demonstrate, and what might be the underlying reasons for misbehaviors that impede instruction and socialization? How can educators convince young adolescents to assume greater responsibility for their own behavior?

What responses do young adolescents demonstrate, and what might be the underlying reasons for misbehaviors that impede instruction and socialization? How can educators convince young adolescents to assume greater responsibility for their own behavior? Assuming that the burden of appropriate behavior is a shared responsibility, how can middle school educators best promote positive behavioral responses?

Charles (2002) listed several categories of student misbehavior: 1) goofing off, 2) class disruptions, 3) defiance of authority, and 4) aggression. While the most serious offenses (e.g., physical assaults) are more likely to make headlines, teachers most often deal with far less significant problems such as non-compliance, calling out, and inattention. Although these problems may seem to be relatively innocuous, they routinely interfere with instruction and challenge teachers to come up with strategies and techniques in response (Charles, 2002).

In examining Charles's four categories of behavior, the most misunderstood problem is what Charles (2002) called goofing off—students sit idly, they talk to friends, and/or they fail to complete their work. The reasons for such behavior are many and varied. For example, whole-group instruction often fails to account for diverse student abilities. This can result in frustration and lead some students to withdraw from, or actively avoid, instruction. In other cases, the curricular content may lack relevance to students; or, it may be at odds with students' cultural and linguistic backgrounds (Cartledge et al., 2002). These and other factors can set the stage for what appears to be goofing off behavior.

Creating a Positive Middle School Learning Environment

Media headlines appear to suggest that schools today are hotbeds of aggressive and violent behavior. In fact, statistics show that these incidents, fortunately, occur very infrequently, and that schools remain the safest place for middle school students. Nevertheless, school personnel have a responsibility to recognize the effects of lesser yet more predictable misbehaviors on learning, and to take deliberate action to create a positive school environment. There is a growing consensus that a positive and safe learning environment is one that emphasizes cooperation, collaboration, and peaceful existence, and is one that is free from threats of psychological or physical harm—that is, an environment that reflects caring and concern for all students (Manning, 2000).

The current significance being attached to the school environment stems from several sources. First, several middle school documents (Carnegie Council on Adolescent Development, 1989; Jackson & Davis, 2000; Manning, 2000; National Middle School Association, 1995; Payne, Conroy, & Racine, 1998) underscore the benefits of a positive school environment on young adolescents' academic achievement and positive socialization. Second, a burgeoning amount of information on early adolescence suggests that 10- to 15-year-olds have a critical need for a positive atmosphere in which to socialize and learn (Manning & Bucher, 2001). Third, mounting recognition exists that schools must accept a larger responsibility to establish and strengthen positive interpersonal relationships between students and teachers, as well as among learners themselves (Kerr & Zigmond, 1986; Manning & Bucher, 2001).

Drawing upon the accumulated literature, we found evidence that effective learning environments usually:

- Recognize and accept the differences among young adolescents' physical, psychosocial, and cognitive development, and provide developmentally appropriate instruction

- Place value on gender, sexual orientation, cultural, and linguistic differences, and provide classroom organization and instructional approaches that account for these differences
- Provide curriculum that enhances young adolescents' acceptance of self and others, and that enables them to accept differences and similarities among people
- Provide instruction that ensures a high degree of academic engagement and success for all young adolescents
- Utilize management procedures that emphasize the idea that students constitute a community of learners, all of whom should accept (or be taught to accept) responsibility for their behavior
- Provide direct instruction to sub-groups or individual students who are unable or unwilling to comply with schedules and routines of instruction
- Recognize the importance of self-esteem and its influence on academic achievement, socialization, and overall personal development
- Encourage a sense of collaboration among students and educators
- Emphasize teamwork and trust, predicated on the principle that being fair to everyone means treating no two students exactly the same
- Recognize that each student brings diverse experiences to the classroom and possesses varied strengths and interests
- Help teachers teach more than academics so that students feel a commitment toward each other as well as a positive affiliation toward the school. (Manning & Bucher, 2001)

Table 1 summarizes strategies that teachers can use to prevent behavior problems among young adolescents.

Educators seeking to achieve positive educational outcomes face the challenge of making fundamental, systemic changes in schools. At the middle school level, education personnel must work to create environments that support young adolescents' social, academic, and emotional development and blunt the onset of behavior problems. Administrators and teachers can be made aware of the benefits associated with building-wide and classroom-level student supports and social interactions with parents, teachers, and peers. They also can recognize the importance of taking specific steps to rectify a problem situation (e.g., a focused intervention plan stemming from an assessment of behavior when so-called "universal supports" are not effective).

Specific Developmentally Appropriate Management Strategies

Creating school environments that are conducive to learning and positive behavior may require school personnel to redefine both the structure and culture of the school (e.g., Gable & Manning, 1996). In redefining the school environment to accentuate positive aspects of students' behavior, the focus shifts from dealing with inappropriate, unacceptable, or disruptive behavior to creating a setting that supports the learning and practice of more appropriate behavior. This is accomplished in various ways. Typically, educators reframe classroom and

Table 1

Proactive Strategies for Supporting and Maintaining Positive Student Behavior

CREATE A MIDDLE SCHOOL LEARNING ENVIRONMENT THAT SUPPORTS POSITIVE STUDENT BEHAVIOR

- Acknowledge and promote appropriate behavior throughout the day in all school settings (e.g., classes, advisory programs, and exploratories)
- Define behavioral expectations for appropriate school behavior
- Understand and plan for the effects of development on young adolescent behavior
- Teach students appropriate replacement skills for misbehavior so they have acceptable behaviors that serve the same function
- Affirm students' strengths, skills, and abilities—both academic and non-academic
- Acknowledge and support young adolescents' diversity of all types (e.g., developmental, cultural, gender, social class, and sexual orientation)

SUPPORT YOUNG ADOLESCENTS' SOCIALIZATION SKILLS

- Listen to young adolescents—their problems, concerns, and challenges
- Respond positively to student communication (e.g., respond to both verbal and non-verbal initiations)
- Use positive and nurturing affect (e.g., responsiveness, sensitivity) in interactions
- Teach positive social/communication skills so that students know positive, age-appropriate ways to interact
- Model appropriate social/communication strategies and build upon what the young adolescent says (e.g., expanding or seeking additional information)
- Teach developmentally appropriate conflict resolution skills for young adolescents acting angrily toward students and/or teachers
- Be consistent in implementing behavioral support strategies over time and in all settings, but take into account individual student strengths/weaknesses/differences

school rules/expectations for behaviors and directly teach all students specific expectations (Horner, 2000). Coupled with this strategy is the prolific use of positive affirmation (at least four times as many affirmations as there are acknowledgments of negative behaviors) with students adhering to these expectations (Lewis, Sugai, & Colvin, 1998). Some teachers have found it necessary to abandon longstanding practices (e.g., nagging or reprimanding students) (Shores et al., 1993), and instead directly engage students in interactions that support social/communication skills (Kaiser & Hester, 1997).

A review of the literature indicates that in order to create the most appropriate learning environment and apply the most effective classroom management practices, middle school educators should consider young adolescents' developmental characteristics. Ample evidence indicates that the behavior of young adolescents is affected by changes in self-esteem, as seen in greater desire for increased socialization, peer approval, and general social interaction (Manning, 1999/2000). These and other developmental characteristics can have a powerful impact on young adolescents' behavior. For example, a low self-esteem stemming from academic failure or subsequent peer rejection might cause a student to bully others in an attempt to feel more powerful. A strong need for peer approval might motivate

another student to disobey a teacher. Furthermore, a long-standing pattern of academic problems may lead some students to avoid (either passively or actively) tasks that they perceive to be irrelevant or too challenging. By understanding how overall development, along with specific contextual events, affect student behavior, teachers can better organize classes to promote opportunities for socialization and collaborative learning—both of which can benefit young adolescents, especially those from culturally and linguistically diverse backgrounds (Cartledge et al., 2002).

Effective middle school educators increase the predictability of daily routines. By providing clear schoolwide expectations and consistently acknowledging appropriate student behavior, teachers can eliminate a major obstacle to effective instruction—namely, the lack of stability and predictability over time. And, in establishing a stable teaching/learning environment, educators are able to make better use of limited instructional time, energy, and resources. In short, predictability in daily routines/expectations; consistency in implementation of intervention strategies; and proactive, systematic, and situational support of appropriate social/communication skills are fundamental to preventing student behavior problems (Colvin, Sugai, & Patching, 1993; Gable, Quinn, Rutherford, & Howell, 1998; Kerr & Nelson, 2002).

Most teachers recognize the importance of providing students with a structured classroom environment (e.g., Kerr & Nelson, 2002). Such a setting includes a clearly defined schedule, preparation for student transitions, delineation, and instruction in appropriate responses to adults and peers, along with regular opportunities for students to learn and practice positive social/ communication skills. Indeed, these classroom attributes are prerequisite to effective academic and nonacademic instruction (Kerr & Nelson, 2002; Reitz, 1994).

Effective middle school educators give clear instructions, demonstrate consistency, model behavioral expectations, and follow through on consequences. Research in classroom management demonstrates the value of offering precise instruction, spelling out the consequences for both compliance and noncompliance, and consistently implementing these procedures (e.g., Alberto & Troutman, 1999). The most successful teachers give simple, straightforward instructions so that students know exactly what is expected of them. Then, teachers follow through each and every time. Although teachers must recognize that different students have varying capacities to respond appropriately, failure to react in some way to inappropriate behavior gives the student tacit approval to repeat it. For example, if a student ignores a specific direction (such as, "Kevin, please pay attention to your own work"), the teacher might have to repeat the direction. If Kevin fails to respond to the direction the second time, the teacher might: 1) move into closer physical proximity, 2) verbally prompt him to comply with the direction, and 3) acknowledge the appropriate behavior of a classmate. If Kevin demonstrates the requested behavior, the teacher would praise his cooperation. While consistency and predictability are critical supports for all students, teacher expectations should reflect pupils' specific strengths and weaknesses. Teacher decisions regarding specific demands should be predicated on a careful review of all available information about the students. Educators can elicit positive behavior by encouraging students to participate actively in the rule-making process, to develop a rationale for specific rules/expectations, and to model behavior expectations for one another.

Unless a student is taught alternative strategies to accomplish a particular outcome (e.g., gain attention)—one that works better than the inappropriate behavior—he or she will likely persist in behaving inappropriately.

Effective middle school educators teach students appropriate replacement behaviors that serve the same function as the misbehavior. Absent more appropriate strategies, adults' attempts to address inappropriate student behavior sometimes are reactive and consist of some kind of punitive consequences (e.g., reprimands, time-outs, revoked privileges) (Conroy, Clark, Gable, & Fox, 1999). While these strategies temporarily may serve to suppress an inappropriate behavior (e.g., calling out), they fail to teach students more acceptable replacement behaviors (such as raising one's hand in order to be acknowledged). Accordingly, there is a high probability that the misbehavior will recur. Unless a student is taught alternative strategies to accomplish a particular outcome (e.g., gain attention)—one that works better than the inappropriate behavior—he or she will likely persist in behaving inappropriately. Classroom interventions will be effective only to the extent that they successfully compete with and triumph over "existing contingencies" that support inappropriate behavior (e.g., calling out gains more attention than correct answers) (e.g., Gable, Quinn, Rutherford, & Howell, 1998; Mace, Lalli, & Lalli, 1991). Therefore, the traditional distinction between academic and non-academic instruction may need to be blurred, so that school personnel will routinely teach both academic and non-academic behavior (Gable, Hendrickson, Tonelson, & Van Acker, in press).

Knowledge of students' academic and non-academic needs can be gained in various ways. For example, by observing students throughout the day, teachers can identify "early warning" signs of problems and determine how best to intervene proactively and instructionally before the little problems escalate and become major challenges. Such a proactive approach to instruction (or to non-academic issues) may be applied to a group of students or to an individual, depending on the behavior. For instance, some young adolescents may lack the necessary skills to negotiate a particular social interaction (e.g., initiate a positive verbal exchange with a classmate). To successfully address this problem, students must be directly and systematically taught the appropriate social skills (Reitz, 1994), usually through teacher modeling, role play/behavioral rehearsal, and individual interaction sessions in which the student learns specific communication skills for interacting with others (Kaiser & Hester, 1997).

In that there are a range of possible skills to be taught, selection of specific skills should depend on which behavior best fits the situation and is most likely to be reinforced not only in the classroom, but also beyond it. Another criterion relates to efficiency—how much effort must go into teaching/learning behavior "X" versus behavior "Y." The more manageable both students and teachers perceive the instructional process to be, the greater the likelihood of a successful outcome (Gable et al., in press). Some skills that educators see as important may have little or no significance for students at home or in the community. We must acknowledge that fact to the student, underscore the need to make choices according to the setting, and teach students different skills for different settings. Indeed, such discrimination skills are a critical part of the socialization process. We know that these goals exceed the scope of traditional instruction. Nevertheless, teachers often discover that students' behavior improves as they experience greater feelings of success and higher rates of positive peer- and teacher-student interactions (Shores et al., 1993).

Effective middle school educators affirm positive behavior. Social reinforcement can be a powerful way to teach more acceptable behaviors. For example, specific praise can help facilitate everything from spelling and math skills to positive communication strategies and self-help skills (Alberto &

Troutman, 1999). Despite its documented effectiveness, teacher use of social reinforcement to acknowledge appropriate behavior and promote specific skills is often at such low rates as to be essentially ineffective (Gable, Hendrickson, Young, Shores, & Stowitschek, 1983; Shores et al., 1993). It is also important to recognize that neither praise nor punishment alone teaches students new behaviors (Kerr & Nelson, 2002). A positive comment or verbal command may signal that a certain consequence will follow a specific student response. But in no way does it ensure that the student will engage in the behavior if she or he does not know it, or if he or she sees it as less reinforcing than another response. In other words, direct instruction of a particular behavior, coupled with multiple opportunities to engage in it, can encourage students to engage in appropriate behavior over time and across settings.

Effective middle school educators teach developmentally appropriate socialization skills. In addition to structuring a classroom environment that affords students positive support, middle school educators can provide experiences that improve young adolescents' socialization skills. Changes in social characteristics and situations that normally occur during early adolescence can have a profound impact on young adolescents. Middle school educators are finding it increasingly useful to teach developmentally appropriate socialization skills, even though such skills are not part of their traditional instructional responsibilities. Socialization skills can be taught informally through friendships and social interaction under various conditions (e.g., cooperative learning activities) or formally through direct, systematic instruction. Sometimes, young adolescents may wish to work alone, and should be given the opportunity to do so. At other times, educators should encourage students to interact in more socially oriented situations. To do so, a teacher might allow students to choose their learning groups, and they might encourage students' social interaction through participation in extracurricular activities.

A shift in young adolescents' allegiance from adults (especially, parents and teachers) to peers and friends is a natural part of early adolescence, a change that warrants educators' understanding and acceptance. This shift in allegiance, accompanied by various peer pressures, becomes a powerful influence on young adolescents' daily socialization. Young adolescents' quest for freedom and independence also should be addressed as part of socialization skills instruction. In responding to this desire for increased freedom and independence, educators can provide students with routine opportunities to engage in decision making that reinforces the understanding that with freedom comes responsibilities. Once we recognize that students differ with regard to their repertoire of age appropriate social skills, it becomes easier to establish group-individual instructional priorities. School personnel can provide various students with opportunities to behave responsibly in specific ways and to demonstrate their growing capacity for self-control and self-management in safe and psychologically secure settings (Manning, 2002). Students who are unable or unwilling to demonstrate appropriate socialization skills will need additional instruction. Various traditional classroom management strategies, including the use of punishment, may exacerbate an al-

ready difficult instructional situation. Rather than teaching a student specific skills, the use of punishment can negatively affect adult-student relationships, causing students to avoid future interactions and, in turn, diminish the number of opportunities for teachers to demonstrate and reinforce appropriate behaviors. Furthermore, the use of punishment as a disciplinary tool can trigger in students feelings of anger, defiance, or a desire for revenge.

Recently, we observed a 6th-grade teacher working deliberately to build a positive, learner-centered classroom that would demonstrate that students could be managed without threats or punishments. She faced an especially difficult task because her students had learned during their previous school experiences to equate school with adult coercion, manipulation, and control. In seeking to change student perspectives on schooling, the teacher worked daily to promote positive teacher-student and student-student collaboration, and to encourage students to make appropriate decisions about their learning. To ensure active engagement and high rates of student success, she took steps to align curricular content and instruction with the academic interests and needs of her class. Although by no means a simple undertaking, the teacher found that, over time, the benefits of redefining a positive classroom environment were well worth her efforts. In the weeks that followed, students' overall perspectives toward schooling improved, consonant with their progress in both academics and socialization skills (Manning, 2002).

Concluding Remarks

Middle school educators today must deal with an increasingly diverse population of young adolescents (Manning, 1999/2000). Addressing the myriad challenges associated with students' diverse academic and social skills needs can consume a tremendous amount of time and energy. Effective middle school educators strongly support routine proactive approaches to improve student deportment as well as promote positive interactions between young adolescents and teachers. Without dismissing the significance of outside factors, the real burden of prevention/intervention rests with school personnel. Fortunately, the accumulated evidence clearly demonstrates that quality, sustained instruction can overcome virtually all potentially negative influences on student performance (e.g., socioeconomic status) (Greenwood, 2002). Such instruction should occur at the classroom and schoolwide levels. However, system-wide intervention means changing the school, the classroom, and the daily instruction in ways that teach, reinforce, and otherwise strengthen appropriate student behavior (e.g., Lewis et al., 1998). System-wide supports require that teachers establish nurturing classroom environments conducive to positive student behavior and successful academic performance. To accomplish that goal, school personnel must integrate the social, behavioral, and academic aspects of group-individual instruction. In all, a successful school environment reflects clear expectations, high rates of student engagement and academic success, and teacher acknowledgment of appropriate behaviors, as well as direct systematic instruction of positive behavior to replace disruptive behavior.

The authors have argued that middle school educators can exercise a tremendous amount of control over the nature and quality of daily instruction. Although by no means a simple undertaking, we must strive to support and nurture appropriate student behaviors in ways that account for their diverse learning and behavioral characteristics. It is reassuring to know that teachers are finding new ways to approach and interact with young adolescents to create conditions that are conducive to positive outcomes for all students.

References

Alberto, P. A., & Troutman, A. C. (1999). *Applied behavior analysis for teachers.* Upper Saddle River, NJ: Prentice-Hall.

Asher, S. R., & Coie, J. D. (1990). *The rejected child.* New York: Cambridge University Press.

Cantwell, D. P., & Baker, L. (1987). Prevalence and type of psychiatric disorder and developmental disorders in three speech and language groups. *Journal of Communication Disorders, 20,* 151–160.

Carnegie Council on Adolescent Development. (1989). *Turning points: Preparing American youth for the 21st century.* Washington, DC: Author.

Cartledge, G., Tam, K. Y., Loe, S. A., Miranda, A. H., Lambert, M. C., Kea, C. D., & Simmons-Reed, E. (2002). *Culturally and linguistically diverse students with behavioral disorders.* Arlington, VA: Council for Children with Behavioral Disorders.

Charles, C. M. (2002). *Building classroom discipline* (7th ed.). Boston: Allyn and Bacon.

Colvin, G., Sugai, G., & Patching, B, (1993). Precorrection: An instructional approach to managing predictable problem behavior. *Intervention in School and Clinic, 28,* 143–150.

Conroy, M., Clark, D., Gable, R. A., & Fox, J. (1999). A look at IDEA 1997 discipline provisions: Implications for change in the roles and responsibilities of school personnel. *Preventing School Failure, 43,* 64–70.

Delaney, E. M., & Kaiser, A. P. (2001). The effects of teaching parents blended communication and behavior support strategies. *Behavioral Disorders, 26,* 93–116.

Dodge, K. A. (1993). The future of research on the treatment of conduct disorder. *Development and Psychopathology, 5,* 311–319.

Gable, R. A., Hendrickson, J. M., Tonelson, S., & Van Acker, R. (in press). Integrating academic and nonacademic instruction for students with emotional/behavioral disorders. *Education and Treatment of Children.*

Gable, R. A., Hendrickson, J. M., Young, C. C., Shores, R. E., & Stowitschek, J.J. (1983). A comparison of teacher approval and disapproval statements across categories of exceptionality. *Journal of Special Education Technology, 6,* 15–22.

Gable, R. A., & Manning, M. L. (1996). Facing the challenge of aggressive behaviors in young adolescents. *Middle School Journal, 27,* 19–25.

Gable, R. A., Quinn, M. M., Rutherford, R. B., & Howell, K. (1998). Addressing problem behaviors in schools: Use of functional assessments and behavior intervention plans. *Preventing School Failure, 42,* 106–119.

Greenwood, C. M. (2002). Science and students with learning and behavior problems. *Behavioral Disorders, 27,* 37–52.

Horner, R. H. (2000). Positive behavior supports. In M. L. Wehmeyer & J. R. Patton (Eds.), *Mental retardation in the 21st century* (pp. 181–196). Austin, TX: Pro-Ed.

Jackson, A. W., & Davis, G. A. (2000). *Turning points 2000: Educating adolescents in the 21st century.* New York: Teachers College Press.

Kaiser, A. P., & Hester, P. P. (1997). Prevention of conduct disorders through early intervention: A social-communicative perspective. *Behavioral Disorders, 22,* 117–130.

Kauffman, J. M. (2001). *Characteristics of emotional and behavioral disorders of children and youth* (7th ed.). Upper Saddle River, NJ: Prentice-Hall.

Kerr, M. M., & Nelson, C. M. (2002). *Strategies for managing behavior problems in the classroom* (4th ed.). Upper Saddle River, NJ: Pearson Education.

Kerr, M. M., & Zigmond, N. (1986). What do high school teachers want? A study of expectations and standards. *Education and Treatment of Children, 9,* 239–249.

Lewis, T. J., Sugai, G., & Colvin, G. (1998). Reducing problem behavior through a school-wide system of effective behavioral support: Investigation of a school-wide social skills training program and contextual interventions. *School Psychology Review, 27,* 446–459.

Mace, F. C., Lalli, J. S., & Lalli, E. P. (1991). Functional analysis and treatment of aberrant behavior. *Research in Developmental Disabilities, 12,* 155–180.

Manning, M. L. (1999/2000). Developmentally responsive multicultural education for young adolescents. *Childhood Education, 76,* 82–87.

Manning, M. L. (2000). Child-centered middle schools: A position paper. *Childhood Education, 76,* 154–159.

Manning, M. L. (2002). *Developmentally appropriate middle level schools* (2nd ed.). Olney, MD: Association for Childhood Education International.

Manning, M. L., & Bucher, K. T. (2001). *Teaching in the middle school.* Columbus, OH: Prentice-Hall.

National Middle School Association. (1995). *This we believe: Developmentally responsive middle level schools.* Westerville, OH: Author.

Nelson, C. M., Scott, T. M., & Polsgrove, L. (1999). *Perspective on emotional/behavioral disorders: Assumptions and their implications for education and treatment. What works for children and youth with E/BD: Linking yesterday and today with tomorrow.* Arlington, VA: Council for Children with Behavioral Disorders.

Patterson, G. R., Capaldi, D., & Bank, L. (1989). An early starter model for predicting delinquency. In D. J. Pepler & K. H. Rubin (Eds.), *The development and treatment of childhood aggression* (pp. 139–168). Hillsdale, NJ: Lawrence Erlbaum.

Payne, M. J., Conroy, S., & Racine, L. (1998). Creating positive school climates. *Middle School Journal, 30,* 65–67.

Reitz, A. L. (1994). Implementing comprehensive classroom-based programs for students with emotional and behavioral problems. *Education and Treatment of Children, 17,* 312–331.

Shores, R. E., Jack, S. L., Gunter, P. L., Ellis, D. N., DeBriere, T. J., & Wehby, J. H. (1993). Classroom interaction of children with behavior disorders. *Journal of Emotional and Behavioral Disorders, 1,* 27–39.

Webster-Stratton, C. (2000). Oppositional-defiant and conduct-disordered children. In M. Hersen & R. T. Ammerman, (Eds.), *Advanced abnormal child psychology* (2nd ed., pp. 387–412). Hillsdale, NJ: Lawrence Erlbaum.

Peggy Hester is Associate Professor and Robert A. Gable is Professor, Early Childhood, Speech Pathology, and Special Education, and M. Lee Manning is Professor, Department of Educational Curriculum and Instruction, Old Dominion University, Norfolk, Virginia.

The Key to Classroom Management

By using research-based strategies combining appropriate levels of dominance and cooperation and an awareness of student needs, teachers can build positive classroom dynamics.

Robert J. Marzano and Jana S. Marzano

Today, we know more about teaching than we ever have before. Research has shown us that teachers' actions in their classrooms have twice the impact on student achievement as do school policies regarding curriculum, assessment, staff collegiality, and community involvement (Marzano, 2003a). We also know that one of the classroom teacher's most important jobs is managing the classroom effectively.

A comprehensive literature review by Wang, Haertel, and Walberg (1993) amply demonstrates the importance of effective classroom management. These researchers analyzed 86 chapters from annual research reviews, 44 handbook chapters, 20 government and commissioned reports, and 11 journal articles to produce a list of 228 variables affecting student achievement. They combined the results of these analyses with the findings from 134 separate meta-analyses. Of all the variables, classroom management had the largest effect on student achievement. This makes intuitive sense—students cannot learn in a chaotic, poorly managed classroom.

Research not only supports the importance of classroom management, but it also sheds light on the dynamics of classroom management. Stage and Quiroz's meta-analysis (1997) shows the importance of there being a balance between teacher actions that provide clear consequences for unacceptable behavior and teacher actions that recognize and reward acceptable behavior. Other researchers (Emmer, Evertson, & Worsham, 2003; Evertson, Emmer, & Worsham, 2003) have identified important components of classroom management, including beginning the school year with a positive emphasis on management; arranging the room in a way conducive to effective management; and

identifying and implementing rules and operating procedures.

In a recent meta-analysis of more than 100 studies (Marzano, 2003b), we found that the quality of teacher-student relationships is the keystone for all other aspects of classroom management. In fact, our meta-analysis indicates that on average, teachers who had high-quality relationships with their students had 31 percent fewer discipline problems, rule violations, and related problems over a year's time than did teachers who did not have high-quality relationships with their students.

The quality of teacher-student relationships is the keystone for all other aspects of classroom management.

What are the characteristics of effective teacher-student relationships? Let's first consider what they are not. Effective teacher-student relationships have nothing to do with the teacher's personality or even with whether the students view the teacher as a friend. Rather, the most effective teacher-student relationships are characterized by specific teacher behaviors: exhibiting appropriate levels of dominance; exhibiting appropriate levels of cooperation; and being aware of high-needs students.

Appropriate Levels of Dominance

Wubbels and his colleagues (Wubbels, Brekelmans, van Tartwijk, & Admiral,

1999; Wubbels & Levy, 1993) identify appropriate dominance as an important characteristic of effective teacher-student relationships. In contrast to the more negative connotation of the term *dominance* as forceful control or command over others, they define dominance as the teacher's ability to provide clear purpose and strong guidance regarding both academics and student behavior. Studies indicate that when asked about their preferences for teacher behavior, students typically express a desire for this type of teacher-student interaction. For example, in a study that involved interviews with more than 700 students in grades 4–7, students articulated a clear preference for strong teacher guidance and control rather than more permissive types of teacher behavior (Chiu & Tulley, 1997). Teachers can exhibit appropriate dominance by establishing clear behavior expectations and learning goals and by exhibiting assertive behavior.

Establish Clear Expectations and Consequences

Teachers can establish clear expectations for behavior in two ways: by establishing clear rules and procedures, and by providing consequences for student behavior.

The seminal research of the 1980s (Emmer, 1984; Emmer, Sanford, Evertson, Clements, & Martin, 1981; Evertson & Emmer, 1982) points to the importance of establishing rules and procedures for general classroom behavior, group work, seat work, transitions and interruptions, use of materials and equipment, and beginning and ending the period or the day. Ideally, the class should establish these rules and procedures through discussion and mutual consent by teacher and students (Glasser, 1969, 1990).

Along with well-designed and clearly communicated rules and procedures, the teacher must acknowledge students' behavior, reinforcing acceptable behavior and providing negative consequences for unacceptable behavior. Stage and Quiroz's research (1997) is instructive. They found that teachers build effective relationships through such strategies as the following:

- Using a wide variety of verbal and physical reactions to students' misbehavior, such as moving closer to offending students and using a physical cue, such as a finger to the lips, to point out inappropriate behavior.
- Cuing the class about expected behaviors through prearranged signals, such as raising a hand to indicate that all students should take their seats.
- Providing tangible recognition of appropriate behavior—with tokens or chits, for example.
- Employing group contingency policies that hold the entire group responsible for behavioral expectations.
- Employing home contingency techniques that involve rewards and sanctions at home.

Establish Clear Learning Goals

Teachers can also exhibit appropriate levels of dominance by providing clarity about the content and expectations of an upcoming instructional unit. Important teacher actions to achieve this end include

- Establishing and communicating learning goals at the beginning of a unit of instruction.
- Providing feedback on those goals.
- Continually and systematically revisiting the goals.
- Providing summative feedback regarding the goals.

The use of rubrics can help teachers establish clear goals. To illustrate, assume that a teacher has identified the learning goal "understanding and using fractions" as important for a given unit. That teacher might present students with the following rubric:

4 points. You understand the characteristics of fractions along with the different types. You can accurately describe how fractions are related to decimals and

percentages. You can convert fractions to decimals and can explain how and why the process works. You can use fractions to understand and solve different types of problems.

3 points. You understand the basic characteristics of fractions. You know how fractions are related to decimals and percentages. You can convert fractions to decimals.

2 points. You have a basic understanding of the following, but have some small misunderstandings about one or more: the characteristics of fractions; the relationships among fractions, decimals, and percentages; how to convert fractions to decimals.

1 point. You have some major problems or misunderstandings with one or more of the following: the characteristics of fractions; the relationships among fractions, decimals, and percentages; how to convert fractions to decimals.

0 points. You may have heard of the following before, but you do not understand what they mean: the characteristics of fractions; the relationships among fractions, decimals, and percentages; how to convert fractions to decimals.

The clarity of purpose provided by this rubric communicates to students that their teacher can provide proper guidance and direction in academic content.

Exhibit Assertive Behavior

Teachers can also communicate appropriate levels of dominance by exhibiting assertive behavior. According to Emmer and colleagues, assertive behavior is

the ability to stand up for one's legitimate rights in ways that make it less likely that others will ignore or circumvent them. (2003, p. 146)

Assertive behavior differs significantly from both passive behavior and aggressive behavior. These researchers explain that teachers display assertive behavior in the classroom when they

- Use assertive body language by maintaining an erect posture; facing the offending student but keeping enough distance so as not to appear threatening and matching the facial expression with the content of the message being presented to students.
- Use an appropriate tone of voice, speaking clearly and deliberately in a

pitch that is slightly but not greatly elevated from normal classroom speech, avoiding any display of emotions in the voice.

- Persist until students respond with the appropriate behavior. Do not ignore an inappropriate behavior; do not be diverted by a student denying, arguing, or blaming, but listen to legitimate explanations.

Appropriate Levels of Cooperation

Cooperation is characterized by a concern for the needs and opinions of others. Although not the antithesis of dominance, cooperation certainly occupies a different realm. Whereas dominance focuses on the teacher as the driving force in the classroom, cooperation focuses on the students and teacher functioning as a team. The interaction of these two dynamics—dominance and cooperation—is a central force in effective teacher-student relationships. Several strategies can foster appropriate levels of cooperation.

Provide Flexible Learning Goals

Just as teachers can communicate appropriate levels of dominance by providing clear learning goals, they can also convey appropriate levels of cooperation by providing flexible learning goals. Giving students the opportunity to set their own objectives at the beginning of a unit or asking students what they would like to learn conveys a sense of cooperation. Assume, for example, that a teacher has identified the topic of fractions as the focus of a unit of instruction and has provided students with a rubric. The teacher could then ask students to identify some aspect of fractions or a related topic that they would particularly like to study. Giving students this kind of choice, in addition to increasing their understanding of the topic, conveys the message that the teacher cares about and tries to accommodate students' interests.

Teachers with effective classroom management skills are aware of high-needs students and have a repertoire of specific techniques for meeting some of their needs.

Take a Personal Interest in Students

Probably the most obvious way to communicate appropriate levels of cooperation is to take a personal interest in each student in the class. As McCombs and Whisler (1997) note, all students appreciate personal attention from the teacher. Although busy teachers—particularly those at the secondary level—do not have the time for extensive interaction with all students, some teacher actions can communicate personal interest and concern without taking up much time. Teachers can

- Talk informally with students before, during, and after class about their interests.
- Greet students outside of school—for instance, at extracurricular events or at the store.
- Single out a few students each day in the lunchroom and talk with them.
- Be aware of and comment on important events in students' lives, such as participation in sports, drama, or other extracurricular activities.
- Compliment students on important achievements in and outside of school.
- Meet students at the door as they come into class; greet each one by name.

Use Equitable and Positive Classroom Behaviors

Programs like Teacher Expectations and Student Achievement emphasize the importance of the subtle ways in which teachers can communicate their interest in students (Kerman, Kimball, & Martin, 1980). This program recommends many practical strategies that emphasize equitable and positive classroom interactions with all students. Teachers should, for example,

- Make eye contact with each student. Teachers can make eye contact by scanning the entire room as they speak and by freely moving about all sections of the room.
- Deliberately move toward and stand close to each student during the class period. Make sure that the seating arrangement allows the teacher and students clear and easy ways to move around the room.
- Attribute the ownership of ideas to the students who initiated them. For instance, in a discussion a teacher might say, "Cecilia just added to Aida's idea by saying that...."

- Allow and encourage all students to participate in class discussions and interactions. Make sure to call on students who do not commonly participate, not just those who respond most frequently.
- Provide appropriate wait time for all students to respond to questions, regardless of their past performance or your perception of their abilities.

Awareness of High-Needs Students

Classroom teachers meet daily with a broad cross-section of students. In general, 12–22 percent of all students in school suffer from mental, emotional, or behavioral disorders, and relatively few receive mental health services (Adelman & Taylor, 2002). The Association of School Counselors notes that 18 percent of students have special needs and require extraordinary interventions and treatments that go beyond the typical resources available to the classroom (Dunn & Baker, 2002).

Although the classroom teacher is certainly not in a position to directly address such severe problems, teachers with effective classroom management skills are aware of high-needs students and have a repertoire of specific techniques for meeting some of their needs (Marzano, 2003b). Figure 1 summarizes five categories of high-needs students and suggests classroom strategies for each category and subcategory.

- *Passive* students fall into two subcategories: those who fear *relationships* and those who fear *failure*. Teachers can build strong relationships with these students by refraining from criticism, rewarding small successes, and creating a classroom climate in which students feel safe from aggressive people.
- The category of *aggressive* students comprises three subcategories: *hostile, oppositional,* and *covert.* Hostile students often have poor anger control, low capacity for empathy, and an inability to see the consequences of their actions. Oppositional students exhibit milder forms of behavior problems, but they consistently resist following rules, argue with adults, use harsh language, and tend to annoy others. Students in the covert sub-category may be quite pleasant at times,

but they are often nearby when trouble starts and they never quite do what authority figures ask of them. Strategies for helping aggressive students include creating behavior contracts and providing immediate rewards and consequences. Most of all, teachers must keep in mind that aggressive students, although they may appear highly resistant to behavior change, are still children who are experiencing a significant amount of fear and pain.

- Students with *attention* problems fall into two categories: *hyperactive* and *inattentive*. These students may respond well when teachers contract with them to manage behaviors; teach them basic concentration, study, and thinking skills; help them divide tasks into manageable parts; reward their successes; and assign them a peer tutor.
- Students in the *perfectionist* category are driven to succeed at unattainable levels. They are self-critical, have low self-esteem, and feel inferior. Teachers can often help these students by encouraging them to develop more realistic standards, helping them to accept mistakes, and giving them opportunities to tutor other students.
- *Socially inept* students have difficulty making and keeping friends. They may stand too close and touch others in annoying ways, talk too much, and misread others' comments. Teachers can help these students by counseling them about social behaviors.

The most effective classroom managers did not treat all students the same; they tended to employ different strategies with different types of students.

School may be the only place where many students who face extreme challenges can get their needs addressed. The reality of today's schools often demands that classroom teachers address these severe issues, even though this task is not always considered a part of their regular job.

In a study of classroom strategies (see Brophy, 1996; Brophy & McCaslin, 1992), researchers examined how effective classroom teachers interacted with specific types of students. The study found that the most effective classroom managers did not

	FIGURE 1 Categories of High-Needs Students		
Category	**Definitions & Source**	**Characteristics**	**Suggestions**
Passive	Behavior that avoids the domination of others or the pain of negative experiences. The child attempts to protect self from criticism, ridicule, or rejection, possibly reacting to abuse and neglect. Can have a biochemical basis, such as anxiety.	**Fear of relationships:** Avoids connection with others, is shy, doesn't initiate conversations, attempts to be invisible. **Fear of failure:** Gives up easily, is convinced he or she can't succeed, is easily frustrated, uses negative self-talk.	Provide safe adult and peer interactions and protections from aggressive people. Provide assertiveness and positive self-talk training. Reward small successes quickly. Withhold criticism.
Aggressive	Behavior that overpowers, dominates, harms, or controls others without regard for their well-being. The child has often taken aggressive people as role models. Has had minimal or ineffective limits set on behavior. Is possibly reacting to abuse and neglect. Condition may have a biochemical basis, such as depression.	**Hostile:** Rages, threatens, or intimidates others. Can be verbally or physically abusive to people, animals, or objects. **Oppositional:** Does opposite of what is asked. Demands that others agree or give in. Resists verbally or nonverbally. **Covert:** Appears to agree but then does the opposite of what is asked. Often acts innocent while setting up problems for others.	Describe the student's behavior clearly. Contract with the student to reward corrected behavior and set up consequences for uncorrected behavior. Be consistent and provide immediate rewards and consequences. Encourage and acknowledge extracurricular activities in and out of school. Give student responsibilities to help teacher or other students to foster successful experiences.
Attention problems	Behavior that demonstrates either motor or attentional difficulties resulting from a neurological disorder. The child's symptoms may be exacerbated by family or social stressors or biochemical conditions, such as anxiety, depression, or bipolar disorders.	**Hyperactive:** Has difficulty with motor control, both physically and verbally. Fidgets, leaves seat frequently, interrupts, talks excessively. **Inattentive:** Has difficulty staying focused and following through on projects. Has difficulty with listening, remembering, and organizing.	Contract with the student to manage behaviors. Teach basic concentration, study, and thinking skills. Separate student in a quiet work area. Help the student list each step of a task. Reward successes; assign a peer tutor.
Perfectionist	Behavior that is geared toward avoiding the embarrassment and assumed shame of making mistakes. The child fears what will happen if errors are discovered. Has unrealistically high expectations of self. Has possibly received criticism or lack of acceptance while making mistakes during the process of learning.	Tends to focus too much on the small details of projects. Will avoid projects if unsure of outcome. Focuses on results and not relationships. Is self-critical.	Ask the student to make mistakes on purpose, then show acceptance. Have the student tutor other students.
Socially inept	Behavior that is based on the misinterpretation of nonverbal signals of others. The child misunderstands facial expressions and body language. Hasn't received adequate training in these areas and has poor role modeling.	Attempts to make friends but is inept and unsuccessful. Is forced to be alone. Is often teased for unusual behavior, appearance, or lack of social skills.	Teach the student to keep the appropriate physical distance from others. Teach the meaning of facial expressions, such as anger and hurt. Make suggestions regarding hygiene, dress, mannerisms, and posture.

Source: Marzano, R. J. (2003). *What works in schools: Translating research into action* (pp. 104–105). Alexandria, VA: ASCD.

treat all students the same; they tended to employ different strategies with different types of students. In contrast, ineffective classroom managers did not appear sensitive to the diverse needs of students. Although Brophy did not couch his findings in terms of teacher-student relationships, the link is clear. An awareness of the five general categories of high-needs students and appropriate actions for each can help teachers build strong relationships with diverse students.

Don't Leave Relationships to Chance

Teacher-student relationships provide an essential foundation for effective classroom management—and classroom management is a key to high student achievement. Teacher-student relationships should not be left to chance or dictated by the personalities of those involved. Instead, by using strategies supported by research, teachers can influence the dynamics of their classrooms and build strong teacher-student relationships that will support student learning.

References

Adelman, H. S., & Taylor, L. (2002). School counselors and school reform: New directions. *Professional School Counseling, 5*(4), 235–248.

Brophy, J. E. (1996). *Teaching problem students.* New York: Guilford.

Brophy, J. E., & McCaslin, N. (1992). Teachers' reports of how they perceive and cope with problem students. *Elementary School Journal, 93,* 3–68.

Chiu, L. H., & Tulley, M. (1997). Student preferences of teacher discipline styles.

Journal of Instructional Psychology, 24(3), 168–175.

Dunn, N. A., & Baker, S. B. (2002). Readiness to serve students with disabilities: A survey of elementary school counselors. *Professional School Counselors, 5*(4), 277–284.

Emmer, E. T. (1984). *Classroom management: Research and implications.* (R & D Report No. 6178). Austin, TX: Research and Development Center for Teacher Education, University of Texas. (ERIC Document Reproduction Service No. ED251448)

Emmer, E. T., Evertson, C. M., & Worsham, M. E. (2003). *Classroom management for secondary teachers* (6th ed.). Boston: Allyn and Bacon.

Emmer, E. T., Sanford, J. P., Evertson, C. M., Clements, B. S., & Martin, J. (1981). *The classroom management improvement study: An experiment in elementary school classrooms.* (R & D Report No. 6050). Austin, TX: Research and Development Center for Teacher Education, University of Texas. (ERIC Document Reproduction Service No. ED226452)

Evertson, C. M., & Emmer, E. T. (1982). Preventive classroom management. In D. Duke (Ed.), *Helping teachers manage classrooms* (pp. 2–31). Alexandria, VA: ASCD.

Evertson, C. M., Emmer, E. T., & Worsham, M. E. (2003). *Classroom management for elementary teachers* (6th ed.). Boston: Allyn and Bacon.

Glasser, W. (1969). *Schools without failure.* New York: Harper and Row.

Glasser, W. (1990). *The quality school: Managing students without coercion.* New York: Harper and Row.

Kerman, S., Kimball, T., & Martin, M. (1980). *Teacher expectations and student achievement.* Bloomington, IN: Phi Delta Kappan.

Marzano, R. J. (2003a). *What works in schools.* Alexandria, VA: ASCD.

Marzano, R. J. (with Marzano, J. S., & Pickering, D. J.). (2003b). *Classroom management that works.* Alexandria, VA: ASCD.

McCombs, B. L., & Whisler, J. S. (1997). *The learner-centered classroom and school.* San Francisco: Jossey-Bass.

Stage, S. A., & Quiroz, D. R. (1997). A meta-analysis of interventions to decrease disruptive classroom behavior in public education settings. *School Psychology Review, 26*(3), 333–368.

Wang, M. C., Haertel, G. D., & Walberg, H. J. (1993). Toward a knowledge base for school learning. *Review of Educational Research, 63*(3), 249–294.

Wubbels, T., Brekelmans, M., van Tartwijk, J., & Admiral, W. (1999). Interpersonal relationships between teachers and students in the classroom. In H. C. Waxman & H. J. Walberg (Eds.), *New directions for teaching practice and research* (pp. 151–170). Berkeley, CA: McCutchan.

Wubbels, T., & Levy, J. (1993). *Do you know what you look like? Interpersonal relationships in education.* London: Falmer Press.

Robert J. Marzano is a senior scholar at Mid-continent Research for Education and Learning in Aurora, Colorado, and an associate professor at Cardinal Stritch University in Milwaukee, Wisconsin; (303) 796–7683; robertjmarzano@aol.com. His newest book written with Jana S. Marzano and Debra J. Pickering is *Classroom Management That Works* (ASCD, 2003). **Jana S. Marzano** is a licensed professional counselor in private practice in Centennial, Colorado; (303) 220–1151; janamarzan@aol.com.

Corporal Punishment
Legalities, Realities, and Implications

PATRICIA H. HINCHEY

For some time now, I have been talking to practitioners about corporal punishment in schools, especially middle and high schools. Practitioner responses to my questions about the legal status of paddling and other physical discipline in their states have fallen into two categories: surprise that I would ask about the subject as if practices such as paddling still existed anywhere, and surprise that I would ask about the topic as if paddling weren't common in every school in the country. Most teachers appear to assume that the status of corporal punishment in their own school or state is a national standard—a perception that is far from contemporary reality. The following quiz will help readers determine the reliability of their own perceptions relating to this topic:

True or False?

- The issue of corporal punishment has reached the United States Supreme Court, which has upheld the practice as constitutional.
- Military personnel and criminals have the right to due process before corporal punishment can be imposed; as a matter of federal law, schoolchildren, on the contrary, do not.
- Early in his term in office, President George W. Bush promoted legislation that would protect educators who had beaten children form lawsuits. Both teachers' unions, the NEA (National Education Association) and the NFT (National Federation of Teachers), opposed this legislation, intended to protect their members.

- Researchers have demonstrated that corporal punishment can constitute a form of sexual abuse.

However unlikely it may seem to many readers, the answer in every case is "true."

U.S. Courts and Corporal Punishment

The Supreme Court case that now provides the foundation for corporal punishment policies is *Ingraham v. Wright* (1977). Two students, James Ingraham and Roosevelt Andrews, suffered severe paddlings in their Florida junior high school that left Ingraham needing medical attention for severe pain and bruising and Andrews unable in one instance to use his arm for a week. Their suit argued that the paddlings were unconstitutional, in violation of the Eighth Amendment's prohibition of cruel and unusual punishment and also of the Fourteenth Amendment's guarantee of due process. The Court, however, rejected both arguments. Because corporal punishment has long been common among parents and school officials alike, the Court found, it could not be classified as "cruel and unusual." Moreover, the Court found that the Eighth Amendment is intended to protect criminals, not schoolchildren, and that children who suffered severe punishment could gain redress by prosecuting officials on such charges as assault and battery, a recourse thought to be sufficient protection for children.

Although many parents and students have indeed sought legal redress for severe beatings, they rarely win in court—

making it especially difficult to understand why President Bush has supported a legislative effort to prohibit lawsuits against educators (Breaking 2001; Spare 2001). Courts have found in favor of schools and teachers even when the punishment they imposed included paddling a nine-year-old seven times within half an hour; sticking a straight pin into a student's arm; confining children in closets and other small, dark spaces; slamming them into walls; and stuffing and/or taping children's mouths (Hyman and Snook 1999). Parents have also been dismayed to lose cases filed after a child was paddled without parental permission. Unless a school chooses to abide by parental wishes, parents in states where corporal punishment is legal can protect their children from beatings only by removing them from schools that employ paddling.

Sometimes the offenses against children are so egregious that it seems unbelievable that courts would find for schools and against the family, but it routinely happens. For example, one seventeen-year-old female, who was both an honor student and a senior with no prior record of misbehavior, skipped school. This young adult was forced to bend over a desk and submit to several blows inflicted by an adult male coach whom she had trusted until the incident. For the girl, consequences included not only the physical pain of the beating, but also menstrual hemorrhaging and long-lasting emotional trauma. Despite arguments that the case involved not only physical but also sexual abuse, the school won the case (Hyman and Snook 1999). In fact, over and over again corporal punishment has been linked to sexual abuse, although many state legislators who could outlaw the practice apparently remain unmoved by such arguments (see Donahue 2001, for example, or Johnson 1994, and others listed on Project NoSpank's Web page "Spanking Can Be Sexual Abuse," available at <http://nospank.net/ 101.htm >).

Nor is any special consideration offered to students with disabilities, for whom courts have upheld paddling, isolation, and mouth taping as punishments. In one case, a disabled student was forced to do exercise so rigorous that it led to his death (Hyman and Snook 1999). Rather than finding such incidents a cause for restraining corporal punishment, legislators have blithely moved forward toward solidifying educators' legal right to impose physical punishment on students with disabilities. In June 2001, a bill enabling discipline of the disabled was introduced by U.S. Senator Jeff Sessions of Alabama and passed the United States Senate.

As the following examples illustrate, courts rarely punish abusive educators in states that allow corporal punishment.

Worldwide and Nationwide Legality

It is perhaps telling that the United States is one of two countries worldwide that have not yet ratified the Convention on the Rights of the Child, adopted by the United Nations General Assembly in November 1989. The other is Somalia. The document calls for multiple protections of the human rights of children, including the right to be protected from violence.

As other countries of the world move toward greater and greater protection of their children, with Northern Ireland and Scotland strengthening laws against corporal punishment in 2001, the United States retains its dubious distinction of being one of very few developed countries whose national policy allows corporal punishment in schools. Over one hundred organizations joined forces to call this fact to national attention in a widely publicized letter to the president of the United States: "Throughout the developed, industrial world, and in many developing nations, the use of corporal punishment against schoolchildren is forbidden. No European country permits the practice" (Open Letter to the President, available at <http:// nospank.net/endcp.htm>). Organizations signing the letter included the American Academy of Pediatrics, the National Congress of Parents and Teachers Association, the National Mental Health Association, the American Psychological Association, the American Association of Physicians for Human Rights, the National Association of School Psychologists, the American School Counselor Association, and the National Committee for Prevention of Child Abuse.

However, the organizations' plea that the president "instruct the Secretary of the U.S. Department of Education to take expeditious and forceful action to deny federal assistance to any school, school district, or other educational entity that authorizes the use of corporal punishment" has fallen on deaf ears. The effort has also been undermined both by President Bush's support for legislation protecting those who beat children and by Senator Session's efforts to make sure that all children are equally subject to such beatings. A *Houston Chronicle* story reported the case of several Canadian parents who moved to Ohio and Indiana to escape the Canadian law prohibiting the use of such objects as paddles, sticks, and belts to inflict punishment on children. In Ohio and Indiana, parents (and others) are free to strike children with such instruments (Clairborne 2001).

For those concerned about the physical safety and mental health of children, the good news is that legislators in twenty-seven states and the District of Columbia have heeded the research and advice of pediatricians, parents, educators, and others and have passed state laws prohibiting corporal punishment in schools. However, that leaves children in nearly half of all states still subject to the abuses of corporal punishment with little or no practical means of prevention or redress. The box identifies states that continue to allow physical punishment of schoolchildren, despite its dangers.

Although defenders of corporal punishment argue that few incidents are excessive, a review of news reports indicates otherwise—and that the extreme cases are sufficiently horrifying to justify exclusion of corporal punishment, whatever the rate of incidence.

States That Allow Corporal Punishment

*Alabama	*Mississippi
Arizona	*Missouri
*Arkansas	New Mexico
Colorado	North Carolina
Delaware	Ohio
Florida	*Oklahoma
*Georgia	Pennsylvania
Idaho	South Carolina
Indiana	*Tennessee
Kansas	*Texas
Kentucky	Wyoming
*Louisiana	

Note: *States listed in the top ten pupil-battering states in both the 1996–97 and 1997–98 Elementary and Secondary School Civil Rights Compliance Reports.

Source: Danger Zones: States in the U.S. that Permit Pupil-Beating, Jordan Riak, .<http://nospank.net/eddpts.htm>

The Realities of Corporal Punishment in the United States

All of the following incidents were reported in newspapers during 2001. In the context of cases with results as severe as death, some cases seem almost trivial by comparison. Still, it is likely that most parents would be greatly upset by the actions of a California teacher who, despite a ban on corporal punishment, taped a first-grader's mouth shut and threatened to tie her up (McLellan 2001); and of an Arizona teacher who tried to force a sixth-grader to chew gum already chewed by others and saved in a jar for the purposes of this punishment (Mother 2001). Such bodily indignities, however, are the least of what a child may suffer in school, as other reported incidents nationwide reveal.

An Oklahoma Christian school teacher struck a 12-year-old with a 3-foot long dowel because he was passing notes in class and inflicted bruises that hospital doctors characterized as "severe" (Martin 2001). A parent in Louisiana was unsuccessful in filing a criminal action against an assistant principal who broke a paddle on a 13-year-old (Shackleford 2001). A parochial school director in Florida was arrested after using a wooden board to paddle an 8-year-old, leaving a mark some 4 inches wide and 6 inches long and welts as high as a quarter of an inch (Port 2001). In another Florida incident, a dean at an elementary school was found guilty of misdemeanor battery for excessively beating an 8-year-old; he was required to take an anger-management course and subsequently returned to his role as school leader—although after this incident, the school did ban corporal punishment (Hustead 2001). In Michigan, another state where corporal punishment is legally restricted, a 15-year-old freshman football player did not return to school for weeks after he received 10 blows with a paddle that eventually cracked. Some six or seven other player were also hit, one approximately 12 or 13 times (Potts 2001). In Tennessee, a school employee faced criminal charges after hitting a 15-year-old in the arm with a baseball bat (Armstrong 2001).

A national antispanking group called for a civil rights audit of students in Mobile, Alabama because black children in recent years have received 65 to 70 percent of all paddlings there, although they make up slightly less than half of all students. Statistics also indicated that on the whole, for the 1998–99 school year, 73 percent of paddlings administered statewide in Alabama were to the black students who make up only 41 percent of its total school population (Catalanello 2001).

If all reports related to religious schools and alternative "boot-camp" type schools were included, this list would be much longer.

Implications: What Teachers Can Do

When I work with education students, tomorrow's teachers, I try to impress on them that becoming a professional educator means accepting responsibility for protecting the rights and interests of children in classrooms. To do less is to fall short of the trust placed in us by our students, their parents, and our profession. A classroom teacher who is willing to take even one of the following steps is, on the other hand, acting to meet professional responsibilities.

1. Become familiar with the information made available by Parents and Teachers against Violence in Education (PTAVE) and by Temple University's National Center for the Study of Corporal Punishment and Alternatives (NCSCPA). Web sites sponsored by these organizations offer a complete library of resources, including news and research articles. The more teachers know about corporal punishment, the better they can counter arguments for it with evidence of the danger it poses to children.

- PTAVE's Project No Spank, <http://nospank.net/>
- Temple University's NCSCPA, <http://temple.edu/education/nespca/NCSCPA.html>

2. Become familiar with print resources as well. Among the most important books on corporal punishment is Hyman and Snook's *Dangerous Schools: What We Can Do About the Physical and Emotional Abuse of Our Children*. Although that book is possibly the most important print resource detailing the dangers of physical punishment, there are several others that also can be helpful:

- Greven, P. 1991. Spare the child: The religious roots of punishment and the psychological impact of physical abuse. New York: Random House.
- Straus, M., and D. Donnelly. 1993. Beating the devil out of them: Corporal punishment in American families. San Francisco: Jossey-Bass.
- Males, M. 1996. The scapegoat generation: America's war on adolescents. Monroe, MA: Common Courage Press.

3. Monitor Project No Spank. Because this is one of the most important sources of information for children's advocates, signing on to its mailing list can be an important step in staying informed and involved.

4. Accept the need to be political in a variety of ways, in a variety of arenas. Develop relationships with colleagues, parents, administrators, school board members and politicians who have the power to help change policy and laws. Find allies and work with them to bring change on local and state levels, using voting power judiciously.

Educate your colleagues at every opportunity. Raise your concerns with other teachers and share what you know about the dangers of corporal punishment. Have them read what you have read, and try to enlist their support and build a strong core of opposition.

Promote efforts to be sure your school is safe for children. Research local policy. If corporal punishment is allowed, consider working for change; meanwhile, try to determine if guidelines are being followed and promote compliance if they are not. In schools where corporal punishment is not permitted, try to determine if the reality of classroom life conforms to regulations; if you find discrepancies, do what you can to spark awareness and promote adherence to policy.

Seek union support. If you are in a local union affiliated with the National Education Association (NEA), ask union representatives to begin publicizing the NEA stance against corporal punishment because of its dangers. The NEA was, in fact, the first major national education organization that called for banning corporal punishment in a 1992 resolution (NEA 1998). If you are affiliated with the American Federation of Teachers, work to persuade that union to join in the NEA public stance.

Enlist the help of your parents and teachers association. Be sure that local chapters are familiar with *Corporal punishment: Myths and realities* (National PTA, 1991) <http://nospank.net/pta.htm>. This National PTA document discusses the dangers of corporal punishment.

Parting Thoughts

As teachers, we must always act as advocates for children's welfare. We have many avenues to help ensure that schools are safe for children—or to protest and publicize existing dangers loudly and frequently, seeking a change in policy. To help end the legal beatings of children in schools teachers must become thoroughly educated on the issue and then assume the role of

change agents, pursuing restraint and reform at every opportunity. Certainly parents, administrators, and school board members share teachers' commitment to the welfare of children. By learning and then sharing the extensive evidence against corporal punishment, teachers may be able to counter the ubiquitous argument that "a little swat on the behind never hurt anybody." Lawmakers and courts have failed to ensure that schools are safe places for the children entrusted to our care. These children cannot afford teachers to fail as their advocates and protectors as well.

Key words: corporal punishment, teachers as advocates, abuse, child welfare

REFERENCES

Armstrong accused of hitting teen with baseball bat. 2001. Associated Press State & Local Wire. 6 September. Retrieved 28 January 2002, from Lexis-Nexis database.

Bragg, R. 2001. Christian school questioned over discipline for wayward. *New York Times.* 5 July. Retrieved 28 January 2002, from <http://nospank.net/n-i03.htm>

Breaking the hickory stick. 2001. Editorial, *New York Times,* Late Edition (East Coast): A.16. 7 May.

Catalanello, R. 2001. National group seizes on racial disparity in punishment at Mobile schools. *Mobile Register.* 21 July. Retrieved 28 January 2002, from <http://nospank.net/n-i13.htm>.

Clairborne, W. 2001. Canadians from sect flee to U.S. over right to spank. 2 August. *Houston Chronicle:* 7.

Donahue, J. 2001. Spanking as sexualized abuse. *Counseling Today.* May. Retrieved 29 October 2001 from <http://nospank.org/donahue.htm>.

Hustead, J. 2001. "Excessive" spanking gets Dawkins probation. 10 April. *Press Journal* (Vero Beach, FL): A3.

Hyman, I., and P. Snook. 1999. *Dangerous schools: What we can do about the physical and emotional abuse of our children.* San Francisco: Jossey-Bass.

Johnson, T. 1994. The sexual dangers of spanking children. Retrieved 29 October 2001, from <http://nospank.org/s-dngr.htm.>

Martin, L. 2001. Teacher charged with injury. *Tulsa World.* 11 October. Retrieved 25 January 2002, from Lexis-Nexis database.

McLellan, D. 2001. Tustin district bars substitute who allegedly taped girl's mouth shut. *Los Angeles Times:* B3. 22 May.

Mother says child was ordered to chew someone else's used gum. 2001. *Associated Press State & Local Wire.* 12 April. Retrieved 28 January 2002, from Lexis-Nexis database.

National Education Association (NEA). 1998. *Child Abuse and Neglect.* Retrieved 20 February 2002, from <http://www.nea.org/issues/safescho/childabus.html>.

Parents and Teachers Against Violence in Education (PTAVE). *Project No Spank.* Retrieved 29 October 2001, from <http://www.nospank.net>.

Port Charlotte school director arrested for paddling student. 2001. *Associated Press State & Local Wire*. 3 July. Retrieved 28 January 2002, from Lexis-Nexis database.

Potts, L. February 5, 2001. Football coach accused of paddling student is suspended. *Associated Press State & Local Wire*. Retrieved January 28, 2002, from Lexis-Nexis database.

Shackleford, C. 2001. Principal won't face charges over paddling. *Chattanooga Times:* B2. 13 September.

Spare the rod: Washington shouldn't encourage corporal punishment, 2001. Editorial in Pittsburgh *Post-Gazette*. 21 May. Retrieved 25 January 2002, from <http://nospank.net/n-h81.htm>.

Stockwell, J. 2001. Boy's death at school a homicide. *Washington Post*. 5 July. Retrieved 28 January 2002, from <http://nospank.net/n-i04.htm>.

Patricia H. Hinchey is an associate professor of education at Penn State University.

From *The Clearing House*, January/February 2003. Reprinted with permission of the Helen Dwight Reid Foundation. Published by Heldref Publications, 1319 Eighteenth St. NW, Washington, DC 20036-1802. © 2003.

UNIT 6
Assessment

Unit Selections

36. **Fundamental Assessment Principles for Teachers and School Administrators**, James H. McMillan
37. **Are We Measuring Student Success With High-Stakes Testing?**, Kathleen Anderson Steeves, Jessica Hodgson, and Patricia Peterson
38. **The Seductive Allure of Data**, W. James Popham
39. **Teaching About Performance Assessment**, Judy Arter
40. **Classroom Assessment for Learning**, Stephen Chappuis and Richard J. Stiggins
41. **Helping Standards Make the Grade**, Thomas R. Guskey

Key Points to Consider

• What fundamental concepts from contemporary learning and motivation theories have specific implications for how teachers assess their students? Are such practices consistent with what is promulgated with standardized tests?

• What are some important principles for using standardized test scores to improve instruction? What are some limitations of standardized tests?

• What are some examples of performance assessment? What are the strengths and limitations of these assessments?

• Many educators believe that schools should identify the brightest, most capable students. What are the assessment implications of this philosophy? How would low-achieving students be affected?

• What principles of assessment should teachers adopt for their own classroom testing? Is it necessary or feasible to develop a table of specifications for each test? How do we know if the test scores teachers use are reliable and if valid inferences are drawn from the scores?

• How can teachers grade thinking skills such as analysis, application, and reasoning? How should objectives for student learning and grading be integrated? What are some grading practices to avoid? Why?

 **Links: www.dushkin.com/online/**
These sites are annotated in the World Wide Web pages.

Awesome Library for Teachers
http://www.neat-schoolhouse.org/teacher.html

Phi Delta Kappa International
http://www.pdkintl.org

Washington (State) Center for the Improvement of Student Learning
http://www.k12.wa.us/

In which reading group does Jon belong? How do I construct tests? How do I know when my students have mastered the course objectives? How can I explain test results to Mary's parents? Teachers answer these questions, and many more, by applying principles of assessment. Assessment refers to procedures for measuring and recording student performance and constructing grades that communicate to others levels of proficiency or relative standing. Assessment principles constitute a set of concepts that are integral to the teaching-learning process. Indeed, a significant amount of teacher time is spent in assessment activities, and with more accountability has come a greater emphasis on assessment.

Assessment provides a foundation for making sound evaluative judgments about students' learning and achievement. Teachers need to use fair and unbiased criteria in order to assess student learning objectively and accurately and to make appropriate decisions about student placement. For example, in assigning Jon to a reading group, the teacher will use his test scores as an indication of his skill level. Are the inferences from the test results valid for the school's reading program? Are his test scores consistent over several months or years? Are they consistent with his performance in class? The teacher should ask and then answer these questions so that he or she can make intelligent decisions about Jon. On the other hand, will knowledge of the test scores affect the teacher's perception of classroom performance and create a self-fulfilling prophecy? Teachers also evaluate students in order to assign grades, and the challenge is to balance "objective" test scores with more subjective, informally gathered information. Both kinds of evaluative information are necessary, but both can be inaccurate and are frequently misused.

The first article in this unit summarizes some fundamental assessment concepts that are the foundation for valid, reliable, and fair assessment. The next article discusses the importance of standards-based testing and how this kind of testing may be related to classroom instruction. It has become increasingly clear that high-stakes testing will be required, and understanding the limitations as well as negative consequences of this kind of testing is needed. W. James Popham, a expert in testing for many years, argues for much more emphasis on classroom assessment. Two other experts in testing argue for student self-assessment as a technique that engages students in learning and provides excellent formative feedback to teachers.

Performance-based assessment is promoted in the article by Judy Arter. This form of assessment has great potential to integrate measurement procedures with instructional methods more effectively and to focus student learning on the application of thinking and problem-solving skills in real-life contexts. Arter demonstrates this through a thorough review of all aspects of performance assessment, including scoring criteria, rubrics, and principles of grading. She also shows how performance assessment, in comparison to other kinds of assessment, is based on constructivistic learning theory.

In the last article, Thomas R. Guskey examines grading practices and makes suggestions for how to assign grades so that the results provide accurate and helpful information as well as motivate students in the context of our standards-oriented school environment.

Article 36

Fundamental assessment principles for teachers and school administrators

James H. McMillan
Virginia Commonwealth University

While several authors have argued that there are a number of "essential" assessment concepts, principles, techniques, and procedures that teachers and administrators need to know about (e.g. Calfee & Masuda,1997; Cizek, 1997; Ebel, 1962; Farr & Griffin, 1973; Fleming & Chambers, 1983; Gullickson, 1985, 1986; Mayo, 1967; McMillan, 2001; Sanders & Vogel, 1993; Schafer, 1991; Stiggins & Conklin, 1992), there continues to be relatively little emphasis on assessment in the preparation of, or professional development of, teachers and administrators (Stiggins, 2000). In addition to the admonitions of many authors, there are established professional standards for assessment skills of teachers (*Standards for Teacher Competence in Educational Assessment of Students* ([1990]), a framework of assessment tasks for administrators (Impara & Plake, 1996), the Code of Professional Responsibilities in Educational Measurement (1995), the Code of Fair Testing Practices (1988), and the new edition of *Standards for Educational and Psychological Testing* (1999). If that isn't enough information, a project directed by Arlen Gullickson at The Evaluation Center of Western Michigan University will publish standards for evaluations of students in the near future.

The purpose of this article is to use suggestions and guidelines from these sources, in light of current assessment demands and contemporary theories of learning and motivation, to present eleven "basic principles" to guide the assessment training and professional development of teachers and administrators. That is, what is it about assessment, whether large-scale or classroom, that is fundamental for effective understanding and application? What are the "big ideas" that, when well understood and applied, will effectively guide good assessment practices, regardless of the grade level, subject matter, developer, or user of the results? As Jerome Bruner stated it many years ago in his classic, *The Process of Education*: "...the curriculum of a subject should be determined by the most fundamental understanding that can be achieved of the underlying principles that give structure to that subject." (Bruner, 1960, p.31). What principles, in other words, provide the most essential, fundamental "structure" of assessment knowledge and skills that result in effective educational practices and improved student learning?

Assessment is inherently a process of professional judgment.

The first principle is that professional judgment is the foundation for assessment and, as such, is needed to properly understand and use all aspects of assessment. The measurement of student performance may seem "objective" with such practices as machine scoring and multiple-choice test items, but even these approaches are based on professional assumptions and values. Whether that judgment occurs in constructing test questions, scoring essays, creating rubrics, grading participation, combining scores, or interpreting standardized test scores, the essence of the process is making professional interpretations and decisions. Understanding this principle helps teachers and administrators realize the importance of their own judgments and those of others in evaluating the quality of assessment and the meaning of the results.

Assessment is based on separate but related principles of measurement evidence and evaluation.

It is important to understand the difference between measurement evidence (differentiating degrees of a trait by description or by assigning scores) and evaluation (interpretation of the description or scores). Essential measurement evidence skills include the ability to understand and interpret the meaning of descriptive statistical procedures, including variability, correlation, percentiles, standard scores, growth-scale scores, norming, and principles of combining scores for grading. A conceptual understanding of these techniques is needed (not necessarily knowing how to compute statistics) for such tasks as interpreting student strengths and weaknesses, reliability and validity evidence, grade determination, and making admissions decisions. Schafer (1991) has indicated that these concepts and techniques comprise part of an essential language for educators. They also provide a common basis for communication about "results," interpretation of evidence, and appropriate use of data. This is increasingly important given the pervasiveness of standards-based, high-stakes, large-scale assessments. Evaluation concerns merit and worth of the data as applied to a specific use or context. It involves what Shepard (2000) has described as the systematic analysis of evidence. Like students, teachers and administrators need analysis skills to effectively interpret evidence and make value judgments about the meaning of the results.

Assessment decision-making is influenced by a series of tensions.

Competing purposes, uses, and pressures result in tension for teachers and administrators as they make assessment-related decisions. For example, good teaching is characterized by assessments that motivate and engage students in ways that are consistent with their philosophies of teaching and learning and with theories of development, learning and motivation. Most teachers want to use constructed-response assessments because they believe this kind of testing is best to ascertain student understanding. On the other hand, factors external to the classroom, such as mandated large-scale testing, promote different assessment strategies, such as using selected-response tests and providing practice in objective test-taking (McMillan & Nash, 2000). Further examples of tensions include the following.

- Learning vs auditing
- Formative (informal and ongoing) vs summative (formal and at the end)
- Criterion-referenced vs norm-referenced
- Value-added vs absolute standards
- Traditional vs alternative
- Authentic vs contrived
- Speeded tests vs power tests
- Standardized tests vs classroom tests

These tensions suggest that decisions about assessment are best made with a full understanding of how different factors influence the nature of the assessment. Once all the alternatives are understood, priorities need to be made; trade-offs are inevitable. With an appreciation of the tensions teachers and administrators will hopefully make better informed, better justified assessment decisions.

Assessment influences student motivation and learning.

Grant Wiggins (1998) has used the term 'educative assessment' to describe techniques and issues that educators should consider when they design and use assessments. His message is that the nature of assessment influences what is learned and the degree of meaningful engagement by students in the learning process. While Wiggins contends that assessments should be authentic, with feedback and opportunities for revision to improve rather than simply audit learning, the more general principle is understanding how different assessments affect students. Will students be more engaged if assessment tasks are problem-based? How do students study when they know the test consists of multiple-choice items? What is the nature of feedback, and when is it given to students? How does assessment affect student effort?

Answers to such questions help teachers and administrators understand that assessment has powerful effects on motivation and learning. For example, recent research summarized by Black & Wiliam (1998) shows that student self-assessment skills, learned and applied as part of formative assessment, enhance student achievement.

Assessment contains error.

Teachers and administrators need to not only know that there is error in all classroom and standardized assessments, but also more specifically how reliability is determined and how much error is likely. With so much emphasis today on high-stakes testing for promotion, graduation, teacher and administrator accountability, and school accreditation, it is critical that all educators understand concepts like standard error of measurement, reliability coefficients, confidence intervals, and standard setting. Two reliability principles deserve special attention. The first is that reliability refers to scores, not instruments. Second, teachers and administrators need to understand that, typically, error is underestimated. A recent paper by Rogosa (1999) effectively illustrates the concept of underestimation of error by showing in terms of percentile rank probable true score hit-rate and test-retest results.

Good assessment enhances instruction.

Just as assessment impacts student learning and motivation, it also influences the nature of instruction in the classroom. There has been considerable recent literature that has promoted assessment as something that is integrated with instruction, and not an activity that merely audits learning (Shepard, 2000). When assessment is integrated with instruction it informs teachers about what activities and assignments will be most useful, what level of teaching is most appropriate, and how summative assessments provide diagnostic information. For instance, during instruction activities informal, formative assessment helps teachers know when to move on, when to ask more questions, when to give more examples, and what responses to student questions are most appropriate. Standardized test scores, when used appropriately, help teachers understand student strengths and weaknesses to target further instruction.

Good assessment is valid.

Validity is a concept that needs to be fully understood. Like reliability, there are technical terms and issues associated with validity that are essential in helping teachers and administrators make reasonable and appropriate inferences from assessment results (e.g., types of validity evidence, validity generalization, construct underrepresentation, construct-irrelevant variance, and discriminant and convergent evidence). Of critical importance is the concept of evidence based on consequences, a new major validity category in the recently revised *Standards*. Both intended and unintended consequences of assessment need to be examined with appropriate evidence that supports particular arguments or points of view. Of equal importance is getting teachers and administrators to understand their role in gathering and interpreting validity evidence.

Good assessment is fair and ethical.

Arguably, the most important change in the recently published *Standards* is an entire new major section entitled "Fairness in Testing." The *Standards* presents four views of fairness: as absence of bias (e.g., offensiveness and unfair penalization), as equitable treatment, as equality in outcomes, and as opportunity to learn. It includes entire chapters on the rights and responsibilities of test takers, testing individuals of diverse linguistic backgrounds, and testing individuals with disabilities or special needs. Three additional areas are also important:

- Student knowledge of learning targets and the nature of the assessments prior to instruction (e.g., knowing what will be tested, how it will be graded, scoring criteria, anchors, exemplars, and examples of performance).
- Student prerequisite knowledge and skills, including test-taking skills.
- Avoiding stereotypes.

Good assessments use multiple methods.

Assessment that is fair, leading to valid inferences with a minimum of error, is a series of measures that show student understanding through multiple methods. A complete picture of what students understand and can do is put together in pieces comprised by different approaches to assessment. While testing experts and testing companies stress that important decisions should not be made on the basis of a single test score, some educators at the local level, and some (many?) politicians at the state and at the national level, seem determined to violate this principle. There is a need to understand the entire range of assessment techniques and methods, with the realization that each has limitations.

Good assessment is efficient and feasible.

Teachers and school administrators have limited time and resources. Consideration must be given to the efficiency of different approaches to assessment, balancing needs to implement methods required to provide a full understanding with the time needed to develop and implement the methods, and score results. Teacher skills and knowledge are important to consider, as well as the level of support and resources.

Good assessment appropriately incorporates technology.

As technology advances and teachers become more proficient in the use of technology, there will be increased opportunities for teachers and administrators to use computer-based techniques (e.g., item banks, electronic grading, computer-adapted testing, computer-based simulations), Internet resources, and more complex, detailed ways of reporting results. There is,

however, a danger that technology will contribute to the mindless use of new resources, such as using items on-line developed by some companies without adequate evidence of reliability, validity, and fairness, and crunching numbers with software programs without sufficient thought about weighting, error, and averaging.

To summarize, what is most essential about assessment is understanding how general, fundamental assessment principles and ideas can be used to enhance student learning and teacher effectiveness. This will be achieved as teachers and administrators learn about conceptual and technical assessment concepts, methods, and procedures, for both large-scale and classroom assessments, and apply these fundamentals to instruction.

Note

An earlier version of this paper was presented at the Annual Meeting of the American Educational Research Association, New Orleans, April 24, 2000.

References

Black, P., & Wiliam, D. (1998). Inside the black box: Raising standards through classroom assessment. *Phi Delta Kappan*, 80(2), 139–148.

Bruner, J. S. (1960). *The process of education.* NY: Vintage Books.

Calfee, R. C., & Masuda, W. V. (1997). Classroom assessment as inquiry. In G. D. Phye (Ed.) *Handbook of classroom assessment: Learning, adjustment, and achievement.* NY: Academic Press.

Cizek, G. J. (1997). Learning, achievement, and assessment: Constructs at a crossroads. In G. D. Phye (Ed.) *Handbook of classroom assessment: Learning, adjustment, and achievement.* NY: Academic Press.

Code of fair testing practices in education (1988). Washington, DC: Joint Committee on Testing Practices (American Psychological Association). Available http://ericae.net/code.htm

Code of professional responsibilities in educational measurement (1995). Washington, DC: National Council on Measurement in Education. Available http://www.unl.edu/buros/article2.html

Ebel, R. L. (1962). Measurement and the teacher. *Educational Leadership*, 20, 20–24.

Farr, R., & Griffin, M. (1973). Measurement gaps in teacher education. *Journal of Research and Development in Education*, 7(1), 19–28.

Fleming, M., & Chambers, B. (1983). Teacher-made tests: Windows on the classroom. In W. E. Hathaway (Ed.), *Testing in the schools*, San Francisco: Jossey-Bass.

Gullickson, A. R. (1985). Student evaluation techniques and their relationship to grade and curriculum. *Journal of Educational Research*, 79(2), 96–100.

Gullickson, A. R. (1996). Teacher education and teacher-perceived needs in educational measurement and evaluation. *Journal of Educational Measurement*, 23(4), 347–354.

Impara, J. C., & Plake, B. S. (1996). Professional development in student assessment for educational administrators. *Educational Measurement: Issues and Practice*, 15(2), 14–19.

Mayo, S. T. (1967). Pre-service preparation of teachers in educational measurement. U.S. Department of Health, Education and Welfare. Washington, DC: Office of Education/Bureau of Research.

McMillan, J. H. (2001). *Essential assessment concepts for teachers and administrators.* Thousand Oaks, CA: Corwin Publishing Company. Available Amazon.com

McMillan, J. H., & Nash, S. (2000). Teachers' classroom assessment and grading decision making. Paper presented at the Annual Meeting of the National Council of Measurement in Education, New Orleans.

Rogosa, D. (1999). How accurate are the STAR national percentile rank scores for individual students?—An interpretive guide. Palo Alto, CA: Stanford University.

Sanders, J. R., & Vogel, S. R. (1993). The development of standards for teacher competence in educational assessment of students, in S. L. Wise (Ed.), *Teacher training in measurement and assessment skills*, Lincoln, NB: Burros Institute of Mental Measurements.

Schafer, W. D. (1991). Essential assessment skills in professional education of teachers. *Educational Measurement: Issues and Practice*, 10, (1), 3–6.

Shepard, L. A. (2000). The role of assessment in a learning culture. Paper presented at the Annual Meeting of the American Educational Research Association. Available http://www.aera.net/meeting/am2000/wrap/praddr01.htm

Standards for educational and psychological testing (1999). Washington, DC: American Educational Research Association, American Psychological Association, National Council on Measurement in Education.

Standards for teacher competence in educational assessment of students. (1990). American Federation of Teachers, National Council on Measurement in Education, National Education Association. Available: http://www.unl.edu/buros/article3.html

Stiggins, R. J. (2000). Classroom assessment: A history of neglect, a future of immense potential. Paper presented at the Annual Meeting of the American Educational Research Association.

Stiggins, R. J., & Conklin, N. F. (1992). *In teachers' hands: Investigating the practices of classroom assessment*. Albany, NY: State University of New York Press, Albany.

Wiggins, G. (1998). *Educative assessment: Designing assessments to inform and improve student performance*. San Francisco: Jossey-Bass. Available Amazon.com

Contact Information:

James H. McMillan
Box 842020
Virginia Commonwealth University
Richmond, VA 23284-2020

Are We Measuring Student Success with High-Stakes Testing?

by Kathleen Anderson Steeves,
Jessica Hodgson,
and Patricia Peterson

A researcher, whether scientific, political, or educational, will tell you that evaluative measures begin with a working theory of the expected outcome. If high-stakes standardized exams and tests of similar ilk are intended to measure student success, why then have we not seen more discussion and careful thought placed on understanding what the outcomes of such testing actually mean and say about our students? What, in effect, do such tests actually set out to measure in our children?

Should we not, as teachers, administrators, and community leaders, be more worried about the measures and results of these annual "intelligence" tests that are increasingly being used to label students? FairTest (2002) recently noted that the United States already tests more children more often than any other nation. As a FairTest (1998) survey concluded, "There are more regulations governing the food we feed our pets than the tests used to make decisions about our children."

Should we not, as educators, insist on the time to step back and answer some fundamental questions? What is a successful student? What constitutes successful student habits, knowledge, abilities, and work? How can high-stakes testing be used more appropriately as a powerful tool for teachers to assist student learning?

Should we not open the debate about whether high-stakes tests, as they currently exist in most states, are accurate measures of what we want our students to be able to do before grade promotion or graduation? Do we want to stay on a path of instruction in which decisions are made about student intelligence, teacher ability, and school value based on a one-time test of general knowledge that has not been clearly defined or examined? As a country adopting more standardized testing, should we not see if its outcomes meet its admittedly high goals?

As educators who see the real effects of the tests on a daily basis, we believe that redefining and reexamination is overdue. Only after reevaluation and setting the parameters for student success can we go on to say definitively that such tests adequately measure the intended variables. This reevaluation must be undertaken before current testing trends, which may label students unfairly and inaccurately, become further entrenched in our society as the all-encompassing measure of a good student.

HISTORICAL DEFINITIONS OF THE SUCCESSFUL STUDENT

Though the specific details of student success have varied throughout the history of education—from the Puritan's scripture-citing prodigy to the Industrial Revolution's well-oiled cog of a learner—certain variables have remained intact (McNergney and Herbert 1995). As Goodlad (1984, 36) stated, there are a "broad array of educational goals in four [predominant] areas that have emerged in this country over more than 300 years." Though not nationally recognized, these four areas have become educationally institutionalized. They represent a logical first step in the search for the "successful" student, including, as Goodlad (1984, 51) noted, "A. Academic Goals (including: 1. Mastery of Basic Skills and Fundamental Processes, and 2. Intellectual Development); B. Vocational Goals; C. Social, Civic, and Cultural Goals; and D. Personal Goals."

According to Goodlad (1984), both parents and teachers have ranked academic goals of schooling as their top priority. These goals consisted of enabling students to: read, write, and solve basic arithmetic problems; acquire ideas from reading and listening; learn to communicate ideas through writing and speaking; utilize available sources of information; employ problem-solving skills, principles of logic, and different modes of inquiry; use and evaluate knowledge through critical and independent skills; accumulate a general fund of knowledge; and develop a positive attitude toward intellectual development.

Of the eight sub-skills constituting academic success, only one—enabling students to "accumulate a general fund of knowledge"—suggests that student success is connected to the mere "knowing" (or testing) of general information. Instead, Goodlad's goals point to a student's ability to "do" as the keystone to academic success. Words like "acquire," "problem-solve," "utilize," "analyze," and "inquire" rest at the helm of a student's successful navigation and eventual completion of school.

Currently, standards in all disciplines *are* academically rigorous. In describing their own standards for student success, national learning organizations have defined success in terms of what the student can "do":

- Apply reflective thinking and decision making when analyzing current civic/social events (National Council for the Social Studies 1993).
- Develop the abilities that characterize science as inquiry (Center for Science, Mathematics, and Engineering Education 1996).
- Investigate, make sense of, and construct meanings from new situations; make and provide arguments for conjectures; and use a flexible set of strategies to solve problems from both within and outside mathematics (National Council of Teachers of Mathematics 1989).
- Apply a wide range of strategies to comprehend, interpret, evaluate, and appreciate texts, including drawing on prior experience, interactions with other readers and writers, knowledge of word meaning of other texts (National Council of Teachers of English 1996).
- Use English to communicate in social settings, to achieve academically in all content areas and in socially and culturally appropriate ways (Teachers of English to Speakers of Other Languages 1997).

Indeed, teacher conceptions of the "successful" student appear to be aligned with those of the community, parents, and employers, each defining success as a student's ability to solve problems, seek solutions, and create and understand meaningful texts. A research study of employers in Oxon Hill, Maryland (Walker 1999), found that employers, like teachers, defined a successful student as one able to acquire and apply knowledge, such as: 1) locating and using meaningful information, 2) deciphering written and spoken language, 3) employing English in a context-appropriate manner, and 4) working with others in a professional manner.

Members of the National Education Goals Panel (1994) imagined successful students as those "practicing the scientific method, solving problems as a group, analyzing data, expressing their findings in writing, and defending their analysis in discussion." Educators such as Theodore R. Sizer and Ernest Boyer have envisioned similar learning environments and roles for the "successful" student. For Sizer (1992, 72), "The residue of serious learning is a mixture of awareness and logic. One exercises qualities of the mind with specifics, but the qualities themselves are the end to be pursued." In short, the goal of learning for Sizer is not the knowledge garnered but rather the process of learning to garner it. As Boyer (in Fiske 1991, 65), former president of the Carnegie Foundation for the Advancement of Teaching, has argued, "The key to problem solving is not to figure out the answer to a question that someone else hands you, but to define the right problem. An educated person

today is someone who knows the right questions to ask." When so many seem to agree on the current definition of a successful student, what's the problem?

HIGH-STAKES TESTING IN PRACTICE

Since U.S. educators first invented the modern standardized norm-referenced test, as Debra Meier (2000, 25) recently declared:

> *Our students have been taking more tests more often than any nation on the face of the earth, and schools and districts have been going public with test scores starting almost from the moment children enter school. From the third- or fourth-grade level (long before any of our international counterparts bother to test children) we have test data for virtually all schools, by race, class, and gender. We know exactly how many kids did better or worse in every subcategory. We have test data for almost every grade thereafter in reading and math, and to some degree in all other subjects. This has been the case for nearly half a century.*

Current trends in testing, though still tentative because there has not been enough time for in-depth study, include: use of multiple-measure assessments, emphasis on reading, and some sort of transitional accountability system as an interim step to mandatory state testing (Anderson, Fiester, Gonzales, and Pechman 1996). According to FairTest (2002), as of 1999, 17 states had graduation tests and five more were planning to implement such tests. Of the 15 states south of the Mason-Dixon line, 11 required students to pass graduation tests. In all, 39 states give either a criterion-referenced or norm-referenced test to determine their students' proficiency level. Almost all states are in the process of implementing proficiency tests of some kind, a process required now by the new federal education legislation. Illustrations from several jurisdictions provide a snapshot of some of the issues for teachers and students in this high-stakes testing trend.

In the District of Columbia, principals' and teachers' evaluations are initially to be based on student scores and improvement on the Stanford-9 (SAT-9) test battery, a multiple choice test adopted in 1996 to measure student achievement in reading and mathematics. A committee that included several teachers argued that the SAT-9 test matched the district's public schools curriculum, which is now aligned with national standards. The SAT-9 is available with various sets of empirical, normative information; ironically, none of the individual tests apply specifically to urban school districts (Harcourt Brace Educational Measurement 1999).

In Maryland, the state's School Performance Assessment Program (MSPAP), established in 1990 as the result of the Governor's Commission on School Performance, tests students' mastery in math, reading, and writing. Tasks require students to respond to questions or directions that lead to a solution to a problem, a recommendation, a decision, an explanation, or a rationale for the students' response to the task or question (Maryland State Department of Education [MSDOE] 1998). Once hailed for offering one of the first "performance-based" school tests in the nation, few states have followed Maryland's lead with MSPAP (Argetsinger and Nakashima 1998), finding such tests to be too expensive and time-consuming. MSPAP critics have complained that the test is used only to rate schools and does not measure individual student performance. An analysis of the 2001 MSPAP scores for the eighth-grade exam showed a dramatic decline in scores that left educators without an explanation. As a result, schools were given an option as to whether to use it or not. Questions were raised about the test's validity and the reliance on one test as a measure of teacher and school success (Shulte 2002). Starting with the class of 2004, high school students will be required to pass the Maryland Functional tests in content courses as a requirement for graduation (MSDOE 1998).

Massachusetts has spent $20 million on the development of the Massachusetts Comprehensive Assistance System, which will be required of all tenth-graders beginning in 2003. The state test will include multiple-choice and open-response questions. A newly formed group, the Coalition for Authentic Reform in Education, is actively opposing the notion that one test should be the only measure of student achievement (Public Broadcasting Service [PBS] 2002).

In Virginia, public schools began using the Standards of Learning (SOL) tests to assess students and schools in 1998. Students are tested in English, mathematics, history/social studies, science, and computer/technology in grades 3, 5, and 8 and at the end of core courses in high school. Beginning with the class of 2004, passing the SOL tests will be a determinant of earning a high school diploma. In addition, by 2006, a school's accreditation will depend on a 70 percent student-passing percentage on the SOL tests (Virginia Department of Education [VDOE] 1999–2001). In the second year of testing, 93 percent of public schools failed to reach the approved benchmark. The state was considering ways to adjust its timetable to implement sanctions (Mathews 1999). At this point, about half of the schools have achieved a passing rate on the required core SOL exams—though ESL students' scores were not included (VDOE 2001). In an effort to comply with expected requirements of President Bush's (2001) "No Child Left Behind" federally backed education legislation, Virginia is moving to expand the SOL testing to grades 4, 6, and 7.

HIGH-STAKES TESTING MAY FAIL STUDENTS AND TEACHERS

If these high-stakes tests are to be the measure of students, as well as of schools, it is imperative that we assess the effect of such testing on student academic success. When our country looks blindly to one test to tell us all we hope to know about students, teachers, and schools, then educators must demand a closer look at the actual meaning of these test results. Many educators know the flaws in the system firsthand. For example, when important consequences—such as student graduation and school accreditation—are linked to high-stakes testing, teachers are likely to respond by "teaching to the test" (Gordon and Reese 1997, 346). To ensure that students pass the assessment, teachers cover material that they believe will most likely be included on the test. However, teaching to these high-stakes tests has several negative consequences for both teachers and students.

When teaching to the test, the test does not become an assessment of a student's mastery of content; it is, instead, a powerful curricular tool. The teacher is forced to make instructional decisions that are not based on prior professional experience, or what is of academic importance, or what is in the best interest of the student; instead, decisions are based on what is most likely to be included on a standardized test (Shepard 1991). In essence, the test becomes a teacher's filter for making instructional decisions. As the curriculum becomes more narrow, content and skills that are not on the standardized assessment are eliminated. In fact, teachers feel pressure to make sure classroom activities correspond to material on the assessment even though they may know other materials will better prepare students for success in the world.

Gordon and Reese (1997) conducted a study on the effects of high-stakes testing on teachers in Texas. In this case, the high-stakes assessment became the object of instruction rather than the outcome of previous instruction. The Texas Assessment of Academic Skills (TAAS) evaluates schools based on the results of the assessment and gives cash awards to schools with high test scores, while poorly performing schools face "sanctions and intervention" (Gordon and Reese 1997, 348). These researchers found that one way Texas teachers have responded to high-stakes testing is to emphasize skills on the test. Teachers tended to spend more time on "drill and practice" and less time on "hands-on activities" found in the curriculum standards. Teachers in Texas complained that the TAAS made them accountable in terms of teaching TAAS-related content, but it did not make them accountable in terms of being effective teachers (Gordon and Reese 1997). Critics of the state's testing procedures have noted that dropout rates have increased, as has cheating (PBS 2002).

Gary Natriello (in Benning 1999), a professor at Columbia University's Teachers College, has argued that the new emphasis on testing may discourage teachers from entering the field because they really want to shape young minds rather than raise a test score by a point or two. Furthermore, schools—especially in urban settings—already have difficulty filling teaching positions. If the broad application of high-stakes test scores demoralizes the teachers currently working, and discourages potential teachers from applying, student achievement ultimately suffers.

Students are likewise affected by high-stakes testing. One of the most troubling effects of high-stakes testing is that it "can force students to leave school before they have to take the examination, or after failing it" (Madaus 1991, 229). Another effect is that the performance of principals and superintendents is often linked to the number of students who reach the bar set by the state. Unfortunately, this situation may mean it is in an administrator's best interest to eliminate systematically from the test those students who probably wouldn't make the bar and to keep enrolled discipline-problem students who will get high scores on the test. In fact, in efforts to increase school performance on high-stakes testing, some schools have relied on increased special education placement and retention in grade. This system allows schools to control, to some extent, the student population whose test scores are reflected in school scores (Allington and McGill-Franzen 1992).

Whatever philosophical perspective one has toward high-stakes testing, it is clear that these tests have a significant effect on both teachers and students. In narrowing the curriculum, changing instructional strategies, and impacting the classroom and student demographics, high-stakes testing negatively alters the educational environment for teachers and students.

There is no evidence that passing the current tests equates to student success. Actually, for many, it may even mean the opposite.

Overall, educators understand that the emphasis these tests place on lower-level skills is not in line with what discipline-based organizations are asking their teachers to do in meeting content standards. Given the increased focus on nationwide standards, it must be asked whether schools *are* supplying their students with the skills and knowledge necessary to become "successful." There is no evidence that passing the current tests equates to student success. Actually, for many, it may even mean the opposite. These questions must then be asked: Are we producing students who can problem-solve, analyze, and ask the right questions? Are we evaluating them accordingly? Are these popular and increasingly endorsed "high-stakes" tests, which neatly tell us who has succeeded and who has failed, attuned to our definition of a successful student or to the philosophy of success that shapes current practice?

RETHINKING HOW WE MEASURE SUCCESS

With the current rush toward adoption of high-stakes testing forms that align with state standards, we must encourage important and necessary public discussion about the outcomes and what we are actually trying to assess in our students today (U.S. Department of Education 1998). As schools hurriedly move toward the narrow use of standardized tests to determine eligibility for graduation and school and teacher evaluation, we argue that it still has not been made clear what these tests really measure and if they actually come close to identifying our society's agreed-upon definition of a successful student.

It is necessary to reopen the discussion on testing, not as a measure to be removed, but as something that must be reexamined for what test results actually do mean and how the billions in testing dollars could be spent best in assessing our students. We must begin a discussion about what a successful student is and whether a revamped test or a restructured system of accounting for the results could more accurately measure this success.

As part of the call to reenergize this important discussion, various issues must be considered. The discussion has begun in a number of states, but it must be expanded.

How do we increase the validity of these tests? Most research employs a margin of error. Why is that not true in high-stakes tests? A student scoring one point below the cut-off score (defined in no logical way) gets no credit, while the student scoring at the cut-off point or one point above gets full credit and is promoted.

Which standards are we using to measure success? All content areas include important skills and knowledge, but what consistent measure of comparison is being used (state, county, district, or national standards)?

What are the long-term effects of high-stakes testing on students who do not graduate or drop out before they fail yet again? Do we have the collective will across the board in urban, suburban, and rural schools to use the test data to make a difference and assist students who need additional instructional time and resources to achieve the standards?

In the end, we must ask one another if we have developed a clear, agreed-upon definition of a successful student so that we may really put required resources into achieving success for all students. We must be certain that the promise to "leave no child behind" is not just overlooked by current community leaders and politicians who herald the tests unchanged. We must insist that high-stakes, standardized testing becomes less a political tool for finger pointing and assessing student and school failure and more of a reasoned way to help pinpoint why these students are failing and where resources are needed to produce the truly successful students we all want!

REFERENCES

Allington, R. L., and A. McGill-Franzen. 1992. Does high-stakes testing improve school effectiveness? *ERS Spectrum* 10(2): 3–12.

Anderson, L., L. Fiester, M. Gonzales, and E. Pechman. eds. 1996. *Improving America's schools: Newsletter on issues on school reform* (Spring). Washington, D.C.: Improving America's Schools Association. Available at: *http://www.ed.gov/pubs/IASA/newsletters/standards*.

Argetsinger, A., and E. Nakashima. 1998. In Md., the 'bubble' test has burst: Analytical exam gains favor over multiple-choice format. *Washington Post,* 11 May, A1.

Benning, V. 1999. Teachers wary of new exams. Poll finds support for D.C. program. *Washington Post*, 5 July, A1.

Bush, G. W. 2001. No child left behind. Washington, D.C.: U.S. Department of Education. Available at *http://www.ed.gov/offices/OESE/esea/nclb/titlepage.html*.

Center for Science, Mathematics, and Engineering Education, 1996. *National science education standards*. Washington, D.C.: National Academy Press.

FairTest: The National Center for Fair & Open Testing. 1998. FairTest applauds National Research Council report opposing high-stakes tests and endorsing tougher regulation of exam use. Press release, 3 Sept. Cambridge, Mass.: FairTest. Available at *http://www.fairtest.org/pr/nrc-pr.htm*.

FairTest:The National Center for Fair & Open Testing. 2002. Will more testing improve schools? Fact sheet. Cambridge, Mass.: FairTest. Available at: *http://www.fairtest.org.facts/Will%20More%20Testing%20Improve%20Schools.html*.

Fiske, E. B. 1991. *Smart schools, smart kids. Why do some schools work?* New York: Simon & Schuster.

Goodlad, J. I. 1984. *A place called school: Prospects for the future.* New York: McGraw-Hill.

Gordon, S. P., and M. Reese. 1997. High-stakes testing: Worth the price? *Journal of School Leadership* 7(4): 345–68.

Harcourt Brace Educational Measurement. 1999. Stanford-9 Achievement Test Series: It's like nothing you've ever seen before. San Antonio: HBEM.

Madaus, G. F. 1991. The effects of important tests on students. *Phi Delta Kappan* 73(3): 226–31.

Maryland State Department of Education. 1998. Maryland school performance report, 1998: State and school systems. Annapolis: MSDOE. ERIC ED 429 348.

Mathews, J. 1999. Va. schools may get reprieve on standards. *Washington Post,* 16 September, B1.

McNergney, R. F., and J. M. Herbert. 1995. *Foundations of education: The challenge of professional practice.* Boston: Allyn & Bacon.

Meier, D. 2000. *Will standards save public education?* Boston: Beacon Press.

National Council for the Social Studies. 1993. Social studies online: Standards and position statements. Washington, D.C.: NCSS.

National Council of Teachers of English. 1996. *Standards for the English Language Arts.* Urbana, Ill.: NCTE and the International Reading Association.

National Council of Teachers of Mathematics. 1989. Curriculum standards for grades 9–12. Reston, VA: NCTM. Available at *http://standards.nctm.org/Previous/CurrEvStds/currstand9-12.htm.*

Public Broadcasting Service. 2002. Frontline: Testing our schools. Television program, 28 March.

Shepard, L. A. 1991. Will national tests improve student learning? *Phi Delta Kappan* 73(3): 232–38.

Shulte, B. 2002. County questions drop in MSPAP scores: Despite new initiatives, district's results decline. *Washington Post,* 31 January, T14.

Sizer, T. R. 1992. *Horace's School: Redesigning the American high school.* Boston: Houghton Mifflin.

Teachers of English to Speakers of Other Languages. 1997. ESL standards for pre-K–12 students. Alexandria, Va.: TESOL. ERIC ED 420 991.

U.S. Department of Education. 1998. Turning around low-performing schools. A guide for state and local leaders. Washington, D.C.: USDE. ERIC ED 420 119.

Virginia Department of Education. 1999–2001. Standards of learning discussion forum. SOLs unfair to students. Richmond: VDOE. Available at: *http://www.vdoe.vipnet.org/messages/23/36.html? 996190534.*

Virginia Department of Education. 2001. Spring 1999 Standards of Learning test results. Richmond: VDOE. Available at: *http://www.pen.k12.va.us/sol99.*

Walker, L. 1999. A community case study. GWU class, Teacher Education, SPED #233, Professor West, Washington, D.C.

Kathleen Anderson Steeves *is Associate Professor of History/Social Studies Education at George Washington University in Washington, D.C. Her research interests include secondary history and social studies, education reform and standards, teacher leadership, and the history of education.*

Jessica Hodgson *teaches social studies at Chantilly High School in Fairfax County, Virginia. She is currently involved in research on using writing as a learning tool in the history classroom.*

Patricia Peterson *teaches 7th- and 8th-Grade English at Garner-Patterson Middle School in Washington, D.C. Her focus is on literacy development through poetry, music, and service learning. Ms. Peterson recently established a student Poetry Club connecting students with community artists and writers.*

From *The Educational Forum,* Spring 2002, pp. 228-235. © 2002 by Kappa Delta Pi, International Honor Society in Education. Reprinted by permission.

The Seductive Allure of Data

Most state accountability tests fail to produce the kinds of data that will improve teaching and learning. Teachers can get the data they need from classroom assessments—if they know how to design instructionally useful tests.

W. James Popham

The word *data*, at least to most educators, simply reeks of goodness. Although probably less heart-warming than *children, smaller classes*, and *summer vacation*, the term *data* inclines most educators to think good thoughts laced with notions of evidence, science, and rigor. Indeed, the theme of this issue of *Educational Leadership* reflects educators' belief that data play a central role in improving student achievement. In any education lexicon these days, the term *data* is inarguably one of our most positively loaded nouns.

Data Scorned?

But *data* shouldn't elicit automatic obeisance from right-thinking educators. Indeed, we should spurn some data. In the following analysis, I intend to dismiss certain sorts of data. I want educators to realize that the wrong kinds of data, even if warmly applauded by many, can actually stifle teachers' pursuit of accurate evidence regarding their students' achievement.

Currently, teachers are buffeted by messages that the often undecipherable test results they receive are, in fact, the data they need to make instructional deci-

sions. Is it any wonder when, after trying in vain to make sense of such opaque test data, many teachers simply quit believing in the instructional utility of data? To avoid becoming disillusioned with all data, teachers must learn how to distinguish between instructionally delightful and instructionally dismal data.

At the Top of the Heap: Test Data

Although all sorts of data might help to improve instruction, the most important data in the United States these days are *test data*—particularly data describing students' performance on achievement tests. That's because schools increasingly employ those data to evaluate educators' effectiveness.

State-determined achievement tests increasingly serve as the centerpiece of state accountability systems. But data from most states' accountability tests, unfortunately, have almost no value for improving teaching and learning. More dangerously, such tests lull educators into believing that they have appropriate data when, in fact, they do not. As a consequence, many educators fail to ask for more meaningful, instructionally valuable data that would help them teach students better.

Instructionally Beneficial Data

Instructionally beneficial data can only come from instructionally useful tests. Here are five attributes of an instructionally useful test, which apply to large-scale assessments as well as to teacher-made classroom assessments.

Significance. An instructionally useful test measures students' attainment of a worthwhile curricular aim—for instance, a high-level cognitive skill or a substantial body of important knowledge. It makes no sense to assess students' mastery of such trifling knowledge as esoteric scientific terms or dates associated with obscure historical events. (I suppose that someone might come up with a cogent argument for asking students to memorize state capitals. I've never been able to.)

Teachability. An instructionally useful test measures something teachable. Teachability means that most teachers, if they deliver reasonably effective instruction aimed at the test's assessment targets, can get most of their students to master what the test measures. For instance, an instructionally useful test should not measure students' innate intelligence. In standardized achievement tests, we frequently encounter items requiring students to engage in such spatial visualization tasks as mentally "folding" letters or geometric shapes into two equal halves. Such tasks clearly depend on a student's inherited visualization aptitude.

Similarly, certain high-level inference skills are extraordinarily difficult to teach because the cognitive processes central to those skills usually depend on the idiosyncratic nature of a particular student's prior experiences. It simply makes no sense to assess students' mastery of essentially unteachable outcomes.

Describability. A useful test provides or is directly based on sufficiently clear descriptions of the skills and knowledge it measures so that teachers can design properly focused instructional activities. These descriptions must not only be provided in plain language, but must also be sufficiently succinct so that they are not off-putting to busy teachers.

If a test is based on an already clearly described set of content standards, and if teachers can tell which of those content standards the test will cover, then no further descriptive information is needed. But if the content standards are not clear enough to unambiguously let teachers identify those curricular targets, then lucid descriptions of what the test will assess must accompany any instructionally useful test. A content standard such as "Students will read a variety of different types of texts" communicates little of instructional value to the teacher.

It makes no sense to assess students' mastery of ill-defined curricular targets or to force teachers to play an annual guessing game about which of the state's content standards the statewide accountability tests will assess.

Reportability. An instructionally useful test yields results at a specific enough level to inform teachers about the effectiveness of the instruction they provide. A national commission has urged that any education accountability test report its results on a standard-by-standard basis for individual students (Commission on Instructionally Supportive Assessment, 2001). Such per-standard reporting of results would enable teachers to identify those parts of their instruction that were successful or unsuccessful on the basis of students' post-instruction test data.

It makes no sense to provide teachers with data so general that those teachers cannot evaluate and improve their own instructional efforts. Similarly, it makes no sense for assessors to contend that they have assessed the complete array of a state's content standards when, in fact, they have measured some standards either by only a handful of items or by no items at all.

Nonintrusiveness. In clear recognition that testing time takes away from teaching time, an instructionally useful test shouldn't take too long to administer—it should not intrude excessively on instructional activities. For instance, if a state-level test of students' reading skills is administered each spring, it should be administrable in one, or at most two, class periods. Longer tests simply soak up too much instructional time. It makes no sense to test students interminably, diverting several weeks of precious instructional time each year to assessment.

In review, we are most likely to obtain instructionally useful data through the use of instructionally useful tests. The five attributes of an instructionally useful test are its significance, teachability, describability, reportability, and nonintrusiveness. The data derived from an instructionally useful test will enable teachers to do a better job of instructing their students. And that, after all, should be the reason we test students in the first place.

Detecting Dismal Data

As suggested earlier, tests that don't produce instructionally useful data can disincline educators to demand data that are instructionally beneficial. In the following three common assessment situations, the wrong kinds of data—provided by the wrong kinds of tests—have diminished the quality of education that we provide to our students.

Nationally Standardized Achievement Tests

Today's nationally standardized tests miss the mark dramatically with respect to three of the attributes of instructionally useful assessment:

- *Describability.* All nationally standardized achievement tests have been constructed according to a traditional measurement approach aimed at providing a comparative picture of students' relative performances. The developers try to devise a "one-size-fits-all" test and describe it in a manner that will make it attractive to many potential purchasers. As a result, nationally standardized tests don't include

properly tied-down descriptions of what they assess. Teachers can't aim their instruction accurately if they have murky assessment targets.

- *Teachability.* In order to produce the score spread on which comparative score interpretations depend, nationally standardized tests contain many instructionally insensitive items that are linked to students' socioeconomic status or inherited academic aptitudes. It is particularly difficult for teachers to increase students' performance on such items.

- *Reportability.* Nationally standardized achievement tests almost always report their results at levels of generality altogether unsuitable for teachers' day-to-day instructional decision making. Some national tests do a better job than others when it comes to reporting students' results. But in no case do these tests provide data that teachers can easily use to appraise their own instructional effectiveness.

I believe that nationally standardized achievement tests have a role in education. Both parents and teachers can benefit from data indicating a student's relative strengths and weaknesses. But the genuine instructional yield of nationally standardized tests is much more modest than the publishers of these tests would have us believe.

Standards-Based Tests

There is a charade currently going on in the way the United States carries out its education assessment activities. Its name is "standards-based assessment." Standards-based tests supposedly measure students' mastery of a state's officially approved content standards—the skills and knowledge constituting the state's curricular aims. Yet because most states have adopted too many content standards and stated them too vaguely, most states' standards-based tests just don't do a decent job determining a student's mastery of those standards.

Pretending that a one- or two-hour state test can provide a meaningful fix on a student's mastery of myriad, often fuzzy content standards is patently hypocritical. Today's standards-based assessments constitute a serious violation of any sort of truth-in-advertising precept. Standards-based tests don't measure what they pretend to measure.

The data yielded by today's standards-based tests have another equally serious shortcoming. Those data almost never provide any indication of *which* content standards a student has or hasn't mastered. In the absence of such data, how can teachers tell which parts of their instruction they need to modify?

Teachers don't learn much of instructional value when the standards-based test results tell them that Johnny is "not proficient" with respect to his mastery of a set of 17 language arts content standards. Teachers cannot discern which of the 17 content standards their students have mastered (hence, which standards have been well taught) and which of the 17 content standards their students have not mastered (hence, which standards have not been well taught).

So most of today's standards-based tests fall down seriously on several attributes of an instructionally useful test. They often lack significance because, in a fruitless effort to measure all of a state's sprawling content standards, they simply do not assess students' mastery of the most important content. Standards-based tests also get low grades on describability—they usually fail to describe their assessment targets satisfactorily, because these tests are based on a plethora of too many, insufficiently clear content standards. And perhaps most seriously, standards-based tests often lack reportability—they fail to provide standard-by-standard reports to teachers, students, or students' parents.

Teachers' Classroom Assessments

Given the enormous pressure placed on teachers these days to boost their students' scores on external exams, teachers understandably tend to give less attention to their own classroom assessments. That's a mistake—but only if the teacher's classroom tests are instructionally useful.

Teachers can judge the instructional utility of their classroom assessments by using the same five attributes of an instructionally useful test that I just applied to large-scale external exams. Teachers should ask themselves the following questions:

- Do my classroom assessments measure genuinely worthwhile skills and knowledge?

- Will I be able to promote my students' mastery of what's measured in my classroom assessments?

- Can I describe what skills and knowledge my classroom tests measure in language sufficiently clear for my own instructional planning?

- Do my classroom assessments yield results that allow me to tell which parts of my instruction were effective or ineffective?

- Do my classroom tests take up too much time away from my instruction?

Clearly, the answers to these questions will vary from teacher to teacher. Generally, teachers who employ their classroom assessments most appropriately adopt a "less is more" approach. They focus on measuring only a modest number of curricular aims, but make certain that those aims deal with genuinely significant outcomes that students can master with adequate instruction. As a dividend of focusing on a smaller number of significant outcomes, those outcomes can then be clearly described to help the teacher target instruction and assessment.

Teachers must deal with one additional consideration if they intend to use their classroom data to supplement results from external exams: Unless classroom tests provide credible data, skeptics will rush to dismiss the results as "self-interested home cooking." I'm not talking about tests that teachers use only to inform themselves about their ongoing instruction, but rather about the more significant sorts of data that schools use to judge a teacher's instructional effectiveness.

One straightforward way for teachers to collect credible evidence of their own effectiveness is to use a pretest/posttest design in which they give identical assessments at the start of a semester and again at its conclusion. Students must use the same kind of paper if the test calls for a constructed response (such as writing an essay). Students do not date their responses. The teacher codes the pretests and posttests so they can be subsequently identified, and then mixes them all together so that a scorer cannot discern which responses are pretests and which are posttests.

Data from most states' accountability tests, unfortunately, have almost no value for improving teaching and learning.

At this point the teacher calls on a nonpartisan scorer (for instance, another teacher or a parent) to blind-score the students' responses. Only after all the shuffled papers have been scored does the teacher sort them into pretests and posttests. The improvement between the pretests and posttests constitutes credible evidence of the teacher's instructional success (Popham, 2001).

What Can Educators Do?

In response to today's increasingly important assessment concerns, I suggest a two-stage course of action. First, educators should disregard data from any test that isn't instructionally useful. Second, they should push for the installation of instructionally useful tests so that the data that those assessments yield will lead to better-taught students.

Although most of today's standards-based tests are not instructionally useful, that need not be the case. A national commission recently described how to create accountability tests that are both accurate and instructionally useful (Commission on Instructionally Supportive Assessment, 2001). Many states assess students' written composition competence by requiring students to generate original writing samples, which are then evaluated according to scoring guides (rubrics) based on teachable criteria. Almost all of today's writing samples are instructionally beneficial. If you live in a state where such instructionally useful tests do not exist, lobby aggressively for their introduction.

If you live in a state that uses nationally standardized achievement tests for accountability purposes, try your hardest to get them replaced with more appropriate, instructionally useful accountability tests.

Teachers should also bring common sense to the scrutiny of their own classroom assessments. In general, a quest for assessment sanity will lead teachers to adopt a less-is-more measurement approach. However, if the resultant data will be used for instructional evaluation, then teachers must collect those data in a manner sufficiently credible to persuade even non-believers of the data's validity.

To educators, the wrong data can often be seductively appealing. But the right data will, in fact, help teachers do a better job with students. *Those* are the data we need.

References

Commission on Instructionally Supportive Assessment. (2001). *Building tests that support instruction and accountability: A guide for policymakers.* Washington, DC:

Author. [Online]. Available: www.nea.org/accountability/buildingtests.html

Popham, W. J. (2001). *The truth about testing: An educator's call to action.* Alexandria, VA: ASCD.

W. James Popham is a professor emeritus at the University of California, Los Angeles, Graduate School of Education and Information Studies; wpopham@ucla.edu.

Teaching About Performance Assessment

How should we teach prospective teachers about performance assessment? What are the issues and concerns that new teachers will encounter as they begin their teaching careers? How can assessment and instruction be better integrated in classrooms?

Judy Arter

Northwest Regional Educational Laboratory

If there is anything definite about performance assessment, it is that experts cannot agree on a definition. Because of this, it is prudent to let readers know the definition used in the current article: Performance assessment is assessment based on observation and judgment (Airasian, 1991, p. 252; Stiggins, 1997, p. 175). One observes a performance or a product and then judges its quality. Examples abound, everything from the driver's test and Olympic judging to the multitude of formal and informal observations teachers make in the classroom: skill levels on such things as oral presentations and wrestling, quality of products such as essays and laboratory reports, and affective orientation, including level of effort and desire to learn. Although fairly broad, this definition is not intended to include *all* constructed-response-type items (especially short answer and fill in the blank), but, admittedly, the line between constructed response and performance assessment is thin. (This is probably why there are so many attempts at definition.)

Performance assessment is not new. Teachers have always observed student performances and products and made judgments about them. However, there are recent developments that highlight the current importance of teaching teachers to do performance assessment well (Herman, 1997). Although undoubtedly familiar to readers, I mention them briefly because they set up major themes for the text that follows.

1. Teachers are being asked to assist students to acquire more complex skills than ever before. Witness the content standards being developed by many states and professional organizations. Students are to read with comprehension, write well, be critical thinkers, be lifelong learners, be collaborative workers, be able to communicate their mathematical understanding, and so forth. Such complex learning targets for students require complex assessments, including performance assessments.

2. Teachers are being asked to use formal performance assessments on a daily basis, and for purposes other than grading. It is not enough to wait until the year-end, large-scale assessment to see what percentage of students meet "mastery." Continuous classroom monitoring of student progress toward important, and frequently complex, learning targets is the essence of standards-based instruction and education.

3. Since performance assessments are increasingly being used for additional purposes, some of which are high stakes, there have been many efforts to make this essentially subjective form of assessment as objective as possible. Familiar examples are standardization of tasks and criteria, careful training of those judging work, and technical work on thorny issues such as sampling and generalizability. Although the focus for this work is generally large-scale assessment, the resulting refinement of performance assessment methods has implications for improving classroom practice as well.

4. There is tantalizing preliminary evidence that performance assessments can be used for more than simply

providing information about students for decision making (as important as this is). Developing and using performance assessments can have positive impacts on instruction and student attitudes and learning, even to the point that performance assessment materials and methods can be used to help students acquire the very skills being assessed (e.g., Arter, Spandel, Cuiham, & Pollard, 1994; Borko et al., 1997; Clarke & Stephens, 1996; Khattri, 1995; Office of Educational Research and Improvement, 1997).

Because of these trends and findings, teachers need to know how to do performance assessment well (i.e., prudently, efficiently, validly, and with positive consequences for students). Yet, studies continue to show that K–12 teachers lack skill in assessing their students (Hills, 1991; Impara, Plake, & Fager, 1993; Plake, Impara, & Fager, 1993) and that they feel unprepared and uncomfortable in terms of their knowledge of assessment practices (Shafer, 1993; Wise, Lukin, & Roos, 1991; Zhang, 1997). Additionally a recent study (Fager, Plake, & Impara, 1997) found that even in those institutions where preservice course work is required or offered, there is a certain amount of feeling that it does not cover what teachers will really need to know and be able to do and that the courses are not taught by those most familiar with assessment issues and developments. Given the importance of effective assessment, we must all continue to think about and discuss what teachers need to know and be able to do with respect to classroom assessment, the best ways to assist them in learning it, and how we will know when they are competent.

Based on the experience of the Northwest Regional Educational Laboratory (NWREL) in conducting thousands of workshops for teachers on assessment and the fruitful ideas of other preservice and in-service instructors (such as Airasian, 1991; Marzano & Kendall, 1996; McTighe, 1996; and Stiggins, 1997), this article describes seven topics that should be included in a course on performance assessment and provides some ideas for teaching them. The focus is on performance assessment as practiced in the classroom; because teachers also need to know about large-scale assessments, however, this topic is discussed as well.

The following is a series of questions to consider: Do you believe that good classroom assessment can improve student achievement? Do you believe that assessing students well will make teachers' lives easier? Do you believe that it is possible to use assessment as a tool that can directly influence student learning as well as a tool for making educational decisions about students? Do you believe that assessment and instruction can be integrated? If we believe these things, then we have to be ready to demonstrate them to teachers or they will not engage in the process of learning to do classroom assessment differently. I propose that we can demonstrate all of these things with performance assessment if we approach it correctly. Not that these things cannot be demonstrated

with other forms of assessment. Rather, performance assessment especially lends itself to these ideas, can draw teachers into the topic of assessment in general, and is the focus of this article.

What Teachers Need to Know and Be Able to Do With Respect to Performance Assessment

The *Standards for Teacher Competence in Educational Assessment of Students* (American Federation of Teachers, National Council on Measurement in Education, and National Education Association, 1990) provide a good starting place for describing what teachers need to know and be able to do with respect to performance assessment. The *Standards* specify that teachers be competent in seven areas:

1. Choosing assessment methods appropriate for instructional decisions.
2. Developing assessment methods appropriate for instructional decisions.
3. Administering, scoring, and interpreting results of assessments.
4. Using assessment results when making decisions.
5. Developing valid pupil grading procedures.
6. Communicating assessment results to students and others.
7. Recognizing unethical, illegal, and inappropriate assessment methods and uses.

The *Standards* are a good place to start and provide a wealth of detail on the specific knowledge and skills teachers should have in these areas, but they do not adequately cover several important topics, those especially relevant to performance assessment.

First, the document does not mention the central necessity of having a clear conception of what is to be assessed and being sure that these targets are the best ones to shoot for. How can one assess (or teach) something if it is not clear exactly what knowledge or skills a student is to possess? Having clear targets means more than merely stating that a learning goal for students is "writing" or "problem solving." Rather, *clarity* of targets requires knowing, for example, what good writing looks like, how students develop toward this target, and what adequate (and weak) writing looks like at various grade levels.

In my work with teachers, I am becoming more and more convinced (along with others, such as Stiggins, 1997, chap. 3, and Marzano & Kendall, 1996, p. 27) that improving classroom assessment has less to do with the actual mechanism of developing assessments than with being clearer on what is to be assessed. As one reviewer of an earlier version of this article stated, "If you can hammer away on exactly what it is the teacher wants the student to be able to do, sometimes the assessment sort of pops out of the discussion." For example, in writing

Table 1

Summary of Performance Assessment Knowledge and Skills

General topic	Specific subtopics	Relationship to standards	Relationship to 3 additional topics
What performance assessment is and why we should care	Definitions Two mandatory parts to a performance assessment: tasks and criteria	Standards 1, 2	Clear targets Use as a tool for learning
When to use performance assessment	Which student learning targets are best assessed with a performance assessment and which with another method Balance—performance assessment not always the answer Balance—ideal against practical	Standards 1, 2	Target-method match Use as a tool for learning
Design options	Design options for tasks Design options for criteria	Standard 2	
The nature of quality and why we should care	Quality in tasks and when to use various design options Quality in performance criteria and when to use various designs Consistency in scoring Sampling Avoiding possible sources of bias and distortion Building in features that result in positive consequences for teachers, instruction, and students	Standards 1-4, 7	Clear targets Target-method match Use as a tool for learning
How to develop tasks and criteria	Practice developing tasks and criteria	Standard 2	Clear targets
Use as an instructional methodology	How to use criteria to assist students to self-assess, and features of criteria that maximize this use How to teach criteria to students The role of performance criteria in standards-based education		Clear targets Use as a tool for learning
Grading and reporting	Converting rubric scores to grades Ways to report on student progress besides grades	Standards 5, 6	

teachers need to grapple with the balance between assessing enabling skills for writing well (e.g., spelling, grammar, good sentence structure, developing a main idea with details, different ways to organize ideas) and determining whether students can use these skills in concert to actually write. Both probably need to be addressed, but exactly which skills and in what balance?

The second topic, not emphasized strongly enough in the *Standards*, is "target-method match." The *Standards* stress matching purposes with methods (see Standards 1 and 2) but not choosing the assessment method that best matches the skills and knowledge to be assessed. The

third topic not covered well in the *Standards* is the use of assessment as a tool for learning.

Keeping all of this in mind, Table 1 presents a summary of what classroom teachers need to know and be able to do with respect to performance assessment. The first column lists general topics for instruction, the second column provides subtopics, the third column cross references the topics to the *Standards for Teacher Competence,* and the final column cross references topics to the three additional areas described earlier: clear and appropriate targets, target-method match, and using assessment as a tool for learning.

Table 1 provides an outline for the remainder of the article. It is impossible in a short article to completely describe such a unit on performance assessment, including ideas on how to teach each topic. Therefore, I try here to (a) hit the high points and major things that seem to confuse teachers, (b) provide some ideas on where to begin so that the order is not only logical but immediately engaging to the adult learner, (c) describe how topics interrelate, and (d) provide references to other documents I have found to be particularly useful. I also emphasize the classroom instructional uses of performance assessment, since that topic has been less well developed by others. To avoid confusion, I refer to child learners as "students" and preservice or in-service teachers as "teachers" or "adult learners."

What Performance Assessment Is and Why We Should Care

Performance Assessment "Kick Off" Readings

Three papers useful for beginning a unit on performance assessment are those of Rudner and Boston (1994), Wiggins (1992), and Stayter and Johnston (1990). The Rudner and Boston article is a balanced overview of the rationale for performance assessment, what various groups are doing with respect to performance assessment, and current issues. (Much of this is still relevant, although descriptions of activities in specific states have changed somewhat since 1994.) The basic message of the Wiggins article is that quality matters. The point of the Stayter and Johnston chapter is that assessment affects kids; if we want it to have a positive effect, we need to pay close attention to design issues. Teachers find these articles accessible, informative, and provocative. As they read, teachers can make notes on what ideas they like, find problematic, and want to know more about. This "kick-off" activates prior knowledge, sets the tone that learning will be cooperative, provides the instructor with information about adult learners' prior knowledge and attitudes, and emphasizes the major themes of the unit.

Using Performance Assessment Definitions to Emphasize Why We Should Care

A useful way to proceed is to familiarize teachers with the definition of performance assessment and ask them to cite examples in daily life and the classroom. This provides an excellent opportunity to point out that performance assessment is not fundamentally new, to outline changes in performance assessment (as outlined in the introduction), and to emphasize the need for balance in assessment (performance assessment is simply one tool, not a cure-all). Regardless of the specific definition of performance assessment one uses, it is important to emphasize early on that there are two parts to a performance assessment: tasks and criteria. It is not assessment if it does not include both.

The Importance of Criteria. One consistently encounters "performance assessments" from supposedly reputable organizations that are simply tasks. For example, a recent Association for Supervision and Curriculum Development (ASCD) publication (Checkley, 1997) extolled the virtues of the following geography "authentic assessment." The teacher asked his students to research the name of their town. The students found other towns all across the United States with the same name. The students wrote to each of these towns and prepared a research paper and a museum display. This process purportedly assessed research skills, geographic knowledge, and communication skills. However, there were no criteria for judging the quality of student performance on any of these skills in the context of this task. So, why is this assessment? Granted, this might be a rich, "authentic," engaging task for students in which they might actually learn something about research skills, geography, and communication. But there is no way to know what, in fact, they learn.

Teachers tend to be better at developing rich, interesting tasks in which to engage students than they are at developing the criteria that describe quality performance on the task. This point is made repeatedly by those assisting teachers in developing performance assessments:

> Respondents claim that an important purpose of portfolios is valid assessment of student progress and growth, yet nowhere in the packets have we found a clear account of how achievement is to be measured. None of the portfolio guide books... [provide] help in analysis, scoring, or grading. (Calfee & Perfumo, 1993, p. 534)

> Teachers [frequently] ask the wrong question first... "What do we do?"—putting the focus immediately on designing tasks—when they need to ask, "What do we want kids to know and be able to do? How well? What does quality look like?" [We] need to ask these questions very clearly first. (Hibbard, 1996, p. 5)

In my work with teachers, it is the skill of "rubric writing" which is most elusive. Perhaps it's because we're used to assigning single grades for complex assignments, knowing what an "A" looks like in our heads, but rarely "putting it to paper" so that our students can see it as well. Perhaps the difficulty in writing scoring criteria also lies in the challenge of describing just what it really looks like to perform well, or better yet, to perform at a variety of levels of competency. Nevertheless, it is the use of rubrics as an indispensable part of the instructional process which completes the vital link between assessment and instruction. Until we invest the time discerning for ourselves what excellence in writing, or speaking, or dancing, or singing, or whatever looks like, we are unable to fully "teach" our students to achieve at these levels. (Mendel, undated)

High-quality performance criteria are essential for providing consistency between raters and for use with students as a learning tool. Good ways to illustrate the importance of criteria for these two uses are provided in the next two sections.

Using Performance Criteria to Provide Consistency Between Raters. Give adult learners a performance to assess; for example, show them a student giving an oral presentation. Ask them to evaluate the quality of performance on that task without providing them any criteria. Have them discuss their frustrations, ideas, and solutions in small groups. Then provide illustrations of good-quality performance criteria for oral presentations (Massachusetts State Department of Education, 1983; Usrey, 1998) and ask the adult learners to again evaluate performance on the task. Have them discuss the differences that good criteria make.

This activity points to the first need for criteria: to provide consistency between raters and within the same rater over time and across tasks. This activity can also lead to a good discussion of the desirability of standard criteria for use by all teachers in a grade, building, district, or department. Furthermore, it can result in a useful discussion about how high-quality criteria define complex learning targets; in fact, high-quality criteria are the final definition of complex learning targets. Teachers can then discuss how having such clear definitions might decrease their anxiety level by helping them to see desired student learning targets more clearly. Finally, the activity of scoring performance both with and without criteria can lead to a fruitful examination of the need to include the correct indicators in the criteria; the criteria must describe what we mean by quality performance. If they do not, teachers will teach to the wrong targets.

Using Performance Criteria to Improve Student Achievement. Discuss the criteria used on a driver's test. Actually contact the Department of Motor Vehicles and ask what the criteria are. (If an individual is to obtain a driver's license in the state of Washington, for example, the examiner must ultimately decide that the individual has adequate skill, has not caused congestion, and has not caused a danger.) Ask the adult learners whether it would be important for students to "know" these criteria in advance and, if so, why. The answer is typically a resounding "yes," because criteria help students know what counts so that they can practice. This decreases student anxiety levels.

Then ask the adult learners what it means to "know" criteria. Is it enough simply to hand the criteria to prospective drivers as they begin their test? (Teachers always say "no.") If students are to *know* criteria, they must be discussed beginning on the first day of class, practiced

with feedback, be illustrated with examples of good and poor performance on each important trait or dimension, modeled by the teacher, used by the students to assess their own work and that of others, and used to guide the revision of performance.

This activity points to the second major use for performance criteria: helping students understand the nature of the skills they are to master and providing a standard of comparison against which students can measure their progress. In short, performance criteria can be a tool to help students acquire the very skills assessed.

These two activities—"scoring with and without performance criteria" and "the driver's test"—begin right away to emphasize the use of performance criteria (a) to clarify the targets of instruction, (b) to track student progress toward these targets, and (c) as an instructional tool in the classroom, as noted in Table 1.

The Importance of Tasks. The other half of the performance assessment equation involves the tasks assigned to students. Tasks elicit a product or performance that can then be assessed with the criteria. Much has been written about developing rich, engaging, real-life tasks, tasks that are capable of eliciting the desired complex performances on the part of the student (e.g., McTighe, 1996). One point about performance tasks that is frequently confusing to teachers is that the task can be *any* activity during the course of which the quality of performance will be observed; it does not necessarily have to be something that occurs separately at the end of instruction. There is a place for these summative, separate assessments, but much "observation and judgment" will occur during the course of regular instruction; for example, how well is a student reading today, or how effective is group collaboration on a particular activity? The key to having daily observation be sound assessment is to have high-quality criteria that teachers have internalized to the extent that they can consistently judge performances, regardless of the context. The presence of criteria makes daily "anecdotal records" actually mean something.

When to Use Performance Assessment

Good assessment means balanced assessment: having a clear idea of what one wants to assess and then choosing the best way to assess it (target-method match; see Table 1). A rule of thumb is that simple learning targets involve simple assessment and complex learning targets involve complex assessment. For example, knowledge and simple skills (e.g., long division) can be assessed well via multiple-choice, matching, true-false, and short answer formats. However, a performance assessment is probably needed to assess writing, mathematical problem solving, science process skills, critical thinking, oral presentations, and group collaboration skills.

Good treatments of matching methods to targets can be found in Stiggins (1997, p. 81) and Marzano and Kendall (1996, p. 311). Stiggins, for example, matches meth-

Table 2

Matching Learning Targets to Assessment Methods

	Selected response	Essay	Performance assessment	Personal communication
Knowledge mastery	X	X		X
Reasoning proficiency	O	X	X	X
Skills			X	X
Ability to create products			X	
Dispositions	X	O	O	X

ods to targets as shown in Table 2. An *X* denotes a good match. An *O* denotes a partial match. A complete treatment of the reasons for the *X*s and *O*s is outside the scope of this article (and has already been done very well in the sources just cited). However, it is useful to note here that the best way to think of "good" matches is as follows: prudent, efficient, valid, and having positive consequences. Thus, although one could use performance assessment to assess all student outcomes, one probably should not because it would not be very efficient or prudent or necessarily have positive outcomes for instruction and students. It is best to save the power of performance assessment for the outcomes most needing it, especially those situations in which having written criteria for complex skills and products will help students understand the nature of the targets they are to reach.

It is useful to show adult learners examples of attempts to assess targets such as reasoning or reading comprehension in a multiple-choice format. Then show them performance assessments aimed at the same target and discuss what each format is—and is not—capable of assessing. Fixed response assessments, even when done well, tend to address decontextualized skills in isolation, while performance assessments, if done well, require students to select skills to use in concert to produce a product or perform an act. Both are useful, depending on what it is one wants to assess. It always goes back to being clear enough about the target to be assessed.

Three examples of thinking skills assessments that involve different methods and could be compared in the manner described above are: the Cornell Critical Thinking Test (multiple choice; Ennis, Millman, & Tomko, 1985), the Test on Appraising Observations (choose an answer and then justify one's choice; Norris, 1990), and performance criteria for judging the "intellectual quality" of student work (Newmann, Secada, & Wehlage, 1995).

Design Options

The tasks and performance criteria used in performance assessments vary widely. The following are the major ways in which I have seen tasks vary. (I include variations in both stimulus and response because both represent task demands on the student; examples of these types are detailed in Regional Educational Laboratories, 1998, chap. 3.)

- A single correct answer or multiple, equally good answers
- Group work, individual work, or a combination of both
- All written versus manipulatives and equipment
- Amount of choice on how to respond (written, picture, oral, etc.)
- Format/length/complexity (on demand, project, portfolio)
- Amount of scaffolding: steps and processes spelled out or left to the student
- Student choice of which task to perform

The major ways in which performance criteria appear to vary include the following:

- Task-specific or general. Task-specific performance criteria spell out separately what responses should look like on each task; there is a separate scoring guide for each task (e.g., the open-ended math items on the Constructed Response Supplement to the Iowa Tests, 1997). In general performance criteria, the same rubric is used across similar tasks (e.g., the six-trait model for writing; see the Appendix).
- Holistic or analytic trait. In holistic performance criteria, there is one score for the overall product or performance (e.g., the math rubrics on the Constructed Response Supplement to the Iowa Tests, 1997). In analytical trait performance criteria, there are multiple scores for a single performance or product, one for each important dimension or trait (e.g., the reading rubrics used in the Oregon state assessment or the six-trait model in the Appendix).

- Number of score points. Generally there are from three (e.g., several items on the Washington Assessment of Student Learning [Washington Commission on Student Learning, 1998]) to six (e.g., Oregon state assessments [Oregon Department of Education, 1997]).

- Amount of detail used to describe each score point. Some performance criteria are extremely skimpy (e.g., Washington state's writing rubric [Washington Commission on Student Learning, 1998]), while others attempt to be extremely descriptive (e.g., the six-trait model for assessing writing; see the Appendix).

- Type of detail used to describe each score point. There are some rubrics (e.g., early attempts in Vermont [Vermont Mathematics Portfolio Project, 1991]) for which the only distinctions between score point levels are words such as *inappropriate, appropriate, workable*, and *efficient* or *rarely, sometimes, frequently*, and *extensively*. It is difficult for performance raters to know when "extensively" has occurred, which can result in low rater consistency. It is also difficult for students to understand how to improve a performance or product if they are told only that their work "rarely exhibits a sense of personal expression." Other rubrics (e.g., the six-trait model) use extensive detail to describe the specific features of work that are indicators of quality. This helps in making meaning clearer, both to raters of performance and to students trying to learn the nature of quality. (In all fairness to Vermont, the Department of Education has supplied many samples of student work to demonstrate the levels and has, through the years, worked to define the levels more thoroughly.)

- Quantitative versus qualitative descriptions of score points. A quantitative score point description might be as follows: "to get an excellent, the paper must have 10 references" (for an example, see Baker, Aschbacher, Niemi, & Sato, 1992, pp. 73–74). Although amount might sometimes be a good indicator of quality, I generally dislike this type of rubric because 3 really good references might be better than 10 bad ones.

- Presence or absence of preset performance standard. On some performance criteria, the score points represent performance standards by definition (4 = "exceeds expectations," 3 = "meets expectations," 2 = "partially meets expectations," 1 = "expectations are not met"; e.g., North Dakota Fourth Grade Writing Assessment [North Dakota Department of Public Instruction, 1998]). Developers define 3 as "meeting standards" and then go about defining characteristics of such work and finding samples to illustrate what they mean. A con-

trasting procedure is to first develop a scale that defines the range of quality products or performances (I have seen scales ranging from 3 to 6 points) and then go back and decide where on this scale performance is good enough to meet various performance standards. This is the approach taken by the Oregon Department of Education (1998). Oregon developed a 6-point scale to define the range of quality and then went back to determine where the performance standards would be. In writing, for example, performance standards range from "3" to "4" depending on grade level.

Before teachers can discuss why assessment developers make the choices they do, they need to be able to recognize variations. An instructor may ask teachers to do a type of "scavenger hunt" activity in which they look for as many examples of each variation as possible. After adult learners are able to distinguish the options, the questions to be addressed are as follows: Why do developers make these choices? What are the advantages and disadvantages of each? Choices are usually made by balancing an ideal choice (for users, uses, and learning targets) against practical considerations and throwing in technical concerns for good measure. The next two sections elaborate considerations when making choices.

The Nature of Quality and Why We Should Care

Teaching the Characteristics of Quality Performance Assessment

Many thorough lists of quality considerations for performance assessments exist (Table 3 summarizes what others have said; another good source is Herman, 1996). Note that such lists include the need for clear and appropriate learning targets, matching performance assessment choices to targets, and use as a tool for learning (see Table 1, "The nature of quality," col. 4).

Coming up with a list of quality features of performance assessment is the easy part. Teaching adult learners the nature of quality and why they should care is the tricky part. A strategy that does not seem to be effective is that of showing teachers the list of quality considerations and lecturing one's way from beginning to end. What seems to work better is to engage adult learners in a bad performance assessment and let *them* articulate what the problems are.

One example of this is a learning activity written for use by teacher trainers and instructors (Regional Educational Laboratories, 1998, Activity 1.5: Clapping Hands): In this fishbowl activity four or five teachers are the "assessees" and three to five teachers are the "assessors." Assessees are asked to perform a simple task, but each is treated differently via providing them with more infor-

Table 3
Criteria for Performance Assessments

Dimension	Yes	Somewhat	No
1. Content/skill coverage and correct method The assessment: • Clearly states skills and content to be covered • Correctly uses performance assessment to measure these skills and content • Avoids irrelevant and/or unimportant content • Deals with enduring themes or significant knowledge • Matches statements of coverage to task content and performance criteria	3	2	1
2. Performance criteria • Include everything of importance and omit irrelevant features of performance • State criteria clearly and provide samples of student work to illustrate them • Are stated generally, especially if the intent is used as an instructional tool • Are analytical traits, especially if the intent is used as an instructional tool	3	2	1
3. Performance tasks General • Elicit the desired performances or work • Recreate an "authentic" context for performance • Exemplify good instruction • Are reviewed by others (students, peers, experts) Sampling/representativeness/generalizability • Cover the content or skill area well; results can be generalized • Sample performance in a way that is representative of what a student can do Bias and distortion • Avoid factors that might get in the way of students' ability to demonstrate what they know and can do	3	2	1
4. Fairness and rater bias Performance tasks • Have content and context that are equally familiar, acceptable, and appropriate for students in all groups • Tap knowledge and skills all students have had adequate time to acquire in class • Are as free as possible of cultural, ethnic, or gender stereotypes • Are as free as possible of language barriers Performance criteria and rater training • Ensure that irrelevant features of performance do not influence how other, supposedly independent features are judged • Ensure that knowledge of the type of student does not influence judgments about performance quality • Ensure that knowledge of individual students does not affect judgements about performance quality	3	2	1
5. Consequences The assessment: • Communicates appropriate messages • Results in acceptable effects on students, teachers, and others • Is worth the instructional time devoted to it; students learn something from doing the assessment and/or using the performance criteria • Provides information relevant to the decisions being made • Is perceived by students and teachers as valid	3	2	1
6. Cost and efficiency The assessment: • Is cost efficient—the results are worth the investment • Is practical	3	2	1

Note. Copyright 1998 by Northwest Regional Educational Laboratory. Adapted with permission.

mation and help as the activity progresses. Likewise, assessors are given more information as the activity progresses. At the end, each participant describes what he or she was thinking and feeling as the activity progressed, and the entire group is invited to comment and provide examples from their own experience of occasions when they were in the position of one of the volunteers. Finally the group generates a list of what it takes to avoid the problems demonstrated in the activity: characteristics of quality tasks, performance criteria, preparation of raters, preparation of students, and reporting. Special attention is given to potential sources of bias and distortion that could lead one to draw an inappropriate conclusion about a student's achievement. These teacher-generated lists are essentially "criteria" for quality performance assessments.

A teacher more readily understands sampling, bias, unclear tasks, and unclear performance criteria when he or she personally experiences their effects. Table 4 shows a list of quality characteristics (criteria) for performance assessments generated by several teacher groups. Teachers can compare their list of criteria with that experts use for guiding the quality development of performance assessments (e.g., the list of criteria included in Table 3). In this way teachers can relate what they already know to a larger conceptual scheme.

After teachers have described for themselves what constitutes sound performance assessment, it is important for them to practice applying their criteria for quality performance assessments to actual sample assessments. It is useful to find performance assessments that are weak and strong on each dimension (trait) that is to be emphasized (e.g., tasks, criteria) and ask the teachers to critique each as a group. Then ask the adult learners what advice they would give the author of the assessment to make the assessment better on a particular trait and have them work in groups to improve the assessment using their own suggestions. It is important to focus on only a few features at a time so that teachers do not become overwhelmed with having to notice and fix everything all at once.

When the adult learners have had experience with this, have them develop their own tasks and criteria and work in peer review groups to improve their efforts. Learners could even keep a portfolio on their efforts and reflect on how their ability to develop and critique assessments has improved with time.

The interesting part of the process of (a) developing criteria for performance assessments, (b) critiquing and revising examples of anonymous performance assessments, (c) developing one's own performance assessments with peer input, and (d) keeping a portfolio is that this is exactly the same way to teach any criteria to any group of adults or students. Thus, in essence, this process models, for prospective or active teachers, what they should do with their own students in the future.

The Need to Consider Use When Determining Quality

An added complexity in discussions of quality is that use must be taken into account. Performance assessments that are adequate for one use might not be appropriate for another. For example, the features most desirable in tasks or criteria used for a large-scale, high stakes assessment might not be those most desirable in a classroom assessment that will also be used instructionally. Thus, learners will need to critique sample assessments with a specific use in mind.

As an example of how use affects assessment design, consider the various design options for performance criteria described earlier. Many large-scale performance assessment developers use task-specific, holistic criteria because (a) raters can be trained more quickly, (b) scores can be computed more quickly, and (c) it is believed that such criteria will result in higher agreement rates among raters. More useful in the classroom, however, are generalized, analytical trait criteria, which help teachers and students articulate the features of solid work that can be generalized from task to task. The value of generalized criteria for instruction has been noted in recent studies by Arter et al. (1994) and the Office of Educational Research and Improvement (1997, p. *xx*).

Consider another example of how use affects the design of performance criteria. If the purpose of the assessment is to make overall judgments about student competence, the criteria only need to be detailed enough to ensure consistent rating. If, however, the assessment is to be used to diagnose student strengths and learning needs or for instruction, all essential aspects of performance must be present, and descriptive detail is essential. Descriptive detail is important because the criteria are being used to communicate with students about the features that contribute most to the quality of a product or performance. What is left out of the criteria will be left out of the performance or product. Furthermore, this descriptive detail must be in language that students can understand, so there should be "student-friendly" versions.

An example of performance criteria that are instructionally useful (analytical trait, general, detailed, and having student-friendly versions) can be found in the six-trait model for assessing writing (NWREL, 1990, 1997; Spandel & Culham, 1998; Spandel & Stiggins, 1997). The adult version of the six-trait model is included in the Appendix.

How to Develop Performance Tasks and Criteria

A good source for assisting teachers to develop performance tasks and a variety of associated rubric types is Jay McTighe's work with the Maryland Assessment Consortium (McTighe, 1996). Here I concentrate on three ways to develop the generalized, analytical trait, detailed performance criteria that are most useful for instruction.

Table 4

Performance Assessment: The Meaning of Quality (Typical Teacher Responses)

Area	Responses
Designing tasks	Be careful of public performances; treat all students equitably; put the performance into a realistic context; be specific on instructions; open-ended; meaningful to students; consider how to handle diversity and differences (e.g., special education, cultures, gender, learning styles); the task itself is a learning experience; nonthreatening; matched to valued outcomes; equity; enough time; proper resources and equipment; can be approached by the student in a variety of ways; responses can be given in a variety of ways
Designing performance criteria	Matched to valued outcomes; clearly stated; elaboration on how to assign points; agreement on what the criteria should be; models/examples; rater buy-in; match performance criteria to task; define range of score points; covers only the important stuff; provides a "picture" of what performance would look like; has many descriptors of quality
Preparing raters	Practice; discuss differences of opinion; have models/examples of different score points; have the raters do the assessment themselves; have raters explain their ratings; calibrate the raters; check consistency over time
Preparing students	Share criteria well ahead; give students the opportunity to add to criteria; train students on what the criteria mean and how it looks when performance is good or poor; use models; do formative assessments with feedback; make the assessment purpose clear; students must have prerequisite skills; students need to trust the raters; self-assessment using the criteria
Reporting results	Make sure the scores have meaning; treat students equitably; be specific and descriptive; provide evidence; allow time for discussion; emphasize what students can do, not what they can't do; nonthreatening; meaningful to students or parents
Overall	Avoid potential sources of bias and distortion: bias in tasks, criteria, or administration; criteria that don't cover the right "stuff"; poor training of raters; poor student preparation; tasks that don't elicit the right performance; sampling inadequacy; student personality; embarrassment with regard to being compared with others; changing criteria; scheduling the assessment at bad times; fatigue of raters or students; poor student or rater motivation; lack of teacher, student, or rater buy-in; rater bias; developmentally inappropriate tasks or criteria; the tendency for raters to score toward the center of the scale; examinee manipulation of the situation or raters; testwiseness; students not knowing the criteria for success; student anxiety; too much teacher help; negative teacher attitude toward the assessment; readability of assessment materials; distractions during assessment; cultural inappropriateness of tasks

Note. Copyright 1998 by Northwest Regional Educational Laboratory. Adapted with permission.

First, given sufficient expertise on the skills for which criteria are being developed, a person can sometimes just sit down and write out the criteria. This process can be illustrated with many common everyday situations. For example, most adults have fun developing criteria for effective whining, room cleaning, or restaurants. In education, most of us are familiar enough with oral presentations that we stand a chance of articulating and writing out decent criteria. And measurement experts usually can write out the criteria for a good-quality performance assessment.

These "off the top of my head" criteria, however, need to be subjected to a reality test. After the criteria have been written down, it is always a good idea to gather samples of the performance under consideration and try to rate them according to one's criteria. This process helps one notice important aspects of performance one has forgotten, borderline cases that need to be clarified through refined statements in the criteria, the need to more clearly specify levels of performance with indicators of quality and so forth. (Note that the criteria for a high-quality performance assessment included in Table 3 do not have levels defined.)

The second way to develop general performance criteria is to simply start with the student work, and this is actually where most teachers begin. Obtain sets of student work that illustrate various levels of quality on the skill in question: writing, communicating mathematical understanding, critical thinking, and so forth. Ask adult learners to sort the work into three performance stacks: strong, medium, and weak. Then have them describe the differences among the stacks (this method is illustrated in detail in Regional Educational Laboratories, 1998, Activity 2.1: Sorting Student Work).

The main problem teachers run into when sorting and describing is using descriptors that are too general. For example, when generating criteria for math problem solving, teachers want to say that one feature of a strong student response is that it is "logical." The challenge is to dig beneath the general descriptor to find the specific characteristics of the work that make one believe it is logical. I usually ask teachers to find a piece they think is logical and point out the aspects that made them think so. They usually mention things such as the following: The student chose the correct information to use, went through from beginning to end without any sidesteps, chose a procedure that would lead to a correct solution, used a problem representation (visual or mathematical) that helped clarify the problem's meaning, restated the problem accurately in his or her own words, seemed to know which representations were right for the problem, and knew when and where to make connections with other knowledge in order to proceed. If such statements can then be connected to actual samples of student work, it provides a powerful instructional tool for teachers and a powerful learning tool for students.

If adult learners have trouble sorting work, they might not have enough of an idea of the construct in question to have formed even intuitive criteria. This leads to the third approach for helping adult learners define performance criteria: They need to read the literature in the content area in question. This frequently occurs, for example, when teachers are attempting to develop criteria for critical thinking. Defining the construct and collecting relevant samples of student work to sort provides a way to profitably interact with preservice content area courses.

Even though developing criteria is a good exercise, it is fortunate that teachers do not always have to start from scratch. There are many good sources of criteria and rubrics. One of my favorites is Perlman (1994). The 70 or so rubrics in this collection provide a good opportunity for adult learners to practice distinguishing good criteria from weak ones and to practice distinguishing criteria that might work for large-scale assessment from those that might be most useful in the classroom.

Use of Criteria as an Instructional Methodology

There are two steps involved in making performance criteria work as tools for learning in the classroom: having a clear notion in one's own mind of what the criteria are and then teaching them to students. The first step was described in the previous section on developing performance criteria. The second step in making performance criteria work as instructional tools in the classroom is to teach them to students. My colleagues have developed seven strategies for teaching criteria to students (Spandel & Culham, 1998; Spandel & Stiggins, 1997). These strategies were developed in the context of writing, but several of them transfer easily to other performances and products.

The first strategy is to *teach students the vocabulary they need to think and speak like writers, communicators, and problem solvers.* Help students understand the nature of quality through engaging them in the kinds of sorting and descriptive activities described earlier. In other words, engage students in developing criteria for quality. Students need to have versions of criteria written in language they can understand (i.e., "student-friendly" rubrics). For example, the six-trait model has student-friendly versions available for primary elementary and secondary students (Regional Educational Laboratories, 1998). I have also seen student-friendly versions of mathematics problem-solving rubrics produced by the Oregon Department of Education and Washington State's Central Kitsap District (1997).

The second strategy is to *read, discuss, and score anonymous samples of student work.* Once criteria are in place, students need to practice using them, noting what is strong and weak in work. They need to not only judge the quality of work but articulate the reasons for their judgment; there is no such thing as a "correct" score, only a justifiable score. To justify their scores, students are asked to find the words in the rubric that describe the work under consideration.

The third strategy is to *practice focused revision*. In addition to being able to notice what is strong or weak in work, students need to know how to fix that which is weak. One procedure is to ask students to give advice to the author and then work in groups to improve the sample performance using the advice given. For example, when working on ideas in writing, students might note that the paper is weak because it is unfocused, emphasizes irrelevant details, or does not include enough descriptive detail to make a point (all descriptors in the trait of "ideas" in the Appendix). The students might advise the author to narrow the topic by selecting one potentially interesting point and elaborating on it using relevant details and anecdotes. Students would then revise the writing using their own advice.

The fourth strategy is to *use reallife samples to illustrate criteria*. In terms of writing, this can be done with various published items (stories, picture books, manuals, instructions, etc.). In helping students learn, for example, the concept of "voice" in writing, one might ask them to match text to authors (Mark Twain, Nathaniel Hawthorne, etc.). Or one could have students compare different writing styles.

The fifth strategy is to *have students help the teacher revise the teacher's products or performances using the criteria for quality*. For example, you could ask your adult learners to critique the performance assessments you use in your class, give you advice on how to improve them, and help you revise them. In K–12, a teacher could ask students to help revise his or her own writing. Sometimes students are amazed to see that writing does not simply emerge full blown from the pen during the first draft.

The sixth strategy is to *allow students opportunities to articulate their emerging notion of quality*. In writing, for example, students could write letters to authors describing why, using the language of the performance criteria, they like the work, or students could describe their progress to parents using the language of the performance criteria.

The final strategy is to *teach minilessons*. For writing, this means organizing regular instructional lessons by trait: ideas, organization, voice, word choice, sentence fluency and conventions. If the criteria really do describe what we mean by quality, why not teach directly to them? Teachers already teach the traits of good writing. What is often lacking is the conscious link between what is being taught and the standards being developed.

Two papers that articulate well the power of using general performance criteria to help students learn are those of Spandel (1996) and Arter (1996).

I have begun asking participants in my workshops (teachers, administrators, and others) to state the most salient characteristics of "standards-based instruction" as they currently understand it. Admittedly an unscientific sample, here is the essence of what they have said.

- There are clearly stated long-term learning targets for students (content standards): what we want students to know and be able to do when they leave K–12 education.
- There are benchmarks along the way so that we know whether we are on track in terms of guiding students to the ultimate level of competency.
- These learning targets are connected to the real world.
- Instruction and assessment are aimed at these important targets and aligned across grade levels to reduce duplication and make it clear how the skills and understandings developed one year will be built upon the next year.
- Standards-referenced descriptions of student learning are used rather than norm-referenced or self-referenced; we define the nature of quality and match student achievement to it in order to judge achievement.
- Everybody—students, teachers, parents, community members — is aware of the nature of excellence and what it takes to succeed. Students can see where they are. Teachers can tell parents at any time how their children are progressing toward "proficiency."

The performance criteria associated with performance assessments can be a prime example of such standards-based instruction.

- Performance criteria help define standards; they are the final definition.
- Developing performance criteria is more than assessment; it helps instruction.
- Performance criteria make standards clear to students (and teachers).
- Teaching criteria to students improves the very skills being assessed.

Grading and Reporting

Grading and reporting is the final topic in Table 1 that should be covered in a course on performance assessment. This topic is covered more thoroughly in the article by Susan Brookhart and so is not discussed at length here. Let me mention, however, that the most frequent question from teachers relating to performance assessment and grading is "How do I convert rubric scores to grades?" Any instruction on performance assessment would be incomplete without helping teachers think about this question. This question is tricky because the purpose of using rubrics to begin with (to help students learn) can be at odds with the purpose of grading (to report student progress or to discipline or reward students), and frequently rubric scores need to be combined with scores from other types of assessment to arrive at a final grade. As pointed out by many authors (e.g., Association for Supervision and Curriculum Development, 1996; Kohn, 1994), teachers need to first think about the purposes for grading: Who are the users? What are the uses? What is grading supposed to accomplish? From this reflection, a method for combining rubric scores with other measures of student achievement to arrive at a "grade" sometimes emerges. One way to involve teachers in this discussion is provided in Activities 4.2 (Putting Grading and Reporting Questions in Perspective) and 4.6 (How to Convert Rubric Scores to Grades) in Regional Educational Laboratories (1998).

Conclusion

Teachers need to know how to construct, administer, score, and use the results from good-quality performance assessments. They need to know these things not just to grade or satisfy some external mandate (although the current climate demands this), but because expertise in performance assessment can make instruction faster, easier, and better. To help teachers see this, instruction on performance assessment must include building the vision of performance assessment as a tool for learning as well as a tool for tracking student progress. There is also a certain immediacy to teachers' need to know about assessment; they literally need information they can use on Monday morning. If we, as preservice and in-service instructors, cannot capture teachers' attention right away and give them something to use immediately, learning to be good assessors will take a back seat to other topics that vie for teacher attention.

What features of performance assessments make them most useful in the classroom as instructional tools? What is the impact on student achievement of using performance assessment in this manner? What approaches to teaching assessment motivate teachers to want to learn more? These are profitable areas for continuing inquiry and research.

Appendix
The Six-Trait Model for Assessing Student Writing

Note. Copyright 1998 by Northwest Regional Educational Laboratory. Adapted with permission.

Ideas and Content (Development)

Level 5: *This paper is clear and focused. It holds the reader's attention. Relevant anecdotes and details enrich the central theme.*

a. The topic is narrow and manageable.

b. Relevant, telling, quality details give the reader important information that goes beyond the obvious or predictable.

c. Reasonably accurate details are present to support the main ideas.

d. The writer seems to be writing from knowledge or experience; the ideas are fresh and original.

e. The reader's questions are anticipated and answered.

f. Insight—an understanding of life and a knack for picking out what is significant—is an indicator of high-level performance, though not required.

Level 3: *The writer is beginning to define the topic, even though development is still basic or general.*

a. The topic is fairly broad; however, you can see where the writer is headed.

b. Support is attempted but doesn't go far enough yet in fleshing out the key issues or story line.

c. Ideas are reasonably clear, though they may not be detailed, personalized, accurate, or expanded enough to show in-depth understanding or a strong sense of purpose.

d. The writer seems to be drawing on knowledge or experience but has difficulty going from general observations to specifics.

e. The reader is left with questions. More information is needed to "fill in the blanks."

f. The writer generally stays on the topic but does not develop a clear theme. The writer has not yet focused the topic past the obvious.

Level 1: *As yet, the paper has no clear sense of purpose or central theme. To extract meaning from the text, the reader must make inferences based on sketchy or missing details. The writing reflects more than one of these problems:*

a. The writer is still in search of a topic, brainstorming, or has not yet decided what the main idea of the piece will be.

b. Information is limited or unclear or the length is not adequate for development.

c. The idea is a simple restatement of the topic or an answer to the question with little or no attention to detail.

d. The writer has not begun to define the topic in a meaningful, personal way.

e. Everything seems as important as everything else; the reader has a hard time sifting out what is important.

f. The text may be repetitious, or may read like a collection of disconnected, random thoughts with no discernible point.

Organization

Level 5: *The organization enhances and showcases the central idea or theme. The order, structure, or presentation of information is compelling and moves the reader through the text.*

a. An inviting introduction draws the reader in; a satisfying conclusion leaves the reader with a sense of closure and resolution.

b. Thoughtful transitions clearly show how ideas connect.

c. Details seem to fit where they're placed; sequencing is logical and effective.

d. Pacing is well controlled; the writer knows when to slow down and elaborate and when to pick up the pace and move on.

e. The title, if desired, is original and captures the central theme of the piece.

f. Organization flows so smoothly the reader hardly thinks about it; the choice of structure matches the purpose and audience.

Level 3: *The organizational structure is strong enough to move the reader through the text without too much confusion.*

a. The paper has a recognizable introduction and conclusion. The introduction may not create a strong sense of anticipation; the conclusion may not tie up all loose ends.

b. Transitions often work well; at other times, connections between ideas are fuzzy.

c. Sequencing shows some logic, but not under control enough that it consistently supports the ideas. In fact, sometimes it is so predictable and rehearsed that the structure takes attention away from the content.

d. Pacing is fairly well controlled, though the writer sometimes lunges ahead too quickly or spends too much time on details that do not matter.

e. A title (if desired) is present, although it may be uninspired or an obvious restatement of the prompt or topic.

f. The organization sometimes supports the main point or story line; at other times, the reader feels an urge to slip in a transition or move things around.

Level 1: *The writing lacks a clear sense of direction. Ideas, details, or events seem strung together in a loose or random fashion; there is no identifiable internal structure. The writing reflects more than one of these problems:*

a. There is no real lead to set up what follows, no real conclusion to wrap things up.

b. Connections between ideas are confusing or not even present.

c. Sequencing needs lots and lots of work.

d. Pacing feels awkward; the writer slows to a crawl when the reader wants to get on with it, and vice versa.

e. No title is present (if requested), or if present, does not match well with the content.

f. Problems with organization make it hard for the reader to get a grip on the main point or story line.

Voice

Level 5: *The writer speaks directly to the reader in a way that is individual, compelling, and engaging. The writer "aches with caring," yet is aware and respectful of the audience and the purpose for writing.*

a. The reader feels a strong interaction with the writer, sensing the person behind the words.

b. The writer takes a risk by revealing who he/she is and what he/she thinks.

c. The tone and voice give flavor and texture to the message and are appropriate for the purpose and audience.

d. Narrative writing seems honest, personal, and written from the heart. Expository or persuasive writing reflects a strong commitment to the topic by showing why the reader needs to know this and why they should care.

e. This piece screams to be read aloud, shared, and talked about. The writing makes you think about and react to the author's point of view.

Level 3: *The writer seems sincere, but not fully engaged or involved. The result is pleasant or even personable, but not compelling.*

a. The writing communicates in an earnest, pleasing manner.

b. Only one or two moments here or there surprise, delight, or move the reader.

c. The writer seems aware of an audience but weighs ideas carefully and discards personal insights in favor of safe generalities.

d. Narrative writing seems sincere, but not passionate; expository or persuasive writing lacks consistent engagement with the topic to build credibility.

e. The writer's willingness to share his/her point of view may emerge strongly at some places, but is often obscured behind vague generalities.

Level 1: *The writer seems indifferent, uninvolved, or distanced from the topic and/or the audience. As a result, the paper reflects more than one of the following problems:*

a. The writer speaks in a kind of monotone that flattens all potential highs or lows of the message.

b. The writing is humdrum and "risk free."

c. The writer is not concerned with the audience, or the writer's style is a complete mismatch for the intended reader.

d. The writing is lifeless or mechanical; depending on the topic, it may be overly technical or jargonistic.

e. No point of view is reflected in the writing.

Word Choice

Level 5: *Words convey the intended message in a precise, interesting, and natural way. The words are powerful and engaging.*

a. Words are specific and accurate; it is easy to understand just what the writer means.

b. The words and phrases create pictures and linger in your mind.

c. The language is natural and never overdone; both words and phrases are individual and effective.

d. Striking words and phrases often catch the reader's eye—and linger in the reader's mind. (You can recall a handful as you reflect on the paper.)

e. Lively verbs energize the writing. Precise nouns and modifiers add depth and specificity.

f. Precision is obvious. The writer has taken care to put just the right word or phrase in just the right spot.

Level 3: *The language is functional, even if it lacks much energy. It is easy to figure out the writer's meaning on a general level.*

a. Words are adequate and correct in a general sense; they simply lack much flair and originality.

b. Familiar words and phrases communicate, but rarely capture the reader's imagination. Still, the paper may have one or two fine moments.

c. Attempts at colorful language show a willinguess to stretch and grow, but sometimes it goes too far (thesaurus overload!).

d. The writing is marked by passive verbs, everyday nouns and adjectives, and lack of interesting adverbs.

e. The words are only occasionally refined; it's more often "the first thing that popped into my mind."

f. The words and phrases are functional—with only a moment or two of sparkle.

Level 1: *The writer struggles with a limited vocabulary, searching for words to convey meaning. The writing reflects more than one of these problems:*

a. Language is so vague that only a limited message comes through.

b. "Blah, blah, blah" is all that the reader reads and hears.

c. Words are used incorrectly, making the message secondary to the misfires with the words.

d. Limited vocabulary and/or frequent misuse of parts of speech impair understanding.

e. Jargon or cliches distract or mislead. Persistent redundancy distracts the reader.

f. Problems with language leave the reader wondering what the writer is trying to say. The words just don't work in this piece.

Sentence Fluency

Level 5: *The writing has an easy flow, rhythm, and cadence. Sentences are well built, with strong and varied structure that invites expressive oral reading.*

a. Sentences are constructed in a way that underscores and enhances the meaning.

b. Sentences vary in length as well as structure. Fragments, if used, add style. Dialogue, if present, sounds natural.

c. Purposeful and varied sentence beginnings add variety and energy.

d. The use of creative and appropriate connectives between sentences and thoughts shows how each relates to and builds upon the one before it.

e. The writing has cadence; the writer has thought about the sound of the words as well as the meaning. The first time you read it aloud is a breeze.

Level 3: *The text hums along with a steady beat, but tends to be more pleasant or businesslike than musical, more mechanical than fluid.*

a. Although sentences may not seem artfully crafted or musical, they get the job done in a routine fashion.

b. Sentences are usually constructed correctly; they hang together; they are sound.

c. Sentence beginnings are not all alike; some variety is attempted.

d. The reader sometimes has to hunt for clues (e.g., connecting words and phrases like *however, therefore, naturally, after a while, on the other hand, to be specific, for example, next, first of all, later, but as it turned out, although*, etc.) that show how sentences interrelate.

e. Parts of the text invite expressive oral reading; others may be stiff, awkward, choppy or gangly.

Level 1: *The reader has to practice quite a bit in order to give this paper a fair interpretive reading. The writing reflects more than one of the following problems:*

a. Sentences are choppy, incomplete, rambling, or awkward; they need work. Phrasing does not sound natural. The patterns may create a sing-song rhythm or a chop-chop cadence that lulls the reader to sleep.

b. There is little or no "sentence sense" present. Even if this piece were flawlessly edited, the sentences would not hang together.

c. Many sentences begin the same way—and may follow the same patterns (e.g., subject-verb-object).

d. Endless connectives (*and, and so, but then, because, and then,* etc.) or a complete lack of connectives create a massive jumble of language.

e. The text does not invite expressive oral reading.

Conventions

Level 5: *The writer demonstrates a good grasp of standard writing conventions (e.g., spelling, punctuation, capitalization, grammar, usage, paragraphing) and uses conventions effectively to enhance readability. Errors tend to be so few that just minor touch-ups would get this piece ready to publish.*

a. Spelling is generally correct, even on more difficult words.

b. The punctuation is accurate, even creative, and guides the reader through the text.

c. A thorough understanding and consistent application of capitalization skills are present.

d. Grammar and usage are correct and contribute to clarity and style.

e. Paragraphing tends to be sound and reinforces the organizational structure.

f. The writer may manipulate conventions for stylistic effect—and it works! The piece is very close to being ready to publish.

Note: Grades 7 and up only—The writing is sufficiently complex to allow the writer to show skill in using a wide range of conventions. For writers at younger ages, the writing shows control over those conventions that are grade/age appropriate.

Level 3: *The writer shows reasonable control over a limited range of standard writing conventions. Conventions are sometimes handled well and enhance readability; at other times, errors are distracting and impair readability.*

a. Spelling is usually correct or reasonably phonetic on common words, but more difficult words are problematic.

b. End punctuation is usually correct; internal punctuation (commas, apostrophes, semicolons, dashes, colons, parentheses) is sometimes missing/wrong.

c. Most words are capitalized correctly; control over more sophisticated capitalization skills may be spotty.

d. Paragraphing is attempted but may run together or begin in the wrong places.

e. Problems with grammar or usage are not serious enough to distort meaning but may not be correct or accurately applied all of the time.

f. Moderate (a little of this, a little of that) editing would be required to polish the text for publication.

Level 1: *Errors in spelling, punctuation, capitalization, usage and grammar, and/or paragraphing repeatedly distract the* reader and make the text difficult to read. The writing reflects more than one of these problems:

a. Spelling errors are frequent, even on common words.

b. Punctuation (including terminal punctuation) is often missing or incorrect.

c. Capitalization is random, and only the easiest rules show awareness of correct use.

d. Errors in grammar or usage are very noticeable, frequent, and affect meaning.

e. Paragraphing is missing, irregular, or so frequent (every sentence) that it has no relationship to the organizational structure of the text.

f. The reader must read once to decode, then again for meaning. Extensive editing (virtually every line) would be required to polish the text for publication.

References

Airasian, P. W. (1991). *Classroom assessment.* New York: McGraw-Hill.

American Federation of Teachers, National Council on Measurement in Education, and National Education Association. (1990). *Standards for teacher competence in educational assessments of students.* Washington, DC: Authors.

Arter, J. (1996). Using assessment as a tool for learning. In R. Blum & J. Arter (Eds.), *Student performance assessment in an era of restructuring.* Alexandria, VA: Association for Supervision and Curriculum Development.

Arter, J., Spandel, V., Culham, R., & Pollard, J. (1994). *The impact of training students to be self-assessors of writing.* Paper presented at the annual meeting of the American Educational Research Association, New Orleans, LA.

Association for Supervision and Curriculum Development. (1996). *Communicating student learning* (T. Guskey, Ed.). Alexandria, VA: Author.

Baker, E. L., Aschbacher, P. R., Niemi, D., & Sato, E. (1992). *CRESST performance assessment models: Assessing content area explanations.* Los Angeles: CRESST.

Borko, H., Mayfield, V., Marion, S., et al. (1997). Teachers' developing ideas and practices about mathematics performance assessment: Successes, stumbling blocks, and implications for professional development. *Teaching and Teacher Education, 13,* 259–278.

Calfee, R., & Perfumo, P. (1993). Student portfolios: Opportunities for a revolution in assessment. *Journal of Reading, 36,* 534.

Central Kitsap School District. (1997). *The student friendly guide to mathematics problem solving.* Silverdale, WA: Author.

Checkley, K. (1997). Assessment that serves instruction. *Education Update, 39*(4), 1.

Clarke, D., & Stephens, M. (1996). The ripple effect: The instructional impact of the systemic introduction of performance assessment in mathematics. In M. Birenbaum & F. Dochy (Eds.), *Alternatives in assessment of achievements, learning processes and prior knowledge.* Norwell, MA: Kluwer Academic.

Constructed Response Supplement to the Iowa Tests. (1997). Itaska, IL: Riverside.

Ennis, R. H., Millman, J., & Tomko, T. (1985). *Cornell Critical Thinking Tests* (3rd ed.). Pacific Grove, CA: Midwest.

Fager, J. J., Plake, B. S., & Impara, J. C. (1997). *Examining teacher educators' knowledge of classroom assessment: A pilot study.*

Paper presented at the NCME national conference, Chicago, IL.

Herman, J. (1996). Technical quality matters. In R. Blum & J. Arter (Eds.), *Student performance assessment in an era of restructuring*. Alexandria, VA: Association for Supervision and Curriculum Development.

Herman, J. (1997). *Assessing new assessments: How do they measure up?* Los Angeles: Graduate School of Education and Information Studies, University of California, Los Angeles.

Hibbard, M. (1996). *Education Update, 38*(4), p. 5.

Hills, J. R. (1991). Apathy concerning grading and testing. *Phi Delta Kappan, 72*, 540–545.

Impara, J. C., Plake, B. S., & Fager, J. J. (1993). Teachers' assessment background and attitudes toward testing. *Theory into Practice, 32*, 113–117.

Khattri, N. (1995). *Performance assessments: Observed impacts on teaching and learning*. Washington, DC: Pelavin Associates.

Kohn, A. (1994, October). Grading: The issue is not how but why. *Educational Leadership*, pp. 38–41.

Marzano, R. J., & Kendall, J. S. (1996). *Designing standards-based districts, schools and classrooms*. Aurora, CO: Mid-Continent Regional Educational Laboratory.

Massachusetts State Department of Education. (1983). *Development of the state speaking assessment instrument: Reliability and feasibility*. Malden, MA: Author.

McTighe, J. (1996). Performance-based assessment in the classroom: A planning framework. In R. Blum & J. Arter (Eds.), *Student performance assessment in an era of restructuring*. Alexandria, VA: Association for Supervision and Curriculum Development.

Mendel, S. (undated). *Creating portraits of performance*. Aurora, CO: Peakview Elementary School.

Newmann, F., Secada, W., & Weblage, G. (1995). *A guide to authentic instruction and assessment*. Madison: School of Education, University of Wisconsin.

Norris, S. P (1990). *Test on Appraising Observations*. St. John's, Newfoundland: Memorial University of Newfoundland.

North Dakota Department of Public Instruction. (1998). *North Dakota fourth grade writing calibration packet*. Bismarck, ND: Author.

Northwest Regional Educational Laboratory. (1990). *Writing assessment: Training in analytical scoring* [video]. Los Angeles: lOX.

Northwest Regional Educational Laboratory. (1997). *Seeing with new eyes* [video]. Los Angeles: lOX.

Office of Educational Research and Improvement. (1997). *Studies of education reform: Assessment of student performance*. Washington, DC: Author.

Oregon Department of Education. (1997). *Read Informative and Literary Texts—Official scoring guides*. Salem, OR: Author.

Oregon Department of Education (1998). *Performance standards*. Available: http://www.open.k12.or.us/jitt/standards/perform.htm

Perlman, C. (1994). *The CPS performance assessment idea book*. Chicago: Chicago Public Schools.

Plake, B. S., Impara, J. C., & Fager, J. J. (1993). Assessment competencies of teachers: A national survey. *Educational Measurement: Issues and Practice, 12*(4), 10–12, 39.

Regional Educational Laboratories. (1998). *Improving classroom assessment: A toolkit for professional developers* (2nd ed.). Portland, OR: Northwest Regional Educational Laboratory.

Rudner, L., & Boston, C. (1994). Performance assessment. *ERIC Review, 3*(1), 2–12.

Shafer, W. D. (1993). Assessment in teacher education. *Theory into Practice, 32*, 118–126.

Spandel, V. (1996, January). Criteria: The power behind revision. *Writing Teacher*, pp. 9–25.

Spandel, V., & Culham, R. (1998). *Writing workshop materials*. Portland, OR: Northwest Regional Educational Laboratory.

Spandel, V., & Stiggins, R. J. (1997). *Creating writers: Linking writing assessment and instruction*. New York: Longman.

Stayter, F., & Johnston, P. (1990). Evaluating the teaching and learning of literacy. In T. Shanahan (Ed.), *Reading and writing together: New perspectives for the classroom*. Norwood, MA: Christopher-Gordon.

Stiggins, R. J. (1997). *Student-centered classroom assessment* (2nd ed.). Columbus, OH: Merrill.

Usrey, P (1998). *The traits of a competent oral communicator*. Portland, OR: Northwest Regional Educational Laboratory.

Vermont Mathematics Portfolio Project. (1991). *Resource book*. Montpelier: Vermont Department of Education.

Washington Commission on Student Learning. (1998). *Assessment sampler Grade 7*. Olympia, WA: Author.

Wiggins, G. (1992, May). Creating tests worth taking. *Educational Leadership*, pp. 26–33.

Wise, S. L., Lukin, L. E., & Roos, L. L. (1991). Teacher beliefs about training in testing and measurement. *Journal of Teacher Education, 42*, 37–42.

Zhang, Z. (1997). *Assessment Practices Inventory: A multivariate analysis of teachers' perceived assessment competency*. Paper presented at the NCME national conference, Chicago, IL.

Judy Arter is Assessment Unit Manager, Northwest Regional Educational Laboratory, 101 SW Main Street, Suite 500, Portland, OR 97204. Her specializations are classroom assessment and performance assessment.

From *Educational Measurement: Issues and Practices*, Summer 1999, pp. 30-44. © 2000 by the National Council on Measurement in Education. Reprinted by permission of the publisher.

Classroom Assessment for Learning

Classroom assessment that involves students in the process and focuses on increasing learning can motivate rather than merely measure students.

Stephen Chappuis and Richard J. Stiggins

Imagine classroom assessment as a healthy part of effective teaching and successful learning. At a time when large-scale, external assessments of learning gain political favor and attention, many teachers are discovering how to engage and motivate students using day-to-day classroom assessment for purposes beyond measurement. By applying the principles of what is called *assessment for learning*, teachers have followed clear research findings of the effects that high-quality, formative assessment can have on student achievement.

We typically think of assessment as an index of school success rather than as the cause of that success. Unfortunately, largely absent from the traditional classroom assessment environment is the use of assessment as a tool to promote greater student achievement (Shepard, 2000). In general, the teacher teaches and then tests. The teacher and class move on,

leaving unsuccessful students, those who might not learn at the established pace and within a fixed time frame, to finish low in the rank order. This assessment model is founded on two outdated beliefs: that to increase learning we should increase student anxiety and that comparison with more successful peers will motivate low performers to do better.

By contrast, assessment for learning occurs during the teaching and learning process rather than after it and has as its primary focus the ongoing improvement of learning for all students (Assessment Reform Group, 1999; Crooks, 2001; Shepard, 2000). Teachers who assess for learning use day-to-day classroom assessment activities to involve students directly and deeply in their own learning, increasing their confidence and motivation to learn by emphasizing progress and achievement rather than failure and defeat (Stig-

gins, 1999; 2001). In the assessment for learning model, assessment is an instructional tool that promotes learning rather than an event designed solely for the purpose of evaluation and assigning grades. And when students become involved in the assessment process, assessment for learning begins to look more like teaching and less like testing (Davies, 2000).

Student-Involved Assessment

Research shows that classroom assessments that provide accurate, descriptive feedback to students and involve them in the assessment process can improve learning (Black and Wiliam, 1998). As a result, assessment for learning means more than just assessing students often, more than providing the teacher with assessment results to revise instruction. In assessment for learning, both teacher and student use classroom assessment information to modify teaching and learning activities. Teachers use assessment information formatively when they

- Pretest before a unit of study and adjust instruction for individuals or the entire group.
- Analyze which students need more practice.
- Continually revise instruction on the basis of results.
- Reflect on the effectiveness of their own teaching practices.
- Confer with students regarding their strengths and the areas that need improvement.
- Facilitate peer tutoring, matching students who demonstrate understanding with those who do not.

We tend to think of students as passive participants in assessment rather than engaged users of the information that assessment can produce. What we should be asking is, How can students use assessment to take responsibility for and improve their own learning?

Student involvement in assessment doesn't mean that students control decisions regarding what will or won't be learned or tested. It doesn't mean that they assign their own grades. Instead, student involvement means that students learn to use assessment information to manage their own learning so that they understand how they learn best, know exactly where they are in relation to the defined learning targets, and plan and take the next steps in their learning.

Student-involved assessment means that students learn to use assessment information to manage their own learning.

Students engage in the assessment for learning process when they use assessment information to set goals, make learning decisions related to their own improvement, de-

velop an understanding of what quality work looks like, self-assess, and communicate their status and progress toward established learning goals. Students involved in their own assessment might

- Determine the attributes of good performance. Students look at teacher-supplied anonymous samples of strong student performances and list the qualities that make them strong, learning the language of quality and the concepts behind strong performance.
- Use scoring guides to evaluate real work samples. Students can start with just one criterion in the guide and expand to others as they become more proficient in scoring. As students engage in determining the characteristics of quality work and scoring actual work samples, they become better able to evaluate their own work. Using the language of the scoring guide, they can identify their areas of strength and set goals for improvement—in essence, planning the next steps in their learning.
- Revise anonymous work samples. Students go beyond evaluating work to using criteria to improve the quality of a work sample. They can develop a revision plan that outlines improvements, or write a letter to the creator of the original work offering advice on how to improve the sample. This activity also helps students know what to do before they revise their own work.
- Create practice tests or test items based on their understanding of the learning targets and the essential concepts in the class material. Students can work in pairs to identify what they think should be on the test and to generate sample test items and responses.
- Communicate with others about their growth and determine when they are nearing success. Students achieve a deeper understanding of themselves and the material that they are attempting to learn when they describe the quality of their

own work. Letters to parents, written self-reflections, and conferences with teachers and parents in which students outline the process they used to create a product allow students to share what they know and describe their progress toward the learning target. By accumulating evidence of their own improvement in growth portfolios, students can refer to specific stages in their growth and celebrate their achievement with others.

Effective Teacher Feedback

"You need to study harder." "Your handwriting is very nice." "Good job." Traditionally, teachers use such statements to register their approval or disapproval of student performance. But such evaluative feedback, long a classroom staple, is of limited value for improving student learning and can actually have negative effects on students' desire to learn. And grades, those traditional coded symbols and markings—B-, 71 percent, 4/10, Satisfactory, F— actually communicate even less about what students have done well or need to do to improve. By contrast, teacher comments that focus on student work and not on individual student characteristics can increase students' motivation and desire to learn.

Black and Wiliam (1998) point to the benefits of replacing judgmental feedback with specific, descriptive, and immediate feedback. When the goal is to increase student motivation and learning, productive feedback tells students what they are doing right, pinpointing strengths and helping learners develop those strengths even further. For some students, receiving this feedback in writing and having time to reflect on it is sufficient. Other students need face-to-face teacher feedback to reinforce what they have done well.

Effective teacher feedback describes why an answer is right or wrong in specific terms that students understand. Students can also generate their own descriptive feedback by comparing their work with teacher-provided exemplars or posted samples. They can then compare their own feedback with that of their teacher.

Descriptive feedback should provide ways for students to improve in clear, constructive language. Instead of simply labeling student errors or omissions, effective feedback guides students to better performance throughout the learning process. Useful comments focus specifically on improving only one area at a time.

Finally, teacher feedback for learning draws an even bigger picture by telling students where they are now relative to the defined learning targets—and where teachers ultimately want them to be. By modeling for students a variety of suggestions designed to narrow the gap between where they are and where they should be headed, teachers can help students learn to generate their own strategies for improvement.

The Skills of Self-Assessment

Eventually, we want students to be able to direct their own learning. Yet it often seems unclear just how students will achieve this goal. Assessment for learning helps students become self-directed learners by developing their self-assessment skills. The principles of assessment for learning are interrelated: Just as involving students in the assessment process helps make assessment more like instruction, students need to learn to self-assess so that they can use the descriptive feedback from the teacher to its best advantage. Sadler (1989) and Atkin, Black, and Coffey (2001) describe a model of formative assessment in which learners continually ask themselves three questions as they self-assess.

Where Am I Trying to Go?

Students need clearly articulated, concise learning targets to be able to answer this first question. Learning is easier when learners understand what goal they are trying to achieve, the purpose of achieving the goal, and the specific attributes of success. Teachers should continually help students clarify the intended learning as the lessons unfold—not just at the beginning of a unit of study. Teachers share learning intentions with students when they

- Phrase objectives in terms that begin with "We are learning to…" or "I can…"
- Ask students to read the objectives aloud and ask clarifying questions.
- Separate what they want students to do—the instructions for completing the task—from what they want students to learn. Otherwise, the directions might overshadow the intended learning.
- Inform students why they need to learn what comes next and how it connects to previous and future learning.
- Display the learning objectives in the classroom.
- Provide students with examples of outstanding work as well as samples of lesser quality so that they can see the differences.
- Ask students to rephrase the learning targets or describe what attainment of a target looks like (Arter & Busick, 2001; Clarke, 2001).

Where Am I Now?

Students can practice comparing their work to models of high-quality work and trying to identify the differences. They can use teacher feedback from formative assessments to gather evidence of what they know and can do relative to the defined learning target. They can use teacher questions designed to prompt students to reflect on what they have learned individually relative to the intended learning. All of these strategies help students ascertain—and, even more important, learn *how* to ascertain—where they are and where they need to be, an awareness that is central to their ultimate success.

> Teachers share learning intentions with students when they separate what they want students to do—the instructions for completing the task— from what they want students to learn.

How Do I Close the Gap?

Assessment for learning helps students know what to do to move from their current position to the final learning goal. To meet learning goals, students must participate fully in creating the goals, analyzing assessment data, and developing a plan of action to achieve the next goal (Clarke, 2001).

Students should learn question-and-answer strategies that they can use to close the gap: What do I need to change in my work to improve its quality? What specific help do I need to make these changes? From whom can I get help? What resources do I need?

Sadler (1989) notes that a steady flow of descriptive feedback to students encourages continual self-assessment around what constitutes quality. Keeping students connected to a vision of quality as the unit of study progresses helps them close the gap by formulating their next steps in learning.

All Students Learning Well

The habits and skills of self-assessment are within the grasp and capabilities of almost every student. Students take greater responsibility for their own learning when they regularly assess themselves (Shepard, 2001). In the hands of trained teachers, assessment for learning breeds confidence in learning. It provides students with opportunities for monitoring and communicating to others their own progress.

Educators open the door to using assessment in more productive ways when they acknowledge that students respond differently to the use of test scores as threats of punishment or promises of reward. Those who succeed keep striving; those who fail may give up. By contrast, most students respond positively to classroom assessment environments that promote success rather than simply measure it.

Students demonstrate unprecedented score gains on standardized assessments when their teachers apply the principles of assessment for learning in the classroom (Black and Wiliam, 1998). With appropriate training, teachers can improve the accuracy of their day-to-day assessments, make their feedback to students descriptive and informative, and increase the involvement of students in the entire assessment process. In this way, classroom assessment for learning becomes a school improvement tool that helps create responsible, engaged, and self-directed learners.

References

Arter, J. A., & Busick, K. U. (2001). *Practice with student-involved classroom assessment*. Portland, OR: Assessment Training Institute.

Assessment Reform Group. (1999). *Assessment for learning: Beyond the black box*. Cambridge, England: University of Cambridge.

Atkin, J. M., Black, P., & Coffey, J. (2001). *Classroom assessment and the National Science Education Standards*. Washington, DC: National Academy Press.

Black, P., & Wiliam, D. (1998). Inside the black box: Raising standards through classroom assessment. *Phi Delta Kappan, 80*(2), 139-148.

Clarke, S. (2001). *Unlocking formative assessment*. London: Hodder and Stoughton.

Crooks, T. (2001). *The validity of formative assessments*. Leeds, England: British Educational Research Association.

Davies, A. (2000). *Making classroom assessment work*. Merville, British Columbia, Canada: Connections Publishing.

Sadler, R. (1989). Formative assessment and the design of instructional systems. *Instructional Science, 18*, 119-144.

Shepard, L. A. (2000). The role of assessment in a learning culture. *Educational Researcher, 29*(7), 4-14.

Shepard, L. A. (2001, July). *Using assessment to help students think about learning*. Keynote address at the Assessment Training Institute Summer Conference, Portland, OR.

Stiggins, R. J. (1999). Assessment, student confidence, and school success. *Phi Delta Kappan, 81*(3), 191–198.

Stiggins, R. J. (2001). *Student-involved classroom assessment* (3rd ed.). Upper Saddle River, NJ: Merrill-Prentice Hall.

Stephen Chappuis is Director of Professional Development and **Richard J. Stiggins** is President and Founder of the Assessment Training Institute, 317 SW Alder St., Ste. 1200, Portland, OR 97204; (800) 480–3060; ati@assessmentinst.com.

Helping Standards Make the
GRADE

*When reporting on student work, educators need a clear,
comprehensive grading system that shows how students
are measuring up to standards.*

Thomas R. Guskey

The issue of grading looms on the horizon for standards-based education. With standards and assessments now in place, educators face the daunting task of how best to grade and report student learning in terms of those standards. Most educators recognize the inadequacies of their current grading and reporting methods (Marzano, 2000). Few, however, have found alternatives that satisfy the diverse needs of students, parents, teachers, school administrators, and community members.

Standards don't lessen the responsibility of educators to evaluate the performance of students and to report the results. Nevertheless, the focus on standards poses unique challenges in grading and reporting. What are those challenges, and how can educators develop standards-based grading and reports that are accurate, honest, and fair?

Criterion-Referenced Standards

The first challenge is moving from norm-referenced to criterion-referenced grading standards. *Norm-referenced* standards compare each students's performance to that of other students in the group or class. Teachers first rank students on some measure of their achievement or performance. They assign a set percentage of top-ranked students (usually 10 to 20 percent) the highest grade, a second set percentage (perhaps 20 to 30 percent) the second highest grade, and so on. The percentages typically correspond to an approximation of the bell-shaped, normal probability curve, hence the expression "grading on the curve." Most adults experienced this type of grading during their school days.

Criterion-referenced standards, in contrast, compare each student's performance to clearly stated performance descriptions that differentiate levels of quality. Teachers judge students' performance by what each student does, regardless of how well or poorly their classmates perform.

Using the normal probability curve as a basis for assigning grades yields highly consistent grade distributions from one teacher to the next. All teachers' classes have essentially the same percentages of *A*s, *B*s, and *C*s. But the consequences for students are overwhelmingly negative. Learning becomes highly competitive because students must compete against one another for the new high grades that the teacher distributes. Under these conditions, students see that helping others threatens their own chances for success. Because students do not achieve high grades by performing well, but rather by doing better than their classmates, learning becomes a game of winners and losers, and because teachers keep the number of rewards arbitrarily small, most students must be losers (Haladyna, 1999; Johnson & Johnson, 1989). Strong evidence shows that "grading on the curve" is detrimental to relationships—both among students and among teachers and students (Krumboltz & Yeh, 1996).

In a standards-based system, grading and reporting must be criterion-referenced. Teachers at all levels must identify what they want their students to learn and be able to do and what evidence they will use to judge that achievement or performance. Grades based on clearly stated learning criteria have direct meaning and communicate that meaning.

Differentiating Grading Criteria

A second challenge is to differentiate the types of grading criteria that teachers will use. Although teachers and students generally consider criterion-referenced grading to be more fair and equitable (Kovas, 1993), the specific grading criteria that teachers use may be very diverse. We can classify these criteria into three broad categories: *product*, *process*, and *progress* (Guskey, 1996).

Standards don't lessen the responsibility of educators to evaluate the performance of students and to report the results.

Product criteria relate to students' specific achievements or levels of performance. They describe what students know and are able to do at a particular point in time. Advocates of standards generally favor product criteria. Teachers using product criteria base students' grades or reports exclusively on final examination scores; final products, such as reports, projects, or portfolios; overall assessments of performance; and other culminating demonstrations of learning.

Process criteria relate not to the final results, but to how students got there. Educators who believe that product criteria do not provide a complete picture of student learning generally favor process criteria. For example, teachers who consider student effort, class behavior, or work habits are using process criteria. So are those who count daily work, regular classroom quizzes, homework, class participation, punctuality of assignments, or attendance in determining students' grades.

Progress criteria relate to how much students actually gain from their learning experiences. Other terms include learning gain, improvement grading, value-added grading, and educational growth. Teachers who use progress criteria typically look at how far students have come rather than where students are. Others attempt to judge students' progress in terms of their "learning potential." As a result, progress grading criteria are often highly individualized among students.

Because they are concerned about student motivation, self-esteem, and the social consequences of grading, few teachers today use product criteria solely in determining grades. Instead, most base their grading on some combination of criteria, especially when a student

receives only a single grade in a subject area (Brookhart, 1993; Frary, Cross, & Weber, 1993). The majority of teachers also vary the criteria they use from student to student, taking into account individual circumstances (Truog & Friedman, 1996). Although teachers do so in an effort to be fair, the result is often a hodgepodge grade that includes elements of achievement, effort, and improvement (Brookhart, 1991). Interpreting the grade or report thus becomes difficult for parents, administrators, community members, and even the students (Friedman & Frisbie, 1995). An *A*, for example, may mean that the student knew what the teacher expected before instruction began (product), didn't learn as well as expected but tried very hard (process), or simply made significant improvement (progress).

Measurement experts generally recommend using product criteria exclusively in determining students' grades. They point out that the more process and progress criteria come into play, the more subjective and biased grades are likely to be (O'Connor, 1999; Ornstein, 1994). How can a teacher know, for example, how difficult a task was for students or how hard they worked to complete it?

Many teachers, however, point out that if they use product criteria exclusively, some high-ability students receive high grades with little effort, whereas the hard work of less-talented students is seldom acknowledged. Others say that if teachers consider only product criteria, low-ability students and those who are disadvantaged—students who must work the hardest—have the least incentive to do so. These students find the relationship between high effort and low grades unacceptable and, as a result, often express their displeasure with indifference, deception, or disruption (Tomlinson, 1992).

A practical solution to this problem, and one that increasing numbers of teachers and schools are using, is to establish clear indicators of product, process, and progress, and then to report each separately (Stiggins, 2001; Wiggins, 1996). Teachers separate grades or marks for learning skills, effort, work habits, or progress from grades for achievement and performance. Parents generally prefer this approach because it gives them more detailed and prescriptive information. It also simplifies reporting for teachers because they no longer have to combine so many diverse types of information into a single grade. The key to success, however, rests in the clear specification of those indicators and the criteria to which they relate. This means that teachers must describe how they plan to evaluate students' achievement, effort, work habits, and progress, and then must communicate these plans directly to students, parents, and others.

Reporting Tools

A third challenge for standards-based education is clarifying the purpose of each reporting tool. Although report cards are the primary method, most schools today use a variety of reporting devices: weekly or monthly progress reports, open-house meetings, newsletters, evaluated projects or assignments, school Web pages, parent-teacher conferences, and student-led conferences (Guskey & Bailey, 2001). Each reporting tool must fulfill a specific purpose, which requires considering three vital aspects of communication:

- What information do we want to communicate?
- Who is the primary audience for that information?
- How would we like that information to be used?

Many educators make the mistake of choosing their reporting tools first, without giving careful attention to the purpose. For example, some charge headlong into developing a standards-based report card without first addressing core questions about why they are doing it. Their efforts often encounter unexpected resistance and rarely bring positive results. Both parents and teachers perceive the change as a newfangled fad that presents no real advantage over traditional reporting methods. As a result, the majority of these efforts become short-lived experiments and are abandoned after a few troubled years of implementation.

Efforts that begin by clarifying the purpose, however, make intentions clear from the start. If, for instance, the purpose of the report card is to communicate to parents the achievement status of students, then parents must understand the information on the report card and know how to use it. This means that educators should include parents on report card committees and give their input careful consideration. This not only helps mobilize everyone in the reporting process, it also keeps efforts on track. The famous adage that guides architecture also applies to grading and reporting: *Form follows function.* Once the purpose of functions is clear, teachers can address more easily questions regarding form or method (Guskey & Bailey, 2001).

Developing a Reporting Form

The fourth challenge for standards-based education is developing the centerpiece of a standards-based reporting system: the report card. This typically involves a four-step process. First, teams of educators identify the major learning goals or standards that students are expected to achieve at each grade level or course of study. Second, educators establish performance indicators for those learning goals or standards. In other words, educators decide what evidence best illustrates students' attainment of each goal or standard. Third, they determine graduated levels of quality for assessing student performance. This step involves identifying incremental levels of attainment, sometimes referred to as benchmarks, as students progress toward the learning goals or standards (Andrade, 2000; Wiggins & McTighe, 1998). Finally, educators, often in collaboration with

parents, develop a reporting form that communicates teachers' judgments of students' progress and achievement in relation to the learning goals or standards.

Many parents initially respond to a standards-based reporting form with, "This is great. But tell me, how is my child doing *really*?"

Identifying Reporting Standards

Identifying the specific learning goals or standards on which to base grades is probably the most important, but also the most challenging, aspect of standards-based grading. These learning goals or standards should stipulate precisely what students should know and be able to do as a result of their learning experiences. In earlier times, we might have referred to cognitive skills, learning competencies, or performance outcomes (Guskey, 1999). Teachers frequently list these learning goals in their lesson plans, make note of them on assignments and performance tasks, and include them in monthly or weekly progress reports that go home to parents.

A crucial consideration in identifying learning goals or standards is determining the degree of specificity. Standards that are too specific make supporting forms cumbersome to use and difficult to understand. Standards that are too broad or general, however, make it hard to identify students' unique strengths and weaknesses. Most state-level standards, for example, tend to be broad and need to be broken down or "unpacked" into homogeneous categories or topics (Marzano, 1999). For grading and reporting purposes, educators must seek a balance. The standards must be broad enough to allow for efficient communication of student learning, yet specific enough to be useful (see Gronlund, 2000; Marzano & Kendall, 1995; Wiggins & McTighe, 1998).

Another issue is the differentiation of standards across marking periods or grade levels. Most schools using standards-based grading develop reporting forms that are based on grade-level learning goals or standards. Each standard has one level of complexity set for each grade that students were expected to meet before the end of the academic year. Most parents, however, are accustomed to grading systems in which learning standards become increasingly complex with each marking period. If the standard states "Students will write clearly and effectively," for example, many parents believe that their children should do this each marking period, not simply move toward doing so by the end of the academic year. This is especially true of parents who encourage their children to attain the highest mark possible in all subject areas every marking period.

To educators using such forms, students who receive 1 or 2 on a 4-point grading scale during the first or second marking period are making appropriate progress and are on track for their grade level. For parents, however, a report card filled with 1s and 2s when the highest mark is a 4, causes great concern. They think that their children are failing. Although including a statement on the reporting form, such as "Marks indicate progress toward end-of-the-year learning standards," is helpful, it may not alleviate parents' concerns.

Example of a Double-Mark, Standards-Based Reporting Form

Elementary Progress Report

Reading	**1st**	**2nd**	**3rd**	**4th**
Understands and uses different skills and strategies	1+	2++		
Understands the meaning of what is read	1++	2+		
Reads different materials for a variety of purposes	1-	2-		
Reading level		1++	2+	
Work habits	S	S		
Writing	**1st**	**2nd**	**3rd**	**4th**
Writes clearly and effectively	1+	2++		
Understands and uses the steps in the writing process	1++	2++		
Writes in a variety of forms for different audiences and purposes	1+	2-		
Analyzes and evaluates the effectiveness of written work	N	1+		
Understands and uses the conventions of writing: punctuation, capitalization, spelling, and legibility	1-	2-		
Work habits	S	S		
Communication	**1st**	**2nd**	**3rd**	**4th**
Uses listening and observational skills to gain understanding	1+	2-		
Communicates ideas clearly and effectively (formal communication)	1-	2+		
Uses communication strategies and skills to work effectively with others (informal communication)	N	1+		
Work habits	U	S		

This report is based on grade-level standards established for each subject area. The ratings indicate your student's progress in relation to the year-end standard.

Evaluation Marks

4 = Exceptional
3 = Meets standard
2 = Approaches standard
1 = Beginning standard
N = Not applicable

Level Expectation Marks

++ = Advanced
+ = On level
− = Below level

Social Learning Skills & Effort Marks

E = Exceptional
S = Satisfactory
U = Unsatisfactory

Facilitating Interpretation

Many parents initially respond to a standards-based reporting form with, "This is great. But tell me, how is my child doing *really?*" Or they ask, "How is my child doing compared to the other children in the class?" They ask these questions because they don't know how to interpret the information. Further, most parents had comparative, norm-based reporting systems when they were in school and are more familiar with reports that compare students to their classmates. Above all, parents want to make sense of the reporting form. Their fear is that their children will reach the end of the school year and won't have made sufficient progress to be promoted to the next grade.

To ensure more accurate interpretations, several schools use a two-part marking system with their standards-based reporting form (see example). Every marking period, each student receives two marks for each standard. The first mark indicates the student's level of progress with regard to the standard—a *1, 2, 3,* or *4,* indicating *beginning, progressing, proficient,* or *exceptional.* The second mark indicates the relation of that level of progress to established expectations at this point in the school year. For example, a ++ might indicate *advanced for grade-level expectations,* a + might indicate *on target* or *meeting grade-level expectations,* and a − would indicate *below grade-level expectations* or *needs improvement.*

The advantage of this two-part marking system is that it helps parents make sense of the reporting form each marking period. It also helps alleviate their concerns about what seem like low grades and lets them know whether their children are progressing at an appropriate rate. Further, it helps parents take a standards-based perspective in viewing their children's performances. Their question is no longer "Where is my child in comparison to his or her classmates?" but "Where is my child in relation to the grade-level learning goals and expectations?"

The one drawback of the two-part marking system is that expectations must take into account individual differences in students' development of cognitive skills. Because students in any classroom differ in age and cognitive development, some might not meet the specified criteria during a particular marking period—even though they will likely do so before the end of the year. This is especially common in kindergarten and the early primary grades, when students tend to vary widely in their entry-level skills but can make rapid learning progress (Shuster, Lemma, Lynch, & Nadeau, 1996). Educators must take these developmental differences into consideration and must explain them to parents.

Choosing Performance-Level Descriptors

Standards-based reporting forms that use numerical grading scales also require a key or legend that explains the meaning of each numeral. These descriptors help parents and others understand what each numeral means.

A common set of descriptors matches performance levels *1, 2, 3,* and *4* with the achievement labels *beginning, progressing, proficient,* and *exceptional.* If the standards reflect behavioral aspects of students' performance, then teachers more commonly use such descriptors as *seldom, sometimes, usually,* and *consistently/independently.* These labels are preferable to *above average, average,* and *below average,* which reflect norm-referenced comparisons rather than criterion-referenced standards.

Such achievement descriptors as *exceptional* or *advanced* are also preferable to *exceeds standard* or *extending* to designate the highest level of performance. Educators can usually articulate specific performance criteria for an *exceptional* or *advanced* level of achievement or performance. *Exceeds standard* or *extending,* however, are much less precise and may leave students and parents wondering just what they need to do to exceed or extend. Descriptors should be clear, concise, and directly interpretable.

Many reporting forms include a fifth level of *not applicable* or *not evaluated* to designate standards that have not yet been addressed or were not assessed during that particular marking period. Including these labels is preferable to leaving the marking spaces blank because parents often interpret a blank space as an item that the teacher missed or neglected.

Maintaining Consistency

A final challenge is consistency. To communicate with parents, most schools and school districts involved in standards-based grading try to maintain a similar reporting format across grade levels. Most also use the same performance-level indicators at all grade levels so that parents don't have to learn a new set of procedures for interpreting the reporting form each year as their children move from one grade level to the next. Many parents also see consistency as an extension of a well-designed curriculum. The standards at each grade level build on and extend those from earlier levels.

While maintaining a similar format across grade levels, however, most schools and school districts list different standards on the reporting form for each level. Although the reporting format and performance indicators remain the same, the standards on the 1st grade reporting form are different from those on the 2nd grade form, and so on. This gives parents a clear picture of the increasing complexity of the standards at each subsequent grade level.

An alternative approach is to develop one form that lists the same broad standards for multiple grades. To clarify the difference at each grade level, a curriculum guidebook describing precisely what the standard means and what criteria are used in evaluating the standard at each grade level usually accompanies the form. Most reporting forms of this type also include a narrative section, in which teachers offer additional explanations. Although this approach to standards-based grading simplifies the reporting form, it also requires significant parent training and a close working relationship among parents, teachers, and school and district leaders (Guskey & Bailey, 2001).

Advantages and Shortcomings

When we establish clear learning goals or standards, standards-based grading offers important information about students' achievement and performance. If sufficiently detailed, the information is useful for both diagnostic and prescriptive purposes. For these reasons, standards-based grading facilitates teaching and learning better than almost any other grading method.

At the same time, standards-based grading has shortcomings. First and foremost, it takes a lot of work. Not only must educators identify the learning goals or standards on which grades will be based, but they also must decide what evidence best illustrates students' attainment or each goal or standard, identify graduated levels of quality for assessing students' performance, and develop reporting tools that communicate teachers' judgements of learning progress. These tasks may add considerably to the workload of teachers and school leaders.

A second shortcoming is that the reporting forms are sometimes too complicated for parents to understand. In their efforts to provide parents with rich information, educators can go overboard and describe learning goals in unnecessary detail. As a result, reporting forms become cumbersome and time-consuming for teachers to complete and difficult for parents to understand. We must seek a crucial balance in identifying standards that are specific enough to provide parents with useful, prescriptive information, but broad enough to allow for efficient communication between educators and parents.

A third shortcoming is that the report may not communicate the appropriateness of students' progress. Simply reporting a student's level of proficiency with regard to a particular standard communicates nothing about the adequacy of that level of achievement or performance. To make sense of the information, parents need to know how that level of achievement or performance compares to the established learning expectations for that particular grade level.

Finally, although teachers can use standards-based grading at any grade level and in any course of study, most current applications are restricted to the elementary level where there is little curriculum differentiation. In the middle grades and at the secondary level, students usually pursue more diverse courses of study. Because of

these curricular differences, standards-based reporting forms as the middle and secondary levels must vary from student to student. The marks need to relate to each student's achievement and performance in his or her particular courses or academic program. Although advances in technology, such as computerized reporting forms, allow educators to provide such individualized reports, relatively few middle and high school educators have taken up the challenge.

The standards must be broad enough to allow for efficient communication of student learning, yet specific enough to be useful.

New Standards for Grading

As educators clarify student learning goals and standards, the advantages of standards-based grading become increasingly evident. Although it makes reporting forms more detailed and complex, most parents value the richness of the information when the reports are expressed in terms that they can understand and use. Reporting forms that use a two-part marking system show particular promise—but such a system may require additional explanation to parents. Teachers must also set expectations for learning progress not just at the grade level, but also for each marking period.

Successfully implementing standards-based grading and reporting demands a close working relationship among teachers, parents, and school and district leaders. To accurately interpret the reporting form, parents need to know precisely what the standards mean and how to make sense of the various levels of achievement or performance in relation to those standards. Educators must ensure, therefore, that parents are familiar with the language and terminology. Only when all groups understand what grades mean and how they are used to improve student learning will we realize the true value of a standards-based approach to education.

References

Andrade, H. G. (2000). Using rubrics to promote thinking and learning. *Educational Leadership, 57*(5), 13–18.

Brookhart, S. M. (1991). Grading practices and validity. *Educational Measurement: Issues and Practice, 10*(1), 35–36.

Brookhart, S. M. (1993). Teachers' grading practices: Meaning and values. *Journal of Educational Measurement, 30*(2), 123–142.

Frary, R. B., Cross, L. H., & Weber, L. J. (1993). Testing and grading practices and opinions of secondary teachers of academic subjects: Implications for instruction in measurement. *Educational Measurement: Issues and Practice, 12*(3), 23–30.

Friedman, S. J., & Frisbie, D. A. (1995). The influence of report cards on the validity of grades reported to parents. *Educational and Psychological Measurement, 55*(1), 5–26.

Gronlund, N. E. (2000). *How to write and use instructional objective's* (6th ed.). Upper Saddle River, NJ: Merrill.

Guskey, T. R. (1996). Reporting on student learning: Lessons from the past—Prescriptions for the future. In T. R. Guskey (Ed.), *Communicating student learning: 1996 Yearbook of the Association for Supervision and Curriculum Development* (pp. 13–24). Alexandria, VA: ASCD.

Guskey, T. R. (1999). Making standards work. *The School Administrator, 56*(9), 44.

Guskey, T. R., & Bailey, J. M. (2001). *Developing grading and reporting systems for student learning.* Thousand Oaks, CA: Corwin Press.

Haladyna, T. M. ('1999). *A complete guide to student grading.* Boston: Allyn & Bacon.

Johnson, D. W., & Johnson, R. T. (1989). *Cooperation and competition: Theory and research.* Endina, MN: Interaction.

Kendall, J. S., & Marzano, R. J. (1995). *The systematic identification and articulation of content standards and benchmarks: Update.* Aurora, CO: McREL.

Kovas, M. A. (1993). Make your grading motivating: Keys to performance-based evaluation. *Quill and Scroll, 68*(1), 10–11.

Krumboltz, J. D., & Yeh, C. J. (1996). Competitive grading sabotages good teaching. *Phi Delta Kappan, 78*(4), 324–326.

Marzano, R. J. (1999). Building curriculum and assessment around standards. *The High School Magazine, 6*(5), 14–19.

Marzano, R. J. (2000). *Transforming classroom grading.* Alexandria, VA: ASCD.

O'Connor, K. (1999). *How to grade for learning.* Arlington Heights, IL: Skylight.

Ornstein, A. C. (1994). Grading practices and policies: An overview and some suggestions. *NASSP Bulletin, 78*(559), 55–64.

Shuster, C., Lemma, P., Lynch, T., & Nadeau, K. (1996). A *study of kindergarten and 1st grade report cards: What are young children expected to learn?* Paper presented at the annual meeting of the American Educational Research Association, New York.

Stiggins, R. J. (2001). *Student-involved classroom assessment* (3rd ed.). Upper Saddle River, NJ: Merrill/Prentice Hall.

Tomlinson, T. (1992). *Hard work and high expectations: Motivating students to learn.* Washington, DC: Office of Educational Research and Improvement, U.S. Department of Education.

Truog, A. L., & Friedman, S. J. (1996). *Evaluating high school teachers' written grading policies from a measurement perspective.* Paper presented at the annual meeting of the National Council on Measurement in Education, New York.

Wiggins, G. (1996). Honesty and fairness: Toward better grading and reporting. In T. R. Guskey (Ed.), *Communicating student learning: 1996 Yearbook of the Association for Supervision and Curriculum Development* (pp. 141–176). Alexandria, VA: ASCD.

Wiggins, G., & McTighe, J. (1998). *Understanding by design.* Alexandria, VA: ASCD.

Thomas R. Guskey is Professor of Educational Policy Studies and Evaluation, College of Education, University of Kentucky, Lexington, KY 40506; guskey@pop.uky.edu.

From *Educational Leadership*, September 2001, pp. 20-27. Reprinted with permission of the Association for Supervision and Curriculum Development (ASCD). © 2001 by ASCD. All rights reserved.

Index

Test Your Knowledge Form

We encourage you to photocopy and use this page as a tool to assess how the articles in *Annual Editions* expand on the information in your textbook. By reflecting on the articles you will gain enhanced text information. You can also access this useful form on a product's book support Web site at *http://www.dushkin.com/online/*.

NAME: _____ DATE: _____

TITLE AND NUMBER OF ARTICLE: _____

BRIEFLY STATE THE MAIN IDEA OF THIS ARTICLE:

LIST THREE IMPORTANT FACTS THAT THE AUTHOR USES TO SUPPORT THE MAIN IDEA:

WHAT INFORMATION OR IDEAS DISCUSSED IN THIS ARTICLE ARE ALSO DISCUSSED IN YOUR TEXTBOOK OR OTHER READINGS THAT YOU HAVE DONE? LIST THE TEXTBOOK CHAPTERS AND PAGE NUMBERS:

LIST ANY EXAMPLES OF BIAS OR FAULTY REASONING THAT YOU FOUND IN THE ARTICLE:

LIST ANY NEW TERMS/CONCEPTS THAT WERE DISCUSSED IN THE ARTICLE, AND WRITE A SHORT DEFINITION:

We Want Your Advice

ANNUAL EDITIONS revisions depend on two major opinion sources: one is our Advisory Board, listed in the front of this volume, which works with us in scanning the thousands of articles published in the public press each year; the other is you—the person actually using the book. Please help us and the users of the next edition by completing the prepaid article rating form on this page and returning it to us. Thank you for your help!

ANNUAL EDITIONS: Educational Psychology 04/05

ARTICLE RATING FORM

Here is an opportunity for you to have direct input into the next revision of this volume.
We would like you to rate each of the articles listed below, using the following scale:

1. **Excellent: should definitely be retained**
2. **Above average: should probably be retained**
3. **Below average: should probably be deleted**
4. **Poor: should definitely be deleted**

Your ratings will play a vital part in the next revision.
Please mail this prepaid form to us as soon as possible.
Thanks for your help!

RATING	ARTICLE
	1. Good Teachers, Plural
	2. What I Hope for in My Children's Teachers: A Parent's Perspective
	3. What Urban Students Say About Good Teaching
	4. Helping Children Cope With Loss, Death, and Grief: Response to a National Tragedy
	5. Shaping the Learning Environment: Connecting Developmentally Appropriate Practices to Brain Research
	6. To Be Successful-Let Them Play!
	7. The School and the Child and the Child in the School
	8. Differing Perspectives, Common Ground: The Middle School and Gifted Education Relationship
	9. 'Mom, Will Kaelie Always Have Possibilities?'-The Realities of Early Childhood Inclusion
	10. Into the Mainstream: Practical Strategies for Teaching in Inclusive Environments
	11. Challenges of Identifying and Serving Gifted Children With ADHD
	12. Beyond the Gifted Stereotype
	13. Celebrate Diversity!
	14. Lessons on Multicultural Education from Australia and the United States
	15. Cultural Influences on the Development of Self-Concept: Updating Our Thinking
	16. Students Remember…What They Think About
	17. Beyond Learning By Doing: The Brain Compatible Approach
	18. Ability and Expertise: It's Time to Replace the Current Model of Intelligence
	19. It's No Fad: Fifteen Years of Implementing Multiple Intelligences
	20. Caution-Praise Can Be Dangerous
	21. Webs of Skill: How Students Learn
	22. Invitations to Learn
	23. The Tyranny of Self-Oriented Self-Esteem
	24. Concept Mapping as a Mindtool for Critical Thinking
	25. Teachers Bridge to Constructivism
	26. Making Students as Important as Standards

RATING	ARTICLE
	27. The Integration of Instructional Technology Into Public Education: Promises and Challenges
	28. Using Data to Differentiate Instruction
	29. Intrinsic Versus Extrinsic Motivation in Schools: A Reconciliation
	30. Do Students Care About Learning? A Conversation with Mihaly Csikszentmihalyi
	31. What Engages Underachieving Middle School Students in Learning?
	32. When Children Make Rules
	33. A Positive Learning Environment Approach to Middle School Instruction
	34. The Key to Classroom Management
	35. Corporal Punishment: Legalities, Realities, and Implications
	36. Fundamental Assessment Principles for Teachers and School Administrators
	37. Are We Measuring Student Success With High-Stakes Testing?
	38. The Seductive Allure of Data
	39. Teaching About Performance Assessment
	40. Classroom Assessment for Learning
	41. Helping Standards Make the Grade

(Continued on next page)

BUSINESS REPLY MAIL
FIRST CLASS MAIL PERMIT NO. 551 DUBUQUE IA

POSTAGE WILL BE PAID BY ADDRESEE

McGraw-Hill/Dushkin
2460 KERPER BLVD
DUBUQUE, IA 52001-9902

NO POSTAGE
NECESSARY
IF MAILED
IN THE
UNITED STATES

ABOUT YOU

Name

Date

Are you a teacher? ❐   A student? ❐
Your school's name

Department

Address   City   State   Zip

School telephone #

YOUR COMMENTS ARE IMPORTANT TO US!

Please fill in the following information:
For which course did you use this book?

Did you use a text with this ANNUAL EDITION? ❐ yes ❐ no
What was the title of the text?

What are your general reactions to the *Annual Editions* concept?

Have you read any pertinent articles recently that you think should be included in the next edition? Explain.

Are there any articles that you feel should be replaced in the next edition? Why?

Are there any World Wide Web sites that you feel should be included in the next edition? Please annotate.

May we contact you for editorial input? ❐ yes ❐ no
May we quote your comments? ❐ yes ❐ no